The Intrigue of Ethics

Perspectives in Continental Philosophy
John D. Caputo, series editor

1. John D. Caputo, ed., *Deconstruction in a Nutshell: A Conversation with Jacques Derrida.*
2. Michael Strawser, *Both/And: Reading Kierkegaard—From Irony to Edification.*
3. Michael Barber, *Ethical Hermeneutics: Rationality in Enrique Dussel's Philosophy of Liberation.*
4. James H. Olthuis, ed., *Knowing* Other-*wise: Philosophy at the Threshold of Spirituality.*
5. James Swindal, *Reflection Revisited: Jürgen Habermas's Discursive Theory of Truth.*
6. Richard Kearney, *Poetics of Imagining: Modern and Postmodern.* Second edition.
7. Thomas W. Busch, *Circulating Being: From Embodiment to Incorporation—Essays on Late Existentialism.*
8. Edith Wyschogrod, *Emmanuel Levinas: The Problem of Ethical Metaphysics.* Second edition.
9. Francis J. Ambrosio, ed., *The Question of Christian Philosophy Today.*
10. Jeffrey Bloechl, ed., *The Face of the Other and the Trace of God: Essays on the Philosophy of Emmanuel Levinas.*
11. Ilse N. Bulhof and Laurens ten Kate, eds., *Flight of the Gods: Philosophical Perspectives on Negative Theology.*
12. Trish Glazebrook, *Heidegger's Philosophy of Science.*
13. Kevin Hart, *The Trespass of the Sign.* Second edition.
14. Mark C. Taylor, *Journeys to Selfhood: Hegel and Kierkegaard.* Second edition.
15. Dominique Janicaud, Jean-François Courtine, Jean-Louis Chrétien, Michel Henry, Jean-Luc Marion, and Paul Ricoeur, *Phenomenology and the "Theological Turn": The French Debate.*
16. Karl Jaspers, *The Question of German Guilt.* Introduction by Joseph W. Koterski, S.J.
17. Jean-Luc Marion, *The Idol and Distance: Five Studies.* Translated with an introduction by Thomas A. Carlson.

THE INTRIGUE OF ETHICS

A Reading of the Idea of Discourse in the Thought of Emmanuel Levinas

JEFFREY DUDIAK

Fordham University Press
New York
2001

Perspectives in Continental Philosophy, No. 18
ISSN 1089–3938

Library of Congress Cataloging-in-Publication Data

Dudiak, Jeffrey.
The intrigue of ethics : a reading of the idea of discourse in the thought of Emmanuel Lévinas / Jeffrey Dudiak.
p. cm.—(Perspectives in continental philosophy ; no. 18)
Includes bibliographical references (p.) and index.
ISBN 0-8232-2092-3 (hardcover)—ISBN 0-8232-2093-1 (pbk.)
1. Lévinas, Emmanuel—Contributions in philosophy of language and languages. 2. Language and languages—Philosophy—History—20th century. 3. Ethics. I. Title. II. Series.
B2430.L484 D83 2001
194—dc21 00-048468

Printed in the United States of America
01 02 03 04 05 5 4 3 2 1

For Ruth, my mother.
"Love is love in this antecedence."

CONTENTS

Acknowledgments ix

Preface: Dialogue and Peace xi

PART I: THE IDEA OF DISCOURSE

1. The Impasse of Dialogue 3
   I. Dialogue as *Dia-logos:* The Ontological Model 5
   II. Dialogue Problematized 27

2. Original Plurality: The Terms of Discourse 57
   I. Allergy and Separation 59
   II. The Ethical Transcendence of the Other 62
   III. The Separation of the Same as Enjoyment 79

3. Discourse as the Condition of Possibility for Dialogue 109
   I. The Relation of Discourse 109
   II. Discourse Produces the *Logos* 118
   III. The Economy of the Same and the *Logos* 128
   IV. Discourse Founds Dialogue 140

PART II: THE POSSIBLE IMPOSSIBILITY

Introduction to Part II 167
   I. Conditions of Possibility and Impossibility 167
   II. From "Discourse" to "The Saying" 169

4. The Two Aspects of Language: The Saying and the Said 178
   I. Language As the Said 178
   II. Language As the Saying 193

5. The Two Directions in Language: The Reductive and the Re-constructive 224
   I. From the Said to the Saying: Reduction 224
   II. Intermezzo: Between Movements 230
   III. From the Saying to the Said: Re-construction 233

IV. The Saying in Justice: Inspiration and Betrayal 240
V. Discourse: A Possible Impossibility 247

6. The Moment of Responsibility: Time and Eternity 263
I. From Simultaneity to Postponement 265
II. From Postponement to Recurrence 279
III. A Temporary Conclusion 289
IV. At This Very Moment 291
V. The Moment of Responsibility 300

PART III: DISCOURSE, PHILOSOPHY, AND PEACE

7. Levinas's Philosophical Discourse 317
I. Levinas's Philosophy As Discourse 320
II. Levinas's Discourse As Philosophy 352

8. The Im/possibility of Peace 403
I. Incredulities 403
II. Offerings 404
III. Testimonies 408

Bibliography 421

Index 433

ACKNOWLEDGMENTS

To Prof. James Olthuis, mentor and friend, for his patient and enthusiastic encouragement, for his singular gift of being-with me throughout this long, sometimes trying, but always enriching writing process . . .

To Prof. Theo de Boer of the Vrije Universiteit, Amsterdam, whose readings of Levinas and comments upon my own text have been a consistent challenge and inspiration to me . . .

To the intellectual and spiritual community at the Institute for Christian Studies, to all of its members, for the innumerable nourishments I have received . . .

To the members of the faculty of the Institute, present and past, and particularly, in my case, Professors Hendrik Hart, Calvin Seerveld, and William Rowe (now of Scranton University, and who introduced me to the work of Levinas), for the many things they have taught me . . .

To my former student colleagues at the I.C.S., for the invaluable contributions they have made to my life and work, and above all to the closest among these, Ronald Kuipers (who made a number of wise suggestions regarding this text), Nik Ansell, Janet Wesselius, and Shane Cudney . . .

To other special teachers and supporters, Professors Robert Gibbs of the University of Toronto (who generously read this work and has encouraged and challenged me to take it further), David Goicoechea of Brock University, and John D. Caputo of Villanova University . . .

To The King's University College, Edmonton, an undergraduate institution devoted to both teaching and faculty research, for providing me with an academic environment conducive to the final preparations of this text for publication . . .

To my editor Anthony Chiffolo at Fordham University Press and my copyeditor David Anderson for their efficient and generous help . . .

To my parents, Michael and Ruth Dudiak, for continuing to give me life . . .

To my wife, Julie Robinson, for teaching me what redemption means . . .

To many others, special friends, and special Friends, who know who they are, for the lightness and grace they have brought to my life and work . . .

And, finally, to Emmanuel Levinas himself, whose graciousness to me in our too brief acquaintance, and the inspiration left across a life's work, have been a marvelous testimony to me of the intrigue of ethics . . .

. . . my sincerest and deepest gratitude.

PREFACE

Dialogue and Peace

From the macro-cosmic levels of international relations, through national, democratic politics, down through labor-management negotiations, to the micro-levels of marital and even personal therapies, twentieth-century humanity places a great deal of faith and hope in dialogue as a way of peacefully settling conflicts and resolving tensions that threaten to devolve, or have already devolved, into violence.[1] There would, moreover, appear to be some warrant for this faith: Sometimes, treaties are signed, the transition of power is smoothly accomplished, work sites are productive, and marriages and persons are healed. But dialogue also, sometimes, fails—either in breaking down or in failing to get underway at all: There are wars, revolutions, strikes, divorces, and enduring personal brokenness.

Need it be argued, or could it even be argued,[2] that peace—that is, genuine peace,[3] and not some or other form of violence parading under that name (and despite a certain and seemingly natural human proclivity for romanticizing bellicosity)—is better than war? And if, as we (many? most?) Westerners believe, dialogue can be a boon to the prospects for peace, might it not serve us to seek to understand why dialogue is seemingly[4] so efficacious in some instances, and not at all so in others? Might we identify the conditions of possibility of dialogue, and thereby promote (at least a deeper understanding of the workings of) dialogue, and thereby contribute to the promotion of peace? This work has as its ultimate motivation the hope of making some modest contribution to this project, with a trust (however tempered by the "harsh reality" that being as war imposes "at the very moment of its fulguration when the drapings of illusion burn" (TI 21 [IX])) in the blessing promised to those, and by those, who undertake peacemaking, a trust that can, nevertheless, perhaps only take the form of a testimony[5] with dirt under its fingernails.

More specifically, we[6] come to this work with the hope of making some progress in thinking through what we shall refer to as "the problem of interparadigmatic dialogue"—that is, the possibility of dialogue between those whose fundamental understandings of and approaches to the world are sufficiently divergent that the potential interlocutors are incapable of finding a common point of appeal that would serve to mediate between, and effectively sort out, their differences, and where these differences create a conflict with respect to some or other aspect of the ongoing fullness of life for those involved.[7] The problem of interparadigmatic dialogue, we shall argue, creates a particular problem for dialogue as this term is conceived of in the philosophical tradition, in that with the problem of interparadigmatic dialogue the very status of the *logos* upon which *dia-logos* is built is called into question; that is, in the problem of interparadigmatic dialogue, the "difference" between interlocutors that it is precisely the role of the *logos* of *dia-logos* to reduce or eliminate imposes itself precisely as incapable of being reduced, at least insofar as the interlocutors retain their difference, that is, remain themselves.[8]

Our question, then, is this: How is dialogue between those holding to divergent paradigm positions possible? Or, again: What are the conditions of possibility for interparadigmatic dialogue? Our thesis, following upon the work of Emmanuel Levinas, and in opposition to the predominant part of the Western philosophical tradition, is that the fundamental condition of possibility for dialogue is not, as the tradition maintains, that I be "more rational" (that is, more attentive to the *logos* that, as we shall see, governs *dia-logos*), but that I be "more good," ethically better (that is, more attentive to the other to whom the *logos* of *dia-logos* is spoken). That is, we shall argue, following Levinas, that the condition of possibility of dialogue, including interparadigmatic dialogue, is not a more robust *logos* (reason), but "a non-allergic, ethical relationship with the other," a relationship that Levinas will call "discourse," and much of this work will therefore unfold as an exposition and examination of this relationship, and its relationship to the possibility of dialogue. We shall argue, in effect, that dialogue is only possible to the extent that I undertake a dialogue, in Levinas's phrase, as the "one-for-the-other" of responsibility, that is, as an asymmetrical exposure/vulnerability/sacrifice to a meaning that originates in—that *is*—the other in his or her alterity, rather than as the securing of myself in the self-certainty of my own (rational) meanings, and attempting to proceed toward the other from there. For Levinas, communication, eidetically, "is possible only in sacrifice, which is the approach of the other for which one is responsible. Communication with the other can be transcendent only as a dangerous life, a fine risk to run" (OTB 120 [154]). Here, then, the possibility of dialogue will be revealed as a risk, a supreme risk to the egoity of the ego—but, as Levinas writes, as a beautiful risk to run, a risk that, as the condition of possibility for dialogue, opens up upon the possibility of peace, or that, as we shall see in the final chapter, is itself the very gesture of peace.

We shall begin, then, in part I ("The Idea of Discourse"), by analyzing the idea of discourse (and, specifically, this idea as it pertains to the questions surrounding the possibilities for dialogue and peace we have here set out to address) as this idea comes to expression in Levinas's 1961 study *Totality and Infinity,* arguing our first thesis—that discourse is the condition of possibility for dialogue—across three chapters: first, by indicating, by way of a Levinasian analysis, the impasse into which the philosophical tradition of the West runs when faced with the problem of interparadigmatic dialogue (chapter 1: "The Impasse of Dialogue"); second, by setting out the terms—the same and the other—that as separated would be capable of sustaining the relationship of discourse (chapter 2: "Original Plurality: The Terms of Discourse"); and finally by following Levinas in his description of how the *logos* of *dia-logos,* and thus dialogue itself, depends for its meaning (and for its very possibility as meaningful) upon the ethical relationship of discourse (chapter 3: "Discourse as the Condition of Possibility of Dialogue").

Then, in part II ("A Possible Impossibility") we will attempt to deepen these analyses by reading the idea of discourse as it emerges in *Totality and Infinity* through the modified vocabulary and problematics of Levinas's 1974 text *Otherwise Than Being or Beyond Essence,* arguing a second thesis—that the idea of discourse in Levinas is well thought as a possible impossibility—across three chapters: first, by analyzing the "new" terms in terms of which "discourse" is said otherwise (chapter 4: "The Two Aspects of Language: The Saying and the Said"); second, by bringing these terms and the question of their complex interrelationships to bear upon the question of the possibility/impossibility of discourse (chapter 5: "The Two Directions in Language: The Reductive and the Re-constructive"); and, finally, by showing how this possible impossibility that is discourse is illuminated and deepened in Levinas's analysis of temporality (chapter 6: "The Moment of Responsibility: Time and Eternity"). It is in these three chapters that what we shall call "the intrigue of ethics," while foreshadowed in the opening three chapters, will begin to take shape as the non-ontological, religio-familial "horizon" in terms of which discourse itself will be shown to be im/possible as a non-allergic relationship with the other.

In part III ("Discourse, Philosophy, and Peace"), we shall argue (in chapter 7: "Levinas's Philosophical Discourse") that Levinas's philosophical discourse is well read as itself a performative example of discourse, as itself a non-allergic, ethical relationship with the other (in the form of testimony and prophecy to the intrigue of ethics in which this thought finds itself implicated). In this chapter we shall further argue that the particular radicalization of transcendental philosophy practiced by Levinas is precisely in the service of this ethical performative. Finally, we shall conclude (in chapter 8: "The Im/possibility of Peace") by revisiting the question of peace, the issue with which we begin and that guides the research—however far afield it appears at times to go—and suggest that peace itself is well described, on Levinas's accounting, as a possible impossibility. There we shall venture to follow out this thought and examine its implications with respect to our hopes for, and calling to, peace, and to the possibility of a dialogue that—we pray—opens us up upon the intrigue of ethics that is its very condition.

Notes

1. An obvious example of this faith in action at the macro-level is the institution of the United Nations. The idea of a "government of

governments" is, of course, not limited to the twentieth century, and the notion of dialogue as the way to peace (through truth) runs as deeply as the roots of Western rationalism. Plato already gives us Socratic dialogue as the way to truth, and peace (for almost the whole of the subsequent tradition—although the exceptions to this truth-peace progression, of which Levinas finds an indication in Plato himself, will be of considerable importance to Levinas) is grounded in this "truth," a movement we will be at some pains to trace here. We shall argue in this work, however, and ironically, that the rationalism that inspired this faith (or at least the rationalist articulation of this faith whose inspiration comes from "elsewhere") is not, in itself, up to making it work, is not up to delivering upon its promise of peace. That this has been recognized, increasingly, in our century (in the work, e.g., of Rosenzweig, Buber, Marcel) is, Levinas claims, testified to by a "new orientation" for dialogue in philosophy (and elsewhere), indeed, for a "philosophy of dialogue" that is opposed to "the philosophical tradition of the unity of the Ego or of the system and of the self-sufficience of immanence." (Wherein truth is thought of as subordinate to the relationship of dialogue, as its product, rather than as productive of it?) Levinas provides a possible historical explanation for the ubiquity, in academic circles and elsewhere, of this "new orientation": "The value that an entire series of philosophers, theologians and moralists, politicians, and even the general public attaches to the notion, the practice, and, in each case, to the word 'dialogue,' to the face-to-face discourse that people undertake, calling upon one another and exchanging pronouncements and objections, questions and responses, attests a new orientation of the idea that, perhaps following the trials of the twentieth century since the First World War, occidental society makes of the essence of the meaningful and the spiritual" (Emmanuel Levinas, "Le dialogue," in *De dieu qui vient à l'idée* [Paris: Librairie philosophique J. Vrin, 1986], p. 211, our translation; hereafter, references to this work will be indicated by the short form DVI, and citations from this text—untranslated at the time of writing—will appear in French in our text, with our translation provided in the notes). Perhaps. Perhaps it is the horror of our century's technical and moral capacity for large-scale violence that has driven us to seek in dialogue, in an unprecedented manner (increasingly, and with a revised manner of thinking of dialogue), a way to peace, a recourse to dialogue driven by a commitment—"Never again" (and after each relapse: "Again, never again")—a commitment the exigency of which has been augmented, one would have to think, by the ominous specter of nuclear war, an unthinkable possibility that, paradoxically, may have put an end to any large-scale war, forcing us to seek nonviolent ways to settle our conflicts. (Or, has it simply driven us to have recourse to other, more subtle forms of violence?)

2. We shall later argue, following Levinas, that such an argument cannot be made, that one cannot (sensibly) give reasons for that which provides the condition of possibility for reason itself, even though it has been the obsession of Western philosophy to do so, and which, in so doing, has buried the (pre)origin of meaning beneath a superstructure of derivative meanings.

3. By "peace" we mean not simply that positivity implied by the doubly negative term "nonviolence," a certain laissez-faire "live and let live" (a hardly credible idea given the global implications of our contemporary environmental/economic interconnectedness), but rather peace as a double positive, entailing both nonviolence and positive "curative help." (This latter phrase is taken from Emmanuel Levinas, "Useless Suffering," trans. R. Cohen, in *The Provocation of Levinas: Rethinking the Other,* ed. R. Bernasconi and D. Wood [New York: Routledge, 1988], p. 158.) That is to say that peace in the fullest sense, what Levinas will refer to as "messianic peace" (Emmanuel Levinas, *Totality and Infinity: An Essay on Exteriority,* trans. Alphonso Lingis [The Hague: Martinus Nijhoff, 1979], p. 22 [Emmanuel Levinas, *Totalité et infini: essai sur l'extériorité* (La Haye: Martinus Nijhoff, 1961), p. X]; hereafter, references to this text will be indicated with the short form TI followed by page references to the English translation, and references to the French text in square brackets), is not merely the absence of war ("Peace . . . cannot be identified with the end of combats that cease for want of combatants, by the defeat of some and the victory of the others, that is, with cemeteries or future universal empires" (TI 306 [283])), but implies the ideas of reconciliation and a community of those living in mutually supportive ways, notions that we will argue—against an "individualistic" reading—are central to Levinas's whole project.

4. It is also possible that even in those instances where it has seemed to succeed, where recourse to dialogue has put an end to or averted a violent outbreak, that it has simply been—by threat, by ruse, or by rhetoric—the imposition of another form of violence, where "interlocutors" have been forced to accept the terms of an "agreement" against their wishes and best interests. Levinas refers to such a "peace" as the peace founded upon war—e.g., "The peace of empires issued from war rests on war. It does not restore to the alienated beings their lost identity" (TI 22 [X])—and, while he admits that such "peace" is better than war, it is not to be confused with genuine, or messianic, peace, which, indeed, inspires or animates whatever peacefulness "the peace of empires" is capable of delivering: "Commerce is better than war, for in

peace the Good has already reigned" (Emmanuel Levinas, *Otherwise Than Being or Beyond Essence,* trans. Alphonso Lingis [The Hague: Martinus Nijhoff, 1981], p. 5 [Emmanuel Levinas, *Autrement qu'être ou au-delà de l'essence* (La Haye: Martinus Nijhoff, 1974), p. 5]; hereafter, references to this text will be indicated by the short form OTB, followed by the page number of the English translation and the page number of the French edition in square brackets). And this confusion need be avoided, perhaps, because this "peace as commerce" is, at least in a certain aspect, still war—not the violence of war waged, but the tyranny of war won. We shall have to address these problems.

5. We shall be preparing throughout this work for a description of the import, both ethical and philosophical, of this testimony, a description that will attain explicit expression only in our chapter 7 wherein its structure, and a tracing of that to which it testifies, will be revealed across the thesis that the whole of Levinas's philosophical discourse needs be read as testimonial/prophetic.

6. In this work I, Jeffrey Dudiak, shall adopt the convention of using the too formal, editorial "we" when I mean "me," the one writing this piece, despite the fact that this convention contravenes much of what is argued for in the work itself. The reason for this adoption is technical: the desire to save "I" for the I of Levinas's discourse. Problems surrounding Levinas's employment of the personal pronoun "I" will be discussed at some length in our chapter 7.

7. That is to say, we are interested specifically in the dilemma surrounding those cases where one is not able simply to say "live and let live," "let be," since the point of contention bears upon the very life of the opposing parties (e.g., diverse peoples who "share" a holy city or ancestral land that, according to the tenets of the different ethno-religio-ideological traditions, can be possessed only by its own followers, like the situation of the Jews and Palestinians with respect to Jerusalem, or that of the Catholics and Protestants regarding Northern Ireland). Whether these differences be religious, ethnic, political, "philosophical" in the broad sense, or what have you, we are thinking for the most part of differences in what is most commonly today referred to as ideology. We shall argue, however, that, contrary to the "rational-liberal" viewpoint, seeking a reduction of ideologies is no way to proceed here, since this viewpoint imposes its own, even if more subtle (in denying that it is an ideology), ideology—ultimately adding to, rather than reducing, the problem of conflicting ideological viewpoints.

8. As we shall see, it is, and from the perspective of the tradition paradoxically, precisely this difference—that which for the tradition impedes the success of dialogue and must therefore be overcome—that for Levinas opens up the very possibility of dialogue.

PART I
The Idea of Discourse

1

The Impasse of Dialogue

DIALOGUE, as the transmission of meaningful thought contents between interlocutors, is, etymologically, *dia-logos,* a transmission mediated *dia* ("through") the *logos* ("word," or "reason"). As such, the very notion of dialogue presupposes an a priori commonality of access to a shared *logos* for all prospective participants in the desired dialogue. The *logos,* if it is to effectively perform its mediatory function, must be shared, must be the same *logos* accessible to each. If dialogue, after its etymological sense, is to be possible, I must be able to speak a word (a *logos*) whose meaning for me corresponds to the meaning that that same word evokes in the other, that is to say, that I and my interlocutor must share both a lexicon of same-signifying signs, and the faculty, namely reason (*logos*), for the processing of such signs into thought contents and back, the faculty whereby such signs are linked to thoughts, and thoughts one to another. That in Greek, the language philosophy speaks,[1] the same word, *logos,* signifies at once "the word by which the inward thought is expressed," and "the inward thought or reason itself,"[2] need be given some attention, for it is in the alibi of this ambiguity that, traditionally, language has been made subordinate to thought.[3] Nor can we ignore the presence of this word at the root of the word 'dialogue', itself the progeny of Greek language/thought. *Logos* inhabits the very word, and our notion, of dialogue, founds its possibility, is the lifeblood of *dia-logos.* A *shared* language, mutual recourse to a series of signs that signify identically across the range of potential interlocutors by providing the external medium for linking up shared, inward thoughts, and the *common* means of processing such signs, are the conditions of possibility for dialogue as *dia-logos.*

But does dialogue not also require a difference between the interlocutors, in that dialogue, the very necessity of dialogue, makes sense only where one of the interlocutors lacks that which the other is capable of providing, necessitating the transmission that dialogue names? Identical terms would have nothing to offer to each other. If we were all the same, if our inward thoughts were identical, dialogue would be rendered superfluous. Is this not what Husserl saw when he denied that the experience of internal dialogue was anything more than a semblance? In the intimacy of the self-same philosophical subject, in "solitary mental life," thought is, according to Husserl, immediately self-present to itself, and no signs—signs, for Husserl, being that by which inward thought is externalized—are therefore required.[4] The same need not communicate with the same. Consequently, would not dialogue, insofar as it were real communication—a transmission of meanings between interlocutors—and not the semblance of language that, according to Husserl, is soliloquy, require, at once, *both* identity in the *logos, and* a difference among the terms in dialogue, that is to say, an identity in difference, or a difference in identity? What might such a locution mean? What might this at least seemingly oxymoronic exigency reflect?[5]

According to Emmanuel Levinas, the Western philosophical tradition has predominantly and overwhelmingly emphasized the identity aspect of this dual exigency for dialogue, emphasizing the common *logos* explicit in *dia-logos* at the expense of the implicit (but no less necessary) difference.[6] For the tradition, the difference requisite for dialogue is taken be a function of—either as a fall away from or as a step in the movement toward—a more primordial or originary[7] identity, resulting in a view of dialogue that Levinas, as we shall shortly see, refers to as the "dialogue of immanence," that is, a view whereby dialogue is part and parcel of the process of reducing all difference to identity, of reducing all transcendence to immanence, or of reducing the other to the same. This process, Levinas claims, endemic to philosophy as ontology, the overwhelmingly predominant mode in which Western philosophy has been transacted, is accomplished precisely by recourse to a term independent of the terms in relation but common to each, such as, for instance, the mediatory logos of *dia-logos,* that, we have been so far suggesting, is the condition of possibility for dialogue. As such, we shall argue, the conception of dialogue as *dia-logos* (by which we shall mean dialogue as predicated upon the a priori commonality of the *logos* for all potential interlocutors, as the condition of possibility for dialogue) is but one manifestation of the Western philosophical/ontological project.

It is the purpose of this opening chapter to trace Levinas's account of dialogue after this philosophically predominant conception, and to indicate the impasse into which this model leads regarding the possibility of giving an adequate account of dialogue, and, in particular, the possibility of giving an adequate account of the possibility of interparadigmatic dialogue. In this chapter the problem of interparadigmatic dialogue will be presented precisely as problematic (that is, problematic for dialogue after the ontological model) in presenting us with a dialogical situation (or at least a situation that calls for dialogue) where the a priori commonality of the *logos* that dialogue as *dia-logos* presupposes is precisely that which is in question, where the conceptual presuppositions of the ontological conception of dialogue are disturbed insofar as the requisite common *logos*, at least for practical purposes, cannot be effectively located, and is thus rendered incapable of performing its mediatory function. For if we are, even in practice, incapable of locating the *logos* as our common point of appeal, what becomes of the possibility of *dia-logos?* That is to say that the challenge of interparadigmatic dialogue brings to the fore the difference between interlocutors that, even while required for dialogue, has, according to Levinas, been suppressed by the tradition. The practical, theoretical, and ethical problems with this suppression will, in this chapter, be addressed in turn. It is, moreover, as we shall see in subsequent chapters, precisely to this difference that Levinas will turn as a starting point for his alternative account of dialogue. But first, we turn to the tradition out of which dialogue as *dia-logos* draws its conceptual resources.

I. Dialogue as *Dia-logos:* The Ontological Model

Levinas gives his reading of dialogue on the model of the philosophical tradition most concisely in a relatively late (1980) article entitled "Le Dialogue,"[8] wherein he describes such a view as "le dialogue de l'immanence." In order to understand what drives an understanding of dialogue conceived after this fashion, it is necessary to take a few pages[9] to introduce and summarize Levinas's reading of what he takes to be the major motif of the Western philosophical tradition, the tradition from which such a view of dialogue emerges, namely, the reduction of the other to the same.

I.1. Ontology as a Reduction of the Other to the Same

According to Levinas, "Western philosophy has most often been an ontology: a reduction of the other to the same by interposition of a middle and neutral term that ensures the comprehension of being" (TI 43 [13]).[10] As this quotation indicates, it is Levinas's thesis that philosophy as it has been predominantly practiced in the West has been, in its deepest spirit and in terms of its dominant motifs (despite a number of significant[11] "lapses"), a reduction of the other to the same,[12] or, which is to say the same (because of Levinas's linking of ethics with respect and responsibility for the dignity of the other qua other—a thesis to be developed in due course), a reduction of ethics to ontology.

To read the history of Occidental philosophy as fundamentally an ontology, and to recognize in this history the reduction of alterity as its systematic result, is to see in ontology a complex of terms and ideas whose interrelations form a matrix of thought whose regime internally promotes this reduction. For Levinas, then, ontology is not only the application of the *logos* to the *ontos*, or the logicizing of the *ontos* (*onto-logos*) in order that being might become intelligible—although it is that. It is also the complicity of *logos* and *ontos* in an attempt to exclude being's "other,"[13] that is, by limiting in advance that which is permitted to have the status of meaning or truth to that which fits into the "theoretical" correlation between the (*logos* endowed) *knower* and the *known* (the *ontos*).[14]

Continuing this quotation, Levinas traces this "reduction"[15] of the other to the same, this primacy of ontology in Western intellectual discourse, to the onset of the classical period of our philosophical tradition—to Socratic maïeutics:[16]

> This primacy of the same was Socrates's teaching: to receive nothing of the Other but what is in me, as though from all eternity I

> was in possession of what comes to me from the outside—to receive nothing, or to be free. Freedom does not resemble the capricious spontaneity of free will; its ultimate meaning lies in this permanence in the same, which is reason. Cognition is the deployment of this liberty; it is freedom. That reason in the last analysis would be the manifestation of a freedom, neutralizing the other and encompassing him, can come as no surprise once it was laid down that sovereign reason knows only itself, that nothing other limits it. The neutralization of the other who becomes a theme or an object—appearing, that is, taking its place in the light—is precisely his reduction to the same. To know ontologically is to surprise in an existent confronted that by which it is not this existent, this stranger, that by which it is somehow betrayed, surrenders, is given in the horizon in which it loses itself and appears, lays itself open to grasp, becomes a concept. (TI 43–44 [13–14])

In this passage several key pillars of the ontological edifice are indicated, elements whose parallel and mutually supportive constructions will constitute what Levinas calls "l'impérialisme ontologique" (TI 44 [15]). We shall organize our discussion of Levinas's characterization of Western thought around three of these, showing their interconnections, and the part that each plays in philosophy as ontology, in philosophy as a reduction of the other to the same: ontology as an expression of freedom, ontology as the unity of Reason, and ontology as the ultimate identity of the free psychism and Reason.

I.1.i. Ontology as an Expression of Freedom As an expression of freedom, or perhaps better, as an expression of the will to freedom (because, for Levinas, the thinking subject never does, despite its ontological "strivings," achieve such autonomy), ontological thought is constituted in such a manner as to permit the thinking subject to assert its independence with respect to anything exterior that might serve to limit it, such that the thinking subject "n'est limitrophe de rien" (TI 61 [32]). This will to freedom that, according to Levinas, is the driving spirit of both Western thought and of Western culture in general[17] is defined by Levinas as the will "to maintain oneself against the other, despite every relation with the other to ensure the autarchy of an I" (TI 46 [16]). Levinas argues that this will to freedom, this will to autonomy, as reflected in Socratic maïeutics, has served as the guiding motif for the greater part of Western thought, and it is this aspiration that determines the way in which the free being relates to exterior being. Not surprisingly, the form that this relation takes in philosophy is the theoretical relation, the theoretical relation *as* a relation between the autonomous agent and exteriority, but this in a way that harbors an irony. For the theoretical relationship with being is, according to Levinas, "first" (d'abord) a relationship that would leave the exterior being "unmarked," that is to say, genuinely exterior, and thus able to be known as it is "in itself"—that which precisely provides it with its metaphysical privilege (where "metaphysics" names that relationship where the other is related to as *other,* as over against the relationship that reduces the other to the same that Levinas names "ontology")—but ends by being a relationship through which exterior being will be subsumed by the free psyche, through which the alterity of the other *as* other, as other absolutely, is suppressed in so far as it is brought into a relationship of correlation with the knowing I, into correlation in its being "known," in much the same manner in which, for Plato of the *Parmenides,* "the relation with the Absolute would render the Absolute relative" (TI 50 [21]). For theory is, at one and the same time, not only an expression of metaphysical desire (where "desire" desires to encounter exteriority as genuinely exterior),[18] but also functions as "intelligence" (which, Levinas argues, compromises the exteriority of being insofar as what it is *taken* to "be," what is *permitted* to have being as its essential attribute, is *taken* as a function of its being known, as if it fulfilled a "need" or "lack" in the knower).[19]

It is not by chance that the theoretical relation has been the preferred schema of the metaphysical relation. Knowledge or theory designates first a relation with being such that the knowing being lets the known being manifest itself while respecting its alterity and without marking it in any way whatever by this cognitive relation. In this sense metaphysical desire would be the essence of theory. But theory also designates comprehension [intelligence]—the *logos* of being—that is, a way of approaching the known being such that its alterity with regard to the knowing being vanishes. The process of cognition is at this stage identified with the freedom of the knowing being encountering nothing that, other with respect to it, could limit it (TI 42 [12]).

The original, "metaphysical" side of this relation (where metaphysics designates the desire to enter into relation with exteriority as genuinely exterior, or other), has, Levinas claims, been largely betrayed by philosophy as ontology[20] in favor of that side of the relation that is here characterized as intelligence, a relation ("ontological" as opposed to "metaphysical") that attains exteriority by means of bringing it into correlation with the knowing psyche, which, as the quotation above indicates, is an expression of the freedom of the knowing subject.

Levinas argues that it is precisely this "intelligence" that overwhelmingly marks, in Western thought, the relationship of the psyche to exteriority, such that "the psychism conceived as knowledge" underlies and dominates all of the psyche's modes of consciousness (up to, and terminating in, consciousness of itself), all of its experience, everything that it "lives":

> C'est dans le psychisme conçu comme savoir—allant jusqu'à la conscience de soi—que la philosophie transmise situe l'origine ou le lieu naturel du sensé et reconnaît l'esprit. Tout ce qui advient dans le psychisme humain, tout ce qui s'y passe, ne finit-il pas par se savoir? . . . Tout le vécu se dit légitimement *expérience*. Il se convertit en "leçons reçues" qui convergent en unité du savoir, quelles que soient ses dimensions et ses modalités. (DVI 212)[21]

Levinas enumerates a wide variety of modalities of experience that, for the tradition, are, he claims, ultimately taken as modalities of "knowing" broadly conceived: contemplation, will, or affectivity; sensibility and understanding; external perception, self-consciousness, and self-reflection; objective thematization and familiarity of that which is not pro-posed; primary or secondary qualities, kinesthetic and cenesthetic sensations; relations with neighbors, social groups, or God (as collective and religious *experiences*); even the indetermination of "to live" and the familiarity of the pure "to exist."[22] In short, all of the modalities of living, of experiencing, come back, for *la philosophie transmise,* according to Levinas, to experiences convertible into "knowledge." Even the secret and the unconscious, "refoulés [repressed] ou altérés [or distorted]"—and thus defined in terms of consciousness—are, according to Levinas, measured or "healed" by consciousness, which it (consciousness) has "lost" or which have lost it: "C'est sans doute ce savoir implicite qui justifie l'emploi large qui, dans les *Méditations,* Descartes fait du terme cogito. Et ce verbe à la première personne dit bien l'unité du Moi où tout savoir se suffit" (DVI 212).[23] That which, according to the tradition, is permitted to have meaning must be found in the knower-known correlation, is either *cogito* or *cogitatum,* and outside of this, outside of meaning, there is nothing, or at least nothing meaningful, nothing of which we might know, or to which we might refer.[24]

The psyche, conceived essentially as *savoir,* as *cogito,* thus approaches exteriority as an object *à savoir,* but with the assurance that that which it meets in exteriority will be correlative with its capacity as knower, that nothing can really surprise it because all exteriority will fit with this capacity, that the *psychisme comme savoir* has already been prepared to receive exteriority "as if from all eternity I possessed that which comes to me from without" (TI 43 [14]):

> En tant que savoir, la pensée porte sur le pensable; sur le pensable appelé être. Portant sur l'être, elle est hors d'elle-même, mais demeure merveilleusement en elle-même ou revient à elle-même. L'extériorité ou l'altérité du soi est reprise dans l'immanence. Ce que la pensée connait ou ce que dans son "expérience" elle apprend, est à la fois l'*autre* et le *propre* de la pensée. On n'apprend que ce que l'on sait déjà et qui s'insère dans l'intériorité de la pensée en guise de souvenir évoquable, re-présentable. Réminiscences et imaginations assurent comme la synchronie et l'unité de ce qui, dans l'expérience soumise au temps, se perd ou est seulement à venir. (DVI 212–13)[25]

The knowing subject here collects every dispersion, gathers everything into itself, including, by means of memory and imagination, the dispersion that is time. The *psychisme comme savoir* is conceived of as being capable of making all exteriority present to itself, brought into its present, as if it were not truly alien, as if it were always already a part of the subject, as if it parted from the subject.[26] Exteriority thus is re-presented, presented as if once again, brought back to its origin, brought home. Every representation is a re-presentation. So the image proper to the sojourn of the psyche into being is a circuitous "Odyssean" one, an odyssey, a journey that ends where it began, rather than an "Abrahamic" adventure, for the psyche in its travels, while it may well be itself enriched, discovers nothing that can surprise it, nothing genuinely new (and is thus no advent-ure). Its discoveries are rediscoveries, a taking back, a taking hold of, that which has really always already belonged to it: maïeutics.

Maïeutic learning is, moreover, not only a (re)learning of that which has always already been in me, but as such a (re)possession: "En tant qu'apprendre, la pensée comporte une saisie, une *prise* sur ce qui est appris et une possession" (DVI 213).[27] Thus, according to Levinas, the etymological foundation found in so many words for knowing relations broadly conceived are not purely metaphorical: ap-*prendre,* Be-*griff,* con-*ception.* Even, as he claims—linking the presentation of an object to its availability for *main*-ipulation[28]—in "La présence se fait main-tenant" (DVI 213). This hand-grasping ["mainmise"], hand-ling of, taking possession of exteriority, is *main*-ifested, moreover, in accordance with the centrality of the *savoir* to consciousness, not only in con-*ception,* but also in every per-*ception,* indeed, for every mode of consciousness, for everything "lived," that is, "known" in the broadest sense, where knowing is finding being already in correlation with, susceptible to as a function of, a freedom whose "taking" of something [as . . .] gives to the "given" its givenness, be that across transcendental forestructures.

Further, and correlatively, the psychism finds in being a willing object; while the knower exercises a grasp upon the known, the known "*se donne*" ("is given," or "gives itself"—in either case, exhibiting a passivity—and perhaps even an active passivity!—with respect to the active knower who takes it) to the knower:

> Le "se donner"—quels que soient les efforts qu'exige la distance "de la coupe aux lèvres"—est à l'échelle de la pensée pensante, lui promet, à travers sa "transcendence" une possession et une jouissance, une satisfaction. Comme si la pensée pensant à sa mesure de par le fait de pouvoir—incarnée—rejoindre ce qu'elle pense. Pensée et psychisme de l'immanence: de la suffisance à soi. (DVI 213)[29]

This *assured* correlation between the thinker and the thinkable, where the thinkable gives itself to the thinker as if it were fulfilling a need in the latter, is, Levinas claims, precisely "the phenomenon of the world," and he claims that it is perhaps this that Husserl expressed in affirming the correlation between the thinker and the world as *the* correlation (DVI 213). In the work of Hegel, too, "où viennent se jeter tous les courants de l'esprit occidental et où se manifestent tous ses niveaux,"[30] Levinas finds this correlation, up to the point where it is, finally, dissolved into self-consciousness. In this philosophy of absolute knowledge and of satisfied man, "Le psychisme du savoir théorétique constitue une pensée qui pense à sa mesure et, dans son adéquation au pensable, s'égale à elle-même, sera consciente de soi." In specific reference to Hegel, then, but also with an eye to the Western philosophical tradition in general, Levinas therefore asserts: "C'est le Même qui se retrouve dans l'Autre" (DVI 214).[31]

I.1.ii. Ontology as the Unity of Reason If the psychism thus claims its freedom (its autonomy) with respect to exterior being by bringing that exteriority into line with itself, into line with its freedom, by assuring a correlation between itself as thinking subject and the object that *se donne* to the *prise* of conception, we must nevertheless note, with Levinas, that this freedom is not, for the tradition, as noted in the quotation regarding Socrates and maïeutics above, "the capricious spontaneity of free will" (TI 43 [14]), the arbitrary freedom of a perfidious will. It is, rather, the expression of a *rational* will, for it is as rational that the psyche is capable of effectuating the correlation with exterior being in terms of which its freedom is exerted: "L'activité de la pensée *à raison* de toute altérité et c'est en cela, en fin de compte que réside sa rationalité même" (DVI 214).[32]

The *je pense* by which exteriority is assumed is not, then, any arbitrary *je veux* constituting its world in any capricious manner it wills, but must correspond to the rational order governing being. By way of example, Levinas indicates that this emphasis has a hold even in the thought of Husserl, the arch advocate of the idea of intentionality, of active, subjective meaning constitution:

> Dans la phénoménologie husserlienne—malgré la spontanéité créatrice conférée à l'Ego transcendental—les modes de la connaissance sont commandés—téléologie de la conscience—

> essentiellement par l'être auquel la connaissance accède. L'esprit c'est l'ordre des choses—ou les choses en ordre—dont la pensée pensante ne serait que le recueillement et le rangement. La possibilité ou l'espoir qu'aurait le *je pense* de ne plus se poser pour soi en face du pensable, de s'effacer devant l'intelligible, serait son intelligence même, sa rationalité, son ultime intériorisation. (DVI 215)[33]

In order to effectuate this correlation with exterior being, therefore, it is necessary for the *je pense* to surrender itself to a term that would mediate the relationship between itself and exteriority, a neutral, middle term that would ensure the correspondence and govern the process of intelligibility, which is, as we shall see, prerequisite to the possibility for the thinking being to exercise its grasp upon (power over) exteriority and thus maintain its freedom. Ironically, then, in order for the psychism to be free, to bring exteriority under the control of the same, it must sacrifice its freedom (as arbitrary and capricious), its particularity, to a third term, a neutral, middle term between itself and exteriority that will "assure the intelligibility of being": "This mode of depriving the known being of its alterity can be accomplished only if it is aimed at through a third term, a neutral term, which itself is not a being; in it the shock of the encounter of the same with the other is deadened. This third term may appear as a concept thought. Then the individual that exists abdicates into the general that is thought" (TI 42 [12]).

This third term, "*moyen et neutre,*" placed between the knower and the known, before which the psyche as arbitrary will must "efface itself" or "abdicate," has, in the history of philosophy, appeared under a number of guises. It has been, according to Levinas, manifested as sensation (as in Berkeley—where all sensible qualities are immersed in the lived experience of affection),[34] as being as distinguished from entities (as in phenomenology—where the entity is disclosed against the horizon that is being),[35] or as rationality, the *logos,* itself.[36] In each instance, however, it functions—and this is the important point here—to provide a framework in which or against which the known being is known, it proffers itself as the system of intelligibility, or as the site of this intelligibility, as the light in which, or as the background against which, exterior being is disclosed. Levinas relates this neutral third to the "intelligible sun" in Plato, to the light outside of the eye and the object that makes seeing possible, a light that itself is not in turn an object (lest another light be necessary to view it).[37] It is in terms of this nonentity that entities are manifested to the *je pense,* in terms of which their alterity is surrendered:

> To know amounts to grasping being out of nothing or reducing it to nothing, removing from it its alterity. This result is obtained from the moment of the first ray of light. To illuminate is to remove from being its resistance, because light opens a horizon and empties space—delivers being out of nothingness. Mediation (characteristic of Western philosophy) is meaningful only if it is not limited to reducing distances. (TI 44 [14])

This neutral third, whatever its particular manifestation, as mediatory, as that by which the "shock" of the meeting of differences is parleyed into assured correlation, opens the way toward the important Levinasian concept of "totality," a term that designates the whole into which everything that is "fits" as parts of this whole, this "fitting" being orchestrated by the neutral third. As such, the idea of totality must be technically (if not practically, as we shall see) distinguished (at least temporarily)[38] from the notion of "the Same," that to which, as we saw in the previous section, all alterity is, in its confrontation with a free ego, reduced. For if "the Same" is a term used to designate all of that that is me, is in me, and is in my grasp,[39] then "totality" is used to designate that system of coherence outside of me that, as it were, has me (as *part*icularized ego, as a "part" of the "whole") in its grasp—as it has in its grasp everything intelligent or intelligible, that is, everything. The neutral third is, as such, as its mediatory role requires, either the unified and universal order of Reason itself, or that upon which this order is founded, and as such yields the possibility of Truth, the assured correlation of knower and known. And this is possible precisely because "La raison est une. . . . rien n'est en dehors d'elle" (DVI 216);[40] and in this way it guarantees the unity of the totality.

The Same, therefore, in order to insulate itself against the other (which will turn out to be a justifying of itself in the face of the other), against exteriority, takes refuge in the totality, sacrifices its arbitrary self to the totality, endeavors

> to apprehend itself within a totality. This seems to us to be the justification of freedom aspired after by the philosophy that, from Spinoza to Hegel, identifies will and reason, that, contrary to Descartes, removes from truth its character of being a free work so as to situate it where the opposition between the I and the non-I disappears, in an impersonal reason. Freedom is not maintained but reduced to being the reflection of a universal order. . . . Knowing would be the way by which freedom would denounce its own contingency, by which it would vanish into the totality. In reality this way dissimulates the ancient triumph of the same over the other. If freedom thus ceases to maintain itself in the arbitrariness of the solitary certitude of evidence, and if the solitary is united to the impersonal reality of the divine, the I disappears in this sublimation. For the philosophical tradition of the West every relation between the same and the other, when it is no longer an affirmation of the supremacy of the same, reduces itself to an impersonal relation within a universal order. . . . Existents are reduced to the neuter state of the idea, Being, the concept. (TI 87–88 [59–60])

I.1.iii. Ontology as the Identity of the Psychism and Reason On the surface of things the abdication of the psyche—as the arbitrary self for itself—in the face of the neutral third would appear to negate the freedom of the psychism along with the alterity of beings, for while the correlation between the thinker and the thought (the thought found in a thinking where the other gives itself to the thinker as the thing thought) is maintained, here it is the thinker that must *se donne* to the system, to the order that governs being—conforming itself to the system of intelligibility. This apparent tension is overcome, however, when we remember that the freedom so negated is merely the freedom of the *arbitrary* will, and not at all that of the *rational* will. On the contrary, the rational will *borrows,* as it were, the rational structure of being in order to put itself in order, which, while corresponding to its disenfranchisement as arbitrary will, serves to confirm it as rational will.

For insofar as the rational will and Reason itself are in perfect correlation—that which *is* the system of intelligibility and the very possibility of Truth—the relation, the cor-relation, can be read indifferently from right to left or from left to right. This relation turns out, then, to be one of mutual borrowing: the psychism borrowing Reason in order to put itself in order as rational (and thus free) will (for, we will recall, it is as rational that the will is able to *a raison de toute altérité,* and thus maintain its freedom), and Reason borrowing the psychism in order to put itself in order through history. Thus Levinas says, in speaking along these lines of Hegel:

> Le *Je pense* où se constitue l'être-en-acte, peut être interprété comme coïncidant avec ce qu'il constitue: la pleine conscience de soi du *je pense,* serait le *système* même du savoir dans son unité d'intelligible. Le pensée pensante qui tend à cet ordre de la raison se dira, dès lors, malgré le labeur de sa recherche et le génie de son invention, comme un détour qu'emprunte le système de l'être pour se mettre en ordre, détour que suivent ses termes et ses structures pour s'arrimer. (DVI 214–15)[41]

This mutual borrowing between Reason and the rational will as an expression of Reason works in smooth complicity because, in the end, there is only one Reason, one discourse, one *cogito,* working itself out historically. It therefore becomes impossible (and this will be of the utmost importance in the discussion of dialogue to follow) to distinguish between my rationality and Reason itself—precisely because these are, when all is said and done, one and the same. In the end there is only one *je pense,* rational thought thought through *me;* in full self-consciousness I, the *je pense,* in being borrowed by the system, am the system of knowledge in its unity of intelligibility itself: " 'I, Plato, am the truth.' That, as Nietzsche said, is philosophy's opening and paradigmatic gesture. The philosopher *is* the truth and he speaks the truth by turning within himself."[42]

This rationalizing of the psychism, this borrowing of the system, far from negating the freedom of the will, is its "ultimate interiorization," that by which it "secures itself," is its affirmation of itself as its truest self—free, rational, and unified. Thus, "[p]ar opposition à l'intériorité des passions sournoises et des perfides secrètes des opinions subjectives, la Raison serait la vraie vie intérieure" (DVI 216).[43] The limitation on the will, the need to subject itself to the intelligible system of being, is a limitation that is, in effect, a self-limitation (which is no real limitation at all), and that ends by confirming rather than betraying its freedom.

Further, not only does the sacrifice of the arbitrary will allow for the retrieval of the rational, or authentic, will, thus confirming its authentic freedom along with its authentic "self," this sacrifice contributes to the freedom of the same in yet a second way. For in compelling the sacrifice of one's arbitrary sovereignty of anarchic will, Western philosophy offers in return another kind of sovereignty, a "practical" freedom, that possible only for a rational will. This abdication, this obedience, permits of a taking up of a posture of power with respect to alterity, which itself shares in the rational order. In becoming its true, rational self, the sovereignty of unbridled will, the *je veux,* gives way to the sovereignty concordant with *ability,* the *je peux,* to the availing oneself of the power of technique[44] made possible in a knowable world because functioning as a rational system. In such a system: " 'I think' comes down to 'I can'—to an appropriation of what is, to an exploitation of reality. Ontology as first philosophy is a philosophy of power" (TI 46 [16]). Aligning myself with rationality opens to me a world susceptible to my powers, or more precisely, to the powers of Reason to which I am now privy, in which I, as myself rational, share.

That I should then demand that the other (here, clearly, the human other) also abdicate his or her capricious will to this term "*moyen et neutre,*" or more precisely, insist that the other's will is already so sacrificed, is not surprising, for my allegiance in this scheme is not to the other, but to Reason, and to its product: Truth. For who am I that I might transgress against Truth? Who is the other that he or she might transgress against Truth? And if peaceful relations between people is conceived of as a matter of their mutual submission to the *logos*/Truth, one cannot but, in the name of peace, insist that the other, like me, submit himself to Reason. Indeed, Western thought, consistent with its commitment, and consistent with the power relations involved in this commitment to the ontological scheme, has instituted sanctions against those who would transgress against Truth, either, at best, relegating the views of such "reprobates" to that of "mere opinion" and simply dismissing them as irrational, or, at worst, insisting that such be officially sanctioned.[45] Here, then, is a philosophical justification, even a philosophical imperative, for reducing the other to the same.

Still, this insistence upon "mutual" subjection nevertheless serves the ends of my liberty, even if it be the obedient liberty of the rational will. The co-implication of the other in the Rational order guarantees that he can no longer surprise me, that he cannot confront me with that which I do not already have access to myself. Here, maïeutics (with its knowledge/power and safety) is guaranteed. The threat of the other, even of the other within myself (that in me which would oppose my will as rational will), is removed. For if there were no neutral third to which the psyche and its other were both subject, the psyche would have to enter into an unregulated competition between capricious wills—thus subjecting itself to the ultimate risk of war.[46] With the institution of the neutral third, not only does the psyche no longer require the other, but so long as the other is following the rational order it cannot hurt the rational psyche, and this because ontology "issues in the State and in the nonviolence of the totality" (TI 46 [16]).[47] Moreover, in entering into this order, the other becomes knowable, becomes an "object" in a world of knowable, because rational, objects. Not only is the other's power over the psyche negated, but the psyche is now capable of exercising a certain power with respect to the other. So, to the "formal" sense of freedom (the psychism being free to be its deepest and truest self), and to the "practical" sense (where the psychism is capable of exercising power over being-things), is added a "political" sense of freedom (the power of the psychism over and against other psychisms).

So, after the ontological scheme that Levinas argues has dominated Occidental thought, the liberty of capricious will, whether it be that of the psyche or that of the other, is read as not being liberty at all, but slavery, slavery to transgression with respect to the Truth that alone can genuinely liberate. There is no room here for transgression, for an outside, for an other. To be free is to be subject, subject to the Truth, even if the Truth ends up, by way of the dialectic here disclosed by Levinas, in the service of the same: "Freedom comes from an obedience to Being: it is not man who possesses freedom; it is freedom that possesses man. But the dialectic which thus reconciles freedom and obedience in the concept of truth presupposes the primacy of the same, which marks the direction of and defines the whole of Western philosophy" (TI 45 [16]).[48]

The subjection to this neutral third leads back to the same in a decisive way that reunites the *je veux* of freedom with the *je pense* of *theoria* and the *je peux* of *phronesis* insofar as consciousness is read ultimately as self-consciousness. Indeed, how could the *temporary* sojourn into being that is consciousness do other than lead back to the psychism, and lead exteriority back to the psychism, when the psychism (at least at its most authentic) would itself have to have been rational from the first in order to enter into the system of intelligibility, in order to have brought itself into line with the system of intelligibility? This possibility indicates the necessity for the psychism to have been rational from the outset, and its relation with exteriority to have been, in fact, from the outset, a relation of self-expression and self-consciousness which confirms, in the end, the freedom with which it began: "The relation with the other is here accomplished only through a third term which I find *in myself* [en moi]. The ideal of Socratic truth thus rests on the essential self-sufficiency of the same, its identification in ipseity, its egoism. Philosophy is an egology" (TI 44 [14], emphasis ours).

The neutral third to which the psyche is to sacrifice itself is, in the end, found in the psyche itself, completing the circle (Odysseus comes home!) and reaffirming it in its freedom, in its freedom expressed in the power to know (and thus control) exteriority, ending in the relation of consciousness that is ultimately consciousness of itself. Thus Levinas claims, speaking of Hegel: "L'unité du *je pense* est la forme ultime de l'esprit comme savoir, dût-il se confondre avec l'être qu'il connaît et s'identifier au système de la connaissance" (DVI 214).[49]

From the original assertion of freedom, to the sacrifice of the arbitrary for the sake of the unity of intelligibility (which delivers another form of freedom), to the identification of the psyche with the very system of intelligibility—for Levinas the main line of the history of Western philosophy is suspended between the originary imperative of Socratic maïeutics to "know thyself" and the Hegelian consummation of this history where all consciousness is ultimately a consciousness of self, is a history that, in being motivated by the will to freedom, has for an effect the reduction of the other to the same.

I.2. Dialogue as the Dialogue of Immanence

Having given an account of Levinas's reading of the predominant emphasis in the Western philosophical tradition, wherein this tradition is read as "L'esprit comme savoir et l'immanence," that is, where the possibility of meaning finds its compass in the correlation between a knower and the known such that the other, in being brought into correlation with the *cogito,* is reduced to the same, we now turn our attention to the matter of dialogue, and specifically to Levinas's account of dialogue after the ontological model, a view of dialogue that Levinas refers to as "le dialogue de l'immanence."[50]

That is to say, if we are to conceive of dialogue along these "ontological" lines, we should not be surprised to discover that this model of dialogue—dialogue as *dia-logos,* dialogue as founded upon the interpretation of the *logos* as the third, neutral, and mediatory term between perspective interlocutors—shares, in repeating the gestures of ontology, in the predominant Occidental preoccupation with the reduction of the other to the same in the name of freedom, in the name of the psychism *as* the truth, as this psychism aligns itself with the System of intelligibility and its Truth. Dialogue after this model, as a function of the unified, rational, system of intelligibility, will reveal itself to be *un discours intérieur*—albeit with two possible manifestations (which, as we shall argue, are ultimately indistinguishable [at least in practice] in so far as they are variant emphases, or perspectives, on one and the same root structure): a discourse interior to the psychism (which utilizes Reason to ensure its own integrity and coherence), and a discourse interior to Reason itself (which uses the psychism to ensure its own integrity and coherence). In this section of the chapter we will examine what, according to Levinas, this interior discourse (or these interior discourses) would look like, in order later to investigate the problems with which such a model of dialogue presents us on practical, theoretical, and ethical levels, especially regarding the issue of interparadigmatic dialogue. We will thus arrive at our primary thesis for this chapter: that dialogue conceived as *dia-logos* is incapable of providing us with a model for dialogue that would be able to explain how dialogue with an other—an other who in being encountered as other is, as we have seen, the very *raison* for dialogue—would be possible, and possible as peace.

I.2.i. The Interior Discourse As we have seen, the psychism on the model of ontology is characterized by Levinas fundamentally as *savoir,* as a bringing of exteriority into coincidence with "consciousness" broadly conceived, as that which leaves itself only to return to itself and find itself wholly intact, enriched, perhaps, but *the same* consciousness. When this psychism "speaks," when it has recourse to language, this recourse is taken to be a function of its essential project: the coherence of knowledge and truth in itself. According to Levinas, then, language on this model, whatever its particular manifestation, "se laisse . . . comprendre dans sa subordination au savoir" (DVI 216):[51]

> Accord et unité du savoir dans la vérité. La pensée encore pensante les cherche par des voies diverses. Elle recourt certes au mots. Mais ce sont des signes qu'elle se donne à elle-même sans parler à quiconque: dans son oeuvre de rassemblement, elle peut avoir à rechercher une présence du pensable au-delà de ce qui se présente immédiatement—"en chair et en os" (leiblich da) ou en image, d'un signifié par signe; de ce qui n'est pas encore présent à la pensée, mais qui n'est plus déjà enfermé en soi. Qu'il n'y ait pas de pensée sans langage ne signifie, dès lors, que la nécessité d'un discours intérieur. (DVI 215)[52]

The production of signs, the origin of language, after this model, is born of the necessity for the psychism, in accord with its project of knowledge as self-consciousness, to bring into presence, to be able to make present to itself, that which is not immediately present, as a way of invoking into presence, or presentifying, the presently absent. Language, then, has nothing, at least not originally, to do with communicating with others, but is—strangely enough—a "communication with oneself," a monologue, a manner of thinking, a "tool" for self-reflection, a detour on the road to the completion of the maïeutic project. Dialogue is, originally, in its subordination to *savoir*, an interior discourse:

> La pensée se scinde pour s'interroger et se répondre, mais le fil se renoue. Elle *réfléchit* sur elle-même en interrompant sa progression spontanée, mais procède encore du même *je pense.* Elle reste la même. Elle passe d'un terme à un terme contraire qui l'appelle, mais la dialectique où elle se retrouve n'est pas un dialogue ou du moins c'est le dialogue de l'âme avec elle-même, procédant par questions et réponses. (DVI 215–16)[53]

Levinas notes that this structure of question and response internal to *le discours intérieur* is precisely that which defined thought for Plato (DVI 16, OTB 25 [31]), and, of course, for Levinas, the connections between thought, dialogue, maïeutics, and the unity of *savoir,* as these find expression in the ontological tradition, are not gratuitous; they are all expressions, functions, of the free ego seeking to effectuate its autonomy: "Selon l'interprétation traditionnelle du discours intérieur qui remonte à cette définition, l'esprit en pensant n'en demeure pas moins un et unique, malgré ses démarches et son va et vient où il peut s'opposer à soi" (DVI 216).[54]

Levinas argues that dialogue on this model is merely another manner of seeking certain truth, another way of accomplishing coincidence with oneself. But how, on this model, is one able to effectuate "the radical reversal, from cognition to solidarity, that communication represents with respect to inward dialogue, to cognition of oneself, taken as the trope of spirituality?" (OTB 119 [152]). When the birth of language is sought beginning from knowledge (to which it would be logically and perhaps chronologically posterior (DVI 218)), how would the language that "effectivement se parle" "à travers la multiplicité empirique des hommes pensants" (DVI 216)[55] be possible? The answer of the tradition, according to Levinas, is by way of apresentation and "sympathy":

> Dans la multiplicité empirique d'êtres existants comme consciences intentionnelles et incarnées, chacun aurait le savoir et la conscience de "quelque chose" et de sa propre conscience, mais arriverait par des expériences apprésentatives et l'*Einfühlung* à prendre conscience des consciences autres c'est-à-dire à connaître

> la conscience que chaque conscience autre a du meme "quelque chose", d'elle-même et de toutes les autres consciences. Ainsi s'établirait la communication: les signes du langage naîtraient de toutes les manifestations expressives des corps signifiants dans l'apprésentation. Le langage naîtrait à partir de l'apprésentation qui est à la fois expérience et lecture des signes. (DVI 218)[56]

That is to say that the signs that one gives to oneself, and that the others give to themselves, become, through appresentation, and a sympathy that allows one to "feel" one's way into the psychism of the other, signs that enter into a general economy of signs, but signs that nevertheless originate in, and return to, the psychism as *savoir.*

Not surprisingly, Levinas makes reference immediately following this quotation to Husserl's "Fifth Cartesian Meditation," which delineates the possibility of the "constitution" of intersubjectivity, claiming that here is to be found "une formulation rigoureuse de la subordination du langage au savoir, réduisant au vécu comme *expérience,* toute modalité indépendente du sens, à laquelle le dialogue pourrait prétendre" (DVI 218).[57] Levinas then quotes a text "caractéristique et remarquable" from Husserl's *Krisis* to illustrate the priority, in Husserl, of the interior discourse to any discourse that might follow from it: "Husserl va jusqu'à prétendre 'loger dans le discours intérieur le discours qui va à tous les autres' : 'ce que je dis là scientifiquement,' écrit-il, 'c'est de moi à moi que je le dis, mais du même coup, de façon paradoxale, je le dis à tous les autres, en tant qu'impliqués transcendantalement en moi et les autres dans les autres' " (DVI 218–19).[58]

Perhaps we might refer to this model for dialogue as "dialogue" proper, that is to say, as dialogue as *dia-logos,* as a dialogue based upon the psychism's *logos*-oriented appropriation of the world, including the appropriation of other persons, who, through appresentation, enter into, without disturbing, the dialogue the psychism is holding with itself.

I.2.ii. The Rational Conversation If the dialogue internal to the psychism can be said to correspond to the ontological search for freedom, where the psychism has recourse to words as a way of furthering its assumptive project, as this project was illustrated above in section I.1.i., then another manifestation of dialogue within the Western tradition can be seen to correspond to the expression of ontology as the unity of Reason as laid out in our section I.1.ii. For just as the psychism, on this conception, gives itself over, at least temporarily, to the system of intelligibility in order to put itself in order, in order to bring itself into line with the Truth, the user of language can be seen as giving himself over to a rational conversation that provides the framework within which this task of self-ameliorization can be accomplished—and it is as having entered into this neutral "exteriority" that speech, as communication with another, becomes possible.

For we will recall that the true interior life of freedom meant not an expression of freedom as "deceitful passions and perfidious secrets," but the expression of a rational will, a will that puts itself in order according to a system of intelligibility exterior to it. After this model, in accord with this strategy of self-ameliorization, "le langage . . . consiste pour chacun des interlocuteurs, à entrer dans la pensée de l'autre, à coïncider dans la *raison,* à s'y intérioriser" (DVI 216).[59] Dialogue remains no less a search for certitude, but certitude (rather than the assurance that all exteriority corresponds to me) is now predicated upon a bringing of oneself into correspondence with the rational System (or with that common term upon which the system of intelligibility is founded), that is, upon submitting oneself to a unified, external truth that as unified is capable of bringing all particular interlocutors under its auspices: "Those who wish to found on dialogue and on an original we the upsurge of egos, refer to an original communication behind the de facto communication . . . , and reduce the problem of communication to the problem of its certainty" (OTB 119–20 [153]). The result is a theory[60] "according to which a prior dialogue sustains the ego which states it, rather than the ego holding forth a conversation" (OTB 119 [153]).

If the dialogue that results from the abdication of individual egoisms in the face of a rational dialogue that transcends them and holds them in its dialogue is to be efficacious, this would require, then, the unity and unicity of Reason. As such, dialogue becomes a dialogue that reason holds with itself, making use of the various psychisms as speakers of parts it alone has written, as passive participants in *its* conversation: "The universal identity in which the heterogeneous can be embraced has the ossature of a subject, of the first person. Universal thought is an 'I think' " (TI 36 [6]). Dialogue on this model is, thus, despite the substitution of Reason for the psychism, strikingly similar to *le discours intérieur* delineated in the previous section—is, *mutatis mutandis,* another instantiation of the interior discourse:

> La raison est une. Elle n'a plus à qui se communiquer, rien n'est en dehors d'elle. Et, dès lors, elle est comme le silence du discours intérieur. Les questions et les réponses d'un tel "échange d'idées" reproduisent ou mettant encore en scène celles d'un dialogue que l'âme tient avec elle-même. Sujets pensants, multiples points obscurs autour desquels se fait un clarté quand ils se parlent et se retrouvent, tout comme, dans le discours intérieur, quand se renoue le fil de la pensée qui avait à s'interroger; clarté où les points obscurs des divers moi's pâlissent, s'estompent, mais aussi se subliment. Cet échange d'idées tiendra, en fin de compte, dans une seule âme, dans une seule conscience, dans un *cogito* que reste la Raison. (DVI 216)[61]

There is no more a "genuine" conversation here than there had been in the interior discourse of the psychism with itself—in either case there is but a single voice. Perhaps we might suggest the technical name of "communication" for this dialogue where interlocutors participate as functionaries of *the* discourse internal to Reason (as we suggested "dialogue"[62] for the discourse internal to the psychism, utilizing the *logos* it finds in itself for its free assumption of exteriority), and this because this version of dialogue presupposes a term "common" to the interlocutors, refers to "an original we," requires an a priori "community" in which each interlocutor participates, requires a prior unity of interlocutors for "commun-ication" to be possible.

I.2.iii. The Unity of the Interior Discourse—So we have two versions of interior discourse in Occidental thought: one being a dialogue of the psychism with itself (which we are calling "dialogue"), and the other being a dialogue of Reason with itself (which we are calling "communication"). We are suggesting, moreover, that these two traditional versions of dialogue correspond to the two sides of rationality (or truth) distinguished by Levinas (and laid out above in our sections I.1.i and I.1.ii): "dialogue" to the assumption of the other by the free, *logos*-endowed psychism, and "communication" to the need for this psychism (ironically, in order to ensure its freedom with respect to the other) to bring itself into line with the system of intelligibility that (it would at least seem) transcends it. We shall not be surprised to discover, then, that just as the freely exercised rationality of the psychism and rationality as the unity of intelligibility turned out to be one and the same rationality insofar as the neutral, third term that would mediate "communication" is found "in me" (see section I.1.iii), the discourse interior to the psychism and the discourse interior to Reason turn out to be one and the same discourse. For while "dialogue" begins its explanation of dialogue from the side of the knower, and "communication" from the perspective of the third term that would mediate between knower and known, each is founded in the ultimate unity of the knower-known correlation, and it is from the original unity of this *savoir* that dialogue, in either case, is described. There is, we are arguing, for the tradition, despite the variant "takes" on it, but one rationality (*logos*), and but one dialogue (*dia-logos*).

For just as the purportedly neutral third that regulates (or is) the system of intelligibility is found "in me," so too is the prior dialogue purportedly mediated by this *terme moyen et neutre.* Insofar as rationality, even when it is that in the face of which the psychism puts itself in order, turns out to be the rationality of the psychism so utilizing it in order to assert itself as freedom, is *le discours intérieur* not also, even when it is taken as the discourse that speaks through the speaker, reappropriated by the speaker and turned into his own interior discourse?

Indeed, after this scheme, how is one to distinguish one's own voice from the voice of Reason?[63] From what standpoint? Is this distinction not necessarily blurred, even as it is necessary to the ontological way of thought? Is the "exteriority" of even the purportedly neutral third itself not, here, at least effectively reduced to the same, along with the interlocutor? "I, Plato, am the truth." With whom need I, nay, can I, speak, except with myself? And insofar as I have, in the fullness of truth, myself to myself, need I even speak at all? These questions need now be addressed in a systematic manner.

II. Dialogue Problematized

Recall that our prevailing concern in this work is with delineating the conditions of possibility for dialogue in the hope that a more precise understanding of these might enhance our chances for engendering dialogue (particularly, in those situations where dialogue presents itself as problematic), and, ultimately, for engendering peace (particularly, in those situations that call out for the institution of dialogue as an alternative to "war"—on whatever scale). We have so far followed Levinas's account of dialogue as it is conceived of within the predominant part of the Western philosophical tradition: as part and parcel of, as an extension of, a single, interior discourse—a discourse that has as its end (both its goal and point of termination) the coincidence of Reason with itself, and consequently (or coincidentally) the reduction of all (apparent or temporary) alterity to this single, unified discourse. It is now our task to examine the resources that this traditional view possesses for giving an account of how dialogue would, in situations of potential conflict, be effectuated and, thus, facilitate, or fail to facilitate, our chances for peace.

It is precisely peace that the tradition promises, a version of peace that Levinas refers to as "peace by truth," or "peace by Reason" (DVI 217). On this view, according to Levinas, "On peut appeler *socialité* l'unité des consciences multiples entrées dans la même pensée où se supprime leur altérité réciproque. C'est le fameux dialogue appelé à arrêter la violence en ramenant les interlocuteurs à la raison, installant la paix dans l'unanimité, supprimant la proximité dans la coïncidence" (DVI 216–17).[64]

Indeed, when the process of self-consciousness fully conscious of itself is complete, when all idiosyncratic particulars have ceded their particularity to the universal, neutral third term that gives them their place in the System, that gives them their true selves, then there is but the One in which the conflicts between particulars are finally resolved in the peace resulting from their coincidence. Everything, every one, has its place and takes his place in the whole that provides it with its ultimate meaning, the meaning toward which all of its partial meanings tend, and in terms of which all of its partial meanings are ultimately meaningful. When all is One, when there are only part-iculars as parts of a whole, violence is excluded, for how can the One being One ultimately be divided against itself (even if such is, for some unknown reason, temporarily necessary, such that we have "history"). Levinas refers to this notion of peace as "la prédilection de l'humanisme occidental," and this peace as the peace "que goûtent les âmes nobles" (DVI 217),[65] but will oppose to this notion, as we shall see in the next chapter, another notion of peace, arguing that this "peace by Reason" is not itself peaceful, but harbors an unsuspected violence—the violence of the totality, which we are, in part, in the course of exploring here. "Ontology . . . issues in the State and in the nonviolence of the totality, without securing itself against the violence from which this nonviolence lives, and which appears in the tyranny of the State" (TI 46 [16]).

For after the ontological conception of dialogue as *dia-logos,* as dialogue founded upon the necessarily a priori commonality of the mediatory *logos,* the process of effectuating a dialogue with an encountered "other"—defined, for the moment, as someone who holds an opposing point of view on some matter of shared concern—is clear: I must simply make an appeal to Reason (the *logos*) that, as the neutral, third term between interlocutors, is, after this conception, necessarily universal, necessarily applicable to everyone (even if, for my part, I find this resource "in me"). And the other, insofar as he or she is rational (and how, as a part-icular in a rational universe, could he or she not be—at least ultimately?), will respond, will, as rational, respond rationally. The success of my appeal to the neutral third is guaranteed in that I am appealing here, in the end, to another *like me,* to another rational being who, as rational, cannot but be compelled and persuaded by an appeal to Reason. The success of my appeal is guaranteed in being an appeal of the same to the same.

But what if this appeal fails? What if an other (a potential interlocutor) does not find my appeal to reason to be, from his perspective, reasonable? Indeed, does this not happen? Is this not the most quotidian of situations? It is precisely at this point that dialogue as *dia-logos* becomes problematic, that effectuating a dialogue becomes a problem. For does not such a situation inject a surd into the tradition's presupposed doctrine of rational coherence by introducing an other who (according to his own testimony) refuses to be reduced to sameness, and who does so precisely by refusing the *logos* that seeks to tame him by accommodating or appropriating his alterity? The other so encountered is other precisely by refusing to "listen to reason." We are referring to this situation as the problem of interparadigmatic dialogue, the situation where my appeals to reason, to what is reasonable, to what after the tradition is universal and necessarily so, fall on deaf ears, where the other fails to acknowledge what is reasonable on my accounting, the *logos* that I find "in me," as reasonable at all. Again, the problem of interparadigmatic dialogue arises precisely at that point where my appeal to the purportedly neutral, third term, the *logos* that governs *dia-logos,* fails to elicit the assent, or perhaps even the recognition, of the other, such that this necessarily common *logos* cannot be found (agreed upon), cannot be invoked to effectively mediate, to reduce or negate, the difference, the otherness, so encountered. And is one not tempted at this juncture to at least entertain the possibility (even if, after the tradition, such could only be a semblance) that the other is governed by a *logos* that differs from my own? That is, the problem of interparadigmatic dialogue at least holds out the possibility that what we are dealing with here is not the *logos,* but *logoi*—and if there is not *logos* but are *logoi,* what becomes of the possibility of *dia-logos?*[66] To be confronted with the problem of interparadigmatic dialogue, to be confronted with dialogue as problematic, to be confronted with interparadigmaticity as we are defining it here, is, in short, the problem of not being able—in the face of a potential interlocutor who refuses to be persuaded by my "reasons"—to effectively locate the neutral third, the common *logos,* that is to mediate the dialogical situation.

It is to this "practical" problem that we shall first turn in our evaluation of the efficacy of the traditional model of dialogue for engendering dialogue, and we shall argue that, faced with this situation in which the stakes for dialogue are raised, dialogue as *dia-logos* fails to deliver at least the practical goods. We shall then suggest, perhaps even more radically, that, even on its own "theoretical" terms, the traditional conception of dialogue yields certain aporias, causing us to question whether this search for the neutral third could, even if it were to succeed, be helpful in facilitating dialogue, or whether it would not rather, even in "success," close down any possibility for dialogue altogether. Finally, a review of the ethical implications of a continued insistence upon the existence and efficacy of this neutral third will lead us to argue that perhaps the search is better abandoned, and that another approach to dialogue might better be pursued.

II.1. Practical Problems

Of course, the tradition rejects the possibility that we could be dealing with *logoi* rather than with the *logos.* Insofar as it is totality thought, ontology, it must reject the possibility that the *logos* is other than singular and unified, and it must propose some other explanation for why dialogue sometimes fails, why there is this "semblance" of *logoi.* In this section we will examine these explanations, and argue that, despite the resources of the tradition, we are left with at least the practical problem that the tradition is incapable of locating (where this "locating" would mean arriving at a reason, a *logos,* that would be universally compelling to all potential interlocutors and as such capable of producing the peace of coherence) the neutral third upon which its account of dialogue depends.

For when, after the tradition, I encounter an other (here, as above, indicating my encountering of someone who holds a viewpoint that is divergent with respect to my own with respect to some matter of shared concern) there are, within the tradition itself, a number of possible explanations for the phenomenon, for this "semblance" of *logoi,* and these can be briefly enumerated as stemming from (1) the adherence to mere opinion rather than to fact or to Truth, which is the result of a certain naïveté; (2) sin, that is, a defiant adherence to one's perfidious will rather than an obedience to the Truth; or (3) incompleteness, based on the premise that all expressions of the Truth are, short of teleological fullness, at present (in time) but partial expressions of the full Truth, even if necessary stages on the way to a final and complete Truth (even if, after some conceptions, that final Truth acts as a regulative ideal in lieu of ever actually arriving). The first two of these proposals, of these explanations for an apparent divergence within the truth, are most compatible with, and would seem to correspond to, it seems to us, a conception of "dialogue" as *dia-logos* as delineated above, where the *logos* is, in its fullness, potentially available *at present* "to all rational agents" (to borrow the idiom of Enlightenment thinkers who share in this explanation), and that it can be invoked as effectively mediatory if it is faithfully attended to by the participants in the dialogue. The third, it seems to us, is more readily compatible with that which we referred to above as "communication," that more historically attuned account (and perfected, perhaps, in Hegel), where the shared *logos* arises as a function of a more deeply shared enrootedness (in *Geist,* in Being, in the Tradition) that unfolds through time. But in no case (need this be reiterated?) is the Truth as unified and as one, in any of these conceptions, called into question. And in each case, in Levinas's phrase, *l'esprit* is qualified fundamentally as *savoir,* as a knowing of this Truth. We shall, nevertheless, address these emphases separately, even as we keep in mind their fundamental complicity. For in neither of these approaches, we are arguing, is *l'esprit* of the individual thinker ultimately, practically, distinguishable from *l'Esprit* as a universal, totality concept—and this is precisely the problem.

For in the case of "dialogue," where the *logos* is, it is claimed, readily available to all rational agents, the failure of the potential interlocutors to coincide in the *logos* must mean that either one or both of them are outside of the Truth of the *logos,* either by clinging to opinion (in naïveté), or by clinging to sin (in willfulness). The problem that arises in such a situation, where one is compelled (perhaps by the desire to avoid some impending violence) to generate a dialogue, is in finding out which of the potential interlocutors is (or if both are), for whatever reason, outside of the Truth. But how is this done? A number of problems arise here, not the least of which is the problem of finding a criterion in terms of which such a judgment could be made. For would not such a judgment require an appeal to the neutral third itself, and is that not precisely what is in question here?

For faced with an other whose viewpoint differs from my own and who does not respond positively to my reason-able appeals, but who claims (either by genuine belief or in a willful lie—and how would I know which?), indeed, to have reason on his side, how am I to mediate between these competing truths? Who, in "truth," is the arbiter, the blessed possessor, of the genuinely neutral and universal third (if anyone)? My appeals to reason as I find it in me are uncompelling to the other, and the truth as he finds it in himself is uncompelling to me. Let us leave aside for the moment the possibility that (insofar as subjectivity is taken into account) my approach to the truth always colors the way in which the truth is framed, and the same is true for the other in his approach (not to mention the possibility that the truth simply *is* a function of one's conceptual framework—and not some objective, external "reality"—a possibility the tradition is not able to entertain insofar as it insists upon the distinction between truth and opinion). We shall deal with this more fully in the comments that follow upon "communication," but it needs be asserted that as far as the tradition of *dia-logos* is concerned, this infection of the truth by subjectivity must be able, by some or other kind of *epoché,* to be ruled out. "Dialogue" as *dia-logos* demands, promises, pure access to the genuinely neutral third: the *logos.* But again, in cases of conflict, of dispute, who shall be deemed to have it, when the criterion upon which it could be decided that one or the other of the disputants have it to the exclusion of the other demands that both already have it for this to be able to be demonstrated? One can only appeal to that which is precisely in dispute.

Indeed, how, ultimately, am I able to distinguish, *even within myself,* opinion from truth? For if I am trapped in opinion, if I am simply naïve, how do I transcend this naïveté and make my way to truth? According to the tradition, by appealing to the Truth that is already within me. But if I am also attracted (by whatever attraction) to opinion (and I must be to have found myself in it at all—and this being in "opinion," at some point, is a condition of possibility for making the transition from opinion to truth, is a condition of possibility for philosophy!), how do I know which is which? And how would I know, for sure, that I had made the transition? What is the point of appeal that would guarantee success in this appeal of self to self? Am I ever really above the corruption of opinion?[67] And even if I were to be, how would I know?

But even if this problem were able to be overcome (for, despite the foregoing, according to the tradition I have no resource, in the end, but to trust the truth that I find "in me," to make a judgment: "I, Plato, am the truth"), by appeal to self-evidence, clear and distinct ideas, intuition, or what have you, a further problem remains: how am I to convince an other, one who does not share this truth (or refuses to acknowledge that he shares this truth that, according to the tradition, is his truth in spite of himself) of this truth? I can only make an appeal to that which the other already refuses, which leads to what Levinas, referring to the attestation of Plato, calls "le grand problème" of this dialogue based upon the accomplishment of *savoir:* "D'amener à ce dialogue des êtres opposés, portés à se faire violence. Il faudrait trouver un dialogue pour faire entrer en dialogue" (DVI 217–18).[68] And this problem takes hold with respect to both opinion and sin. For how, on the one hand, is the other, in error, to be convinced of his error when that which is required to see one's error is being out of error—being already in the truth? And, on the other hand, how is one who chooses to refuse the truth in sin to be convinced of the necessity of giving this up when this being convinced would presuppose one's redemption, conversion? In this case, after the phrasing of Levinas, dialogue "ne serait possible que dans le pur amour de la vérité et de l'intelligibilité d'un univers spinoziste" (DVI 217).[69] The possibility of dialogue presupposes both the possibility and the will on behalf of all interlocutors to transcend their own perspectives and desires (insofar as these are strictly personal and not yet the expression of one's truest self—the rational ego). So to solve the "great problem" of dialogue requires that the problem already be solved, in that the other (like myself) needs to be convinced of the truth in order to be convinced of the truth. For the capacity to lead the other into the *logos* that would lead to the possibility of dialogue (and what language would one employ to accomplish this?) presupposes a yet deeper shared *logos* by which this leading itself would be made possible, and, if this failed, a leading to this deeper *logos* by an even and ever deeper one, etc. . . . Either the problem, the problem of finding a dialogue that would lead to dialogue, is solved always already from the outset, or degenerates into one of infinite regress.

Levinas, in "Le Dialogue," follows his mention of *le grand problème* of dialogue by appearing to suggest that this problem might be overcome, or at least circumvented, by recourse to what we have been referring to as "communication":

> A moins de supposer l'unité préalable d'un savoir souverain et divin, d'une substance qui se pense et qui aurait éclaté en une multiplicité de consciences suffisamment maîtresses d'elles-mêmes, limitées et hostiles les unes aux autres, mais qui, de conflit en conflit, se trouvent astreintes ou conduites aux dialogues qui devront permettre, de proche en proche, la convergence des regards partant de points de vue multiples, mais nécessaires à la plénitude d'une pensée retrouvant sa souveraineté et son *unité* perdues, son *je pense* ou son *système.* (DVI 218)[70]

This model would seem to avoid the problem of locating a common *logos* by asserting that it is not the interlocutors who hold forth a conversation, a *dia-logos* that would require an *appeal* (however much ex- or implicit) to the *logos* as mediatory, but that the conversation has a hold on them, that is, that communication becomes possible in that the respective interlocutors are, whether they recognize or acknowledge it or not, enrooted in their depth in a common ground, and it is in terms of this, their irremissible interconnectedness, that they cannot but participate in the constitution of an eventually common *logos*—this constitution being a function of their very enrootedness. Thus, as "parts" of this "whole" (be it a process rather than a substance) that transcends them, the interlocutors each contribute to *the* conversation in and as the part-ial perspectives they have and are—and no particular need have (or even could have) a view of the whole as it is in itself, given that any such view would, as coming *from somewhere in* the conversation, be partial. But is "the great problem" of dialogue, finding a dialogue that would compel the other to enter into dialogue, really avoided here?

Insofar as this problem presupposes that I am in the Truth and that my task is to find a way to convince the erring other to join into it, this model indeed undercuts the problem by admitting that I am not in the Truth fully—rather, I am in the Truth partially, as is the other. We each have a truth as a share of the Truth, as participants in the Truth, but no one has the Truth fully. Leaving aside for the moment the problem of how anyone could know, from a partial perspective, that their perspective and that of the other(s) were partial manifestations of a whole (for would this knowledge not presuppose some kind of knowledge of the whole such that the judgment of partiality could be made?), let us recall that the problem with which we are dealing in this work is the problem of finding the conditions of possibility for a dialogue in those situations where there is a disagreement that threatens to degenerate into violence should a resolution not be found. And if this is our problem, does an analysis of this model not lead us to ask (before the question of whether this model successfully navigates or navigates around what Levinas has referred to as the great problem for dialogue) a deeper question—the question of from where, after this model, the motivation comes for entering into a peace-generating dialogue at all. For while having faith in a fundamental enrootedness of all prospective interlocutors might well generate a faith in some *final* resolution among them, from where comes the motivation, let alone the power, to invoke that which would bring a dialogue of peace in any *particular* situation? In fact, conflict after this model is *necessary* to the process of peace as each in his partial truth has the obligation of asserting his partial truth with a view toward its integration in the final Truth, a Truth that cannot be final, cannot be Truth, until all such partial truths are so integrated. Thesis and antithesis call for one another and are *both* necessary to their dialectical synthesis. The whole requires the parts and the parts in conflict, a conflict necessary to the final Truth, and *final* peace.

On this model, then, history *is* "just war"[71] and entails all of the structures constitutive of war as delineated by Levinas in the "Preface" to *Totality and Infinity*. From this process, from this war, no one can take distance, as beings are stripped of their freedom, integrated into a process that derives its meaning from its end—teleological peace—an end into which the individual meanings of those involved are assimilated. So, here, do we not meet expositionally for the first time the above mentioned peace of the State, the peace of empires, as a peace founded upon violence?

On this model, what can one do, what *must* one do, in a particular situation, but persist in one's partial truth against the partial truth of the other—the assertion of which is required for the final resolution, for the ultimate fusion of horizons, for the Truth that requires all truths as their ultimate integration? On this model, peace is postponed, deferred, until the end of time, until the end of history defined as the march of the Spirit through time until the Spirit is unified, rests, in the Truth. But so long as there is history, so long as there is time, there is conflict, and conflict that is necessary to peace, such that, on this model, logically pressed, the enemy of (present) conflict is an enemy of (final) peace. The advocate of peace is the enemy of Peace. The peacemaker (the pacifist) commits treason against the State, the peace of the State. "Where violence reveals itself to be reason" (TI 302 [279]), the warrior alone is the (genuine) peacemaker.

Do I not, then, have an "ethical" obligation to take up my particularity into a robust part-icipation in the "just war" of history in the interest of peace? Perhaps. But it might still be possible that seeking peace in the short term need not be at odds with teleological peace. For who says that the necessary conflicts need be of the most destructive variety? Could dialogue (debate) also be a form of conflict, and a more benign, "better," form than all out war?[72] Is a partial fusion of horizons not possible even now—the Kingdom of God among us even while we await the Kingdom of God? But would not this "better" require, as a condition of its possibility, a "vision" of the final peace? Indeed, does not this model require, as the "justification" for the just war of history undertaken in whatever form, just such a "vision"?[73] That is to say that this acknowledgement of the partiality of every truth requires some sort of awareness, some or other kind of "knowledge," of the Truth, such that each part could be conceived as partial, and so that we might confidently proceed in the assurance that our truth is a veritable part of *the* Truth. And since our "glimpse" of this final end, after the tenets of the conception itself, can only be partial, does not this vision of the end become, of necessity, a matter of "faith"—a "religious" vision? An ideology among ideologies, insofar as the end cannot but be "glimpsed" otherwise and from elsewhere? And does this not open up yet another front in the historical war in which one is enlisted to fight? For not only must I now, in accord with this view of history as teleologically directed, participate in this history of conflict in the hope of its resolution (and as my partial self, for how else would I participate?), but I must also do so as someone who has "seen" the Truth, as a believer, against those who have not "seen" (against those, for instance, who refuse to acknowledge that their truth is only partial), for when all have "seen," when we all have a shared "vision," the conflict will be over, and "history" will already have come to an end. But insofar as conflicts remain, am I not compelled, in the name of the final peace I envision, to press others to accept this vision—the accomplishment of which is necessary for, *is,* the accomplishment of peace?

And are we not, then, back where we began—with a conflict whose resolution requires that I appeal to that which I find "in me," and that the other rejects? Peace here, albeit now envisioned as a "final peace," requires, not an appeal to a common *logos* universally and presently present to all, but an appeal to the common enrootedness of the prospective interlocutors in that which founds the possibility of *logos,* and *dia-logos.* But again, it is this commonality—be it of *logos* or founding ontological or spiritual ground that gives rise to the "original *we*"—that, faced with the problem of interparadigmatic dialogue, is in question. In neither of its predominant manifestations does the onto-logical model for dialogue, based upon a prior communality, provide, practically speaking, ultimate and assured access to this purportedly common point of appeal, and thus an explanation of how dialogue might be facilitated in those situations that we are referring to as interparadigmatic, that is, where the prospective interlocutors can enter into a dialogue while retaining their distinctive viewpoints, while not being reduced to some or other a priori "commonality" that would dominate their differences, but as themselves.

All of this could be said yet again, if somewhat differently, in light of what we take to be one of Levinas's most important claims, namely, his assertion that "it is impossible to place oneself outside of the correlation of the same and the other so as to record the correspondence or the noncorrespondence of this going with this return" (TI 36 [6]), or, which is to say the same, the radical impossibility of totalization. While Levinas will present this impossibility in ethical terms, and we have here presented it as an epistemological/ontological problem (two approaches that, we shall have to show, are not, in the thought of Levinas, incompatible, and that in fact flow from one to the other), what is of import here is that dialogue on the ontological model has been presented as an attempt to realize this impossibility, as a perpetual attempt to escape particularity and attain a universal, total and totalizing, viewpoint on the whole in terms of which its constitutive parts might be viewed and regulated. Ontology might well, we are arguing, be defined precisely as a yielding to the temptation to attempt to make possible this impossibility. We take the thought of Levinas, as will become clear as this work progresses, to be a sustained and impressive effort, against the weight of the tradition and its vocabulary, to resist this temptation, even if it will be precisely engaged in the task of describing another possible impossibility.

II.2. Theoretical Problems

In addition to the practical problem of how effectively to locate the common ground that on the ontological model is requisite for *dia-logos,* we should now like to elaborate upon a theoretical aporia (already alluded to in the introduction to this chapter) that arises in the elucidation of this ontological model, and this as yet another reason for calling into question the adequacy of this framework for dealing with the problem of interparadigmatic dialogue: namely, the problem of how, on this model for dialogue, to explain the necessity/possibility of dialogue at all. That is, we wish to ask, in an interconnected way, and given the parameters of the ontological model of dialogue as *un dialogue de l'immanence,* both the "why?" question, and the "how?" question of dialogue. In short, *why* would a subject qualified by *savoir,* by the immanence of self-consciousness, enter into dialogue at all? And even if, for some reason, such a subject would be compelled to do so, *how,* given the premises of the model, would this be done?

To begin, then, *why* dialogue? For in the scheme that we have, after Levinas, been elaborating here, where the *cogito* is seen to hold *un discours intérieur* (be this necessarily confused with *le discours intérieur* of Reason itself), is this discourse not, in the end, the product of a lone soul? For, as Levinas reminds us, "La raison est une. Elle n'a plus à qui se communiquer, rien n'est en dehors d'elle" (DVI 216),[74] and elsewhere: "Reason, speaking in the first person is not addressed to the other, conducts a monologue" (TI 72 [44]), and this because there is no other, no exteriority, to whom it might address itself. Levinas sums up this argument in near bullet-point form in *Totality and Infinity:* "But the community of thought ought to have made language as a relation between beings impossible. Coherent discourse is one. A universal thought dispenses with communication. A reason cannot be other for a reason. How can reason be an I or an other, since its very being consists in renouncing singularity?" (TI 72 [44]).

So, rather than having a communication that "effectivement se parle" (DVI 216)[75] across interlocutors, we are left, as in the "immediate self-presence" that characterizes "consciousness of . . ." for Husserl, with only an internal dialogue, that is, with a dialogue of the same with the same that is effectively a monologue, and, moreover, a monologue that, as always already present to itself, only "resembles" communication. The unity presupposed by the possibility of dialogue as *dia-logos,* therefore, not only renders the requisite common *logos* practically unattainable, but, perhaps even more problematically, would appear to preclude the possibility of the exteriority that dialogue, as communication with an *other,* is intended to reach. If, in short, there is no *other,* but only a single, unified *logos*/discourse, why dialogue?[76]

But even if the subject in its temporal and temporary process toward full self-consciousness should require contact with an exteriority to heal the split within the *logos* that remains so long as there is time, as the means toward the accomplishment of its integrative project, the subject as *savoir* is faced with another, but related, problem: the problem of *how* to enter into a relation with this temporary exteriority that is *not* a genuine exteriority *as* an exteriority, that is, of entering into a communicative relationship that would not, as qualified by knowledge, immediately reduce the other to an object of this knowledge, but maintain the other as an other with whom one might enter into a relationship of solidarity, a relationship of dialogue. How, indeed, Levinas queries, does one, from within *le dialogue de l'immanence,* effectuate "the radical reversal, from cognition to solidarity, that communication represents with respect to inward dialogue, to cognition of oneself, taken as the trope of spirituality?" (OTB 119 [152]) Levinas notes the paradox that would have to be involved in this derivation of communication out of self-coinciding (OTB 118–19 [152]), in this conversion from cognition to solidarity in the operation of the *cogito.* Indeed, according to Levinas, "communication would be impossible if it should have to begin in the ego, a free subject, to whom every other would be only a limitation that invites war, domination, precaution and information" (OTB 119 [152]). Such a monad, concerned with its own certainty, would be, Levinas adds, even if it were for whatever reason to require/desire dialogue with another, "incapable of communication, save by miracle" (OTB 119 [153]).[77]

II.3. The Ethical Problem

We will conclude this chapter by arguing, following Levinas, that insofar as we can even entertain the possibility that there is an "other" (one who refuses the *logos* that dialogue as *dia-logos* attempts to impose, and who lives independently of the unity thus imposed), dialogue on the ontological model cannot but be a suppression of this alterity—that is, violence and domination—and this, moreover, because the ontological model does not leave any room for such a possibility and would thus, insofar as such an alterity were to exist, suppress it, if for no other reason, out of sheer blindness.

But to make this argument is no simple matter, for *within* the ontological model itself, there is, as we have seen, no room for a genuine other.[78] If we are, then, to assert an alterity, must we not have recourse to an "experience"[79] that falls outside of the parameters of ontology in practice, to—in Levinas's phrase—"nonphilosophical experiences,"[80] to experiences that *call into question* the relentless assimilative process that ontology is as the march toward ultimate coherence, toward absolute self-consciousness? What we are suggesting here is that the problem of interparadigmatic dialogue might just present us with such an experience in being a situation where I am confronted with an other who *presents himself* as a refusal of my *logos,* of the *logos* as found in "me." Much more will need to be said about this refusal and of the possibility for relationship (that Levinas will name "discourse") that this refusal opens up in the following chapters, but for now we need only entertain the possibility that this "ethical experience" signifies something that the ontological stress on dialogue as *dia-logos* risks to obscure or to suppress, or to suppress precisely in obscuring it.

For after the ontological model of dialogue, communication, rather than being the means toward, or an expression of, society with a free and independent interlocutor, is, as we have seen, conceived of as, "always another way of seeking certainty, or the coincidence with oneself" (OTB 118 [151–52]). On this scheme, where what counts is "connaissance d'autrui comme d'un objet avant toute socialité avec lui" (DVI 217),[81] the other cannot but be presented (by me to myself) as an object of my knowing, and thus as falling within the realm of my powers as the *grasped* of my con-*ception.* If "meaning" is itself a function of the knower-known relation (and for the tradition, as we have seen, this relation is the natural site of meaning), then the other cannot but be reduced to the meaning that he "borrows" from his being known. So even if there were "another" kind of meaning, a meaning that could not be reduced to a being-known (and Levinas will suggest, as we shall see, that ethical meaning is just such a meaning), the ontological model would, by definition, be incapable of admitting it as experience, and thus be blind to its having/being a meaning at all.

Furthermore, if all meaning is a function of the knower-known relation as mediated by the *logos,* and the one true *logos* is found in me, then violence—far from being conceived of as assimilating the other to my/the system of intelligibility—is rather the presentation of the other as other, the presentation of the other, that is to say, as resistance to my/the Truth. After this conception, why should I not insist upon the other's assimilation, even against his will (which I know not to be his true will, his rational will)? Have I not even an ethical obligation to, and an ontological foundation for, this "logic" of "inquisition"? The other's self-presentation as other must be reduced to the same (and this for his own good!), brought under the sway of the *logos,* if Truth is to have its day.

But since this truth, this triumphant truth for which I am obligated to struggle, is, as noted, always found "in me," does not the encounter of the other who would call into question this truth not, even for a moment, and despite the supreme confidence that the philosophical subject must possess, cause me to call my own truth into question? Perhaps it is, after all, I who is mistaken. And if this is a possibility, must I not also entertain the possibility that judgments, both the other's and my own, about what is true are subject to the "pouvoir de domination et possibilité de ruse, . . . toutes les tentations de la rhétorique trompeuse, de la publicité et de la propagande" (DVI 217)?[82] Can I be so sure that the truth as I find it is not, rather than a naming of what is the case, a function of power relations?[83] Who makes the decisions about who needs to be brought into the truth (from out of their ignorance or sinfulness), the "true" or the "powerful?" Again, in the dialogue where the goal is to make the other "entendre raison" (DVI 216), how am I finally to distinguish between the commonly proffered plea that the other "Listen to reason!" and the *perhaps* more "truthful" one: "Listen to me!"?

Whatever be the case, what Levinas's analyses of dialogue as an extension of ontology make clear is that this dialogue, "installant la paix dans l'unanimité, supprimant la proximité dans la coïncidence" (DVI 217),[84] cannot but be, insofar as the possibility of alterity is entertained, "la suppression de l'altérité" (DVI 217). According to Levinas, after the ontological model, "The function of language would amount to suppressing 'the other,' who breaks this coherence and is hence essentially irrational. A curious result: language would consist in suppressing the other, in making the other agree with the same" (TI 73 [45]).

We have, then, in this opening chapter, after exhibiting the possibilities for dialogue after the ontological model that, according to Levinas, has dominated Western thought, argued that this model is inadequate to account for the possibility of dialogue in those situations that we have described as interparadigmatic, and, therefore, inadequate also for helping us to locate the conditions of possibility for dialogue in such situations, an understanding of which might, we hope, help us to understand how, through dialogue, peace might be facilitated in these situations. And this should perhaps not surprise us, for, to believe Levinas, "being," (the provenance of *onto*-logy) "reveals itself as war to philosophical thought" (TI 21 [IX]).

Our argument has proceeded in three interrelated phases: (1) by showing that the common *logos* requisite for *dia-logos* cannot, after the ontological model, and faced with the situation in which interparadigmatic dialogue is called for, practically, effectively be located in a way that would establish it as a compelling point of appeal for all potential interlocutors, a condition for its being able to play its mediatory role; (2) by showing that, on the ontological model logically pressed, there is neither the necessity nor the possibility of dialogue as genuine communication in that that which is taken as the goal of dialogue after such a model (coherence in the truth) is presupposed by the model, such that, by presupposing that which would render it redundant, dialogue on this model would negate its own necessity/possibility; and (3) by showing that, as an extension of the search for certainty, dialogue on the ontological model cannot but be a suppression or domination of the other, a relating to which dialogue purports to be. How, then, might interparadigmatic dialogue be possible?

Notes

1. Despite the fact that Levinas will insist that "meaning" is irreducible to the categories provided for it by Greek philosophy (and this holds true of even philosophical meaning itself) he does assert that "the essential characteristic of philosophy is a certain, specifically Greek, way of thinking and speaking." Although philosophy is not exclusively this, insofar as (1) other discourses have, historically, been incorporated into philosophy, and (2) philosophical meaning refers from itself beyond itself, one cannot, nevertheless, Levinas insists, undertake philosophy without speaking Greek. See Emmanuel Levinas and Richard Kearney, "Dialogue with Emmanuel Levinas," in *Face to Face with Levinas,* ed. Richard A. Cohen (Albany: State University of New York Press, 1986), pp. 18–19.

2. These two senses for *logos* are taken from *A Lexicon Abridged from Liddell and Scott's Greek-English Lexicon* (Oxford: Clarendon Press, 1980).

3. This will be an essential aspect of Levinas's characterization of dialogue after the ontological model as "le dialogue de l'immanence," that is, as a dialogue in subordination to *savoir,* as we shall show in section I.2 of this chapter.

4. This argument issues from the distinction in the *Logische Untersuchungen* between *Ausdrück* (expression) and *Anzeichen* (indication), where, in solitary mental life, the latter is reduced to the former. We shall return to this issue in section II.2. of this chapter.

5. Does it reflect a contradiction at the root of Western thought? And if so, what might such a contradiction itself reflect? By means of foreshadowing, we suggest that it might well reflect the relation of "the Same" to "the Other" that Levinas will call discourse, or, later, proximity, the latter being described specifically as "the other in the same" (or "difference within identity"), as an exigency that cannot be thought within the confines of Western reason alone, being a "structure" that

imposes itself, on Levinas's account, "prior to" the distinction between difference and identity.

6. In opposition, much of contemporary "postmodern" philosophy emphasizes difference to such an extent that the problem for a theory of dialogue is not in explaining the presence of a difference that would create the necessity for dialogue, but in locating any identity, any commonality, between interlocutors that would render dialogue possible. These issues will be addressed in our chapter 4, where we discuss the distinction Levinas draws in *Otherwise Than Being or Beyond Essence* between "the saying" and "the said."

7. "Primordial" and "originary" are not necessarily "prior" or "original" in any chronological sense, but reflect a certain philosophical/ontological privilege. The primordial or originary, even if they are not chronologically "first," nevertheless exert an influence upon the whole process, either as teleologically (like the oak that inhabits the seed) or ontologically (like the plan from which the house is built) determinative. Their being chronologically first is not, of course, necessarily excluded.

8. "Le Dialogue: Conscience de soi et promité du prochain," in *De Dieu qui vient à l'idée,* pp. 211–30. "Le Dialogue" first appeared in the collection *Esistenza, mito, ermeneutica: Scritti per Enrico Castelli,* vol. 2, Archivio di Filosofia (Padua: Cedem, 1980), pp. 345–57.

9. This Levinas does himself in "Le Dialogue" in a section entitled "L'esprit comme savoir et l'immanence," which sets up his subsequent account of "Le dialogue de l'immanence," in which dialogue after the terms of the tradition is examined. Our account here, as foundational to an understanding of many of the issues dealt with later in this work, will deal with the issues somewhat more exhaustively than does the brief "L'esprit comme savoir et l'immanence," drawing primarily upon the opening sections of *Totality and Infinity* to supplement Levinas's brief account in "Le Dialogue."

10. Levinas never published a comprehensive history of philosophy in which he systematically argued this thesis, although it must be noted that, as Jacques Rolland relates in the "*Avertissement*" to *La Mort et le temps,* the text of one of Levinas's thematic courses on the history of philosophy, he "consecrated the greater part of his teaching to the history of philosophy," and that his work as a whole "is characterized by a singular practice of reference to the tradition," even if this is "far more often a matter of allusion than a matter of analysis properly speaking"; see Jacques Rolland, "*Avertissement,*" to Emmanuel Levinas, *La Mort et le temps* (L'Herne, 1991), p. 5 (our translation). His statements à propos what he takes to be and to have been the case for the history of Western

philosophy thus most often take the form of rather grand, general assertions—albeit punctuated by brief analyses of representative figures—that are presented, not as conclusions to carefully and comprehensively laid out exegeses, but, rather, as if to ask: "Is it not the case that . . . ? Is this not, at root, what has been going on in philosophy?" His "historical allusions," it seems to us, make no attempt at covering every angle, at answering every objection, or at dealing with every exception, but attempt to capture the "spirit" of the tradition, or of a particular representative figure. (Indeed, Levinas is not averse to self-consciously reducing certain of his philosophical interlocutors to the level of caricatures in order to make a point, as has been noted, for example, by Robert Bernasconi in his "Rereading *Totality and Infinity*," in *The Question of the Other,* ed. A. B. Dallery and C. Scott [Albany: SUNY Press, 1989], p. 28.) Do they do so fairly? Without attempting a definitive answer to this complex question, we permit ourselves two comments: (1) Let us at least signal along with Adriaan Peperzak that any "representation of 'Western philosophy' is a risky extrapolation based on a very restricted selection of works. On the basis of the texts we possess of Heidegger, Levinas and Derrida, we may say that their situation is roughly the same as that of the French university [curriculum of the first half of our century]. Patristic and medieval philosophy plays hardly any role in their diagnosis. [Peperzak notes also a relative inattention to Hegel, Marx, and Freud. Although this seems to us hardly the case regarding at least a more recent Derrida, and perhaps also understates the attention paid by Levinas to Hegel.] Philosophy tends to consist, for the three authors, of Plato, Aristotle (4th century b.c.), and Plotinus (4th century a.d.) on the one hand, and the philosophers of the last four centuries (from Hobbes and Descartes to the present) on the other hand" (Adriaan Peperzak, *To the Other: An Introduction to the Philosophy of Emmanuel Levinas* [West Lafayette, Ind.: Purdue University Press, 1993], p. 10, n. 30). (2) We also ask, first, whether such a judgment (about the "fairness" of Levinas's reading) could, in fact, be made. Is there some or other "objective" history of philosophy of which Levinas's or anyone else's reading could be a more or less accurate approximation? Or are there only competing histories of philosophy? To pose these questions is to immerse ourselves already in the problematics that this chapter intends to delineate and will end in a position that answers in the affirmative the second of these questions. Further, given this, we might ask whether a susceptibility to believing Levinas's telling of the story of philosophy is requisite for taking his point, for hearing his message. Insofar as Levinas is arguing against a certain emphasis within this history, a certain possible reading of it (even if for Levinas it might be considered *the* story), we can, we would argue, be taught by this reading whether or not we take his reading, his emphasis, as a credible, or as the most credible, telling of this history.

11. Significant both in the sense of "important" and in the sense of "signifying." The site and meaning of these "lapses" will be important for Levinas, and some of these will have to be traced in the course of this work.

12. Adriaan Peperzak notes that "The set of concepts Same (*tauton*) and Other (*to heteron*) is taken from Plato's *Sophist* (254b–256b), where they figure as highest categories of being" (*To the Other,* p. 91, n. 12). For reasons to be discussed, these categories, at least as "categories of being," will be dropped by Levinas by the time of the writing of *Otherwise Than Being.*

13. This phrasing suggests that ontology itself acts consciously, has volition, "attempts." We would not argue this. However, the locution is meant to suggest that those who have practiced ontology do act consciously, do have volition, and that they have attempted (whether *self*-consciously or not) to exclude alterity, and this, to believe Levinas, in order to maintain their freedom, as we shall shortly see. In short, ontology, or ontologizing, has a political agenda, with ethical consequences.

14. This point is made succinctly and well by Steven G. Smith: "According to Levinas, the Western philosophical tradition is overwhelmingly devoted to the problem of theoretical truth. Its approach may be epistemological, that is, attentive to the necessary structure of knowing, or ontological, that is, attentive to the necessary structure of being; but there is a root complicity between the two emphases. It is the destiny of knowledge to search out and adhere to being, and it is the destiny of being to disclose itself to be known. The bias toward the 'theoretical,' in this inclusive sense, unites such diverse thinkers as Husserl and Heidegger"; Steven G. Smith, "Reason as One for Another: Moral and Theoretical Argument in the Philosophy of Emmanuel Levinas," in *Face to Face with Levinas,* p. 54.

15. Levinas will reemploy the term "reduction," giving it a positive sense, in *Otherwise Than Being* (Chapter II.3.e, "The Reduction," as the reduction of the Said to the Saying), playing there upon the technical usage given the term in Husserlian phenomenology, although deviating from Husserl's meaning. This practice, on the part of Levinas, of reappropriating terms (often in reference to their etymologies) that have been appropriated by the philosophical tradition, will have to be traced at several junctures. For the present, it is important simply to note that, here, regarding "reduction," clearly, no such technical meaning is intended.

16. Not infrequently, Levinas traces this reduction back a little further yet: to Parmenidean monism (e.g., TI 60 [31]).

17. Adriaan Peperzak, commenting on Levinas's "Philosophy and the Idea of the Infinite" (La Philosophie et l'idée de l'Infini), comments: "It is important to realize that the freedom which inspires the 'Western project' precedes both theoretical and practical expressions" (*To the Other*, p. 46). In the essay itself, reprinted (in translation and in French) in Peperzak's volume, Levinas refers to this stress on the "primacy of the same" as "narcissism" (*To the Other*, p. 94 [75]).

18. Levinas reserves to term "desire" to indicate the relation with exteriority that respects exteriority qua exteriority, namely, metaphysics. He opposes this to "need," a term that is employed to indicate the relationship with exteriority where exteriority is stripped of its genuine exteriority in being brought into correlation with me as if its existence corresponded to that which originated in me, and as such were a completion of me as knower, filling up a lack in me as knower, such that this exteriority is reduced to the economy of the same, or ontology. This distinction is particularly important to Levinas in his framing of the early sections of *Totality and Infinity.*

19. The activity of the knower implied by the italicized terms emphasizes how intelligent comprehension is already at odds with a purely passive letting be of being on the part of the subject.

20. "Here theory enters upon a course that renounces metaphysical Desire, renounces the marvel of exteriority from which that Desire lives" (TI 42 [13]). Levinas will argue that philosophy needs to recover its hidden desire for the other qua other, that theory needs recover its metaphysical side, and that the relationship so designated will in fact prove the condition of possibility for philosophy as ontology. We shall trace these arguments in our chapters 2 and 3.

21. "It is in the psychism conceived as knowledge—up to the point of self-consciousness—that traditional philosophy situates the origin or the natural site of meaning and recognizes the spirit. Everything that happens in the human psychism, all that passes through it, does it not finish by being known? . . . Everything lived is legitimately called experience. It is converted into 'lessons received' which converge in the unity of knowledge, whatever its dimensions and modalities" (quotations from texts for which there were no published English translations at the time of writing will appear, for the most part, in the body of our text in French. We have provided our own translations of these in the notes.)

22. "Même réduit à l'indétermination du *vivre* et à la familiarité du pur *exister,* du pur être, le psychisme *vit* ceci ou cela, *est* ceci ou cela, sur le mode du *voir,* de l'éprouver, comme si *vivre* et *être* étaient des verbes transitifs et *ceci* et *cela* compléments d'objects" (DVI 212).

23. "It is without doubt this implicit knowledge which justifies the broad employment which, in the *Meditations,* Descartes made of the term *cogito.* And this verb in the first person says well the unity of the Me where all knowledge suffices to itself."

24. Even "non-sense," after this scheme, would be seen to have its meaning in its being juxtaposed to what makes sense, even if a negative meaning, even if meaningful as the negation of meaning.

25. "As knowledge, thought bears on the thinkable, on the thinkable called being. Bearing on being, it is outside of itself, but remains marvelously in itself or returns to itself. The exteriority or the alterity of the self is retaken in immanence. That which thought knows or that which in its 'experience' it learns is at the same time the other and the possession of thought. We only learn that which we know already and which inserts itself in the interiority of thought in the form of an evocable form, re-presentable. Reminiscences and imaginations assure the synchrony and the unity of that which, in the experience subjected to time, is lost or is only to come."

26. One cannot but be reminded here of Derrida's reading of the history of philosophy as a "metaphysics of presence," a reading that, on at least this point, corroborates that of Levinas.

27. "As learning, thought bears a grasp, a taking of that which is learned and a possession."

28. The "man-" of manipulate, as that of manifest (see below), being derived from *manus,* hand.

29. "The 'being given'—whatever efforts the distance 'from the cup to the lips' requires—is at the measure of the thinking thought, promises to it, across its 'transcendence,' a possession and an enjoyment, a satisfaction. As if the thought thought at its measure by the fact of being able—incarnated—to rejoin that which it thought. Thought and psychism of immanence: self-sufficiency."

30. "Wherein comes to be thrown all the currents of the occidental spirit and where all its levels are manifested."

31. "The psychism of theoretical knowledge constitutes a thought which thinks at its measure and, in its adequation to the thinkable, is equal to itself, will be self-conscious. . . . It is the Same which finds itself in the Other."

32. "The activity of thought 'gets the better of' all alterity, and it is in this, finally, that resides its very rationality."

33. "In Husserlian phenomenology, despite the creative spontaneity conferred on the transcendental ego, the modes of knowledge are ordered—teleology of consciousness—essentially by the being to which the consciousness accedes. The mind is the order of things—or things

in order—of which the thinking thought would be only the collection and the arrangement. The possibility or the hope that the *I think* would have to no longer pose itself for itself in the face of the thinkable, to efface itself before the intelligible, would be its very intelligence, its rationality, its ultimate interiorization."

34. "Berkeley found in the very qualities of objects the hold they offered to the I; in recognizing in qualities, which remove the things from us most, their lived essence he spanned the distance separating the subject from the object. The coinciding of lived experience with itself was revealed to be a coinciding of thought with an existent. The work of comprehension lay in this coincidence. Thus Berkeley immerses all sensible qualities in the lived experience of affection" (TI 44 [14–15]).

35. "It is the Being of existents that is the *medium* of truth; truth regarding an existent presupposes the prior openness to Being. . . . Since Husserl the whole of phenomenology is the promotion of the idea of *horizon,* which for it plays a role equivalent to that of the *concept* in classical idealism; an existent arises upon a ground that extends beyond it, as an individual arises from a concept. . . . The existing of an existent is converted into intelligibility; its independence is a surrender in radiation" (TI 44–45 [15]). And regarding Heidegger: "*Being and Time* has argued perhaps but one sole thesis: Being is inseparable from the comprehension of Being (which unfolds as time); Being is already an appeal to subjectivity" (TI 45 [15]).

36. Levinas does not in these analyses offer any examples of this, but one can think of any number of Enlightenment thinkers who would fit the bill.

37. "As Plato noted, besides the eye and the thing, vision presupposes the light. The eye does not see the light, but the object in the light. Vision is therefore a relation with a 'something' established within a relation with what is not a 'something.' We are in the light inasmuch as we encounter the thing in nothingness. . . . The sensible light qua visual datum does not differ from other data, and itself remains relative to an elemental and obscure ground. A relation with what in another sense comes absolutely from itself is needed to make possible the consciousness of radical exteriority. A light is needed to see the light" (TI 189, 192 [163, 166]). Thus the idea of light, of that element that empties space and makes intelligibility possible, is not the sole provenance of the "*philosophes de la lumière,*" but a ubiquitous "philosophical" notion.

38. It is the aspiration of the same to coincide with the Totality, to, in becoming reason(able), coincide with Reason—in the fullness of time, when time (history) will have been fulfilled (and thus at an end), this coincidence marking this very fulfillment. The distinction between the

same and the totality is temporary, then, in that the temporal—the ongoingness of time—marks precisely the possibility, and necessity, of the distinction.

39. "The Same," as we shall later need to show, will also have to be distinguished from the ego in its solitary enjoyment. We shall argue that the notion of "the Same" is best described as "the economy of the ego."

40. "Reason is one. . . . Nothing is outside of it."

41. "The *I think* where the being-in-act is constituted can be interpreted as coinciding with that which it constitutes: the full self-consciousness of the *I think* would be the very *system* of knowledge in its unity of intelligibility. The thinking thought which tends to this order of reason will be said, then, despite the labor of its research and the genius of its invention, to be like a detour that the system borrows in order to put itself in order, a detour that its terms and its structures follow in order to secure itself."

42. John D. Caputo, *Against Ethics* (Indiana University Press: Bloomington, 1993), p. 12.

43. "As opposed to the interiority of the deceitful passions and secret perfidies of subjective opinions, Reason would be the true interior life."

44. These powers of technique are more generally, or are founded upon, the powers concordant with finding oneself *chez soi* in the world, which, as we shall indicate shortly, is to live the alterity of the world as if it were not really other, to live the alterity of the world as if it were my possession, to reduce the alterity of the world to a part of the Same. Thus, for Levinas, this reference to technical powers applies also to Heidegger despite the latter's critique of the powers of technique in that for Levinas Heidegger's Being-in-the-world is lived as a Being-in-the-world-*chez-soi*. "In denouncing the sovereignty of the technological powers of man Heidegger exalts the pre-technical powers of possession" (TI 46 [17]).

45. One thinks readily here, for example, of the discourses of Foucault on the "insane" and the "criminal," but women, minorities, foreigners, children, and other others have too fallen prey to sanctions for crimes against Reason. We wish here to keep an eye toward the political implications of such "neutrality," as this will play a role in the problems of dialogue to be discussed later in this chapter.

46. Levinas does not say this precisely, but it does fit well with what he has to say in the "Preface" of *Totality and Infinity,* and in several other places, about war as the conflict of wills. It also fits wells with the thought of Nietzsche, for whom having to have recourse to Reason for protection against the other, rather than having the strength and confidence to take up and win the war of all against all, is seen as evidence of Socrates'

weakness, and motivates his designation of Socrates as the first "decadent" in the history of Occidental thought which exists as the legacy and the perpetuation of this decadence. See, for example, Friedrich Nietzsche, *The Twilight of the Idols: Or How to Philosophize with a Hammer* (Harmondsworth: Penguin Books, 1987). Despite the obvious differences in both the content and tone of their respective works, Levinas and Nietzsche are in accord in seeing in philosophy as ontology the expression of an unwillingness to face the other without the mediation of a term that blunts the other's effect upon me, that in some sense protects me from the other, and both desire, for very different reasons, and in highly divergent modalities, the restoration of the relationship as unmediated.

47. This is, of course, not the whole story for Levinas regarding violence, for the quotation continues: "without securing itself against the violence from which this nonviolence lives, and which appears in the tyranny of the State." We shall return to this notion later in the chapter.

48. This quotation is in reference specifically to Heidegger and how the idea of freedom functions in his thinking, but as Levinas is here arguing for the belongingness of Heidegger's thought to the philosophy of the Same, we would argue that this quotation can legitimately be applied, in the spirit or Levinas, in a general way to what he takes to be the predominant trend of Western philosophy at large.

49. "The unity of *I think* is the ultimate form of the spirit as knowing, be it confused with the being that it knows and identify itself with the system of knowledge."

50. These two phrases, "L'esprit comme savoir et l'immanence" and "Le dialogue de l'immanence," are, respectively, we recall, the titles of the first two sections of Levinas's article "Le Dialogue" in *De Dieu qui vient à l'idée.*

51. "Allows itself to be understood in its subordination to knowledge."

52. "Accord and unity of knowledge in the truth. The thought still thinking seeks them by various means. It has recourse to words, certainly. But these are signs that it gives to itself without speaking to anyone: in its work of reassembling, it can have to seek a presence of the thinkable beyond that which presents itself immediately, 'in flesh and blood' (bodily there) or in an image, of a signified by a sign; of that which is not yet present to thought, but which is no longer already locked into itself. That there is no thought without language signifies only, then, the necessity of an interior discourse."

53. "Thought splits itself from itself in order to interrogate itself and respond to itself, but the thread is retied. It *reflects* on itself in interrupt-

ing its spontaneous progression, but proceeds again from the same *I think.* It remains the same. It passes from one term to a contrary term that calls it forth, but the dialectic in which it finds itself is not a dialogue, or at least it is a dialogue of the soul with itself, proceeding by questions and responses."

54. "According to the traditional interpretation of the interior discourse that goes back to this definition, the mind in thinking remains no less one and unique, despite its thought processes and its goings and comings where it can oppose itself to itself."

55. "Is really spoken," "across the empirical multiplicity of thinking persons."

56. "In the empirical multiplicity of existing beings as intentional and incarnated consciousnesses, each would have the knowledge and the consciousness of 'something' and of its own consciousness, but would arrive by way of appresentative experiences and *sympathy* to become conscious of the consciousness of others, that is to say, to know the consciousness that each consciousness has of the same 'thing,' of itself and of all other consciousnesses. Thus communication is established: the signs of language would be born of all of the expressive manifestations of the bodies signifying in appresentation. Language would be born beginning in appresentation, which is, at once, experience and the reading of signs."

57. "A rigorous formulation of the subordination of language to knowledge, reducing to the lived as *experience* every modality independent of meaning to which dialogue would be able to make claim."

58. "Husserl goes so far as to 'lodge in the interior discourse the discourse that goes to all the others': 'that which I say there scientifically,' he writes, 'it is from me to me that I say it, but in the same stroke, I say it to all the others as implicated transcendentally in me, and the others in the others.' "

59. "Language . . . consists, for each of the interlocutors, to enter into the thought of the other, to coincide in *reason,* to interiorize oneself therein."

60. According to Levinas, such a theory can be found from Cassirer to Binswanger (OTB 119 [153]). To these we are suggesting might be added the names of Hegel, Heidegger, and Gadamer who, respectively, could be taken as "grounding" the possibilities for conversation in our mutual—even if in our ignorance—participation in *Geist,* Being, and the Tradition.

61. "Reason is one. It no longer has anyone with whom to communicate; nothing is outside of it. And, thus, it is like the silence of the interior discourse. The questions and responses of such an 'exchange of

ideas' reproduces or stages again those of a discourse that the soul holds with itself. Thinking subjects, multiple obscure points around which forms a clarity when they speak to and find one another, entirely like, in the interior discourse, when is retied the thread of thought which had to interrogate itself; a clarity where the obscure points of the diverse egos fade, become dim, but also are made sublime. This exchange of ideas occurs, when all is said and done, in a single soul, in a single consciousness, in a *cogito* that remains Reason."

62. This nomenclature—"dialogue," "communication"—is admittedly more or less arbitrary (even if some attempt has been made to make these terms "ring" in a way that evokes that to which they refer), and in utilizing it we seek merely the convenience of a shorthanded way of communicating this difference in starting points regarding traditional explanations of dialogue. We might just have readily utilized the terms "epistemological" and "ontological" dialogue, after the distinction made by Smith, and referred to above in note 14. Levinas himself makes no such formal distinction of nomenclature regarding these two "forms" of ontological dialogue, but, we are arguing, recognizes them as distinct and as being modeled upon, respectively, "the ontology of isolated subjectivity" and "the ontology of impersonal reason realizing itself in history" (TI 305 [282]). That is, what we are trying to capture here regarding dialogue is Levinas's claim that "For the philosophical tradition of the West every relation between the same and the other, when it is no longer an affirmation of the same, reduces itself to an impersonal relation with the universal order" (TI 87–88 [60]). By "dialogue," we mean to refer to the first option, by "communication" the second, as these options pertain to how dialogue variously functions within the tradition. Because Levinas himself does not use these terms in the sense in which we are employing them, it would be impracticable for us to attempt, in following Levinas's discourse, to sustain our nomenclature throughout. So we shall place these terms in inverted commas whenever we intend them to be taken in the technical sense here delineated.

63. We shall investigate later (in chapter 7) Levinas's own claim that the law comes to me across my own voice—but in a way that subverts, rather than confirms, my rationality qua identification with Reason.

64. "We can call *sociality* the unity of multiple consciousnesses entered into the same thought where their reciprocal alterity is suppressed. This is the famous dialogue called to put an end to violence in leading the interlocutors back to reason, installing peace in unanimity, suppressing proximity in coincidence."

65. "The predilection of Occidental humanism"; "that noble souls hunger for."

66. We are reminded here of a sentence from Jaspers that seems *à propos:* "If there are truths, then there is no Truth."

67. Levinas seems to equate the notion of opinion to being lost in "the they" of Heidegger's analyses in *Being and Time,* trans. J. Macquarrie and E. Robinson (San Francisco: Harper & Row, 1962). He contrasts, in the "Preface" to *Totality and Infinity,* for instance, opinion to "what [the mind] discovers by itself" (TI 25 [XIII]).

68. "To lead to this dialogue those opposed to it, inclined to do themselves violence. It would be necessary to find a dialogue in order to make [the other] enter into the dialogue."

69. "Would only be possible in the pure love of truth and intelligibility of a Spinozian universe."

70. "Unless one presupposes the pre-given unity of a sovereign and divine knowledge, of a substance thinking itself which would have broken up into a multiplicity of sufficiently self-mastering consciousnesses, limited in their horizons, opposed by their differences and hostile one to another, but which, from conflict to conflict, find themselves compelled or led to dialogues which would have to permit, through ever more nearness, the convergence of the looks parting from multiple points of view, but necessary to the fullness of a thought finding again its sovereignty and its lost *unity,* its *I think* or its *system.*"

71. This phrase, "just war," could be read here as "nothing but war" in the sense that so long as there is history there is conflict, history being conflict, or as "justified war" given that this war is purported to lead to teleological peace.

72. For obliteration of the other—whose integrated partiality is also necessary to final peace—also puts an end to Peace.

73. Levinas will argue that this "vision" is necessarily "eschatological," that is, "moral," even if it is, in philosophy, seen as "teleological." "Morality will oppose politics in history and will have gone beyond the functions of prudence or the canons of the beautiful to proclaim itself unconditional and universal when the eschatology of messianic peace will have come to superpose itself upon the ontology of war. Philosophers distrust it. To be sure they profit from it to announce peace also; they deduce a final peace from the reason that plays out its stakes in ancient and present-day wars: they found morality on politics" (TI 22 [X]).

74. "Reason is one. It no longer has anyone with whom to communicate, nothing is outside of it."

75. "Effectively is spoken."

76. Caputo makes a similar point, albeit in terms of the aim of the tradition rather than in terms of the conditions of possibility for dia-

logue itself (as we are claiming is the case for Levinas) when he, with his usual color, writes: "If we all reached consensus, we would soon be led, after having found that we were all saying the same thing, simply to shut up. That would on occasion certainly have its advantages, but is on the whole an odd thing for a theory of communication to aim at. If what we seek is universal agreement, if we were all to speak with universal reason, we would first be reduced to sameness and then to silence" (Caputo, *Against Ethics,* p. 40).

77. But the idea of "miracle" is not to be overlooked in the thought of Levinas, for it is a kind of miracle, and a miracle that will be precisely applicable to this problem, that Levinas will, as we shall see, offer us in his conception of the subject not only as "the same," but, in its being ethically obligated by the other, as "the other in the same," the subject "realizing these impossible exigencies," that is, from a certain perspective at least, as a kind of miracle.

78. That is, within this model as predominantly conceived. For Levinas will argue that the other already indwells and, across complex structures, even inspires this effort toward unity itself, even as it also breaks it up.

79. "Experience" is another of those terms that Levinas will attempt to wrest from the confines of the philosophical/ontological tradition. For while phenomenology limits the possibility of that which can be experienced to that which corresponds to the subject's transcendental forestructures, defines "experience" in this way, and thus effectively reduces experience to that which fits with the knower-known relation, Levinas argues that experience at its most fundamental level describes a relationship with an absolutely other, with that for whose coming my transcendental forestructures have not prepared me in advance, a relationship he refers to as "experience par excellence." We will discuss at length this distinction between "experience" and "experience" in the Levinasian text in a discussion of Levinas's philosophical method in our chapter 7.

80. In speaking of the origin of his ethical language, that which, he claims, articulates that which is capable of breaking up the closed circle of ontological thought, Levinas asserts: "It does indeed arise from what Alphonse de Waelhens called nonphilosophical experiences, which are ethically independent" (OTB 120 [154]).

81. "Knowledge of the other as an object before any sociality with him."

82. "Power of domination and possibility of ruse, . . . all the temptations of misleading rhetoric, of advertising and propaganda." Levinas notes here that it is the ontological ideal of "effacement before the truth" that makes one susceptible to these possibilities.

83. Across the corpus he has left us, Foucault argues for a negative answer to this question in some impressive detail. But one need not go as far as Foucault to be shaken by it. Already the masters of suspicion (in Ricoeur's phrase)—Marx, Nietzsche, and Freud—displace (even if each in his own way in the end would seem to attempt to save) the self-certain, enlightened, philosophical subject in revealing the powerful undercurrents of the subject that—*à son insu*—rather produce it as their effect.

84. "Installing peace in unanimity, suppressing proximity in coincidence."

2

Original Plurality: The Terms of Discourse

In our opening chapter we argued that the traditional notion of dialogue as *dia-logos* fails to help us make progress in understanding the conditions of possibility for interparadigmatic dialogue insofar as (1) in those situations that we are claiming are qualified by interparadigmaticity, the common *logos* that would be called upon to mediate the difference between interlocutors is precisely that which is in question, that which defines the difference so encountered, such that we are left with appealing to that which is precisely in question, and, thus, with a vicious circle; (2) in presupposing the commonality it is precisely the role of such a dialogue to locate, dialogue as *dia-logos* eliminates its own possibility/necessity; (3) this model precludes a priori the possibility of any genuine alterity, thus violently reducing to the same any alterity with which it would appear to be the task of dialogue to open and sustain relations.

We shall argue that in providing us with an account of the possibility of a dialogue that begins not with commonality (that presupposed by the tradition), but with original difference, that is, with a nonintegratable plurality, Levinas gives us a model for understanding dialogue that responds precisely to the exigencies we encounter in the challenge of interparadigmatic dialogue, that is, when we are challenged to engender a dialogue where the commonality the tradition presupposes is precisely that which is in question. So (recalling our argument in the introduction of chapter 1 that dialogue requires both a commonality, a shared *logos*, that would make *dia-logos* possible, and a difference between interlocutors that would make the relation, as a relation, necessary), if the problem for the tradition is in explaining the possibility of an effective difference (sufficient to warrant the necessity of dialogue) given an original identity (an original identity that, as we have seen in the opening chapter, Levinas argues erodes the difference requisite for a genuine dialogue, that is, a dialogue that would not be the integrative unfolding of an a priori logic but a meeting of terms in difference), the problem for Levinas would appear to be in describing the possibility of a relation (and a relation capable of yielding the commonality requisite to dialogue) from out of an original (and, as it will turn out according to Levinas, irreducible) difference. Such a relation Levinas will call discourse.

In this chapter and the next, which are of a piece, we shall present Levinas's idea of discourse, as this idea is proposed in the pages of *Totality and Infinity,* as providing us with a description of the conditions of possibility for interparadigmatic dialogue, that is, for engendering a dialogue in those situations where the common *logos* that would mediate a *dia-logos* cannot be effectively located, and thus cannot perform its mediatory function. We shall, following Levinas's own definitions, define discourse as "an original, non-allergic, ethical relationship with alterity productive of a meaning capable of founding communal meaning,"[1] and our exposition will follow the elements of this definition in dealing with, in this chapter, the way in which the separated terms requisite for discourse (the relation as "non-allergic") (2.I) are, for Levinas, evinced, first, in the ethical separation (transcendence) of the other from the same and from the system that, as the same, it operates (2.II), and, secondly, in the separation of the same from any system of totality (2.III), and then, in the next chapter, how the existence of these distinct and separated terms opens up the possibility for discourse as an "original," "ethical" relation (3.I), how, from out of this relation, the common *logos* (required for *dia-logos*) is produced (3.II), and how the possibility of dialogue as *dia-logos* is therefore, and remains, rooted in the original relation of discourse (3.III).

That is, we shall argue over the course of the next two chapters a central thesis, namely, that the condition of possibility of dialogue (and interparadigmatic dialogue in particular) is "discourse" conceived of as a unilateral, ethical responsibility of the-one-for-the-other. We shall argue, following Levinas, that what is required, if interparadigmatic dialogue is to be possible, is not that we be, as the philosophical tradition requires, "more clever" (that is, more consistently "rational," more attentive to the *logos*), but "more good" (that is, ethically "better," more attentive to, indeed, in the service of, the other). Interparadigmatic dialogue opens itself up as a possibility, then, only to the extent that one of the potential interlocutors runs that to which, in a later work, *Otherwise Than Being or Beyond Essence,* Levinas refers, for reasons that will become clear, as *un beau risque* (e.g., OTB 94 [119]), the risk of being exposed, defenseless, to the potential violence of the other, but for the sake of peace.

I. Allergy and Separation

If the relation of discourse is "an original, non-allergic/ethical relation with alterity productive of a meaning capable of founding communal meaning," and thus capable of opening a way toward dialogue in difference, as we, following Levinas, are proposing, it is first of all necessary to provide a description of the terms—the same and the other—that would be capable of holding forth such a relation (and it would be inaccurate to say capable of "entering into," since this relation is, for Levinas, "original" [if not, as we shall later see, pre-original]; I am, as will be seen, always already in ethical relation with the other). That is to say, if I and the other are to be capable of relating ethically—where my relation to the other is to be one of responsibility for the other and not a violent reduction of the other to the same—I and the other must exist in what Levinas refers to as an original "pluralism of being," or "multiplicity," that is, I and the other must exist as separated the one from the other, each with his own existence lived independently from his other, outside of participation in a common, third term that would govern (ontologically) the relation and thus the meaning of the terms in relation:

> The pluralism of being is not produced as a multiplicity of a constellation spread out before a possible gaze, for thus it would be already totalized, joined into an entity. Pluralism is accomplished in goodness proceeding from me to the other, in which first the other, as absolutely other, can be produced, without an alleged lateral view upon this movement having any right to grasp of it a truth

> superior to that which is produced in goodness itself. (TI 305–6 [282–83])

It is this ontological "participation" in a "superior (overarching) truth," wherein the meanings of the terms in relation are reduced to a delineation of their place in an a priori system of relations, that Levinas refers to as "allergy," and its consequences for ethics, and for dialogue as an ethically responsible activity, we have already examined at some length in our opening chapter. This allergy, expressed both in the *Schwärmerei* of pagan religion and in the System of philosophy as ontology, where the particular existent loses its singularity (and thus its dignity and responsibility) in participation in that which exceeds it, and thus exists as a function of that to which it belongs and of which it is a mere expression, is Levinas's primary and persistent nemesis—because, he believes, anathema to the possibility of ethics as a singular responsibility to a singularity. For Levinas, then, "[s]eparation opens up between terms that are absolute and yet in relation, that absolve themselves from the relation they maintain, that do not abdicate in favor of a totality this relation would sketch out. Thus the metaphysical relation realizes a multiple existing [un exister multiple]—a pluralism. But," Levinas hastens to add, "this relation would not realize pluralism if the formal structure of relationship exhausted the essence of relationship" (TI 220 [195]), for such would be to leave the terms that were to constitute the plurality in an allergic relation, in a totality, in which pluralism is merely "numerical"—defenseless against a synoptic view.[2]

In this chapter, then, dealing with pluralism as separation over against "allergy," with separation as an antidote to allergy, we will follow Levinas in his attempt to "explicate the power that beings placed in relation have of absolving themselves from the relation" (TI 220 [195]) across his description of the separation, or "transcendence,"[3] of the other from the same (insofar as the ego as the same already functions, as we saw in chapter 1, as knower in the knower-known correlation that qualifies the system of intelligibility), and then the separation of the same itself from "participation" in this ontological system (insofar as such participation would compromise the separation, and thus the plurality, necessary to ethical relating). So while, from a certain perspective (where we begin with the knower-known relation that founds ontology), the separation of the other and that of the same can be seen as "correlative" (the other separating, withdrawing behind the known object that he is to me as knower, and the same separating, withdrawing behind the knowing subject that would constitute the appearance of the other, each taking distance from its place in the knower-known relation), these "separations" cannot be seen as reciprocal, as interdependent, as dialectical reflections, each of the other, where either of these separations would be derived from the other.[4] That is, for Levinas, "the power that beings placed in relation have of absolving themselves from the relation . . . entails a different sense of absolution for each of the separated terms; the Metaphysician is not absolute in the same sense as the Metaphysical" (TI 220 [195]). So the other cannot be seen as being separated from the ontological system of the same in the same sense as the same is separated from the ontological system it operates as knower, and thus from the other. Rather, each withdraws, or is shown to be separated, after its own fashion. For were these separations dependent upon one another—strictly parallel, or reverse sides of the same separation—they would remain functions (dialectically constituted) of the same system from which their respective (but noninterdependent) separations are precisely a separation. Terms capable of ethical relation, terms that would comprise an original plurality, irreducible to their ontological meanings, must, after Levinas's phrase, "be produced as nonintegratable."[5]

We must therefore describe, in this chapter, two nonparallel and nonreciprocal separations, the ethical separation (or transcendence) of the other from the same, and the separation of the same as enjoyment, in an attempt to provide a description of the terms—terms that would have a meaning refractory to the meaning they would garner from ontological participation—that would be capable of holding forth the relationship of discourse as "an original, non-allergic, ethical relationship with alterity productive of a meaning capable of founding communal meaning." In other words, if we are to argue that discourse is the condition of possibility of dialogue, we must first describe the conditions of possibility of discourse itself:[6] the same and the other in an original (irreducible) plurality.

II. The Ethical Transcendence of the Other

II.1. The Same Called into Question

It was not by chance that we concluded our opening chapter (outlining the failure of the ontological model for dialogue to account for the possibility of interparadigmatic dialogue) with a discussion of the ethical implications of dialogue after this model, for it is precisely as an ethical "event" (in the sense of a happening for which no ontological structures have prepared us in advance) that, for Levinas, my naïve assimilation of the other, the reduction of the other to the same that is ontology, is interrupted, and the other qua other (that which would provide dialogue as communication with an *other*—over against dialogue as a reduction of the other to the same—with its raison d'être) (re-)[7] enters the scene.

Levinas insists that this interruption could only be ethical, in that—insofar as my relation with an other is ontologically based, is founded upon my relation to him as knower to known—the free assimilative ego cannot but appropriate all alterity to itself, bringing it into line with its a priori categories for knowing and experiencing, or, to have recourse to a language close to Levinas's own, that of phenomenology, its "transcendental forestructures," which, after the ontological view, constitute the very conditions of possibility for anything "appearing," being "experienced," at all. For Levinas, therefore, the other as other, that is, as an other irreducible to the same, transcending the reach of my transcendental forestructures, can enter the scene, can *se produire* ("be produced," or "produce itself"),[8] only as a *calling into question* of the free exercise of these forestructures, that is, as an ethical calling into question of my capacities as a knower/possessor. Here ethics is taken not as another kind of experience for which I would possess a priori the requisite forestructures, but as a challenge posed to me in my very exercise of such forestructures, a putting into question of the assumptive same that would wish to claim this challenge itself as its own "experience," as its own production, as that which, in the end (as in maïeutics) proceeded from itself. For Levinas, then, "A calling into question of the same—which cannot occur within the egoist spontaneity of the same—is brought about by the other. We name this calling into question of my spontaneity by the presence of the other ethics" (TI 43 [13]).

For left to itself, left unaffected in its root as a *cogito* in relation to objects and potential objects of knowledge, the assumptive ego stays its course—and if its assimilation of the world is frustrated, and it must turn back, it proceeds ever again from the same assumptive ego, forced to be stronger, more ingenious, to create a more powerful technology for overcoming the obstacles that oppose it, but remaining "essentially" the same, still, and unquestioningly, oriented toward the free assimilation of the world, inclusive of the human others that inhabit it. The *cogito* can only be effectively challenged, can only encounter a genuine alterity (that which is refractory to its capacities as a knower, the nonassimilable, the "other"), when, rather than being set back to recoup itself and rethink its strategies, it is called up short as *cogito,* stopped in its tracks, "paralyzed."[9] Over him "I *can*not have power" (je *ne peux* pas pouvoir) (TI 84 [56]).[10] And this, Levinas claims, can come about only when the very assumptive march of the naively spontaneous ego is questioned *as* assumptive, when it is made ashamed of itself,[11] that is, in an ethical encounter with an other that reveals to the ego not its weakness, not its ontological limitations, but its guilt, "where power, by essence murderous of the other, becomes, faced with the other and 'against all good sense,' the impossibility of murder, the consideration of the other, or justice" (TI 47 [18]). More specifically, the other as other, as refractory to my categories for knowing him, as a resistance to being reduced to something known by me, is, according to Levinas, encountered precisely as a calling into question of the assimilative same in the commandment "Thou shalt not commit murder"[12] taken in a broad sense, where the prohibition against murder is not confined to a prohibition against biological annihilation, but extends to what might be called the "spiritual" life of the one who as other issues the command. The prohibition, issued from a freedom, from a being who transcends my constitutive donation, his freedom and transcendence "revealed" in and by this prohibition itself, might read: "Thou shalt not reduce me, an independent, free will, to yourself and to the meanings that have begun in you."

Levinas refers to this self-presentation of the other who, on ethical grounds, calls into question the free exercise of the ego, as "face," where the notion of face clearly transcends any correlation to the face as a phenomenal object offered to my knowing, in that the face in Levinas's sense destroys any such image:

> The way in which the other presents himself, exceeding *the idea of the other in me,* we here name face. This *mode* [our emphasis] does not consist in figuring as a theme under my gaze, in spreading itself forth as a set of qualities forming an image. The face of the Other at each moment destroys and overflows the plastic image it leaves me, the idea existing to my own measure and to the measure of its *ideatum*—the adequate idea. It does not manifest itself by these qualities, but *kath'auto.* It *expresses itself.* (TI 50–51 [21])

The introduction of this new "mode" of presentation, of a "presence" that does not rely upon my making it present, relies upon the distinction between that which I am able to present (make present) to myself as a constituting (meaning giving) knower, and the self-presentation of the other that arrives at the encounter with a meaning of his own, independent of any meaning he would "borrow" from me, a distinction that Levinas often renders as that between the "manifestation" of the other (where the other, in the "plastic image" he presents to me and that can be known, is given to me as an object of knowledge) and "expression" or "manifestation *kath'auto*" (where the other, in his very expression, contests his being taken as an object, contests being reduced to the image he presents to me). In the face, that is to say, the other and the meaning that he expresses coincide—the other in his meaningfulness qua other is there from the first, contemporaneous with his arrival, and does not await my capacities as knower to endow him with a meaning: "*The absolute experience is not disclosure but revelation:* a coinciding of the expressed with him who expresses, which is the privileged manifestation of the Other, the manifestation of a face over and beyond form" (TI 65–66 [37]). That is, in the ethical encounter with the face, the other presents himself as transcendent to any categories I might bring to bear in his regard, as *kath'auto,* not in a borrowed light, but in a light of his own—in a "pure experience":[13]

> Manifestation *kath'auto* consists in a being telling itself to us independently of every position we would have taken in its regard, *expressing itself*. Here, contrary to all the conditions for the visibility of objects, a being is not placed in the light of another but presents itself in the manifestation that should only announce it; it is present as directing this very manifestation—present before the manifestation, which only manifests it. (TI 65 [37])

So, if the other is to *se produire* as other, as irreducible to the same, the other must be produced in what Levinas refers to as a "signification without context" (TI 23 [XII]),[14] must be produced as a "presence" that is irreducible to a making-present. That is, the other as other must interrupt the monopoly of meaning claimed by ontology for the knower-known relation wherein "meaning" is defined by, and is thus limited to, the correlation between a knower and a known, a limitation that emerges from as it confirms the economy of the same. And this monopoly, this hegemony, can only be broken when the other's meaning, the meaning that he himself brings to his own manifestation, is not in its turn a new meaning that I might assume in terms of my transcendental meaning categories, but, qua face, the *calling into question* of these categories themselves—such that the always possible assumption of this meaning in terms of which I might assimilate it to meanings proceeding from me would be, in turn, called into question, up to and including the very categories in terms of which I would *welcome it as* other. To "welcome as . . ." is already to provide the other with a context, to give him a place in relation to the other objects of my consciousness, that against which his self-presentation *as other* is precisely a contestation. Not ontologically "welcomed as . . ." but ethically "welcomed," I encounter the other in what Levinas refers to as a "passivity more passive than all passivity," or "the passivity of passivity," that is, in a passivity that does not retain for itself the power to welcome that which it cannot refuse. The ethical self-manifestation of the other thus destroys, without exception, any and all relation as cor-relation between the same and the other.

That is to say that the meaning of the other as other does not proceed from the same as in ontology, but brings to the same the genuinely new, a novel meaning that the ego has not already prepared itself to receive. Levinas therefore refers to this encounter as a "teaching," a nonmaïeutic teaching[15]—and what this teaching first teaches is not a meaning "content," a fact to be assumed, but the violence of the ego that would attempt to take it as such a content or fact. It teaches this teaching itself: that the other, presenting himself as transcendent, cannot be "learned" (brought into the knower-known relation), at least not without violence: "The first teaching teaches this very height, tantamount to its exteriority, the ethical" (TI 171 [146]). Faced with the face of the other, the ego, according to Levinas, discovers the murderous nature of its naïve spontaneity, discovers the violence of its free assumption or assimilation of the other (insofar as it "by nature" reduces the other to the same, and insofar as it freely assumes that which is of need to the other—a point to which we will return), and it is called up short—already guilty.

As such, the "no" that comes from the face is not the quantitative/ontological "no" of a "you cannot, you lack the power" (which is the [temporary] "no" found in relation to object-things), but the qualitative/ethical "no" of "thou shalt not" (issued only from the human other, *Autrui*).[16] Indeed, the *ethical* nature of this prohibition, that this prohibition can in nowise be read as an ontological one, is evinced in the fact that such ontological/epistemological assumption is not thereby halted; and Levinas readily admits that, despite this prohibition, murder, even "literal," biological murder, is the most banal of events:

> It would be pointless to insist upon the banality of murder, which reveals the quasi-null resistance of the obstacle. The most banal incident of human history corresponds to an exceptional possibility—since it claims the total negation of a being. It does not concern the force that this being may possess as a part of the world. The Other who can sovereignly say *no* to me is exposed to the point of the sword or the revolver's bullet, and the whole unshakable firmness of his "for itself" with that intransigent *no* he opposes is obliterated because the sword or the bullet has touched the ventricles or auricles of his heart. In the contexture of the world he is a quasi-nothing. . . . He thus opposes to me not a greater force, an energy assessable and consequently presenting itself as though it were part of a whole, but the very transcendence of his being by relation to that whole; not some superlative of power, but precisely the infinity of his transcendence. (TI 198–99 [173])[17]

It is this *ethical* prohibition, then—that paradoxically arises in the weakness, the vulnerability, the "powerlessness" of the other, and that thus calls to responsibility in his regard—that produces the separation of the other from the same, that is, the ethical impossibility (which endures as an ontological possibility)[18] of assuming the other under the categories, be they the rational categories, that proceed from me. We can recognize this in what Levinas refers to as "a concrete moral experience: what I permit myself to demand of myself is not comparable with what I have the right to demand of the Other. This moral experience, so commonplace, indicates a metaphysical asymmetry: the radical impossibility of seeing oneself from the outside and of speaking in the same sense of oneself and of the others, and consequently the impossibility of totalization" (TI 53 [24]).[19] But this "radical impossibility" is, of course, ontologically possible.[20] Indeed, it is this possibility that, for Levinas, founds the very real interhuman violence in our world, where one undertakes to speak of the other as one speaks of oneself, totalizes one's own being, and treats the other as a function of, as an extension of, or as an obstacle to, one's own "existence," of one's own "truth." To read Levinas, we are in the course of arguing, is to be sensitized to the ever subtle ways in which this temptation to totality, to violence, is reinstituted against the face of the other that would contest this violence, is to be sensitized to the attempt—undertaken in the name of truth, or God, or Reason, or Being, or what have you—to provide a context for the face whose ethical expression is a calling into question of any such context, however well intentioned or purportedly pacific. For any such attempt is, according to Levinas, to assert again an "allergic," participatory involvement in a totalizing view of being that, for Levinas, as we have noted, "reveals itself as war to philosophical thought" (TI 21 [IX]).

It is only, then, as an *ethical* challenge to the assimilative march of the free ego, and its hegemony over meaning, that the other can resist the totalizing proclivities of the same. And only thus is the separation, the transcendence, of the other produced that would, as we are attempting to show, render possible dialogue as dialogue with an *other,* as opposed to dialogue as a reduction of the other to the same.

Our introduction of alterity, of the other, in chapter 1, in the experience of the problem of interparadigmatic dialogue (that is, as the encountering of an other whose point of view with regard to some or other issue of importance to us both differs from my own) is, therefore, only partially adequate to the notion of "the other" as this idea emerges in the discourse of Levinas. It is inadequate as a description of an encounter with alterity if it is taken as the mere *experience* of another with a differing perspective,[21] for the ontological, constitutional structures of the ego are more than up to the challenge of assimilating this experience as an experience, that is, as that which is yet another known, or potentially known, to me as knower. As an epistemological challenge, as that which I could presentify to myself as the unknown, as that which could be known as the unknown (insofar as I would know that I do not know), the knowing subject would already be on the way to knowing it, on the way to assimilating it to the dialectic of *savoir,* on the way to reducing it to the same. In the dual borrowing between knower and known, as outlined in chapter 1, wherein both are finally put in order according to the system of intelligibility, an epistemological alterity is no enduring challenge to the knowing ego. But if the other in our opening chapter was introduced along these lines, he gains his force only *as other* (and this was strongly hinted at in our opening chapter, although not developed in that we tried there to stay with an internal analysis of *dia-logos* on the ontological model) when the other is encountered as *presenting himself* as a *calling into question* of my *cogito—epistemologically* irrefutable, but able to be called into question *ethically.* When in the first chapter, then, the ego was backed up against itself and forced to ask, "How do I know that I am right (have true access to the universal *logos*) rather than the other?" implicit in this question, or at least implicit in this question to the degree it is able to open me up to a genuine alterity, is another: "How do I know that I am right *over against* the other?" or "How do I know that in my truth I am not doing harm to the truth of the other (who presents himself as a 'truth' that my 'truth' does not govern—but to which I am responsible)?"[22] This encounter with an other is only revelatory of the other as genuinely other (as an other that is not, through the knowing relation, ontologically correlated with the same) when the epistemological challenge is transformed into, or reflects, an ethical one.

This stress on the "ethical" basis for the separation of the other from the same, essential, we are arguing, to a consistent reading of Levinas, leads us to a clarification of two related points in Levinas's discourse that are easily misunderstood, and an understanding of which is essential to an understanding of the ethical relationship that follows from, that is the other side of, this ethically based separation: the first being the meaning of "otherness" and "the other" in Levinas; and the second being the relationship, in this discourse, of the other with "the idea of the infinite."

II.2. A Totally Other Separation

Levinas's insistence that the other be thought of as totally other (as illustrated in his 1990 response to Derrida entitled, simply, "Tout Autrement")[23] has been the cause of both some incredulity and consternation among some of his readers. But if this total alterity is thought, as we are arguing it should be, as an ethical, rather than as an ontological, alterity (even if, as we shall see, this ethical alterity results in a certain "effective" ontological/anthropological alterity), then certain of these concerns can, we think, be avoided.

We are thinking here, for instance, of the objection posed by John D. Caputo in his *Against Ethics*,[24] where, despite his love for Levinas, and despite his love of Levinas's "most important" and "impossible" saying about the other, Caputo, in the context of a discussion of universals and individuals, claims that he does "not quite believe" his own rabbi (Levinas), at least insofar as Levinas speaks of the other as *totally* other.[25] The reason for this incredulity is that Caputo does not believe that it is possible—if one is to speak strictly—to speak about the individual other qua individual other, much less as totally other:

> I cannot speak about the individual, but I must and I do so all the time, since proper names happen. . . . Such a difficulty can be called, with a certain shorthand, "im/possible," i.e., what operates under a dual condition of possibility and impossibility. That is what Derrida calls a "quasi-transcendental" condition. "*Différance*" makes it possible (almost) to speak about the individual, even as it makes it impossible (almost).[26]

It is only across our transcendental forestructures (be this the "quasi-transcendental" of *différance*—a term that Caputo borrows from Derrida in terms of which it is claimed that all meaning is the product of the interplay of differing signifiers each of whose final meanings—since their meanings themselves result only from the play of yet further signifiers, ad infinitum—is therefore always deferred), Caputo claims, that anything can enter into our experience. This is Caputo's reading of Derrida's famous statement, in *De la Grammatologie,* that "there is nothing outside of the text" (il n'y a pas d'hors texte), by which, Caputo assures us, "Derrida does not deny but delimits reference; what he denies is reference-without-difference. Without *différance. Différance* does not lock us up inside anything. On the contrary, *différance* is a doorway, a threshold (*limen*), a door through which everything outgoing (reference, messages sent, etc.) and incoming (messages received, perceptions, etc.) must pass."[27] Now, Levinas's description of the other as the totally other, as absolutely other, and thus "ineffable," therefore strikes Caputo as incredible (not to be believed) insofar as this would claim for the other the status of being a "being without *différance,*"[28] the fulfilling of "the dream of absolute presence in the mode of absolute absence,"[29] the possibility of a fact that would not need to be interpreted like all other "facts,"[30] and this strikes Caputo as a very "metaphysical" gesture, in the sense where "[m]etaphysics has always dreamt of a land of pure individuals, an unexplored, unmarked, untouched, virginal, pristine terrain upon which no philosophical foot has trod, an arctic or antarctic land of pure polar snow, without marks or traces."[31] And such purity is, on Caputo's terms (precisely because all experience comes to us across our transcendental forestructures), impossible, or, as he would have it, im/possible:

> "The individual is ineffable": that is already to get a fix on the individual, to situate the individual thus far and to that extent within our view and within our grasp, in advance. This is already to set our sights on the concrete particular as a kind of gap or caesura within the grids of words and concepts, to fix it within the cross hairs of language. We thereby bring the individual—this is Levinas's nemesis, what he is trying to ward off—within our fore-having, fore-seeing, and fore-grasping. To just this extent, to the extent that we have marked off the singular as unmarked, as pristine and vir-

ginal, we have already anticipated it, made ready its arrival, so that it does not arrive absolutely unannounced, without a proper invitation, as an absolute singularity, an absolute novelty, an absolute surprise.

We cannot be absolutely surprised—that is perhaps the not wholly melancholy implication of *différance.* Were a surprise absolute, were we confronted with something absolutely novel, that would make it impossible to recognize the surprise *as* a surprise. We would not know that we were being surprised or indeed that anything was happening at all.[32]

The implication of this is that, *pace* Levinas (on Caputo's reading), the other cannot be totally other:

> Levinas posits the absolutely Other on one side and he posits the same on the other side, but not as opposites, not oppositionally, for then the dialectical machine would be set off. Still, they are related, and this relation, which is the ethical relation, is what matters most to him. . . . But how can you have an absolute relation to an absolute? Would not the very relation and correlation dissolve the absoluteness? How could anything be cor-related to what is absolutely Other, since the absolute absolves itself of all relation and correlation? If something were, properly speaking, absolutely Other, then it would not be a matter of concern for us and we would simply ignore it, being quite oblivious of it. Now ignoring the Other would greatly distress Levinas, since the Other lays unconditional claim upon us. But that means that the Other is related to us after all, viz., in a very powerful, unconditionally commanding way. We in turn should acknowledge this relationship by responding to it, by answering it and taking it up, decisively and unequivocally. So in fact the absolutely Other is only relatively absolute, almost absolute, not quite absolute. By the absolutely Other, I would mean what is transcendent, quite transcendent, indeed quite a lot, *ad infinitum,* but not absolutely. "Absolute alterity" *ad literam* would be a poetic way of saying *ad infinitum,* which is of course something we never reach.[33]

Now, we take Caputo's point.[34] If the other were (ontologically) absolutely other, we could have no awareness of it, and any relation into which it might enter (even the ethical relationship) would dissolve its absoluteness. But what if the other were not (at least at first blush) ontologically absolutely other, but that its absolute alterity were a function of its being in relation, and in a relationship of a certain kind? "Otherness," whether absolute or not, is not, we are arguing, a property that belongs to individuals, but already a relational term (even definitionally, for something could not be "other" in itself, but only "other than . . .")—and a term that applies to relations of more than a single (e.g., ontological) register. The other is other, for Levinas, we are arguing, not in *ontologically* transcending, ad infinitum,[35] the reach of my transcendental forestructures (but, insofar as it is known, experienced yet in terms of these), but in *ethically* "calling into question" the validity of my transcendental forestructures themselves, and is absolutely other to the extent that any transcendental forestructure that would "welcome" the experience of this "calling into question" would itself, by the same ethical alterity, be called into question. The absolute in relation is not contradictory[36] if this absoluteness, this alterity, is taken, not as an a priori state of affairs that would be compromised by the relation, but as a *product* of the relation itself.[37]

Indeed, we would maintain that Levinas is not arguing that the other is (at least not on first reading) *necessarily* ontologically other at all. On the contrary, Levinas maintains that it is only my fellow human that can be genuinely other:

> The absolutely foreign alone can instruct us. And it is only man who could be absolutely foreign to me—refractory to every typology, to every genus, to every characterology, to every classification—and consequently the term of a "knowledge" finally penetrating beyond the object. The strangeness of the Other, his very freedom! Free beings alone can be strangers to one another. Their freedom which is "common" to them is precisely what separates them. (TI 73–74 [46])

Might this passage suggest that a certain, prior ontological/anthropological similarity (or at least analogy of some kind) is itself a condition of possibility for ethical alterity? Such a proposal is indeed difficult, and perhaps impossible, to reconcile with what follows the above quotation in Levinas's text—and such assertions are a common refrain throughout his text—that the other (he to whom I relate in language) "is wholly by relation to himself, *kath'auto,* a being that stands beyond every attribute, which would precisely have as its effect to qualify him, that is, to reduce him to what is common to him and other beings—a being, consequently, completely naked" (TI 74 [46]). Indeed, the other reveals himself to me as totally other, as without common genre with me, even that of a common "humanity." This should give us pause about our (albeit most tentative) suggestion that a prior ontological similarity is *required* for ethical alterity, and, indeed, it will turn out that what is required for ethical alterity is not a common humanity delineated in any a priori fashion, but rather the capacity for speech, and more precisely, the capacity to call into question the categories I would apply to it (which is a function of its freedom),[38] and it is Levinas's (perhaps empirical) observation that such a capacity adheres only to human beings.[39] But we should also take pause, in light of the fact that the totally other is, for Levinas, only the human other, if we are tempted to conclude that the totally other of his discourse is founded upon an ontological, as over against an ethical, transcendence, for if such were the case then the absolutely other would more feasibly be that which is ontologically furthest from us—germs, dirt, plastic, quarks—rather than our fellow human beings.

Now, that we are dealing here with an at least "effective" ontological alterity cannot be doubted; Levinas's disavowals of a common genre between the same and the other need be heeded. But such statements have an ethical, rather than an ontological, inspiration. For in his ethical capacity to call into question the transcendental forestructures in terms of which I might project his meaning, the other human preserves to himself the right to (ontologically) define himself, to direct and interpret and correct any meaning I might make of his manifestation to me, the ethical right to be what he is on his own interpretation rather than what I would make of him. And this does not *necessarily* preclude ontological similarities between us, even as I am thereby prohibited from, from my side of the relation, commandeering the meanings that would govern any such possible similarities. But as any ontological similarities I would propose to the other are susceptible to being called into question by him, I cannot proceed in my relations with him on the basis of any such proposals as if they were a priori and the basis of the possibility of the relation. As such, the ethical alterity of the other, his very ethical otherness, effectuates a for all practical purposes ontological separation—my inability to capture in a concept or category the "essence" of the other.

Indeed, as we shall shortly see, for Levinas any ontology at all—and thus any ontological similarities or differences between terms—is founded upon, is one of the "products" of, the ethical relation with the other, such that the otherness of the other requisite for ontology could not itself be an ontological category, for ontology could not precede its own conditions of possibility. The delineation of ontological similarities or differences, then, which will be shown to have been worked out as the product of the struggle for truth between free beings in ethical relation, are not forbidden by, or contradictory with, ethical separation—totality thinking is possible (and, as we shall see, even necessary)—but require it. As foundational to ontological similarity, any such similarity cannot then return to dominate, to define, the ethical alterity that is its condition of possibility. Rather, ethical separation rests at the heart of any ontological formulation, evoking it, and any ontological formulation (insofar, as we shall also see later, as it is *said to an other*) reflects this ethical separation, an ethical separation that can always and again, as foundational to it, call such formulations into question. Ontological separation, consequently, is dependent upon a *prior* ethical separation, the latter irreducible to the former.

Further, and along these same lines, we would argue that Levinas does not, *pace* Caputo's implied claim, attempt to "name," to "speak about," or to "get a fix on" the individual other, even in a negative sense, with his designation "the totally other," even if by this description Levinas appears to be naming what cannot be named. This designation names, rather, he who is capable of calling into question all names, even this one, and capable of calling into question, in turn, any subsequent naming ad infinitum, and it is this being called into question that for Levinas is ethics, and that constitutes the absolute alterity of the other. It is not that the other is, in himself, an absolute, or, ontologically, absolutely other. Ethics, for Levinas, is, as we shall see later in this chapter, not a matter of speaking *about* the other, but speaking *to* him,[40] of responding to the ethical challenge that he poses to me.

Levinas is suggesting (and it is this, we are arguing, that Caputo seems to miss) a change in modality or register in his use of the terms other and totally other, and this change in modality is not to be read as the substitution of one (ethical) set of forestructures for another (ontological) one, but as an even more radical displacement. We recall, noting especially the suggestion of a change in modality, the following: "The way in which the other presents himself, exceeding *the idea of the other in me,* we here name face. This *mode* does not consist in figuring as a theme under my gaze, in spreading itself forth as a set of qualities forming an image" (TI 50 [21]). Levinas refers to this self-presentation of the other in the face as "the opening of a new dimension."[41] He identifies the other as he who is capable of reversing, and not only overflowing, the vectors of transcendental meaning constitution that flow from me to the object—"*Revelation* constitutes a veritable inversion [in relation to][42] *objectifying cognition*" (TI 67 [39])—including any meaning I might project by the term "the other" itself. Here, where the thought of the other is conceived on the basis of the Cartesian idea of infinity, "the movement proceeds from what is thought and not from the thinker" (TI 61 [33]). The other, in his calling into question of my categories for meaning, brings into the situation his own ethical meaning (which is this contestation itself), and this ethical meaning, as we shall see, bears upon, founds, ontological meaning itself. Thus Levinas might well concur with Derrida, but perhaps for reasons other than those that attract Caputo, and affirm that there is no-*thing* outside of the text. But perhaps it is not things (objects and potential objects of knowledge) alone that bear meanings.[43] To claim, as Caputo at least seems to, that there is therefore no meaning outside of the text is to decide in advance that ethics is, must in principle be, a function of ontology—that which Levinas's discourse, and his discourse on discourse, precisely contests.[44]

II.3. The Production of Infinity

The argument of the previous section—that the alterity of the other need be read as an ethical, over against an (a priori) ontological, alterity (or as an ontological alterity founded upon an ethical alterity rather than as an ontological alterity that would found ethical separation)—is given credence, we maintain, by Levinas's introductory discussions, in *Totality and Infinity,* of "the idea of the Infinite," an idea that, in being distinguished from the idea of totality, governs the analyses of that work.[45] Here, as we will show, the infinity of the other, which is, Levinas tells us, a philosophical articulation of his transcendence,[46] is shown not to be a property of the other *an sich*—the other is not in ontological fact infinite (on the contrary, it is, as we shall see, precisely his finitude—his susceptibility to suffering and death—that warrants his ethical infinity)—but is *produced* in my ethical relation with him.[47]

Indeed, the introduction of the Cartesian "idea of the infinite" makes its appearance in the body of *Totality and Infinity*[48] in a discussion of "metaphysical alterity," where Levinas is at pains to show that this alterity, this "infinity" of the other, and the transcendence with respect to the same that it implies, is not to be taken merely as a negation of the modes of the same pushed to the limit, such that, for Levinas, as the title of this section puts it, "Transcendence Is Not Negativity":

> One may indeed endeavor to deduce the metaphysical alterity from beings that are familiar to us, and thus contest its radical character. Is not metaphysical alterity obtained by the superlative expression of perfections whose pale image fills the here below? But the negation of imperfections does not suffice for the conception of this alterity. Precisely perfection exceeds conception, overflows the concept; it designates distance: the idealization that makes it possible is a passage to the limit, that is, a transcendence, a passage to the absolutely other. The idea of the perfect is an idea of infinity. The perfection designated by this passage to the limit does not remain on the common plane of the *yes* and the *no* at which negativity operates; on the contrary, the idea of infinity designates a height and a nobility, a transcendence. The Cartesian primacy of the idea of the perfect over the idea of the imperfect thus remains entirely valid. The idea of the perfect and of infinity is not reducible to the negation of the imperfect; negativity is incapable of transcendence. (TI 41 [11–12])

Levinas is here contesting the view that alterity, metaphysical alterity, could be explained as the result of an ontological project,[49] as a "beyond" of ontology ontologically conceived, as a "too much" for ontology, as a negation of the modes of the same which would leave us an alterity as the result of the play of the same even as it would aspire to transcendence, even if, on the basis of this passage itself, Levinas deems it "premature and in any case insufficient to qualify it, by opposition to negativity, as positive" (TI 42 [12]).

When, several pages later (in the section entitled "Transcendence as the Idea of Infinity"), Levinas takes up again the discussion of the idea of the infinite, we discover why, previously, it would have been premature, and even insufficient, to characterize infinity as a positivity. It would have been insufficient because "the infinite" never becomes, for Levinas, a positive infinity if this positivity is read along ontological lines (as Levinas thinks it is for Hegel).[50] But the infinite does reveal itself as a positivity in the *idea* of the infinite, an idea that is *produced* precisely *in relation* to the infinite of which it is the idea:

> This relation of the same and the other, where the transcendence of the relation does not cut the bonds a relation implies, yet where these bonds do not unite the same and the other into a Whole, is in fact fixed in the situation described by Descartes in which the "I think" maintains with the Infinite it can nowise contain and from which it is separated *a relation* called "idea of infinity." To be sure, things, mathematical and moral notions are also, according to Descartes, presented to us through their ideas, and are distinct from them. But the idea of infinity is exceptional in that its *ideatum* surpasses its idea, whereas for things the total coincidence of their "objective" and "formal" realities is not precluded; we could conceivably have accounted for all the ideas, other than that of Infinity, by ourselves. (TI 48–49 [19], emphasis ours)

But if "the idea of infinity" is a *relation* with "the Infinite," it is important to note that, for Levinas, "the transcendence of the Infinite with respect to the I which is separated from it and which thinks it measures (so to speak) its very infinitude. The distance that separates *ideatum* and idea here constitutes the content of the *ideatum* itself. Infinity is characteristic of a transcendent being as transcendent; the infinite is the absolutely other" (TI 49 [20]). Clearly, here, it is the "transcendence" of the Infinite that measures its infinitude, where its infinity is a characteristic of its transcendence—and not an a priori and ontological infinity that constitutes its transcendence. It is this distance, this transcendence, that is the very content (the very infinity) of the infinite.

The infinite is not infinite first, to later enter into relation with the same, but infinite by virtue of its relation with the same; its "infinity" is produced in, is a function of, this relation.[51] Levinas puts this to us again later, perhaps even more explicitly—and already in the specific context of the ethical relation, which for Levinas is *the* relation with transcendence that maintains the transcendent as transcendent, and thus the "concretization" of the idea of infinity—when he writes: "Teaching signifies the whole infinity of exteriority. And the whole infinity of exteriority is not first produced, to then teach: teaching is its very production. The first teaching teaches this very height, tantamount to its exteriority, the ethical" (TI 171 [146]).

That is why, in the next paragraph, Levinas can tell us that "To think the infinite, the transcendent, the Stranger, is hence not to think an object, . . . [but] to do more or better than think" (TI 49 [20]). Consequently, and in opposition to the intentionality that corresponds to objects, "[t]he 'intentionality' of transcendence is unique in its kind" (TI 49 [20]). The designation of this other "intentionality" (where intentionality, which usually designates the constitution of objects, is thus put between scare quotes) suggests the change in register or modality we suggested in our previous section, suggests that we are dealing here with that which is not appropriately described in terms of objectivity at all, is no longer a matter of ontology, as does the "more and better" than thinking that the idea of the infinite evokes in the one who thinks it. And it is to this "modality"—that of the more and better than thinking—that we must turn if we are to concretize, to think positively, the Cartesian notion of the idea of the infinite in its formal ("apparently wholly empty") designation of "a relation with a being that maintains its total exteriority with respect to him who thinks it" (TI 50 [20–21]). This "concretization of the idea of infinity," where the idea of infinity is "not an idea but desire,"[52] is, for Levinas, the ethical relation of "discourse," to an account of which we shall turn in our next chapter: "In the concrete the positive face of the formal structure, having the idea of infinity, is discourse, specified as an ethical relation" (TI 80 [52]).

III. The Separation of the Same as Enjoyment

III.1. The Separation of the Same

But before moving on to a positive account of the relationship of discourse we must, to complete our exposé on Levinas's insistence that the transcendence of the other be taken as an ethical as over against an ontological separation, trace the delineation of another structure that, in *Totality and Infinity,* is taken to be necessary to the production of Infinity, and thus to the relation of discourse as an ethical relation, and that will therefore be important to the ongoing analyses of our next chapter: the ego separated in its enjoyment.[53]

To read Levinas, we are arguing in this chapter, is to be sensitized in the extreme to the ever subtle ways in which totality thinking (that thinking that would pretend to step outside of itself and to view the whole of which it is a part as if from the outside) reasserts its hegemony behind every apparent rupture, a reassertion that Levinas believes, as we attempted to illustrate in our opening chapter, ultimately negates the possibility of any genuine (i.e., nonintegratable) exteriority, and with this the possibility of discourse as an ethical rather than an ontological relationship, and thus the possibility of dialogue as anything other than an allergic relation, a reduction of the other to the same, as anything other than violence. If the other is to be encountered as nonintegratable, as a calling of the same (that would attempt to integrate it) into question, it is necessary, therefore, that the terms involved in this ethical relationship not be conceived of as having already been in an a priori, ontological relationship prior to the ethical one, and that the ethical call of the other would only interrupt—for then the a priori interrelationship that would subtend any interruption would, as the a priori ground of any interruption, persist intact behind any apparent break and subsume this interruption into the totality as a function or mere "moment" of it. Participation in the whole, in the totality, would be the irremissible ground of being, and every conceivable relationship (be it negatively in the relationship of the refusal of relationship) between terms (encompassed by a totality) would be limited to one of reciprocal limitation within a closed system[54]—which, on Levinas's terms, is "war," or its substitute, "politics," wherein the terms limit themselves in exchange for a measure of protection against the threat of the other.[55] But politics is not yet ethics,[56] for in politics, as defined by Levinas, the same is not called into question by the other. The absolute alterity necessary to such questioning is absent under such a regime, and any notion of ethics (as responsibility for the other) is an illusory, if fortunate, "effect," or extension, of an unquestioned self-interest.

It is necessary, then, for ethics (as the calling into question of any totality to which I might make claim), for discourse (as an ethical relationship with an other), and for dialogue (as communication with an exteriority), that *both* the other and the same be produced as nonintegratable, as each having its own separated existence prior to any integration in a shared, and thus encompassing and integrating, ground of existence.[57] Levinas refers to this situation, as we indicated earlier, as an original plurality, and for the Levinas of *Totality and Infinity* this plurality of beings constitutes the ultimate structure in being where "being" here implies, paradoxically and somewhat awkwardly, no prior ontological unity, but the "pre-ontological"[58] existence of separated beings (that will nevertheless be shown to be in *ethical* relation): a plurality of beings, or existents, who exist independently of any encompassing totality structure, be that under the subtle sway of the being of beings that would open the way to a fundamental ontology, or even to an analogy of being among beings. Consequently, this plurality cannot, evidently, be thought as another attempt at ontologically describing the way things at root "are" (where the employment of the verb "to be" would be taken to indicate shared participation in the *ontos*), despite Levinas's persistence in utilizing the terms "beings," or "existents," and "the plurality of being" in describing it, since this thought is precisely an attempt—despite the obvious difficulties[59]—to think the plurality outside any such original, ontological unity, that is, in terms of an *original* plurality, irreducible even to the unity of being.

So if the other is to be capable of expressing himself to the same (in calling the same into ethical question) as separated from (or transcendent to) the same (that which we have argued so far), the same to whom he expresses himself must *also* exist as separated from the other, must exist independently, prior to any correlation with the other, in an existence that is not constituted in correlation—be it a negative correlation—with the other, but as an independent existence, that is, in a separation that is neither equivalent nor parallel to the separation of the other from the same.[60] For if the same is thought solely as a term in the correlation between the knower and the known that is produced as an ontological regime, the same would be constituted in a dialectical relationship to its other, would be what it is in terms of this relationship, defined in terms of the epistemo-onto-logical system of which it is a part. The same under the auspices of the same as a term in correlation cannot be a separated subject, for it is here what it is as over against the other from which it distinguishes itself, its self-reference (indeed, its reference *tout court*) dependent upon, constituted in dialectical tension with, the negation that constitutes the other as other, I and not-I forming a whole that constitutes the *system* of intelligibility:

> The metaphysician [the same] and the other do not constitute a simple correlation, which would be reversible. The reversibility of a relation where the terms are indifferently read from left to right and from right to left would couple them the *one* to the *other;* they would complete one another in a system visible from the outside. The intended transcendence would be thus reabsorbed into the unity of the system, destroying the radical alterity of the other. (TI 35–36 [5–6])

The same as already in ontological relation, as a part of a larger whole, cannot be an existent in an *original* plurality, a term capable of finding itself in an ethical, non-ontological, non-allergic, relationship. For this it is necessary that it exist independently of, or prior to, any a priori participation in an ontological system that would give it its place, its existence, as a part of a system. For this it must exist as separated from any such system, and "separated" where its existence would be an existence as "independence," that is, where its separated existence would not be defined in terms of that from which it is separated (its "separation," therefore, recognized technically only after the fact, and not as constitutive of its existence as separated), but defined only in reference to itself, such that it "maintains itself all by itself" (TI 54 [25]). Levinas goes so far as to refer to this separated existence as "atheist," by which he means to make no comment on the existence or nonexistence of God, but by which he indicates the radicality of the separation of the same, separated even from the designs of God that would implicate it (and the other) in a destiny not its own, and thus compromise its freedom and its responsibility—that is, its capacity to find itself in a non-allergic, ethical relationship with an other.[61]

Now, it is true that in our analyses so far the same that has been called into question by the other has been the same conceived precisely as the knower correlative with a known that the other calls into question by refusing (ethically) to be taken as a known. As such, we have not yet reached a delineation of the same as an independent existence, even if its susceptibility to being called into question would require such separation. And this should not surprise us, for our analyses begin, as do those of Levinas—and how could it be otherwise?—in media res, in a world already populated by objects, by others, and by complex relations between these, in a world already languaged, already ontologically constituted, where the same as "I" already lives the world as "the same" world lived by me and the other, as a system, that is, as already organized in accord with certain a priori structures that precede me.[62] While Levinas will, as we shall see, certainly take his distance from Heidegger, we believe that it would be consistent with Levinas at this point to borrow from Heidegger and suggest—and it seems to us that Levinas does so, albeit implicitly—that our experience of this already finding ourselves in the middle of things is analogous to Heidegger's notion of *in-der-Welt-sein*,[63] a finding ourselves in an already "worlded" world (although, for Levinas, not in the manner of *Geworfenheit*, but *chez soi*).[64] And our finding ourselves such is, as it is for Heidegger (and we shall make more of this later), largely a matter of enculturation.[65] Now, as we are arguing here, were the same merely a product of this enculturating process, if all there were to me was the confluence of influences my culture was exerting upon me, I could never be separate from the process itself, and any subsequent forces, while they might change me, would do so as an extension of this process itself—such that there could be nothing exterior to the I (the I *being* the confluence of the totality of forces acting upon it), and thus no calling into question of the same *itself,* and thus no "ethics." If such an ethical moment is to be posited as possible, it is therefore necessary to trace back, in a kind of "reduction," from our experience of the world as already worlded (and where I and the other would be "functionaries" of this "world") to a separate subject that would make the self-presentation of the other *as other* (encountered, that is, as "not of this world,"[66] as transcendent to the world that *is* the correlation between my transcendental forestructures and their objects) possible, and that would thus subtend the same as *in-der-Welt-sein.*

That is, the same as separated must be distinguished from, extricated from, the same in system, from the same as governing the system of intelligibility as knower in correlation with the known, and such that its separation not be produced as the dialectical (and thus interdependent) opposite of the other from which it is separated, which would leave it within a system, be that a system of differences. So long as the same *is* the system of intelligibility, a knower in correlation with a known object, where this correlation constitutes "being" and yields "truth," that is, so long as the same as my self-identification in system is confused with the Same as *the* System of intelligibility (and we have argued in the opening chapter that this identification is, short of ethical interruption, unavoidable in that this system is always found "in me"),[67] there can be no separation of the other, since (as we have also seen in chapter 1), for the tradition, Reason is one and permits of no exteriority. Levinas must therefore seek for the same a basis of self-reference that is not reducible to the self in correlation, must identify a same that exists separately, independently. That is to say, the ego must itself be thought, must have an existence, independent of the structures that it operates as knowing its world, structures that, if equated with the ego, would draw it into a dialectical relation with the known being where its own "being" would be a function of its place in this relation, and its own separation—necessary for there to be a plurality in being—illusory.[68]

Such a separated same is identified by Levinas as "psychism," or "*cogito*" ("I think"), as the experience of an "inner life" that cannot be equated with, though it is reflected in, the thinking subject in correlation with known objects:

> The separation of the Same is produced in the form of an inner life, a psychism. The psychism constitutes an *event* in being; it concretizes a conjuncture of terms which were not first delineated by the psychism and whose abstract formulation harbors a paradox. The original role of the psychism does not, in fact, consist in only *reflecting* being; it is already *a way of being* [une manière d'être], resistance to the totality. Thought or the psychism opens the dimension this *way* requires. The dimension of the psychism opens under the force of the resistance a being opposes to its totalization; it is the feat of radical separation. (TI 54 [24])

The same, then, in its very being, is a resistance to its own totalization, a separation from, a taking distance from, the very system of a priori structures that it itself operates in an already worlded world. That is, finding itself in a system of meanings that precede it, that it did not delineate, the psychism is capable of taking up a distance from these meanings,[69] of living itself as separated, as a resistance to the meanings that this system, this totality, would impose. And this resistance is correlative with, is produced in, the psychism living in time. To illustrate this, Levinas again has recourse to the exposition of the idea of the infinite in Descartes's *Meditations:*

> The *cogito,* we said, evinces separation. The being infinitely surpassing its own idea in us—God in the Cartesian terminology—subtends the evidence of the *cogito,* according to the third *Meditation.* But the discovery of this metaphysical relation in the *cogito* constitutes chronologically only the second move of the philosopher. That there could be a chronological order distinct from the "logical" order, that there could be several moments in the progression, that there is a progression—here is separation. For by virtue of time the being is not *yet*—which does not make it the same as nothingness, but maintains it at a distance from itself. It is not all at once. Even its cause, older than itself, is still to come. The cause of being is thought or known by its effect *as though* it were posterior to its effect. We speak lightly of the possibility of this "as though," which is taken to indicate an illusion. But this illusion is not unfounded; it constitutes a positive event. The posteriority of the anterior—an inversion logically absurd—is produced, one would say, only by memory or by thought. But the "improbable" phenomenon of memory or of thought must precisely be interpreted as a revolution in being. Thus already theoretical thought—but

> in virtue of a still more profound structure that sustains it, the psychism—articulates separation. (TI 54 [24–25])

This maintaining itself at a distance from itself evinces a separation, a certain freedom of life for the psychism, "an as-for-me, a leave of absence, a postponement, which precisely is interiority" (TI 55 [26]), a "time" irreducible to the time of history (the time of the historiographers wherein the "life" of the individual, at death, is integrated into the whole that is History), a "present" that, while in a site, while *in-der-Welt-sein*

> remains free with regard to that site; posited in a site in which it maintains itself, it is that which comes thereto from elsewhere. The present of the *cogito,* despite the support it discovers for itself *after the fact* in the absolute that transcends it, maintains itself all by itself—be it only for an instant, the space of the *cogito.* That there could be this instant of sheer youth, heedless of its slipping into the past and its recovered self-possession in the future (and that this uprooting be necessary if the I of the *cogito* is to cling to the absolute), in short, that there be the very order or distance of time—all this articulates the ontological separation between the metaphysician and the metaphysical. (TI 54–55 [25])

It is this separation of the same, having time against totalizing historical time, that is "the possibility of an *existent* being set up and having its own destiny to itself, that is, being born and dying without the place of this birth and this death in the time of universal history being the measure of its reality" (TI 55 [26]). It is this separation of the same, further, that permits it, outside of any prior participation, to relate, to "cling," to the other in its otherness, ethically, that opens up the way to plurality, where each existent has its own time, requisite of society as ethical sociability as over against community as enrootedness in the common. For this, "[t]he real must not only be determined in its historical objectivity, but also from interior intentions, from the *secrecy* that interrupts the continuity of historical time. Only on the basis of this secrecy is the pluralism of society possible" (TI 57–58 [29]). And only on the basis of this pluralism is discourse as a non-allergic relationship with a genuine alterity possible.

II.2. The Egoism as Independence

If the description of the psychism and its "as for me" evinces the separation of the same from an allergic participation in a system of interrelations—a participation that, we have been arguing, would belie its separation—we have not yet shown *how,* on the basis of what structure, this separation would be possible. And, indeed, Levinas does not rest with telling us, negatively, what this separated same could *not* be were it to be capable of entering into a non-allergic, ethical relationship with the other, but seeks to provide us with a positive description of an interiority that would render "this secret," this separation possible.[70] That is to say, to exist as separated the same must be seen as being capable of carving out, of establishing, a space for itself—the space of an interiority—that is produced not in contradistinction to other elements in a system of relations—for then, in Caputo's felicitous phrase already quoted, the "dialectical machine would be set off" and the possibility for a genuine separation, and thus for plurality, and thus for alterity (and thus for dialogue as communication with an other—and not as the unfolding of an a priori logic) would be eliminated—but "all by itself," independently, from within. Most concisely, Levinas will argue that this interiority is "positive in enjoyment of itself" (TI 55 [25]), and he describes the ego in this mode of existence as an "egoism." The egoism, then, "will be specified as sensibility, the element of enjoyment," which "provides a principle of individuation" (TI 59 [30]) for a being that exists, and has a meaning, refractory to being integrated into a whole. Indeed, for Levinas, sensibility, or the element of enjoyment, "constitutes the very egoism of the I, which is sentient and not something sensed," and it is this sensation that "breaks up every system" (TI 59 [30–31]), that, in the end, qualifies the ego as separated.

"We live from 'good soup,' air, light, spectacles, work, ideas, sleep, etc. . . . These are not objects of representations. We live from them" (TI 110 [82]). This declaration will function for Levinas as something like a manifesto for the long middle section of *Totality and Infinity* whose analyses it opens, entitled "Interiority and Economy," and whose purpose it is to provide us with a description of the interior life of the same as separated from any system of finality that would compromise its separation, its independence, and render it incapable of ethical relating. And this way of life as "living from . . ." good soup, air, etc., is qualified as enjoyment. That is to say that while I may well represent to myself "soup, air, etc. . . . ," my relationship to these "things" from which I live (which are not, in the mode of enjoyment, properly speaking "objects" since I live them beyond, or beneath, their "objectification") is not first of all qualified by these representations, but by my enjoyment of them, my "living from" them, including my very enjoyment of representing them to myself—an enjoyment that subtends the act of representation itself: the enjoyment of formulating an idea.

That is, the contents that fill my life are not, on Levinas's reading, susceptible to being reduced to any "for the sake of which," but are lived positively in their own right; I take joy in them, and my enjoyment of them makes up the "worth [prix] of my life" (TI 112 [84]). That is, these contents are not lived, or at least my living of them is not exhausted, as a "means to life," as Heideggerian *Zeuge*, subjected to a "utilitarian schematism," for I do not only enjoy the end to which they are subsumed, be that my existence itself, but enjoy the very use of them, even when they are explicitly designated as tools.[71] They are lived, rather, as "objects of enjoyment, presenting themselves to 'taste,' already adorned, embellished" (TI 110 [82]). Here Levinas is describing a meaning—enjoyment, happiness—that is lived outside of a system of finality, that has, that *is*, its own meaning. For, he claims, "[t]he contents from which life lives are not always indispensable to it for the maintenance of life, as a means or as the fuel [carburant] necessary for the 'functioning' of existence. Or at least they are not lived as such. With them we die, and sometimes prefer to die rather than be without them" (TI 111 [82–83]). That is, Levinas attempts to describe the "independence" of happiness from any extrinsic finality, including the finality of the *conatus essendi* itself, by claiming, on the one hand, that this is evinced by the fact that "[h]appiness is not an accident of being [and thus reducible to the categories of being], since being is risked for happiness" (TI 112 [84]), and, on the other, by pointing out that the fullness of life is often more a matter of "frivolity" than a "goal-oriented" activity: "To enjoy without utility, in pure loss, gratuitously, without referring to anything else, in pure expenditure—this is the human [voilà l'humain]" (TI 133 [107]). Recognizing this meaning, Levinas is thus able to state: "Life is not the naked will to be, an ontological *Sorge* for this life. Life's relation with the very conditions of its life becomes the nourishment and content of that life. Life is *love of life,* a relation with contents that are not my being but more dear than my being: thinking, eating, sleeping, reading, warming oneself in the sun" (TI 112 [84]). Life as the love of life, in a radical reversal of Quintilian's famous "non ut edam vivo, sed ut vivam edo,"[72] means further that my very enjoying of the contents of life becomes a content of my life, such that life is the "enjoyment of enjoyment," or "egoism," separated from the totality of involvements.

Yet the structure of this enjoyment remains a "living from . . ." that which is not myself: soup, air, etc. And while it may well be true, as Levinas maintains, that I do not live these solely, or principally, as that which is *necessary* to my life, it remains nevertheless true that they are necessary to me, and without them I die, even if it is also true that "with them I die." But this irrevocable dependence is, Levinas assures us, lived precisely—and paradoxically[73]—in enjoyment as independence, that is, as "a mastery in this dependence" (TI 114 [87]). For, though life "depends on what is not itself, this dependence is not without a counterpart which in the final analysis nullifies it. What we live from does not enslave us; we enjoy it" (TI 114 [86–87]). How so? Levinas claims this is because we live that from which we live as nourishment. "Nourishment, as a means of invigoration, is the transmutation of the other into the same, which is in the essence of enjoyment: an energy that is other, recognized as other, recognized, we will see, as sustaining the very act that is directed upon it, becomes, in enjoyment, my own energy, my strength, me" (TI 111 [83]). That from which I live does not enslave me because it nourishes me—it fills me, not only, or even principally, for the sake of my life, but fills my life itself. "These contents are lived: they feed life. One lives one's life: to live is a sort of transitive verb, and the contents of life are its direct objects. And the act of living these contents is ipso facto a content of life" (TI 111 [83]).

Neither Plato's "simple lack," nor Kant's "pure passivity," my need is thus a "happy dependence" because "capable of satisfaction" (TI 115 [87]): "The human being thrives on his needs; he is happy for his needs," such that "living from . . . is the dependency that turns into sovereignty, into happiness—essentially egoist" (TI 114 [87]). As a living upon that which I live as nourishment, enjoyment is accomplishment—satisfaction rather than suppression (TI 118 [90]), fulfillment rather than ataraxy, "which is worth *more* than ataraxy" (TI 113 [85]): "Happiness is accomplishment: it exists in a soul satisfied and not in a soul that has extirpated its needs, a castrated soul" (TI 115 [87–88]). Happiness, enjoyment, is not the lack of needs, but needs met, the cycle of hunger and satisfaction, or accomplishment, and, therefore, suffering, on Levinas's reading, is not the presence of needs (as Levinas tells us is the case for Plato (TI 114,116 [87,88])) but the pain of needs unfulfilled, which presupposes the possibility of fulfillment, such that for Levinas pain (*la douleur*) presupposes (the primordiality of, and thus the enduring possibility of) happiness.[74] There is, then, in Levinas's phrase, and constitutive of life as the *love of life,* "a pre-established harmony" (TI 145 [118]) between my needs and their future fulfillment, such that when my needs are experienced as pain we are no longer in the realm of the original condition, but suffer as the result of a "disorganized society," that is, we have here been "thrown into" the derivative and "limit case" of *Geworfenheit.*[75]

It is this independence of happiness, the ability of the egoism to live its dependence as independence (living *from* its other), that, moreover, founds the personality of the egoism, that makes it personal, as opposed to being a function of the system in which it finds itself: "Enjoyment, in relation with nourishment, which is the *other* of life, is an independence *sui generis,* the independence of happiness. . . . And because life is happiness it is personal. The personality of the person, the ipseity of the I, which is more than the particularity of the atom and of the individual, is the particularity of the happiness of enjoyment" (TI 115 [87]).

In enjoyment, the ego is singular (that is, particular in the sense of set apart, disconnected, "the refusal of the concept" (TI 118 [90]), rather than part-icular in the sense of a part of a whole, or the particularity of the *tode ti,* "which is on the same plane of the concept" (TI 118 [90])), a "solitude, . . . isolation itself, . . . existing without having a genus" (TI 117–18 [90]), and thus personal, because extracted, in its "being," from every system of reference, living its enjoyment in the glory of disconnected moments where "each happiness comes for the first time" (TI 114 [86]). The ego, structured as enjoyment, as egoism, has reference only to itself, is *pour soi,* not in the sense of being *contre autrui,* but naively, "innocently" egoistic: "In enjoyment I am absolutely for myself. Egoist without reference to the Other, I am alone without solitude, innocently egoist and alone. Not against the Others, not 'as for me . . .' —but entirely deaf to the Other, outside of all communication and all refusal to communicate—without ears, like a hungry stomach" (TI 134 [107]).

In enjoyment the ego is "for itself," not in the sense of for its existence, nor in view of its self-representation, but for its pleasures, as in "every man for himself!" (chacun pour soi) (TI 118 [91]),[76] and, yet, in this innocence, "capable of killing for a crust of bread" (TI 118 [91]).

And this "isolation," this mode of "separated existence," is possible because, for Levinas, that which is enjoyed by the egoism is not, primordially, things in the already constituted world of involvements and interrelations where objects have always already qua objects (as we shall later see) a reference to an other, and thus a place in an a priori system of references: "Enjoyment precisely does not reach them qua things. . . . [Rather, t]hings come to representation from a background from which they emerge and to which they return in the enjoyment we can have of them" (TI 130 [103]). Levinas refers to this "background," this "medium" (milieu), as "the elemental." It is difficult, or rather impossible, to say exactly what the element *is,* for while the elemental is the background (and Levinas does not, but might have, referred to it as a horizon)[77] from which objects emerge, and into which they return, it itself does not become an object, is not objectifiable, because not possessable: "Things refer to possession, can be carried off, are furnishings [meubles]; the medium from which they come to me lies escheat, a common fund or terrain, essentially nonpossessable, 'nobody's'; earth, sea, light, city. Every relation or possession is situated within the nonpossessable which envelopes or contains without being able to be contained or enveloped" (TI 131 [104]).

We are incapable of containing the element, Levinas tells us, because we are not able to circumscribe it adumbrationally. Earth, sea, light, city—the element presents to us but a single side, and withdraws into a "depth . . . inconvertible into the breadth and length in which the side of the element [i.e., "the surface of the sea and the field, the edge of the wind"] extends" (TI 131 [104]).

But more precisely (à vrai dire), Levinas continues: "The element has no side at all. One does not approach it. The relation adequate to its essence discovers it precisely as a medium: one is steeped in it; I am always within the element" (TI 131 [104]). Levinas therefore contends that "the adequate relation with the element is precisely bathing" (TI 132 [105]), an "immersion" that does not permit of the distance necessary to representation, to objectification:[78] "The element presents us as it were the reverse of reality, without origin in a being, although presenting itself in familiarity—of enjoyment—as though we were in the bowels of being" (TI 132 [105]). Not an object, not a "something," the element is a "pure quality," "determining nothing" (TI 132 [105]), "content without form" (TI 131 [104]). And it is this pure quality that "suffices"[79] to enjoyment, to sensibility prior to representation—that has a "destiny," a meaning, independent of and underlying all relations to things: "Enjoyment—an ultimate relation with the substantial plenitude of being, with its materiality—embraces all relations with things" (TI 133 [106]).

So what I as egoism enjoy at root is not already constituted objects, wherein sensibility would be the by-product of system of finality in relation to which sensibility would have a *sens*,[80] but the qualities of objects in their "elemental" (TI 134 [107]) or "pure quality" (TI 132 [105]), "qualities without support" (TI 132 [105]), their adjectivality ("adjectives without substances" (TI 132 [105]), "quality without substance" (TI 135 [108])) released from adherence to objects. I enjoy, bathe in, the spectacle of rich blueness, the piquant, bitter taste, independently of the adherence of these qualities to the lake and the cup of coffee. It is this independent enjoyment of pure qualities, disconnected from any intersubjective reference to objects,[81] that produces the egoism of the ego as sensible self-reference (which does not mean self-consciousness), that makes happiness, enjoyment, strictly personal and allows the egoism to exist as an independence—as the rupture of totality that pluralism demands. In its independence, in its solitude, as personal, enjoyment as sensation "breaks up every system" (TI 59 [30–31]).

Of course, in our everyday, concrete lives, that which we enjoy is already a part of a system of involvements; the lake whose blueness enthralls me is the lake at the end of the street, along which my wife and I walk, and that is too crowded in the summer with tourist traffic, and the coffee that I savor is the coffee that you served to me, and that we enjoy together. Always already, we are *in-der-Welt-sein*. That from which I live is, concretely, already involved in a system of interpersonal relationships, where soup, and even the air that I breathe (as is evidenced by the existence of nonsmokers' rights groups), are shared, and thus contested, and thus (as we shall see), already "objectified." That is, we do not *consciously* live our enjoyments as enjoyments of the elemental. And this for two reasons. First, because consciousness itself is for Levinas (as we shall also see) a function of intersubjectivity, and egoist enjoyment is a structure that "precedes" consciousness. And, secondly, Levinas is making no claim in these analyses of enjoyment to give us a picture of *l'homme concret,*[82] the person in and of the already "worlded world" that we meet and are in our everyday lives. Rather, he is attempting to describe a structure that underlies and makes possible concrete man as we see him in our world. But this does not mean, for Levinas, that the originary structure of being is this being-in-the-world, that sensation is a kind of by-product of, or a means of opening oneself out onto, participation in a system of finality that would transcend it and engulf it and endow it with meaning. Rather, sensation has its own meaning, its own value, independent of any extrinsic finality. The structure of enjoyment is necessary, Levinas would claim, to understand *l'homme concret,* the man who lives his enjoyments egoistically in and through the world of involvements, to explaining an egoistic self-reference (which, clearly, would be prior to self-consciousness) that persists through the interpersonal constitution of objects in a worlded world, to explaining the separation of the psychism from that world, and thus the possibility of relating to an other on the basis of something other than ontological grounds, that which, we will be arguing in the next chapter, is the very condition of possibility for dialogue.

Enjoyment delineates the underlying structure of separation of the same from the system of totality that makes possible the separation of the psychism spoken of only abstractly, negatively, in the previous section: "Enjoyment accomplishes atheist separation; it deformalizes the notion of separation, which is not a cleavage made in the abstract, but the existence at home with itself [l'existence chez soi] of an autochthonous I. The soul . . . acquires its own identity by this dwelling in the 'other' (and not logically, by opposition to the other)" (TI 115 [88]).[83] To delineate this underlying structure as necessary to a description of the life of *l'homme concret* thus requires a certain "reduction" from concrete life (performed in the last two sections as the "negative" and "formal" delineation of the psychism existing as a resistance to totality, and its "positive" description as egoism) that is analogous, though not technically equivalent, to the phenomenological strategy of "transcendental reduction," and we shall have to deal with some of the details of this "method" later.[84] What counts for the moment is to recognize that Levinas, in his "reduction," arrives at a description of a structure that, while necessary to an understanding of life as concretely lived, as being-in-the-world structured ontologically, delineates a meaning that is irreducible to life as being-in-the-world ontologically structured: life as enjoyment, happiness, life as the love of life. And this structure, this modality of existence, irreducible to consciousness (as a condition of possibility for consciousness itself—as we shall show in the following chapter), subtends the same's conscious relationship to the objects of its "world," persists as independent of, and foundational to, objects enjoyed as "objects," when the qualities that are enjoyed are attached—as they always are in concrete life—to objects in a system of reference. Its "priority," its "before," its "originary" character with respect to consciousness does not, then, reflect a chronological priority, but a structural one, where "originary" is meant to designate an irreducible structure rather than any "original" (in the sense of chronologically first) condition. That is, "the same" as egoism subtends, and must be distinguished from, "the same" as consciousness, where the latter is already implicated in, and operates, a system of intelligibility that would pretend to be universal and all-encompassing.

And it is the psychism existing as such, as enjoyment, as sensible self-reference, that underlies its possibility to take up a distance from its involvements, and that thus underlies its susceptibility to being called into ethical question by an other—as independent and personal, not drawing its existence from its involvements, its participation, in a system that would transcend it and give it a place and a meaning, but living for itself. The other can call the same into question because the same (the interior economy of the ego) is not the Same (the rational system of Being), but a separated ego capable of taking up a position with respect to being (and its own being), and thus capable of being called into question by—and thus into ethical relation with—the other. We shall describe in our next chapter the manner in which the common world, the worlded world, of the same already presupposes the face of the other that would call this same into question—how the same as the system of intelligibility is founded upon, is made possible by, the ego in enjoyment faced by the other, how, to borrow one of Levinas's most famous phrases, "ethics precedes ontology." The transcendence of the other, in concert with the egoism in its structure of enjoyment, provides the possibility for a relationship between these terms that is not dialectically constituted, that is free[85] of any a priori participation in a system of totality, and that thus opens the way to conceiving of the relation between terms as other than an ontological one.

In this chapter we have traced the separation (transcendence) of the other from the same (as an "ethical" resistance to my powers of meaning constitution, and thus as possessing its own meaning independent of me) and the separation of the egoism from the totality (as an enjoyment that subtends any such involvement, and thus possesses its own meaning independent of any meanings it might "borrow" from such involvement). As such, neither the separated self, nor the other, nor the plurality they constitute, strictly speaking *are*, if this conjugation of the copula indicates an ontological category, first, because it has been our purpose in this chapter to follow Levinas in showing how the meanings of these terms are neither ontological meanings nor founded upon ontological meanings, and secondly because ontology, and the pronouncements made in its terms, will be shown to be derivative of the ethical relation between these separated terms, even if one must borrow from the derived language in order to name this relation. And so the original plurality that has here been delineated must be considered, strictly speaking—although we are flirting here with a realm in which speech can no longer be strict—as a "pre-ontological" plurality,[86] a plurality that is neither ontological nor non-ontological, since we are tracing here a structure that is prior to the taking hold of ontology, and that is necessary to, is a condition of possibility for, ontology itself.

These "correlative" (in the sense that each is a withdrawal, albeit after its own fashion, from the knower-known relation) but noninterdependent separations—the transcendence of the other and the separation of the same—are both, we have been arguing, necessary to an original plurality, to the existence of existents whose respective (but not equivalent) existences are not a function of a totality but have their ways of existence outside of any a priori system of involvements and are thus, potentially, capable of being described as being in a relationship with one another that is not governed by ontological interdependence: the ethical relationship of discourse. It is to an analysis of this relationship that we now turn.

Notes

1. Discourse is variously defined by Levinas as "a non-allergic relation with alterity" (TI 47 [18]), "a non-allergic relation, an ethical relation" (TI 51 [22]), "an original relation with exterior being," "the production of meaning" (TI 66 [38]).

2. "The dimension of height from which the Metaphysical comes to the Metaphysician indicates a sort of nonhomogeneity of space, such that a radical multiplicity, distinct from numerical multiplicity, can here be produced. Numerical multiplicity remains defenseless against totalization" (TI 220 [195]).

3. Levinas reserves the word "separation" for what we are calling the separation of the same, and he uses the word "transcendence" to name what we are calling the separation of the other. This practice has the advantage of helping the reader avoid the conclusion that these movements are somehow dialectically related to one another—a conclusion that Levinas insists we avoid. We are attempting, perhaps dangerously, to call each of these movements "separation," and we do so because our analyses have begun with the idea of dialogue as governed by the *logos* as system of intelligibility, a system from which *both* the same and the other must be separated if there is to be the possibility for dialogue, or at least an ethically responsible one. This, at least, is our thesis.

4. "Just as the interiority of enjoyment [that which will come to specify what we are here calling the separation of the same] is not deducible

from the transcendent relation [what we are here calling the separation of the other, and what Levinas calls the transcendence of the other], the transcendent relation is not deducible from the separated being as a dialectical antithesis forming a counterpart to the subjectivity, as union forms the counterpart of distinction among two terms of any relation. The movement of separation is not on the same plane as the movement of transcendence" (TI 148 [122]). We have here rendered "la relation transcendente" as "the transcendent relation," over against Lingis's curious "the transcendental relation."

5. The nonparallelism of these separations will be important, not only to showing how terms exist outside of an ontological, allergic relationship (the task of the present chapter), but also to an understanding of the relationship of these separated terms, the relationship called discourse (that will be the subject of our attentions in the following chapter), a relationship that will be shown to be necessarily "asymmetrical," that is, where the terms in relation, the I and the other, will be shown to be in this relation as separated (from each other and from the relationship), as the I and the other, and not as interchangeable terms in a formal and reciprocal relation, the latter being always already and ever again, a totality.

6. There is a strong sense in which this way of phrasing the issue is misleading in that separation is, as we shall shortly see, produced in discourse, and thus could hardly be said to be its condition of possibility. Discourse is, for Levinas, an absolute relation, which is to say without a priori conditions, but itself the condition for any a priori. We use this unfortunately misleading language insofar as we begin our analyses by showing how the same and the other are each separated from the onto-epistemological subject-object relation—separations requisite for discourse even if these separations are possible only if articulated on the basis of an original separation/relation (discourse) that founds the possibility for the knower-known relation itself. In our Part II, we shall attempt to describe the conditions of possibility and impossibility of discourse on the basis of a non–a priori, and nontranscendental, condition.

7. As we shall see, this ethical interruption of the structures of meaning constitution (that take shape in, that "are," the economy of the same) is in fact a reintroduction of the other, since these ontological structures are themselves only possible because there has already been an other who would ground their possibility. Our analyses, like those of Levinas, do not, like the tradition they oppose, attempt to begin at an absolute and sure beginning, but with the "given" in media res, tracing the structures that "support" the given from out of the given itself. More

will be said about this, Levinas's, "phenomenological" method in chapter 7.

8. This phrase, *se produire,* and the notion of production more generally, will be central to Levinas's "presentation" of infinity. It is therefore worth noting that "The term 'production' designates both the effectuation of being (the event 'is produced,' an automobile 'is produced') and its being brought to light or its expression (an argument 'is produced,' an actor 'is produced'). The ambiguity of this verb conveys the essential ambiguity of the operation by which the being of an entity simultaneously is brought about [s'évertue] and is revealed" (TI 26 [XIV]). While there is good reason to render *se produire* in this passage, as Lingis has done, by the passive "is produced," there is also a case to be made, we think, for allowing this verb to reverberate with another of its possible meanings, hearing in it the also (at least grammatically) possible reflexive, "produces itself," since this production comes, as we shall see, to the one for whom it is produced from outside of itself, precisely, from the side of him who in it *se produire,* from the expression of the other.

9. This term, "paralyzed," appears several times in Levinas's texts in this context, for example: "He arrests and paralyzes my violence by his call, which does not do violence, and comes from on high" (TI 291 [266–67]). The encounter with the other, wherein I as meaning constituting subject am called into question, might therefore be thought of as producing a kind of "reduction," an "*epoché,*" wherein the transcendental structures through which the transcendent object is constituted as meaningful are "put out of play" in order to make space for a nonontological, nonconstitutive "meaning." But if we are to think thus, it is important that this *epoché* not be thought of as a reduction actively undertaken by a transcendental ego, but as passively undergone by an otherwise active and assumptive ego.

10. Or again: "The expression the face introduces into the world does not defy the feebleness of my powers, but my ability for power [mon pouvoir de pouvoir]" (TI 198 [172]).

11. As we shall see below (in section I.3), Levinas will develop his "phenomenology" of the encounter with the other along the lines of the Cartesian notion of "the idea of the infinite," that is, as a coming up against "the idea of the perfect." Thus, Levinas will write: "The idea of the perfect is not an ideal but desire; it is the welcoming of the Other, the commencement of moral consciousness, which calls in question my freedom. Thus this way of measuring oneself against the perfection of infinity is not a theoretical consideration; it is accomplished as shame, where freedom discovers itself murderous in its very exercise. It is accomplished in shame where freedom at the same time is *discovered* in the

consciousness of shame and is *concealed* in the shame itself" (TI 84 [56]). We quote this passage here to illustrate the specifically ethical (i.e., nontheoretical) meaning of shame, and the role that this plays in breaking the hegemony of the theoretical/ontological relationship à propos "meaning."

12. "This infinity, stronger than murder, already resists us in his face, is his face, is the primordial *expression,* is the first word: 'you shall not commit murder.' The infinite paralyzes power by its infinite resistance to murder, which, firm and insurmountable, gleams in the face of the Other, in the total nudity of his defenseless eyes, in the nudity of the absolute openness of the Transcendent. There is here a relation not with a very great resistance, but with something absolutely *other:* the resistance of what has no resistance—the ethical resistance" (TI 199 [173]).

13. "The interlocutor alone is the term of pure experience, where the Other enters into relation while remaining *kath'auto,* where he expresses himself without our having to disclose him from a 'point of view,' in a borrowed light" (TI 67 [39]).

14. This phrase, "la signification sans contexte," reappears at OTB 91 [116], again in the context of a discussion of the face.

15. "Teaching is not reducible to maïeutics; it comes from the exterior and brings me more than I contain. In its nonviolent transitivity the very epiphany of the face is produced" (TI 51 [22]).

16. "The idea of infinity exceeds my powers (not quantitatively, but . . . by calling them into question); it does not come from our a priori depths—it is consequently experience par excellence" (TI 196 [170]).

17. The missing phrase is as follows: "But he can oppose to me a struggle, that is, oppose to the force that strikes him not a force of resistance, but the very unforeseeableness of his reaction." Here Levinas is referring to the unanticipatable "dexterity" of the other that marks the danger of war, of the struggle between free but ontologically interrelated beings (but where their ontological interrelatedness clearly cannot "govern" their freedom), each opposed to each as freedoms limiting one another in their respective exercise of freedom. But this struggle that "already overflows the consciousness of struggle . . . *presupposes* the transcendence of expression" (TI 199 [174]), and it is this transcendence, rather than the possibility of the struggle that may result from it, that interests us here.

18. To anticipate, this tension between ethical impossibility and ontological possibility with respect to one and the same event will be precisely the tension reflected in the title of our Part II that presents discourse as a possible impossibility. If murder is, at once, ontologically possible while ethically impossible, discourse is, we will argue, at once, ethically possible while ontologically impossible.

19. It is true that in the pages of *Totality and Infinity* this quotation is meant to show "a separation of the I that is not reciprocal of the transcendence of the other with regard to me," and is not intended, first of all, to illustrate the transcendence of the other in relation to me. But this separation of the other is, though not dialectically "deduced" from the separation of the same, the other side of the "metaphysical asymmetry" here indicated, that is, another of its conditions of possibility. Or at least it is this that we are arguing.

20. It is even, as we shall see, necessary to "justice," where justice is produced, in response to a plurality of "faces," as an ontological transformation of the ethical moment that ontology appears here only to impede. But this necessity emerges only across complex structures we shall have to unfold.

21. "This 'curvature' of intersubjective space in which exteriority is effectuated (we do not say 'in which it appears') as superiority must be distinguished from the arbitrariness of 'points of view' taken upon objects that appear. But the latter, source of errors and opinions, issued from the violence opposed to exteriority, is the price of the former" (TI 291 [267]).

22. As we shall see, an encounter with the other is necessary, according to Levinas, for there to be critique at all. For without the challenge of the other to the very exercise of my transcendental forestructures, there would be no reason to call them into question, and thus no apology, no call to give account or to explain, and thus no "reason," no *logos* (and no *dia-logos*).

23. Emmanuel Levinas, "Wholly Otherwise," trans. S. Critchley, in *Re-reading Levinas,* ed. R. Bernasconi and S. Critchley (Bloomington: Indiana University Press, 1991), pp. 3–10 ("Tout autrement," in *L'Arc,* "Jacques Derrida" special issue [Paris: Librairie Duponchelle, 1990], pp. 33–37).

24. The objections found here to the thought of Levinas echo many of the concerns found in Jacques Derrida, "Violence and Metaphysics," in *Writing and Difference* (Chicago: University of Chicago Press, 1987), pp. 79–153, an article that we shall discuss in part in chapter 7. We have addressed at some length Caputo's reading of Levinas in our "Again Ethics: A Levinasian Reading of Caputo Reading Levinas," in *Knowing Other-wise,* ed. J. H. Olthuis (New York: Fordham University Press, 1997), pp. 172–213.

25. Caputo, *Against Ethics,* p. 82.

26. Ibid., p. 73.

27. Ibid., p. 76.

28. Ibid., p. 74.

29. Ibid., p. 82.
30. Ibid., p. 85.
31. Ibid., p. 74.
32. Ibid., p. 74.
33. Ibid., pp. 80–81.
34. We shall have to return to this point later, reconsidering it in terms of Levinas's attempt to render this "ethical" relation, irreducible to ontological categories, in ontological language, the language of philosophy.
35. Levinas makes it clear that the immemorial past, in terms of which the other is described in *Otherwise Than Being,* is irrecuperable by reminiscence, not because of its "remoteness" (éloignement) from the present, but because of its "incommensurability" with the present (OTB 11 [13]).
36. "To affirm the presence in us of the idea of infinity is to deem purely abstract and formal the contradiction the idea of metaphysics is said to harbor, which Plato brings up in the *Parmenides*—that the relation with the Absolute would render the Absolute relative. The absolute exteriority of the exterior is not purely and simply lost as a result of its manifestation; it 'absolves' itself from the relation in which it presents itself" (TI 50 [21]).
37. Indeed, as we shall see, the absolute, ethical alterity of the other is a function of his susceptibility to violence, and not least of all to the violence that I do to him—and in this sense can hardly be called absolute in the sense of "absolving itself from all relation."
38. This freedom of the other to call into question my categorization of him will be made possible, moreover, by our "fraternity," and we shall have to indicate the manner in which this human fraternity can be conceived of as other than an onto-anthropo-logical category, but as a term meaningful across an ethical intrigue.
39. This point raises some interesting questions. In a 1986 interview, to the question "According to your analysis, the commandment 'Thou shalt not kill' is revealed by the human face; but is the commandment not also expressed in the face of the animal?" Levinas answered: "I cannot say at what moment you have the right to be called 'face.' The human face is completely different and only afterwards do we discover the face of the animal. I don't know if a snake has a face. I can't answer that question. A more specific analysis is needed" (Tamra Wright, Peter Hughes, and Alison Ainley, "The Paradox of Morality: An Interview with Emmanuel Levinas," in *The Provocation of Levinas,* pp. 171–72). But Levinas makes it clear, in the same interview, that despite this ambiguity as to whether or not an animal has a face, we have—on the basis of an

analogy to human suffering—obligations toward animals: "It is clear that, without considering animals as human beings, the ethical extends to all living beings. We do not want to make an animal suffer needlessly and so on. But the prototype of this is human ethics. . . . The animal suffers. It is because we, as human, know what suffering is that we can have this obligation" (p. 172). John Llewelyn discusses this issue in his article (written before the publication of the aforementioned article) "Am I Obsessed by Bobby? (Humanism of the Other Animal)," in *Re-reading Levinas,* pp. 234–45, Bobby being the dog that showed up for a few weeks at the German camp for Jewish prisoners at which Levinas was interned and became a companion of the prisoners, and is referred to in Levinas's article "Nom d'un chien ou droit naturel." Llewelyn writes: "When asked about our responsibilities toward nonhuman sentient creatures, [Levinas] is inclined to reply that our thinking about them may have to be only analogical or that the answer turns on whether in the eyes of the animal we can discern a recognition, however obscure, of his own mortality—on whether, in Levinas' sense of the word, the animal has a face" (p. 240). In an analysis that compares Levinasian and Kantian ethics, Llewelyn argues that, "In the metaphysical ethics of Levinas I can have direct responsibilities only toward beings that can speak, and this means beings that have a rationality that is presupposed by the universalizing reason fundamental in the metaphysics of the ethics of Kant. . . . Both Kant and Levinas are so sensitive to the dangers of the *Schwärmerei* threatened by what Kant calls pathological love that they require an obligating being to be able to make a claim in so many words. No claim goes without saying, even if the saying is the silent saying of the discourse of the face" (p. 241). He concludes: "We have failed to discover any evidence that Levinas allows that Bobby and I can be face to face such that I could read in his own eyes 'Thou shalt not kill.' We must therefore retreat to the question whether in the face-to-face the other man addresses me not only on behalf of himself and other men, but also on behalf of the nonhuman animal; and to the question whether, if what the human face tells me is 'Thou shalt not commit murder,' the legal and quasi-legal connotations of the word 'murder' prevent us saying that the commandment includes the nonhuman animal within its scope" (pp. 243–44). So while Llewelyn acknowledges, in citing other works of Levinas, the possibility in this thought for a certain responsibility to animals based upon a kind of Benthamian analogy of animal and human suffering, he does seem to accuse Levinas of a certain ethical anthropocentrism, and Levinas would not seem to want to deny this, as we see by returning to the interview referred to above: "The being of animals is a struggle for life. A struggle for life without ethics.

. . . However, with the appearance of the human—and this is my entire philosophy—there is something more important than my life, and that is the life of the other" (p. 172). Ethics, for Levinas, is a human phenomenon, and one would assume that for him any prohibitions against vandalism, the de-*facing* of artworks, monuments, sacred objects, etc., would, like the prohibitions against making animals suffer, refer by analogy to the human face.

40. "One does not question oneself concerning him; one questions him" (TI 47 [18]). "The invoked is not what I comprehend: *he is not under a category.* He is the one to whom I speak—he has only a reference to himself; he has no quiddity" (TI 69 [41]).

41. "The face resists possession, resists my powers. In its epiphany, in expression, the sensible, still graspable, turns into total resistance to the grasp. This mutation can occur only by the opening of a new dimension" (TI 197 [172]).

42. Lingis's translation ignores/omits Levinas's phrase "par rapport à," without which the sentence reads awkwardly.

43. Simon Critchley suggests that Derrida's own meaning is perhaps very close to the one we would here attribute to Levinas. See Simon Critchley, *The Ethics of Deconstruction: Derrida and Levinas* (Oxford: Blackwell, 1992), especially pp. 31–32: "*Nothing* exists *outside of a context.* . . . Pursuing Derrida's argument, what interrupts the closure of a determinate context, making that context an open structure, is an unconditional affirmation that intervenes in this context and motivates deconstruction. Such, I would claim, is the ethical moment in Derrida's thinking."

44. That Caputo does not see past this priority of ontology is demonstrated in a paragraph that follows the above quotation (taken from *Against Ethics,* pp. 80–81), but that we have relegated to the notes in that we have yet to discuss Levinas's idea of the "otherwise than being." There we read: "I would say, *pace* Levinas, what is otherwise-than-being cannot help ending up as being-otherwise. . . . What comes to me from on high, across the curved space of ethics (that is a very powerful image), is a face, a phenomenal face, the appearance of the Other, visible and full of flesh. But this face is not a face, is more than a face, is not a matter of flesh and blood, is nothing finite, phenomenal, visible, graspable, perceptually constituted. That is because there is an excess, an infinity, an invisibility. Ergo, what comes to me from on high is more than a face, otherwise than a phenomenal face, a certain *hyperousia,* a superessential face, supereminent and transcendent" (Caputo, *Against Ethics,* p. 81). But why, in terms of what we have been arguing, must this "excess" be interpreted in terms of "being" as "*hyperousia,*" "superes-

sential," rather than as an ethical excess, as a contestation of *ousia* and essence? Might the "constitution" of that (a real, phenomenal, flesh and blood face) which is capable (ethically) of calling into question the validity of meaning constitution not mark the limits of meaning constitution (and the unsurpassability of transcendental forestructures) itself? We are far from finished with these concerns, for there is still the problem, and no small problem at that, of how Levinas is to conduct this discourse on an ethics that not only transcends but contests ontological language within the language of philosophy, a language dominated by ontological categories and concerns. To this issue we shall have to return.

45. "[*Totality and Infinity*] will proceed to distinguish between the idea of totality and the idea of infinity, and affirm the philosophical priority of the idea of infinity" (TI 26 [XIV]).

46. "The rigorously developed concept of this transcendence is expressed by the term infinity" (TI 24–25 [XIII]).

47. Levinas claims that *Totality and Infinity* "will recount how infinity is produced in the relationship of the same with the other, and how the particular and the personal, which are unsurpassable, as it were magnetize the very field in which the production of infinity is enacted. . . . Infinity does not first exist, and *then* reveal itself. Its infinition is produced as revelation, as a positing of its idea in *me.* It is produced in the improbable feat whereby a separated being fixed in its identity, the same, the I, nonetheless contains in itself what it can neither contain nor receive solely by virtue of its own identity" (TI 26–27 [XIV–XV]).

48. Though it has already been introduced in the "Preface" of this work (See TI 23–27 [XI–XVI]).

49. Levinas attributes such a view to both Kant and Heidegger: "The finite is here [in Kant] no longer conceived by relation to the infinite; quite the contrary, the infinite presupposes the finite, which it amplifies infinitely. . . . The Kantian finitude is described positively as sensibility, as the Heideggerian finitude by the being for death. This infinity referring to the finite marks the most anti-Cartesian point of Kantian philosophy as, later, of Heideggerian philosophy" (TI 196 [170]).

50. "Hegel returns [bypassing Kant] to Descartes in maintaining the positivity of the infinite, but excluding all multiplicity from it; he posits the infinite as the exclusion of every 'other' that might maintain a relation with the infinite and thereby limit it. The infinite can only encompass all relations" (TI 196 [170–71]).

51. Thus, when Levinas, in the following sentence, claims: "The transcendent is the sole *ideatum* of which there can be only an idea in us; it is infinitely removed from its idea, that is, exterior, because it is infinite"

(TI 49 [20]), he cannot mean that the infinite is infinitely removed from its idea because it is, in itself, ontologically infinite, but because it is (ethically) produced as infinite by means of its exteriority.

52. "The idea of the perfect is not an idea but desire; it is the welcoming of the Other, the commencement of moral consciousness, which calls into question my freedom" (TI 84 [52]).

53. "Egoism, enjoyment, sensibility, and the whole dimension of interiority—the articulations of separation—are necessary for the idea of Infinity, the relation with the Other which opens forth from the separated and finite being" (TI 148 [122]).

54. "The metaphysical other is other with an alterity that is not formal, is not the simple reverse of identity, and is not formed out of resistance to the same, but is prior to every initiative, to all imperialism of the same. It is other with an alterity constitutive of the very content of the other. Other with an alterity that does not limit the same, for in limiting the same the other would not be rigorously other; by virtue of the common frontier the other, within the system, would yet be the same" (TI 38–39 [9]).

55. "Political theory derives justice from the undiscussed value of spontaneity; its problem is to ensure, by way of knowledge of the world, the most complete exercise of spontaneity by reconciling my freedom with the freedom of others" (TI 83 [55]).

56. Even if Levinas believes politics is inspired by ethics, and that commerce is better than war: "Commerce is better than war, for in peace the Good has already reigned" (OTB 5 [5]).

57. "The plurality required for conversation results from the interiority with which each term is 'endowed,' the psychism, its egoist and sensible self-reference" (TI 59 [30]).

58. As the *logos* that governs onto-logy is (like the *logos* that governs dia-logue that we examined in the first chapter) unified and one, ontology can permit of no original plurality, but already articulates an original unity. Any original plurality must therefore be conceived of as outside of ontology. It is precisely to a pre-ontological "being" that Levinas, we would argue, attempts to refer in his delineation of a being prior to the comprehension or disclosure of being in his concept of the *il y a*, the "there *is*"—that which remains after every possible negation, a being that thus subtends the speaking of being, or onto-logy. It is Levinas's project in *De l'existence à l'existent* (*Existence and Existents,* trans. A. Lingis [The Hague: Martinus Nijhoff, 1978]) to show how beings (existents) emerge from and as over against this being (or existence). It is to being in this pre-ontological sense that Levinas refers in *Totality and Infinity,* we think, when he speaks of a plurality (of existents) in being,

even though being in this work also often refers to the being that is disclosed in ontology, the being of beings. We assert that Levinas, perhaps recognizing the ambiguities and the difficulties of sustaining this dual usage (among other exigencies to be discussed later), surrenders, in his later work, the idea of being to ontology, and decides to trace the "otherwise than being."

59. Of what is Levinas speaking, in what modality, when he speaks, for instance, of this plurality, if this plurality "is" not? These difficulties demand our rapt attention, and we shall have to return to them both later in this chapter, and again in greater detail in chapter 5.

60. "While the atheist independence of the separated being does not posit itself by opposition to the idea of infinity, it alone makes possible the relation denoted by this idea. The atheist separation is *required* by the idea of Infinity, but is not dialectically brought about by it" (TI 60 [31]).

61. "One can call atheism this separation so complete that the separated being maintains itself in existence all by itself, without participation in the Being from which it is separated—eventually capable of adhering to it by belief. The break with participation is implied in this capability. One lives outside of God, at home with oneself; one is an I, an egoism. The soul, the dimension of the psychic, being an accomplishment of separation, is naturally atheist. By atheism we thus understand a position prior to both the negation and the affirmation of the divine, the breaking with participation by which the I posits itself as the same and as I" (TI 58 [29–30]).

62. This is the case, moreover, even if, as we attempted to show in the opening chapter, in our epistemo-onto-logical meditations, these structures are found, and necessarily so, "in me." Their a priori nature is, and we shall have to show how this is the case, not a function of their being embedded in any structure of things that human thought would only reflect, but a result of the fact that the a priori, and being itself insofar as it is ontologically conceived, is a function of interhuman constitution—a function of reason, but where I do not reason alone, where reason itself is a function of interpersonal relations.

63. That is to say, Levinas, in *Totality and Infinity,* never denies the power and prevalence (even the necessity) of totality (as has been noted by several commentators [though perhaps first, to believe T. de Boer, by A. Dondeyne, "Inleiding tot het denken van E. Levinas," *Tijdschrift voor Philosophie* 25 {1963}, p. 555]), the title of the work is *Totality* and *Infinity,* not *Totality* or *Infinity*), of ontological categories, but does contest the idea that ontology is to be taken as equivalent with "the full measure of being." In his *Otherwise Than Being or Beyond Essence,* Levinas will refer

to these structures as "the said" (le dit), whose relationship to ethical expression, "the saying" (le dire)," we will examine in our chapters 4 and 5.

64. The importance and details of this distinction will be clarified as this chapter and the next advance. In short, for Levinas, as opposed to Heidegger, the ego, as enjoyment, lives its world as independence, its distance from the world not as alienation, but as accomplishment.

65. Heidegger writes, for example: "Dasein 'is' its past in the way of *its* own Being, which, to put it roughly, 'historicizes' out of its future on each occasion. Whatever the way of being it may have at the time, and thus with whatever understanding of Being it may posses, Dasein has grown up both into and in a traditional way of interpreting itself: in terms of this it understands itself proximally and, within a certain range, constantly. By this understanding, the possibilities of its Being are disclosed and regulated. Its own past—and this always means the past of its 'generation'—is not something which *follows along after* Dasein, but something which already goes ahead of it"; Martin Heidegger, *Being and Time,* p. 41 [20]. For Levinas too, we will argue, it is this enculturation process that gives to the structures that I live the "a priori" force that they have for me. To anticipate, we will see in Levinas's notion of the discrete presence of the feminine the origins of this process.

66. "His face in which his epiphany is produced and which appeals to me breaks with the world that can be common to us, whose virtualities are inscribed in our *nature* and developed in our existence" (TI 194 [168]). Note that Levinas denies here neither a common world nor a common nature—but these do not constitute an ultimate structure.

67. "The particular I [le moi] is one with [se confonde avec] the same [le Même], coincides with the 'daemon' that speaks to me in thought, and is universal thought. The I of representation is the natural passage from the particular to the universal" (TI 126 [99]).

68. But does not this very illusion not already testify to separation? Levinas thinks so: "Its power for illusion—if illusion there was—constitutes its separation" (TI 55 [25–26]).

69. The question of *how* such "taking distance from" is possible will have to be described, a possibility that will require the presence of the other—but not the other in ontological/dialectical relation, but the other in ethical relation, and ultimately, as the other in the same, which for Levinas qualifies nonassumable time. That Levinas will describe the separation of the same in terms of time, in what follows, should not, then, surprise us.

70. "Separation and atheism, these negative notions, are produced by positive events" (TI 148 [121]).

71. This point is vividly illustrated by the common North American phenomenon of the "handyman hobbyist," who can easily afford to buy anything he could make himself, but chooses to make it for the sheer enjoyment of doing so, taking satisfaction in his possession of a vast array of tools, and in his very use of them. Levinas, a French intellectual and not a North American handyman, opts for the example of the pleasure of having and manipulating a cigarette lighter, even outside of its practical finality of lighting cigarettes (see TI 133 [106]).

72. "I do not live to eat, but eat to live."

73. This, we maintain, is the "paradox" referred to in the already quoted: "The psychism constitutes an *event* in being; it concretizes a conjuncture of terms which were not first delineated by the psychism and whose abstract formulation harbors a paradox" (TI 54 [24]). The paradox is that of a created being—not self-created, but capable nevertheless of taking up a position with respect to its being: "It is certainly a great glory for the creator to have set up a being capable of atheism, a being which, without being *causa sui*, has an independent view and word and is at home with itself. We name 'will' a being conditioned in such a way that without being *causa sui* it is first with respect to its cause" (TI 58–59 [30]).

74. "At the origin there is a being gratified, a citizen of paradise. The 'emptiness' felt implies that the need which becomes aware of it abides already in the midst of an enjoyment—be it the air one breathes. It anticipates the joy of satisfaction, which is *better* than ataraxy. Far from putting the sensible life in question, pain takes place within its horizons and refers to the joy of living. Already and henceforth life is loved" (TI 144–45 [118]).

75. "The limit case in which need prevails over enjoyment, the proletarian condition condemning to accursed labor in which the indigence of corporeal existence finds neither refuge nor leisure at home with itself, is the absurd world of *Geworfenheit*" (TI 146–47 [120]).

76. Lingis, conservatively and uncolorfully, "undertranslates" this phrase as "each for himself."

77. He perhaps does not because of Husserl's tendency to allow the "unsuspected horizons" of thought to become interpreted themselves as "thoughts aiming at objects" (TI 28 [XVII]), and Levinas, contesting this, may have wanted to avoid association with this notion by avoiding the term.

78. "We can, to be sure, represent the liquid or the gaseous to ourselves as a multiplicity of solids, but then we are abstracting from our presence in the midst of the elemental" (TI 132 [105]).

79. "The question what is the 'other side' of what offers us one side

does not arise in the relation maintained with the element. The sky, the earth, the sea, the wind—suffice to themselves" (TI 132 [105]).

80. "It [enjoyment] does not express (as Heidegger would have it) the mode of my implantation—my *disposition*—in being, the tonus of my bearing. It is not my bearing in being, but already the exceeding of being; being itself 'befalls' him who can seek happiness as a new glory above substantiality" (TI 113 [85]).

81. Sounds, colors, shapes, smells, durity, and suppleness are offered to my enjoyment in their pure quality as sensations—*hylé.* And as such they are offered to me alone—for *I* taste, the sensation is mine. I do not taste another's tasting even if I can enjoy that another enjoys what he tastes, enjoying another's enjoyment in a manner that this my enjoyment is not to partake of one and the same enjoyment even when the other enjoys me too; we each retain our own enjoyments, our own sensations, even in enjoying one another or a common object of enjoyment. And in this individuality of enjoyment the element that I enjoy is "mine," not because I have claimed it, but because it is undisputed.

82. "The description of enjoyment as it has been conducted to this point assuredly does not render the concrete man. In reality man has already the idea of infinity, that is, lives in society and represents things to himself" (TI 139 [112]).

83. The manner in which this living *chez soi* is concretized for Levinas will have to be addressed in the following chapter.

84. See chapter 7.

85. "Their freedom which is 'common' to them is precisely what separates them" (TI 73–74 [46]).

86. In *Otherwise Than Being or Beyond Essence,* Levinas will refer to such structures as also "pre-original," ceding even the notion of origin to ontology (to "the said") which, he claims, alone concerns itself with origins.

3

Discourse as the Condition of Possibility for Dialogue

I. The Relation of Discourse

I.1. Discourse as an Ethical Relation

If the separation or "transcendence" of the other from the same is produced as an ethical refusal—coming from the other—of being reduced to the categories of knowing operated by the same, as the prohibition "Thou shalt not kill" in the very expression of the other, then this prohibition also produces, as the inverse side of this transcendence, a relation with the other. For to be called into question (as the assimilative march of the same) is already to be in relation with the other, to find oneself (however more or less consciously) in a relation with the other by means of this calling into question itself, a relation that calls the same to account, that calls the same to responsibility with respect to the other—which is to find oneself (over and above any ontological relation, or better, as we shall see, before and as constitutive of any ontological relation) in an *ethical* relation. And insofar as this relation is produced, as we have seen, in the expression of the other, in his "speaking" (even if nonverbally, by means of the face that, even without words—that is, not as a phenomenal face in the world but as a "facing" that calls the world into question—"speaks") that calls the same to responsibility, Levinas refers to this relation as "discourse." "The face speaks. The manifestation of the face is already discourse" (TI 66 [37]). In the encounter of the face, we are already in the realm of language.

This relation must be ethical insofar as it is produced (as we argued *via negativa* in the previous chapter) precisely as a refusal of any ontological participation, as a refusal of any a priori ontological relation. It is produced as ethical, rather, insofar as the other's expression comes from on high, that is, from an ethical height, across what Levinas refers to as "the primary curvature of being" (TI 86 [59]). Such curvature, such "height," testifies to my inability to reduce this relation to an ontological one, to a "horizontal" relation from being to being (or to a play within the same (being)), to a relation that would be able to be viewed (and thus regulated) from the outside, from the position of a neutral observer outside of the terms in relation[1]—the position to which (starting out from the position of a term from within the relation) the tradition always aspires, and which inevitably results, as we have argued following Levinas, in a reduction of the other to the same, or, which is to say the same thing, in totality.

That is, if this relation is to be produced *as ethical,* it must be produced as an asymmetrical relation, must be produced as *my* ethical responsibility for the other, as my unilateral responsibility for the other. The same is, under this regime, "me" in particular, and not "me" as an instantiation of any "me in general,"[2] for if it were the latter the other would not be genuinely other, but another "me," my alter-ego, his *alterity* articulated on the basis of a *shared egoity,* which would be to reduce the other in advance to the same.[3] For to demand that the other be correlatively responsible for me is to attempt once again to pretend to a position outside of the relation from which it could be viewed and regulated, to pronounce upon the terms in relation as if from the *outside* as a term *inside* the relation: to be at once one of the plaintiffs and the judge in a suit. But if the ethical separation/relation is, as we are claiming, precisely a calling into question of this ability to judge (myself and) the other from a purported outside (but precisely as a being judged by an irreducible outside), the ethical relation with the other imposes itself as an irremissibly asymmetrical one, where the irreducible difference that is implied in the call to ethical responsibility is maintained in the relationship that it evokes. In this relationship the same and the other remain distinct and noninterchangeable: "We are the same and the other" (TI 39 [9]). There is here no possibility of an a priori common basis or point of appeal upon which the relationship would be founded insofar as the relationship itself is a response to the lack of any such common measure. And as the relationship is what it is as a refusal of any common measure, the responsibility that this relationship as ethical evokes cannot be a reciprocal one—which would presuppose a common (ethical) measure between terms—but must be realized (or produced) as *my* responsibility for the other, independently and (as we shall see) prior to any responsibility the other might have for me. It is only as asymmetrical, that is to say, that the relationship of discourse avoids being reduced to an ontological relationship, or an ethical relationship governed by an ontological a priori, that which the other in the relation of discourse as ethical precisely contests. In the relationship of discourse, then, it is I and I alone who—before any responsibility can be demanded of the other—am responsible for the other: me, the me who finds myself in the relation, called into question by the other, called by the other to respond, responsible for the other before being asked for my consent.[4]

Discourse, the ethical relation of my responsibility for the other, is, thus, qualified not by the nominative case (where the other would become an object of knowledge, where the other would fulfill as a known the adequate idea produced in the same),[5] but by the vocative (where the other would—cutting across his manifestation—express himself as a calling upon me), and a vocative that harbors, or that at once is, an imperative, a calling of me to responsibility in the other's, in the face of the other's, *regard.* This ethical call, then, is never appropriately met with a response that would result in an "I know," but by a "*me voici,*" "here I am, at your service (in the name of God),"[6] for it is a call not to knowledge but to responsibility. This ethical relationship is never "viewed," is not "known" in any ontico-epistemo-logical sense (which would include any notion of "lived experience" in the phenomenological sense of this phrase, as an experience undergone by a subject that would assume it), but is, rather, "enacted" (that is, produced as it is en-acted in me—and here as more of a matter of my being acted upon than as a matter of my activity). The ethical call coming from the other demands of me an ethical response. It *is* only to the extent that I take it up.[7]

The relation opened up in this call (of the other to me) is not known because it is a relation that calls knowledge into question. That is to say that the other, in calling upon me, in his speech that establishes his separation/relation that is discourse, never appears as a content of that speech, but withdraws always and again behind the manifestation that he offers, as directing this manifestation itself. For whatever is offered to me of him in terms of a content, in terms of what I am able to make/know of his manifestation in terms of my transcendental forestructures, is precisely what he disturbs *as* speaking, even as these contents are offered: "The life of expression consists in undoing the form in which the existent, exposed as a theme, is thereby dissimulated" (TI 66 [37]). Discourse for Levinas is thus a matter of the "expressive" aspect of language as over against language as the "manifestation" of being (as Levinas argues that it is preeminently for the tradition), a consideration of the fact that language is not only, or even primarily, the "externalization" of thought contents, but a speaking of such contents *to* someone (which will turn out to be a gesture constitutive of meaningful thought contents, which will open up the space in which references to a shared "world" will be meaningful):

> But in its expressive function language precisely maintains the other—to whom it is addressed, whom it calls upon or invokes. To be sure, language does not consist in invoking him as a being represented and thought. But this is why language institutes a relation irreducible to the subject-object relation: the *revelation* of the other. In revelation only can language as a system of signs be constituted. The other called upon is not something represented, is not a given, is not a particular, through one side already open to generalization. (TI 73 [45])

What the other "gives" in terms of his manifestation remains, therefore, ethically within his control—to be interpreted ever again *by him* insofar as I am tempted to dominate him by assimilating his "meaning" to a content known in correlation with me as the one who knows it. His meaning, which is his principle or "first" meaning ("above and beyond the manifested"),[8] as capable of (as being the) calling into question any meaning I would make of his manifestation, is preserved behind any meaning that would be *given* to me and that I would thus constitute; and this meaning, which is an ethical meaning, is precisely his ability to so preserve his meaning—in respect to me—for himself. As such, his speech is fundamentally magisterial, is a teaching which teaches first, as we have noted, before all consideration of content, this teaching itself. As a resistance to my assimilation and domination of his meaning, the other remains, by means of the ethical relation, the prime interpreter of his own speech:[9] "He who manifests himself comes, according to Plato's expression, to his own assistance. He at each instant undoes the form he presents" (TI 66 [37]). The other as other is thus a living speech—a living presence—irreducible to the "dead" meanings that his passing away leaves to the integrative powers of historiography:

> The interpellated one is called upon to speak; his speech consists in "coming to the assistance" of his word—in being *present.* This present is not made of instants mysteriously immobilized in duration, but of an *incessant* recapture of instants that flow by by a presence that comes to their assistance, that answers for them. This *incessance* produces the present, is the presentation, the life, of the present. It is as though the presence of him who speaks inverted the inevitable movement that bears the spoken word to the past state of the written word. Expression is this actualization of the actual. (TI 69 [41])

His withdrawal from the content of his speech as it is interpreted by me is, then, precisely not his "passing away" from it, the irresponsibility of an abandonment, but his ability to keep it alive, his "present-ing" it, his being present with it, to direct it—a mastery to which only his death puts an end. It is this presence of the other—as over against that which is present to me as knower, as irreducible to that which I know—to which I relate in responsibility (rather than epistemo-onto-logically), and that qualifies discourse as a distinctively ethical relationship.

I.2. Ethical Meaning and Truth

It is precisely in the presentation of the face, as the (negative) prohibition against my reduction of the other to the same, and (simultaneously, as we shall see) as the (positive) call to me to responsibility in the other's regard, that Levinas recognizes the production of a meaning that would not be an ontological meaning that I would have already (as a knower constituting meanings) assumed into the same, but an ethical meaning, and an ethical meaning that, as we shall see in the next section, will be requisite for ontological meanings even as this ethical meaning calls the ontological meanings, perpetually and ever again, into question, produces them in and by calling my "constitution" of them into question, by calling me (and the meanings produced in the economy of the same over which I preside as knower) into question:

> This way of undoing the form adequate to the Same so as to present oneself as other is to signify or to have a meaning. To present oneself by signifying is to speak. This presence, affirmed in the presence of the image as the focus of the gaze that is fixed on you, is said. Signification or expression thus contrasts with every intuitive datum precisely because to signify is not to give. Signification is not an ideal essence or a relation open to intellectual intuition, thus still analogous to the sensation presented to the eye. It is preeminently the presence of exteriority. Discourse is not simply a modification of intuition (or of thought), but an original relation with exterior being. . . . It is the production of meaning. Meaning is not produced as an ideal essence; it is said and taught by presence, and teaching is not reducible to sensible or intellectual intuition, which is the thought of the same. To give meaning to one's presence is an event irreducible to evidence. It does not enter into an intuition; it is a presence more direct than visible manifestation, and at the same time a remote presence—that of the other. This presence dominates him who welcomes it, comes from the heights, unforeseen, and consequently teaches its very novelty. (TI 66 [37–38])

Here, faced with the face of the other, a meaning imposes itself upon the same that is clearly not an ontological meaning, not a meaning that would be the product of a knower-known relation, requiring the intuition, the anticipation, of a manifestation, but one that "brings to us a notion of meaning prior to my *Sinngebung*" (TI 51 [22]), unanticipated, teaching its novelty, and thus dominating the same to which it comes. This notion of the possibility of a meaning other than ontological meaning, where the correlation between knower and known is not equated with the full measure of being (as Levinas argues it is for the philosophical tradition), the possibility of a meaning that escapes or transcends this correlation, is a central and persistent tenet of the whole thought of Levinas, and this we attempted to illustrate in our previous chapter by following Levinas through the delineation of the meanings of the ethical transcendence of the other and of the egoism separated in enjoyment as meanings meaningful in independence from ontological meaning. The meaning of transcendence as transcendence (that is, as a refusal of being reduced to immanence in correlation with a knowing ego), we have been in the course of demonstrating, can be produced only as ethical, as a relation with an exteriority to whom I owe responsibility and that calls into question the *conatus essendi* of the ego in its exercise as the same—that is, can be produced only in discourse, as discourse. And it is as a relation with exteriority that discourse animates, is the essential of, both language and truth, insofar as language is a relationship of the exchange of meaning (and not only, or even primordially, ontological meaning) between the same *and exteriority,* and truth an aspiration to, a desire for, exteriority.[10]

So while language can indeed be interpreted as an act, as the exchange of information (as it is for the greater part of the philosophical tradition), Levinas argues that the essential of language is in the ethical relation that breaks the monopoly of meaning exercised in the same and that puts me in a relation with an exteriority—an exteriority that, in the economy of the same, is reduced to a known content, and which is as such never present *kath'auto:* "But then one omits the essential of language: the coinciding of the revealer and the revealed in the face, which is accomplished in being situated in height with respect to us—in teaching" (TI 67 [38]). It is precisely, then, as an ethical calling into question of the same, in teaching, that language, as an exchange of meaning with alterity, begins. Language as an exchange of meanings between terms in original and irreducible difference—as opposed to language as *dia-logos* where the relation with the other is always a finding of, a connecting with, the *logos* that would be common to us, and thus a reduction of the other to the same—arises in the "calling, . . . commanding, . . . obeying" (TI 62 [33]) of the other that calls the same into question and that calls me to responsibility in his regard. It is in the immediacy of the face to face, calling to me back across and as a cutting through of the structures of the same, at counter-current to these structures, that a meaning is imposed that did not originate in the same, and that the possibility of an exchange of meanings with an exteriority that is not a function of the play of the same is introduced, providing language as such an exchange with its *point d'appui:* "The immediate is the interpellation and, if we may speak thus, the imperative of language" (TI 52 [23]).

That is to say that, for Levinas, language is not first of all an exchange of information, nor is it first of all a lexical system of interrelated signs in terms of whose differential play linguistic meaning—and perhaps meaning *tout court*—is produced (as it is for Saussure and, perhaps too, for the early Derrida), but a speaking to the other that any exchange of information, or that any system of meaningful signifiers, presupposes. The other, who is not known, who is not correlative with a knowing but withdraws behind the theme that he offers, is not he *of* whom I speak, but he *to* whom I speak, and even if I speak of him, this speaking of him is at the same time a speaking to him, or a speaking to yet another other: "Already the comprehension of Being is said to the existent, who arises behind the theme in which he is presented. This 'saying to the other'—this relationship with the Other as interlocutor, this relation with an *existent*—precedes all ontology" (TI 47–48 [18]). So this "who" to whom I speak a "what" never becomes a "what" except that another "who" arises ever and again behind this "who as what," the "who to whom" I speak this "who as what." Without this other, without an interlocutor, as we have argued in our chapter 1, speech is superfluous; there would be no (need of) language. And since my "speaking/naming" is speech to an other who is not spoken or named but spoken to, language "breaks the totality" (TI 80 [53]) in referring to that which is irreducible to the same. Discourse is addressed to an interlocutor.

As such, language is an aspiration, desire, for exteriority, which for Levinas is the very essence of "truth." As such, "the ethical relation, opposed to first philosophy which identifies freedom and power, is not contrary to the truth; it goes unto being in its absolute exteriority, and accomplishes this very intention that animates the movement onto truth" (TI 47 [18]). But this "truth" as a going on to exteriority is clearly not, could not be, ontological truth wherein truth is taken as the correlation between knower and known that precisely reduces to the same the exteriority toward which truth on Levinas's terms aspires. It is, rather, an ethical truth, the truth of the face:[11]

> The face brings a notion of truth which, in contradistinction to contemporary ontology, is not the disclosure of an impersonal Neuter, but *expression:* the existent breaks through all the envelopings and generalities of being to spread out in its 'form' the totality of its 'content,' finally abolishing the distinction between form and content. This is not achieved by some sort of modification of the knowledge that thematizes, but precisely by 'thematization' turning into conversation. (TI 51 [21–22])

This ethical truth, as irreducible to an ontological truth (indeed, as a calling into question of ontological truth), must be maintained as ethical, remain at the level of the other who presents himself in the meaning correlative with his presentation as face: a truth, a presence, irreducible to (indeed, foundational to) the categories of truth or falsity taken onto-epistemo-logically:

> It is the frank presence of an existent that can lie, that is, disposes of the theme he offers, without being able to dissimulate his frankness as interlocutor, always struggling openly [à visage découvert]. The eyes break through the mask—the language of the eyes, impossible to dissemble. The eye does not shine; it speaks. The alternative to truth and lying, of sincerity and dissimulation, is the prerogative of him who abides in the relation of absolute frankness, in the absolute frankness which cannot hide itself. (TI 66 [38])

Thus the meaning of the other, the "truth" of the other, is guaranteed by the other in his face and establishes with me an ethical relationship: discourse. The ethical relationship thus has its own meaning independent of, or prior to, any ontological meaning that would name it, for any such "naming" is spoken to the other, seeks his investiture, appeals already to the ethical truth that he is. And this ethical truth is thereby, at least implicitly, recognized by, and is thus refractory to, any assertion of ontological truth.[12]

But this ethical meaning, this ethical truth, is not yet, is not at all, the shared meaning of a universal truth, a meaning that would mean the same to me and to the other, the *logos,* because this ethical meaning arises in the context of the asymmetrical relation that is precisely the refusal of any assertion I might make about an a priori shared or universal, that is, objective, meaning. The meaning of the face of the other, we will recall, is not the meaning that I in turn would have for the other. "We are the same and the other," and remain so. The expression of the other, his call to me to responsibility on his behalf, is not correlative with my call to him to responsibility on my behalf (or at least there is no way that I could know if it was, or ethically enforce such) for this would require appeal to precisely the kind of totalizing vision that the face of the other calls into question. The other's call to me to ethical responsibility calls me to ethical response, and the speech that I offer to the other, my meaning in the context of this ethical relationship, before any meaning content, is an ethical "*me voici,*" a response to the "truth" of the other—which is his right of refusal with respect to any "truth" I might bring to bear in his regard, his unimpeachable right to my responsibility to him *as other.*

II. Discourse Produces the *Logos*

II.1. Objective Meaning and the Truth of Logos

If the ethical relation is established as discourse, as a calling into question of the same, as a calling of the same to responsibility, as an ethical meaning that is not a meaning content (not something known), the universality of the *logos,* required for *dia-logos,* arises, for Levinas, in the consideration of the contents of the speech of he who, in his speech, already presents himself as an ethical meaning, as refractory to any *logos.* For the other, in his poverty, in his *lowly* estate as stranger, widow, and orphan—that is, from ethical *height*—in his call to me not to commit murder, does not merely call me to "let him be"[13] in any laissez-faire sense, but calls me to let him be in the sense of living fully, to let him *exist* in the fullest sense—and for this he requires the elements of the world, the goods that make up the nourishment of existence. His ethical call to me is not only, then, a call to me to allow him to direct his own meanings, to define his own existence, but also a call to responsibly provide him with that which is necessary for his life, a call to address—to the point of supplying his want with "the bread from one's mouth"[14]—his condition as stranger, widow, and orphan. His ethical height, in other words, is a function of his poverty, his neediness, his susceptibility to suffering and outrage, and appears in the fact that he requires for his life the things that are, after the naive spontaneity of the egoism, "mine." It is here that is delineated that place where his ethical height and his empirical lowliness meet or are one, where the negative prohibition against my assimilation of his meanings issued from the face and the call to me to positive, active responsibility on his regard are integrated in what Levinas refers to as the other's "glorious abasement" (TI 251 [229]).[15] That is, his ethical appeal to me is also a reference to the (potentially common) "stuff" of "the world," to the element upon which I feast in *jouissance* as belonging, up to now, exclusively to me, to that which is necessary to my existence, but that I live, as has been seen, not first of all as "objects in the world," but as accomplishment. The ethical call of the other is thus a calling into question of the stuff of my egoistic existence, in which I bathe as enjoyment, and that I, subsequently (and we will have to show how this is so in section III of this chapter), gather and direct in the economy I construct around the perpetuation of my own life, around the assurance, against the cares of the morrow, of my *jouissance.* The "positive" call to responsibility that corresponds to the "negative" prohibition, in the face, against murder, thus demands a concrete response in the form of my offering of what is mine to the other:

> But Desire and goodness concretely presuppose a relationship in which the Desirable arrests the "negativity" of the I that holds sway in the same—puts an end to power and emprise. This is positively produced as the possession of the world I can bestow as a gift on the Other—that is, as a presence before a face. For a presence before a face, my orientation toward the other, can lose the avidity proper to the gaze only by turning into generosity, incapable of approaching the other with empty hands. This relationship henceforth possibly common, that is, susceptible of being said, is the relationship of conversation [discours]. (TI 50 [21])

And it is here, for Levinas—in the "suitability of the mine for the other" (TI 76 [48]), in the other's ethical calling into question of that which is mine, in the contestation of my heretofore naïve possession of the element, and in my offering, in response to the other's need, of that which is mine to the other, in the creation of common objects and places of reference (a "world") that such offering establishes, and around these common objects and places—that community and universality take root, and that the universal aspect of language is founded:

> To recognize the Other is therefore to come to him across the world of possessed things, but at the same time to establish, by gift, community and universality. Language is universal because it is the very passage from the individual to the general, because it offers things which are mine to the Other. To speak is to make the world common, to create commonplaces. Language does not refer to the generality of concepts, but lays the foundation for a possession in common. It abolishes the inalienable property of enjoyment. The world in discourse is no longer what is was in separation, in the being at home with oneself where everything is given to me; it is what I give: the communicable, the thought, the universal. (TI 76 [48–49])

For Levinas, therefore, "Objectivity results from language, which permits putting into question of possession," results from a "disengagement" from the possession proper to enjoyment, a disengagement which "has a positive meaning: the entry of the thing into the sphere of the other. The thing becomes a theme. To thematize is to offer the world to the Other in speech" (TI 209 [184]). That is, in short, "It is in generosity that the world possessed by me—the world open to enjoyment—is apperceived from a point of view independent of the egoist position" (TI 75 [48]). Generosity is the very condition of possibility for objectivity.

So, contrary to the tradition, for which the *logos* is either an a priori shared, or rooted in a more primordial shared enrootedness in some or other totality, that is, in the more primordially shared ground of Being, or History, or Spirit, or what have you, for Levinas, objectivity (the common identification of the object across the *logos*) is a *product* of the interpersonal ethical relationship of discourse as this relationship bears upon the "things in the world," where the delineation of "things" and of "the world" in which they have a reference and a role, are already themselves the product of this intersubjective reference. In an obvious, if nonexplicit, attempt to distance himself from Heidegger on this matter, but where the reference to "finality" might indicate more generally any totality thinking that would read the object as the residue of, as the standing out from, some or other comprehensive and teleologically oriented system of relations, Levinas claims:

> Objectivity, where being is proposed to consciousness, is not a residue of finality. The objects are not objects when they offer themselves to the hand that uses them, to the mouth and the nose, the eyes and the ears that enjoy them. Objectivity is not what remains of an implement or a good when separated from the world in which their being comes into play. It is *posited* in discourse, in a *conversation* [entre-tien] which *proposes* the world. This proposition is held between [se tient entre] two points which do not constitute a system, a cosmos, a totality. (TI 95–96 [68])

Things, therefore, "are fixed by the word which gives them" (TI 139 [112]), and Levinas will stress again in his later *Otherwise Than Being* that objectivity, far from being the outcome of involvements or their failures, is *said,* that is, is a function of *proclamation,* of *kerygma,* is pronounced to an other and seeks (and requires) his confirmation, his investment.[16]

Or again, in distinction from a view, like that of Husserl in his (at least initially) solitary search for essences in correlation with pure subjectivity, where the object is manifested (though not yet as "objective"—which for Husserl too requires intersubjectivity) to the solitary thinking subject who would constitute its being transcendentally: "The generality of the Object is correlative with the generosity of the subject going to the Other, beyond the egoist and solitary enjoyment, and hence making the community of goods of this world break forth from the exclusive property of enjoyment" (TI 76 [48]). For the egoism in enjoyment, as we will recall from the previous chapter, concerns itself neither with "objects" nor with the "world," but lives a pre-reflective existence, bathing in an undifferentiated element.

II.2. Ethics Invests the Truth of Logos

Objectivity, or the truth of objects, and the truth of a thought that would name them, the very rationality of the *logos,* therefore rests upon a reference to the other who, while himself withdrawing from the realm of "objective facts" that he offers or that I offer to him, would produce the objectivity of things that enter into commerce between us, and this by means of his status as teacher:

> Ideas instruct me coming from the master who *presents* them to me: who puts them in question; the objectification and theme upon which objective knowledge opens already rest on teaching. The calling into question of things in a dialectic is not a modifying of the perception of them; it coincides with their *objectification.* The object is *presented* when we have welcomed an interlocutor. The master, the coinciding of the teaching and the teacher, is not in turn a fact among others. The present of the manifestation of the master who teaches overcomes the anarchy of facts. (TI 69–70 [41])

That is to say that the objectivity of the object, the truth of propositions, rests upon the truth that the other qua other, as face, presents to me in speaking to me, that is, upon an ethical truth, the non-ontological meaning that we, following Levinas, attempted to delineate in section I.2 of this chapter: "The relationship between the same and the other, my welcoming of the other, is the ultimate fact, and in it the things figure not as what one builds but as what one gives" (TI 77 [49]). For Levinas, the first truth, the first fact, that which opens the way toward the possibility of truth and factuality in the ontological sense (the ability to say that or what something *is*) is not itself an ontological truth or fact. Objective truth rests on the indisputable "fact" (indisputable because, as foundational to ontological truth, itself neither true nor false ontologically, but an always positive *ethical* truth)[17] of the face of the other, on the ethical, or metaphysical, "factuality" of the other's priority over the same as "irreducible to evidence" insofar as "the face is the evidence that makes evidence possible" (TI 204 [179]). But this originary and ultimate fact is necessary for me to get a start in being, in the truth of being, is—and it is this that we are here trying to show—a necessary starting point for the intellect.[18]

For ontological "facts," "truths" that are presented to my perception or conception, truths not grounded in anything other than phenomena—that is, not "guaranteed" by a truth outside of the phenomena themselves that would, through speech, invest them as true—are, according to Levinas, always anarchical, always susceptible to being the illusory or apparent "facts" offered to the truth seeker as if by Descartes's evil genius:

> But a world absolutely silent that would not come to us from the word, be it mendacious, would be an-archic, without principle, without a beginning. Thought would strike nothing substantial. On first contact the *phenomenon* would degrade into *appearance* and in this sense would remain in equivocation, under suspicion of an evil genius. The evil genius does not manifest himself to *state* his lie; he remains, as possible, behind things which all seem to manifest themselves for good. The possibility of their fall to the state of images or veils codetermines their apparition as a pure spectacle, and betrays the recess that harbors the evil genius; whence the possibility of universal doubt, which is not a personal adventure that happened to Descartes. This possibility is constitutive of apparition as such, whether produced in sensible experience or in mathematical evidence. (TI 90 [63])

One is therefore capable of breaking the spell spun by the always possible, nonmanifest evil genius—the anarchy or ambiguity of silent apparition[19]—only by reference to a principle that is not itself within the field of apparition, but that could introduce a principle, a starting point for knowledge and truth, into this anarchy of appearances. For Levinas, such a principle can only be introduced in the expression of the other:[20]

> The ambivalence of apparition is surmounted by expression, the presentation of the Other to me, the primordial event of signification. To comprehend a signification is not to go from one term of relationship to another, apperceiving relations within the given. To receive the given is already to receive it as taught—as an expression of the Other. . . . The world is offered in the language of the Other; it is borne by propositions. The Other is the principle of phenomena. The phenomenon is not deduced from him; one does not rediscover him by tracing back from the sign the thing would be to the interlocutor giving this sign, in a movement analogous to that leading from the appearance to things in themselves. For deduction is a mode of thinking that applies to objects already given. The interlocutor cannot be deduced, for the relationship between him and me is presupposed by every proof. (TI 92 [64–65])

It is therefore the other, who does not appear but who offers the sign, on whom the sign depends for its meaning even as he is not therein signified, who is capable, through his speech, through his speaking of the world, to endow the world and its objects with a meaning that is not henceforth susceptible to the doubt that would suspect it mere appearance, guaranteeing the objectivity of things in the world by the ethical truth that he is in speaking to me, guaranteeing the truth of objects in his very calling upon me to give them to him: "It is not I, it is the other that can say *yes.* From him comes affirmation; he is at the commencement of experience" (TI 93 [66]). That is to say that for Levinas, "Language thus conditions the functioning of rational thought: it gives it a commencement in being, a primary identity of signification in the face of him who speaks, that is, who presents himself by ceaselessly undoing the equivocation of his own image, his verbal signs" (TI 204 [179]).

Ontological truth, the truth of objects in the world, the truth of the worlding of the world, even the truth of being,[21] therefore refers to the ethical truth of the other who, in calling me into question, in calling me to responsibility, speaks to me, and introduces a principle into the anarchy of appearances, and this by his speaking itself, by his speech that comes to its own assistance, guaranteeing itself:

> Speech introduces a principle into this anarchy. Speech disenchants, for the speaking being guarantees his own apparition and comes to the assistance of himself, attends his own manifestation. His being is brought about in this *attendance.* The speech which already dawns in the face that looks at me looking introduces the primary frankness of revelation. In function of it the world is oriented, that is, takes on signification. In function of the word the world commences, which is not equivalent to the formula: the world issues in speech. The world is *said* and hence can become a theme, can be proposed. The entry of beings into a proposition constitutes the original event of their *taking on signification;* the possibility of their algorithmic expression itself will be established on this basis. Speech is thus the origin of all signification—of tools and all human works—for through it the referential system from which every signification arises receives the very principle of its functioning, its key. (TI 98 [71])

The *logos* as a rational system of thought therefore refers to a more originary *logos:* the "word" offered and guaranteed (in his "attendance" to it, in his answering for it)[22] by the other, a word that is capable of teaching, of thematizing phenomena: "To seek truth I have already established a relationship with a face which can guarantee itself, whose epiphany itself is somehow a word of honor. Every language as an exchange of verbal signs refers already to this primordial word of honor" (TI 202 [177]). The *logos* as system refers, that is, not first of all to an intelligibility *tout fait,* to being as the manifestation of being, but to an intelligence.[23]

Indeed, for Levinas, if it were not for the other calling into question the ego in the naïve spontaneity of its enjoyment, there would not be a question of "truth" at all. For the aspiration to truth presupposes an other from whom this aspiration draws its inspiration (as the very exteriority to which truth aspires) and to whom this truth might be spoken. And this not only because without an other truth would be meaningless in the sense that it would be anything that I would say that it is, and thus indistinguishable from private fantasy, for, without another, there would be no need to say it. Rather, without an other there would be no need, or desire, for the ego in enjoyment to awaken to any such aspiration.[24] The notion of truth only makes sense when I am faced with an other, and Levinas puts this starkly when he writes: "Without separation there would not have been truth; there would have been only being" (TI 60 [31]).[25]

The possibility of truth as objectivity, as a judgment about the being of things, is thus correlative with the possibility of critique, with the possibility of my being called into question, with the possibility that the truths by which I live, that the goods from which I live, indeed, my very existence, can be challenged or claimed by an other. For without an other there would be no impediment to the naive spontaneity of the ego, that which Levinas describes, borrowing a phrase from Hugo's *Hernani,*[26] as "une force qui va" (a force on the move). For it is not only the same in its exercise of its economic/ontological forestructures that is called into question by the other (the same as an ontological system of intelligibility is itself only possible, as we have seen, as a response to an other who has already awakened it to its *logos*) but the freedom of the ego exercising itself at the heart of this economy, as the structure of the same as egoism subtending the same as (economic and ontological) system:

> To approach the other is to put into question my freedom, my spontaneity as a living being, my emprise over things, this freedom of a "moving force" [force qui va], this impetuosity of the current to which everything is permitted, even murder. The "You shall not commit murder" which delineates the face in which the Other is produced submits my freedom to judgment. Then the free adherence to truth, an activity of knowledge, the free will which, according to Descartes, in certitude adheres to a clear idea, seeks a reason which does not coincide with the radiance of this clear and distinct idea itself. A clear idea which imposes itself by its clarity calls for a strictly personal work of a freedom, a solitary freedom that does not put itself in question, but can at most suffer a failure. In morality alone it is put in question. Morality thus presides over the work of truth. (TI 303–4 [280])

It is, then, this calling into question of my freedom by the other that permits of critique (and thus of reason, as of philosophy). And this calling into question, this possibility of critique, is an ethical event, such that for Levinas it is "the freedom that can be ashamed of itself [that] founds truth" (TI 83 [55]). It is, then, ethics (as a calling of the spontaneous same into question) that is the "essence of reason,"[27] and that founds theory itself.[28]

That is, the beginning of the possibility of critique not only opens up, across the element that I enjoy but that is claimed by the other, the possibility of a shared *logos,* but demands of me a *logos* (a word), a response to the other, an *apo-logy* by which I, in response to the other, call upon, in inclining myself before, the other to justify my freedom in making a case for myself, attending to my own offerings to the other by way of this apology itself, calling upon the other to confirm the truth that I offer to him as a gift. The *logos* that will then inhabit *dia-logos* thus contains, as an essential element, my *apo-logos:* "The very fact of being in a conversation consists in recognizing in the Other a *right* over this egoism, and hence in justifying oneself. Apology, in which the I at the same time asserts itself and inclines before the transcendent, belongs to the essence of conversation" (TI 40 [10]).

I would not, without the other, speak a single word (*logos*), would not—because there would be no point—appeal, across the *logos,* to anyone. I would have no reason to speak and no reason with which to speak. The fact of the *logos* already indicates the presence of the other even if that other is not indicated *in* the *logos,* an other who has already called my *jouissance* into question, and required of me the speech that seeks to justify itself:[29] "Speech is not instituted in a homogeneous or abstract medium, but in a world where it is necessary to aid and to give" (TI 216 [191]). To attempt to enter into dialogue is already apology, already to incline myself before the other and seek the investiture of my freedom, and the truth of my *logos* (word).[30] In this, Levinas is working at counter-current to the tradition, for which, as he reads it, freedom requires no justification, but where all must justify itself before freedom.[31] After such a position, pushed to a logical extreme (as, for instance, in Sartre), the other can only be encountered as a "threat" (TI 303 [208]), and as such an obstacle to be overcome, in assimilation, or in war. But in neither case is there dialogue with the other. As such, for Levinas, the *logos,* the truth of *logos,* is not the unfolding of a prior logic, found in me, flowing from myself (or from myself in correlation to a world that would be already true), but interpersonal, where ontology is the struggle with the other to name what is constituted between us, and apology my struggle, faced by the other, to have my freedom justified.

To appeal to the other across the *logos* is, in effect, to ask: "Have we not agreed that . . . ?" and "Do we not still agree that . . . ?" And the other, withdrawing from the themes he has offered, even as he offers them (which is not the sign of any inconsistency or of disloyalty, but flows from the fact that he is, ethically, not correlative with this theme), can always answer: "No," this "no" indicating either "You have mis-taken me," or "I no longer find myself in the theme I have offered," that is, "I do not (any longer) agree." And since ontological truth, despite appearances, has never been anything but such agreement, or the struggle for such agreement, the other is, as a justified freedom ("His justified existence is the primary fact" (TI 84 [56])), always free to withdraw his consent (or perceived consent) and call this "truth" into question by the ethical truth that he, as other, imposes upon me *prior* to any ontological truth. To appeal to the other across the *logos* of *dia-logos* is thus not an appeal to an a priori common given, but to the product of an ethical relationship (discourse) where the other withdraws behind the theme that he offers and remains the master/teacher of that theme, an other who can therefore call into question ever and again[32] any ontological truth that has heretofore been constituted in response to him.

III. The Economy of the Same and the *Logos*

III.1. Objectivity and the Third Party

To round out our analysis of the idea of discourse in Levinas's *Totality and Infinity,* and before proceeding to our conclusion that this ethical relationship be taken as the condition of possibility for dialogue, and for interparadigmatic dialogue in particular, we need to briefly address two (and we shall argue, interrelated) matters whose elucidation is necessary to a fuller understanding of Levinas's model: the presence of the third party, the other of the other; and the discrete presence of the feminine other.

For it is true that, for Levinas, objectivity, and objective truth, are not (as our analyses so far would seem to suggest) constituted solely in the ethical face to face, even if this be a relation across the goods of the world, but requires already the presence of the third party, another other, the other of the other, to whom I am also responsible. For in the "directness" of the face-to-face relation, the claim that the other makes upon the emergent goods of the world, upon that which heretofore I had taken as mine, goes unopposed.[33] The dispute over the material good, that which creates a common referent and thus objectivity, does not yet take hold because, if there were for me but one other, my ethical responsibility would demand of me a total giving of the world that, in the ethical optics of discourse, belongs by rights always already to the other who, as stranger, widow and orphan, lays claim to it. While there might be the necessity of naming here, and thus a kind of objectivity, insofar as the other would identify to me that which in particular he as face would claim, there would not yet be here the commonality of objects *in possible dispute* that the *logos* requires. There would be no dispute. For that, there need be another other, one who also makes a claim upon that which is "mine," instituting on my behalf the necessity of what Levinas will call, in his later work, "a comparison between incomparables" (OTB 16 [20]), a giving of that which is precisely in dispute among the other and the third, and a decision—in the face of this plurality of faces that do not add up to a whole—regarding to whom it is to be given. I am ethically challenged—in what is a challenge to ethics as my unlimited responsibility for the singular other—to mediate between legitimate but conflicting claims: "A question of consciousness. Justice is necessary, that is, comparison, coexistence, contemporaneousness, assembling, order, thematization, the visibility of faces, and thus intentionality and the intellect, and in intentionality and the intellect, the intelligibility of a system, and thence also a copresence on an equal footing as before a court of justice" (OTB 157 [200])—in short, the birth of philosophy. And it is only at the end of this complex process, always beginning in and returning to my ethical responsibility for the other, where I, across these structures, am, "by the grace of God," taken as the other of the other, that I am permitted, even am called upon (in "a command that commands commanding" (TI 213 [188])), to take my share of the goods of this world as objects shared also by me as for me, and enter into the *logos* that would mediate *our* plurality.[34] We shall have to return to the analysis of these structures from a number of diverse perspectives in subsequent chapters. What counts for our present purposes, though, is to notice that the constitution of objectivity and the *logos* is an interpersonal effect of my asymmetrical relationship with the other as this relationship is transacted always already under the influence of the *third person,* and is not the result of some or other a priori enrootedness or participation in a shared, impersonal, neutral, *third term.*[35]

And this is why, as we saw in chapter 2, the ethical transcendence that is necessary for the relation of discourse could be founded on no prior ontological connections, because the common *logos* that governs both *onto-logos* and *dia-logos* is already the product of the ethical relation of discourse, and cannot therefore be presupposed by it. And this is why, for Levinas, as we have seen, "truth presupposes justice" (TI 90 [62]), which is to say that "truth is produced only in veritable conversation or in justice" (TI 71 [43]), and why "ethics is first philosophy."[36] And this is why, as we are in the course of arguing, discourse founds dialogue.

III.2. Economy and the Feminine Other

Now, to understand Levinas on this point, that objectivity and thus the *logos* are the product of the presence of the third party, it is important to keep in mind that for Levinas the presence of the third party is no mere empirical event, a matter of an actual third person showing up at the event of the face to face relation to disturb its "purity."[37] Rather, "[t]he third party looks at me in the eyes of the other—language is justice" (TI 213 [188]). And this is why the "detail" raised in the previous section—of how the single other would be able to name that of mine upon which he would make a claim *prior* to the objectivity that requires the third—need not trouble us; there *is* no situation in which I am "faced" with the other alone.[38] And this is why we are being careful to indicate the "transcendental" (which we shall argue later, in chapter 7, is best conceived of as an ethical, radicalized transcendental) level upon which meanings such as enjoyment and ethics are transacted, prior to, and as foundational for, the "life-world experiences" of *l'homme concret.* To encounter the other is always already to encounter the third. How so?

We believe we can approach this question by addressing ourselves to another question that our analyses have so far only implicitly raised, and an answer to which is necessary to filling out our analyses on the way to arguing our central thesis: that discourse need be seen as the condition of possibility for dialogue, and for interparadigmatic dialogue in particular. For we will recall that in our second chapter we followed Levinas in arguing that the separation of the same (which was qualified as enjoyment) was a necessary condition for the production of infinity, which in turn was necessary to the possibility of relating to an alterity in other than ontological terms, or ethically, a relation that (as we have seen in this chapter) Levinas refers to as discourse, which is the encountering of a truth, a meaning, capable of founding the production of truth as *logos,* as generality and universality, which, in turn, is necessary to *dia-logos.* But is the separation of the same, the "necessary" condition for the production of transcendence, the condition that founds this whole chain of conditions that result in the possibility of dialogue, a "sufficient" condition for the coming on the scene of transcendence? By this we do not mean to ask whether there might be other conditions in addition to that of separation that might too be necessary for the production of transcendence, but rather, why would the same separated in enjoyment, this "citizen of paradise" (TI 144 [118]) "without care for the morrow" (for without time),[39] leave the comfort of this state of satisfaction—of the correlation of needs and satisfactions—and desire an other, a desire that Levinas refers to as "the desire of the undesirable" insofar as the other *as other* is unnecessary (and even antithetical) to my need,[40] is a "luxurious need" (TI 62 [34]), and thus cannot but destroy my "paradisaic" state of undisturbed enjoyment?

Now, in approaching this question it is important to once again remember that the description of the egoism separated in enjoyment undertaken in the last chapter was not a description of *l'homme concret,* but the description of an underlying structure necessary to giving an explanation of the life of concrete humanity as we experience such in an already worlded world (and where else might we experience him?). It is therefore necessary to refine our question, for the same never was in this paradisaic condition as a "state of being" only later to be disturbed by the coming of the other. The other is—and we will have to show how—always already there. Our question is perhaps better, then, put thus: what is the relationship (how and why is there a relationship) between the same as isolated in enjoyment and the other that comes—or that has always already come—to interrupt this isolation? Or, which is perhaps to ask the same thing (as we hope to show): how does the egoism, separated from the other in enjoyment, and thus "prior" to the structures common to myself and the other that constitute a world, find itself in an already worlded world?

We can approach this question only when we recognize that for Levinas the egoism in enjoyment is already being disturbed by the presence of an other manifested across a "concern for the morrow" that should by rights not belong to the egoism qua enjoyment, qua "pre-established harmony" (TI 145 [118]) between the egoism and the element:

> The reversion of all the modes of being to the I, to the inevitable subjectivity constituting itself in the happiness of enjoyment, does not institute an absolute subjectivity, independent of the non-I. The non-I feeds enjoyment; the I needs the world, which exalts it. The freedom of enjoyment thus is experienced as limited. Limitation is not due to the fact that the I has not chosen its birth and thus is already and henceforth in situation, but to the fact that the plenitude of its instant of enjoyment is not ensured against the unknown that lurks in the very element it enjoys, the fact that joy remains a chance and a stroke of luck. . . . The happiness of enjoyment . . . can be tarnished by the concern for the morrow involved in the fathomless depth of the element in which enjoyment is steeped. (TI 144 [117])

That is to say that the egoism, concerning itself for its future, finds itself extended in time, susceptible (in what Levinas will refer to as an extreme passivity) to a temporal stretching that dissolves its (albeit pre-reflexive and pre-reflective) presence to and with itself (which Levinas indicates phenomenologically in the experience of senescence),[41] and thus susceptible to the presence of an other (time)[42] within the same that is irreducible to the enjoyment of the same, irreducible to a presence that would proceed from and thus confirm the same. The threat, internal to enjoyment, opens up time, introduces into enjoyment a temporal stretching, a future, a future in which lurks the threat, but also a time in which the same as the same can constitute itself as and in what Levinas refers to as the economy of the same, constituting a worlded world in correlation with a powerful subject capable of overcoming the care of the morrow by means of economy and labor—both of which, Levinas tells us, are opened up as possibilities from out of a home.

That is, the egoism, already disturbed in its moment of pure *jouissance* by the presence of an other in the same of pure presence, by an uncertain future, manifested by the care the enjoying egoism has for the morrow, is nonetheless capable of overcoming this disturbance by means of the time allotted to the egoism to secure for itself its future, in a time that allows for labor and economy: the tilling of fields, the collecting and storing up of goods, the building of a shelter. That is to say that the separation of the same is *accomplished* as a separation from itself as pure enjoyment, as a suspension of the immediacy of enjoyment, in order to secure for itself its future—and this distancing of the self from itself is accomplished as labor. In labor the immediacy of bathing in the element is suspended (a bathing where all of the element is for me but that also carries me away, "inundates me") by a grasp exercised upon the element (and thus for Levinas the organ of labor is the hand)[43] that detaches some aspect of the element that, rather than being consumed in the present of enjoyment, is placed in reserve as a resource against an uncertain future—as a guarantee of future enjoyments. Consequently, we need to distinguish between two types of possession in Levinas's analysis, corresponding to these two positions regarding the element: first, "the possession without acquisition enjoyed by the sensibility steeped in the element, which 'possesses' without taking" (TI 158 [131]), and second, the "grasp operated on the elemental" (TI 158 [131]) which *is* labor, in which "[t]he uncertain future of the element is suspended" (TI 158 [131]). But this suspension of the element would be impossible, Levinas tells us, for an existent without a dwelling (TI 159 [132]), insofar as acquisition requires a depository in which the acquired could be stored up. That which is detached from the element must be deposited in a home, if the detached elements of the element are to become "things" available for future use. Such "things" are not yet, to be sure, objects, are not yet objectified (that which requires that my possession of them be called into question by an other who names them), but "fixed between the four walls of the home," "calmed in possession," and Levinas suggests that they "can, perhaps, be defined by tranquility—as in a 'still life' " (TI 158 [131]). But their being so possessed is the condition of possibility for their being called into question, and thus of their subsequent (and, again, this "subsequent" does not refer to "lived" time, but to a structural priority) objectification.

The home, then, is the necessary condition for overcoming the uncertainty of the morrow, as the site in which can be stored up the products of labor against the insecurity of being carried away by the element, and, qua home, is itself a kind of protection against the element, the security of a wall that shelters me against the elements. The home, then, like the interiority it concretizes, is a kind of against-nature-within-nature, a haven against the uncertainty within the paradise always already lost of the immediacy of the enjoyment of bathing in the element but disturbed by an other. The home is the possibility of a suspension of enjoyment for the sake of future enjoyments, a security against the threat immanent to enjoyment, the possibility of a contra-nature (as immediate enjoyment), but still in the service of the ego as radically egoistic. But if the home is necessary to the possession of goods and to the taking form of a "world"[44] (which in turn are necessary to these goods being called into question, and thus to objectification, and thus to the *logos,* and thus, ultimately, to *dia-logos*—so one can see where we are headed with all of this), how is the home possible? Indeed, we know *why* an egoism would withdraw into a home—in order to secure itself against an other in the same manifested as an uncertain future—but *how* does this happen?

Levinas argues that "[t]he familiarity of the world does not only result from habits acquired in this world" (TI 154 [128]), that being at home in the world—or having a home in the world—does not result merely from the fact that I have trodden its grounds before, that I know the terrain, but from a deeper familiarity, in fact, from a welcome, and this welcome into a home is offered to the egoism by that which Levinas refers to as the discrete presence of the feminine. Discrete because the feminine other does not, like the other that comes to me from ethical height, speak to me and thus call my possession of the world into question (which establishes objectivity and the *logos* across a more originary possession), but is a presence of the other "in its withdrawal and in its absence" (TI 155 [128]): "The Other who welcomes in intimacy is not the *you* [vous] of the face that reveals itself in a dimension of height, but precisely the *thou* [tu] of familiarity: a language without teaching, a silent language, an understanding without words, an expression in secret" (TI 155 [128–29]).[45] That is, this

> familiarity and intimacy are produced as a gentleness that spreads over the face of things. This gentleness is not only a conformity of nature with the needs of the separated being, which from the first enjoys them and constitutes itself as separate, as I, in that enjoyment, but is a gentleness coming from an affection [amitié] for that I. The intimacy which familiarity already presupposes is an *inti-*

> *macy with someone.* The interiority of recollection is a solitude in a world already human. Recollection refers to a welcome. (TI 155 [128])

And, Levinas tells us, "the other whose presence is discretely an absence, with which is accomplished the primary hospitable welcome which describes the field of intimacy, is the Woman," who, as such, is precisely "the condition for recollection, the interiority of the Home, and inhabitation" (TI 155 [128]). Thus "the home that founds possession" (that is, the possession of movable goods [Bien-meubles]) can itself, in a different sense, be itself possessed, "because it already and henceforth is hospitable for its proprietor," insofar as it "refers us to its essential interiority, and to the inhabitant that inhabits it before every inhabitant, the welcoming one par excellence, welcome in itself—the feminine being" (TI 157 [131]). We believe that this feminine other, who "inhabits before every inhabitant," is better thought, then, not as a "wifely" figure with whom I might "set up house," but as a "maternal" one[46]—welcoming me into a home in a pre-original hospitality, prior to my origin. But whether relying for these analyses upon our experiences of either maternal or wifely figures, it is important to exercise some caution and remember that Levinas is speaking here of "conditions" in a transcendental (or radicalized transcendental) sense, such that "the empirical absence of the human being of 'feminine sex' in a dwelling nowise affects the dimension of femininity which remains open here" (TI 158 [131])—and the defending of such a position Levinas claims would be to "defy ridicule" (TI 157 [131]). Rather, Levinas's analyses of "the feminine" here—though susceptible to the charge of gender essentialism, certainly[47]—refer to a certain kind of transcendental condition, that does not itself reflect any empiricism but "makes every empiricism possible," and does not rest upon, therefore and further, any empirical home, but delineates a transcendental condition for an interiority that makes the dwelling in an empirical home itself possible.

For the egoism in its economy of the same, in its "solitude in a world already human," therefore, the other, in the form of "an intimacy with someone," as the feminine other, has always already come. But we would misinterpret Levinas, we maintain, if we were to interpret this feminine other as anything less than fully other (and by implication as anything less than fully human), that is, as an attenuated or partial alterity that simply laid the foundations for the meeting with a genuine alterity, as if the feminine other ("the Woman") were one kind of other, and the other that presents itself in the face ("the Man"?) another kind. Rather, we believe the feminine other needs be thought of as fully other, as, in fact, "the other" in the full sense that this word bears in Levinas's discourse on ethical alterity, but operating, as feminine, "on another plane" than the other who comes to me from ethical height and that speaks to me, that is, as *the other* in the *modality* of the feminine:

> This [feminine] alterity is situated *on another plane* than language and nowise represents a truncated, stammering, still elementary language. On the contrary, the discretion of this presence *includes all the possibilities of the transcendent relationship with the Other.* It is comprehensible and exercises its function of interiorization *only on the ground of the full human personality,* which, however, in the woman, can be reserved so as to open up the dimension of interiority. And this is a new and irreducible possibility, a delightful lapse in being, and the source of gentleness in itself. (TI 155 [129], emphasis ours)

This reading of the feminine, not as another other than the other as face who calls from an ethical height, but as the other in a particular modality (i.e., in reserve), of which the other as face is another modality, is given credence, we believe, in another passage where the feminine and the face are taken as simultaneous revelations of "the presence of the Other," where this other—referring to *both* the other as face and the other in withdrawal—is in the singular, is one and the same other:

> For the intimacy of recollection to be able to be produced in the oecumenia of being the presence of the Other *must not only* be revealed in the face which breaks through its own plastic image, *but* must be revealed, *simultaneously* with this presence, in its withdrawal and in its absence. This simultaneity is not an abstract construction of dialectics, but the very essence of discretion. (TI 155 [128], emphasis ours)

There is nothing, then, to preclude the possibility, but rather everything to recommend the inevitability, that the other as feminine who discretely welcomes me into a home, at the same time, in the modality of the face, calls my egoistic possession of the world constituted from out of the home into question. And if our suspicions are correct and the feminine other is best thought of as a maternal figure, this simultaneity (in the same person) of welcoming (an investing of my freedom) and calling into question (the discipline of limiting that freedom) would not seem to be incongruent—or at least no more than it is for maternal figures (of either empirical gender) in the concrete life-world.

As such, although we are speaking here of transcendental conditions for the life of *l'homme concret,* the "way back" to concrete life from the structure of *jouissance* (after the delineation of the transcendental condition of *jouissance* that has been phenomenologically deduced from life as lived) goes by way of the presence, within the structure of *jouissance* itself, of the other, always already there, and testified to by the care for the morrow that enjoyment, were it "pure," that is, in relation to no other, would not have "known." And it is precisely this other, always already there, in the mode of the feminine, that welcomes the egoism into a home and that allows it the opportunity to protect itself against the very threat that it, as other, introduces from the beginning (or from before the beginning, if the beginning marks the starting point of an active ego whose activity would already presuppose dwelling) into the same. As such, the other, in the mode of the feminine, is an originary (or pre-originary, according to the analyses of *Otherwise Than Being*) "grace:" my being welcomed into a home and, consequently, given a world, before I even begin. And while "enculturation" in the fullest sense no doubt demands the face that speaks, that teaches me contents (made possible by an ethical teaching that does not itself become a content, as we have seen), the conditions of possibility of this enculturation process could not be other than this being welcomed into a home, being given an orientation point with respect to a world where I can act and fend for myself, and this because "someone" (the feminine, maternal figure) has already fended for me, which is a pre-original grace—a goodness before any dialectic between goodness and evil takes hold, whereby I find myself *chez moi,* with a home in the world, at home in the world, already confirmed in my egoism (as the investment of my freedom that apology calls for)—granted by the feminine presence, this discrete (welcoming rather than challenging) presence. And it is this being *chez moi,* this having been welcomed into a home, this *oiko*-nomy, that opens up the possibilities for possession that are accomplished in labor, which is in turn the condition of possibility for my world (structured around the possessions that feed my *jouissance*) being called into question by the other, that is, for the passage from the isolated economy of interiority into the interpersonal economy of a shared world regulated by a shared *logos.*

So, to refer back to our preceding section, when Levinas informs us that it is only by the grace of God that I am taken as the other of the other (that is, where the asymmetrical responsibility that I have for the other, and that I cannot demand or expect to be reciprocated, is reciprocated, and there is justice for me too), the transcendental structure for this grace is already in place: I am always already the other of the feminine other who has already welcomed me, who has already invested my freedom qua egoism from before my beginning—from the womb.[48] Mothers are (or non-gender-specific maternity is) the grace of God. So when, in justice (that is, after the arrival of the third—a third that, not incidentally, is always already present in the encounter with the other if only in the figure of the feminine other, or the other in the modality of the feminine, who in welcoming me into a home makes the possession that the other qua other calls into question possible and so must have already been structurally present before the encounter),[49] I am, across complex structures, able to be taken as the other of the other, is this "grace of God" not a reenactment, or the very articulation, of feminine graciousness at the level of justice?[50]

But this investment of my freedom as egoism—as an egoism that precedes the alternative between egoism and altruism, and is its condition of possibility—also creates the possibility that this home, this starting point in the world, with which I have been graced (and the intersubjective world constituted around it in its having been claimed by the other) will be assimilated by the egoism for its egoistic purposes, in accord with its isolationist enjoyment, a structure that continues to subtend even the self called to be responsible, indeed, as the condition of possibility for its being so called:

> The identity of the I comes to it from its egoism whose insular sufficiency is accomplished by enjoyment, and to which the face teaches the infinity from which this insular sufficiency is separated. This egoism is indeed founded on the infinitude of the other, which can be accomplished only by being produced as the idea of Infinity in a separated being. The other does indeed invoke this separated being, but this invocation is not reducible to calling for a correlative. It leaves room for a process of being that is deduced from itself, that is, remains separated and capable of shutting itself up against the very appeal that has aroused it. (TI 216 [191])[51]

But if in *Totality and Infinity* we discover that such "shutting itself up" is possible, in the space of separation necessary to the production of Infinity (and ethics), it is not until *Otherwise Than Being* that we discover "why" such shutting itself up would occur, in what Levinas refers to as the ego's "forgetting" of its responsibility for the other in the concern for itself, a concern justified by the presence of the third party:

> The ego can, in the name of this unlimited responsibility, be called upon to concern itself also with itself. The fact that the other, my neighbor, is also a third party with respect to another, who is also a neighbor, is the birth of thought, consciousness, justice, and philosophy. The unlimited initial responsibility, which justifies this concern for justice, for oneself, and for philosophy can be forgotten. In this forgetting consciousness is a pure egoism. (OTB 128 [165])

That is, the egoism, forgetting that its world has been given to it by an other whose presence (as feminine absence) was indispensable to it, and forgetting that its *logos* has been constituted in the calling into question of its world by the presence of the other (coming from ethical height), can turn its being in the world against the other who has made its world possible. It is such forgetting that leads to "egoism" in the colloquial (and nontranscendental) sense, an egoism that lives its egoism as if it were not always already in the presence of the other, responsible for the other. The egoism, as interiority, animated by enjoyment and concretely accomplished as dwelling, forgets that its dwelling (the site of its *je peux*) depends already upon an other (the feminine) in the same, and egoism (as a transcendental structure), in forgetting its other, becomes (or is concretized in the world as) egoistic.

It is such an egoism, believing that it is of itself a justified freedom (and Levinas maintains that this justification of freedom by itself, this not inclining itself to the other who alone can invest it, is an unquestioned tenet of Western thought),[52] that assimilates the *logos* to its own purposes, that perceives the *logos* as the correlation between it as knower to a known world subject to its freedom, and that attempts, therefore, in *dia-logos,* not to reach the other as other, but to reduce the other to the same, to a function of its (my) freedom—and that perpetuates (in not recoiling in shame before the other) the naïve violence of the egoism in *le monde concret.*

We see here, then, the presence of the other always already at the heart of enjoyment and the egoism, an other that, *at once,* breaks up the pure immediacy of enjoyment (manifested as care for the morrow), and, in the mode of the feminine, welcomes the egoism into a home from out of which it has the power to avert immediate danger by means of labor and economy, the same economy that the other as face, that is, in the mode of ethical height, calls into question, thereby establishing the possibility for the egoism to avail itself of objectivity and the *logos* in the shared world, the life-world, of *l'homme concret.* But to give a descriptive account of this world, "the world," in which concrete communications are transacted across an already instituted *logos* (or *logoi,* as we have argued in our opening chapter), it has been necessary to trace out the structures of the ego that would hold forth such communications: a separated egoism in enjoyment already and always in relation to an other who, in the mode of the feminine, invests the freedom of this egoism by welcoming it into a home, that which allows it to construct an (egoistic) economy around its original *jouissance,* and who, in the mode of ethical alterity, by calling into question the freedom of *jouissance* and its egoistic economy, awakens the egoism to its *logos,* to a shared world where it can either remember the call of its pre-original responsibilities, or (in forgetting) exercise unabashedly the violence of the egoism.

IV. Discourse Founds Dialogue

Let us return, then, to the question that has set the agenda for this work and, in light of the foregoing, clarify what we take to be

Levinas's answer to it: What are the conditions of possibility for interparadigmatic dialogue? or How are we to make some progress in understanding how interparadigmatic dialogue might be possible, a dialogue defined, we will recall, as one arising (or aspired to) in a situation in which the common *logos* by means of which dialogue as *dia-logos* is to be mediated cannot be agreed upon, and therefore cannot play its promised mediatory role? We have seen why Levinas would reject the answer to this question offered by the overwhelmingly predominant part of the Western philosophical tradition, as Levinas reads it, insofar as the tradition presupposes precisely that which is in question in the problem of interparadigmatic dialogue—mutual access to an a priori shared *logos,* a presupposition that—as we have attempted to argue following Levinas—in its unquestioning acceptance of the priority and rights of freedom cannot but result in a violent reduction of the other to the same, the other with whom it is precisely the aim of interparadigmatic dialogue to enter into linguistic commerce (chapter 1). In arguing for the priority of the relationship of discourse in my commerce with the other, which does not presuppose a shared *logos* (rather, refuses such on ethical grounds absolutely) but provides a description of the relation between terms in irreducible difference, in arguing that my relationship with the other is first of all a calling into question of my capacities for reducing of the other to the same, in arguing that the other is first of all encountered as *other* in the mode of *ethical* expression (as a refusal to being reduced to a purportedly common term that is, in the end, found in me), Levinas preserves the alterity of the other that would be the "term" of interparadigmatic (or of any) dialogue (chapter 2). But the transcendence produced in the ethical refusal that the other as face presents, far from leaving the terms in some sort of dual solipsism, is already, by virtue of the refusal itself, a relation between terms, albeit a "relation without relation," that is, an ethical relation irreducible to any a priori ontological relation, is already discourse, already appeal and response, the ethical relationship of responsibility (chapter 3). Ethical separation is at once ethical relation—before the interposition or imposition of any ontological categories that, in fact, are produced from out of this "prior" separation-relation (discourse) alone.

That is to say that the *logos* requisite for *dia-logos,* a *logos* that is not the organon of reducing the other to the same but one that is recognized by him, must already be an appeal to the other, an offering or receiving that establishes the objectivity of the object and the intelligibility of ideas, where the very rationality of the *logos* already relies upon the other to invest my reference to the world as shared world with meaning (*onto-logy*), and to invest my freedom (*apo-logy*).[53] Here is the possibility of a *logos* that is shared, because—rather than being found "in me," derived or deduced from my connection to the world in my solitude (a solitude which for Levinas is, consequently, pre-rational, a relationship of enjoyment that precedes any institution of a *logos*)—this *logos* is already and always a response to another's appeal, is an offering made to him, does not proceed from itself or from the ego that possesses it but awaits, is produced in, the investiture, the confirmation, of the other. To appeal to the other across the *logos* of *dia-logos* is to appeal to the other in terms of a *logos* (a word) that is already such an appeal: an appeal to an appeal, a response to an ethical appeal in terms of which this appeal to consent to a *logos* (in the form of a gift offered) would accrue an objective, or "universal," meaning, rather than an appeal to a common meaning that would impose itself upon thought before such an ethical appeal is made. As such, the "objective" or "universal" is precisely not that which appears to me as above question in being clear and distinct, but that which is produced precisely across my being called into question. My *logos* (word) offered to the other creates the possibility for the other's acceptance of my gift, the possibility that my *logos* as word will be invested with ontological meaning, transmuted into the *logos* (as *reason*able to the other), a *logos* that will found and regulate a system of *reason*able references and relations among things in a now common world, and that will open up, across such commonalities, the possibility of a *dia-logos,* insofar as this constitution of a world in common is already *dia-logos.*

To appeal to the other across the *logos* is thus already to recognize his right to call this *logos* into question, or to invest it with meaning, or to invest it with meaning *in* calling it into question—which is already an ethical gesture. And it is so, moreover, implicitly in my very speaking to the other, even if it would pretend to a neutral universality, even if explicitly or seemingly this "right of the other" would be denied, even, Levinas tells us, "to classify him as sick, [or] to announce to him his death sentence,"[54] even in rhetoric, where I appeal to the freedom of the other, solicit his "yes," even as I would attempt to corrupt it.[55] To appeal to the other across the emerging *logos* that inhabits *dia-logos* rests therefore on a communicative relationship that "is therefore not the unfolding of a prefabricated internal logic, but the constitution of truth in a struggle between thinkers, with all the risks of freedom, [that is, insofar as] language is spoken where community between the terms of the relationship is wanting, where the common plane is wanting or is yet to be constituted" (TI 73 [45]). Over against the Socratic dialogue which "already presupposes beings who have decided for discourse, who consequently have accepted its rules" (TI 180 [155]), that is, that already acknowledge a *logos* that would govern the dialogue, on the Levinasian view (which Levinas refers to as after the "Cartesian order" over against the "Socratic order" (TI 180 [155])), dialogue is produced, is born, in discourse, in an original, ethical relation with the other *as other,* that is, with a being who has not already decided for dialogue, who is not already endowed (and a priori) with the *logos* that dialogue requires. Language is born, rather, in the commonality (and the *logos*) produced across the gift of "the object" that the one offers (or is capable of offering) to an other as this other in his need, and as his need, calls upon the one to give it—above and beyond the *logos* that governs in the same as an operation of its immanent economy, and precisely as an interruption of this economy.

Insofar, then, as the *logos* as the system of rationality that objectively names beings is itself the product of the relationship of discourse, dialogue as *dia-logos* presupposes discourse, that is, the rational word is spoken *to* the other who alone can invest its rationality. The condition of possibility of interparadigmatic dialogue (or of any dialogue, for that matter, since for Levinas all dialogue is spoken between terms in irreducible difference) is, therefore, discourse. Discourse precedes the constitution of *logos,* and thus any possibility of *dia-logos.* The universal aspect of language (the shared *logos*) that would, after the analyses of the tradition, be the condition of possibility of *dia-logos* is itself conditioned, and is conditioned by the ethical relationship that produces it. It is, and remains, an appeal to a singularity (to that which refuses reduction to a universal category), is founded upon an ethical inclination that underwrites the possibility of universality, and it is this relationship between discourse and the *logos* of *dia-logos* that founds Levinas's famous claim that "ethics is first philosophy"—that is, ethics makes philosophy as a universal discourse possible.

To facilitate a dialogue in those situations where the other refuses the *logos* to which I would make appeal, in those situations that we are describing as presenting us with the problem of inter-paradigmatic dialogue, it is therefore necessary that one of the terms in relation recognize the other as legitimately calling the *logos* that he has appropriated to his economy of the same into question, and if necessary to sacrifice this *logos,* to reconstitute it in the face of the other to whom, in fact, the very constitution of this *logos* is already an appeal. And it is, as we have stressed, my *logos,* my meanings, my constitution of the world that must be called into question, for the other is always, as face, an already justified freedom. That is to say, as we have seen, that for Levinas the relationship of discourse, the relationship that founds any subsequent constitution of a *logos,* can be produced only as asymmetrical; the responsibility that animates the relationship is, must be, mine alone, for to attribute this same responsibility to the other as a correlative responsibility for me would be already to pretend to have recourse to a neutral, third position from which the relationship could be viewed and judged and from out of which such an attribution could be "objectively" and "justly" made. But such a pretension is precisely that which the relationship of discourse contests insofar as it is a calling into question of any such position I should wish to invoke, of any such position I would have formulated "in me" before encountering the other as other who would call it into question—a calling into question which is, moreover, the condition of possibility for any "objectivity" at all. Indeed, to make such a demand of the other, to insist upon the reciprocity of responsibility, to appeal to a "common" call that the other rejects, is, as we have argued, to condemn myself and the other to the intractable struggles for the superiority of one or the other interlocutor's appropriation of a "truth" that "in (ethical) truth" can only have arisen between us, and to the resultant difficulties in which we found ourselves ensnared after the analyses of our first chapter. This is, we believe, among Levinas's concerns in his refusal of the possibility of escaping one's own perspective as one's own, one's own position with regard to the other, and aspiring to a position of neutrality from which the relationship could be viewed and mediated, which is, he believes, the constant aspiration of the tradition, which, as we have seen, proceeds by way of the insertion of a neutral third term between myself and the other (the *logos*) that would soften the shock of the encounter—but that, despite its pretensions to neutrality, is a function of the ego, is found "in me."

Rather, when the *logos* is conceived of as already a response to and responsibility for the other that precedes any assimilation of this *logos* to an egoism, is conceived of as universal only across giving, is conceived of as an ethical response to the other, the other—he who has solicited this response—is not then able to be dominated by the *logos* that is, at root, rather *for* him. Faced, that is, with an other who refuses the *logos* that I find "in me" (but that is, in fact, already the residue of my already ethical relations to the other), I am not therefore ethically permitted to impose this *logos* on the other. Since the *logos is* only in response to him, the imposition of my *logos* that the other refuses could only be a violence, the imposition of the same on the other by means of that which, by rights, is only between us. I must, if dialogue is to be effectuated in such situations, respond to the ethical meaning of the other who refuses my (assimilation of the) *logos,* and, through offering what is mine to the other—in recognizing his refusal and responding to his condition as stranger, widow, and orphan by giving—reconstitute the world and the *logos* itself in the space of this giving, offering, refusal, investiture, and re-offering. In this way, Levinas's proposals avoid the intractable struggles over which of the terms in the dialogue already possesses the truth in terms of which a dialogue could proceed by giving us a description of these terms in an original but non-allergic relation, in "discourse," and thus in original plurality, and by describing the relation between these terms as prior to, and constitutive of, any "truth" that would purport, in terms of an already constituted *logos,* to govern it: "Better than comprehension, *discourse* relates with what remains essentially transcendent. . . . Language is a relation between separated terms" (TI 195 [169]).

The possibility of interparadigmatic dialogue thus rests upon my capacity to recognize that responsibility for the other, which is (ethical) truth, founds and thus governs the truth of *logos,* precedes and founds dialogue as the possibility of any circulation of information. It is to see the first and governing truth as the good (for the other) rather than the good as correlative with or a completion of what is (speaking from the position of a logic cut off from its ethical source) the true (that is, what falls into line with an ego's egoistic appropriation of the fruits of ethical truth). If interparadigmatic dialogue is to be possible, then, I need allow *my* constitution of the world to be reconstituted in light of the fact that the *logos* that inhabits dialogue is not a priori but constituted in the struggle between beings over that which is between them, that the truth of *logos* is the result of my giving of that which is mine to the other as a gift that can be invested as universal and objective by the other—but this is possible only insofar as I already recognize *my* asymmetrical ethical responsibility to the other, recognize his right to call into question that which is mine, his right to that which is mine, and his right to exist independently of my freedom, that which Levinas refers to as "the profound essence of language" which founds, even as it is hidden by, the reciprocity of dialogue (TI 101 [75]).[56]

To attempt to engender such a dialogue is as such a supreme risk, and precisely a supreme risk *for me* (since I am the one called upon to give the gift), because there is no guarantee that the other will respond in kind and return gift for gift, will invest my understandings and my freedom, will leave me anywhere to live or anything from which to live, in short, no guarantee that the other will acknowledge that I have a right to partake of the goods of the world, a right that the other has inalienably. (Rather, as we have seen, my right, my being recognized as the one for whom the other is responsible, is left, according to Levinas, up to the grace of God.) It is to such certainty that the tradition, according to Levinas, unceasingly aspires, seeking to ground the *logos* and thus *dia-logos* in the absoluteness of a justified egoism (be this in the guise of a certainty provided by the absoluteness of Being, or of God, or what have you to, which the knowing ego would have certain access), and why, according to Levinas, this tradition cannot make space for discourse, which depends upon my certainty being called into question. On the contrary, for Levinas, "Regarding communication and transcendence one can indeed only speak of their uncertainty. Communication is an adventure of a subjectivity, different from that which is dominated by the concern to recover itself, different from that of coinciding in consciousness; it will involve uncertainty." And then, still regarding "communication," Levinas comments, in what could be taken as the statement of our thesis in this work:

> It is by virtue of its eidos [Eidétiquement] possible only in sacrifice, which is the approach of him for which [dont] one is responsible. Communication with the other can be transcendent only as a dangerous life, a fine risk to be run [un beau risque à courir]. These words take on their strong sense when, instead of only designating the lack of certainty, they express the gratuity of sacrifice. In a fine risk to be run, the word "fine" has not been thought about enough. It is as antithetical to certainty, and indeed to consciousness, that these terms take on their positive meaning, and are not the expression of a makeshift [un pis-aller]. (OTB 120 [154])

The way past the impasse of dialogue is thus correlative with the risk of putting myself at the service of the other, but not in any voluntaristic sense (which would presuppose that I had myself to myself first, and that I could then freely choose to give/offer to the other), but in recognizing that I am always already in the service of the other, where my "truth" is this service, where my truth is inseparable from, *is,* my capacity for goodness, and where my being responsible for the other is my deepest "me."[57] And this being at the service of the other means that I am already sacrificed to the other—that my recourse to the *logos* is already (if unknowingly) such sacrifice (as *apo-logy*), and this *logos* cannot, then, without violence and contradiction,[58] return to dominate the other (in *onto-logy*) in whose service it is constituted as *logos.* My service or sacrifice to the other, and thus the way out of the impasse of dialogue, is thus a kind of remembering, a putting of the *logos* at the service of the other in the face of whom it has been constituted, and the recognition (even if implicitly) of whose priority alone permits of its possibility. And Levinas, as we recall from our earlier analyses in this chapter, does refer to the violence of reducing the other to the same as a "forgetting." Levinas's discourse would appear, then, at this level, not as prescriptive (telling me what I should do), but as a descriptive invitation (reminding me of who I am)[59]—delineating a structure in terms of which alone the self can, reminiscent of one of the oldest philosophical aspirations, know itself, to know that in sacrificing itself the self does not lose itself, but finds its own (deepest) self: what Levinas will refer to in his *Otherwise Than Being* as "the one-for-the-other," or "substitution." Thus the sacrifice that is a supreme risk to the egoism and its solitary enjoyment is not a risk that need be taken, it is a risk that has already been taken (whether I recognize it or not); I am always already susceptible to the violence and wounding of the other (identified in *Totality and Infinity* as the egoism's "care for the morrow," and in *Otherwise Than Being* as "sensibility") despite all of my attempts at security. Knowing myself to be such, reminded of my responsibilities to the other, awakened to the fact that my attempts at security are futile and ultimately a betrayal of myself, I am opened up to the possibility of opening myself up (through a remembering of my originary, or pre-originary, openness) to the other, of putting myself at his service in the sacrifice of the *logos* that I operate in my economy of the same, and through this *logos* as it is reconstituted—ever and again as it is repeatedly called into question—as a responsible response to him.

Faced with the problem of interparadigmatic dialogue, then, it seems I can break the impasse only by taking the risk of sacrifice, which means ultimately recognizing that I am already so sacrificed. To cling to my already constituted constitution of the world as the truth, we are arguing, to insist that the *logos* is the *logos* that I find in me, is to remain ensconced in intractable struggles over *whose* constitution of the world will dominate, mine or that of the other, that is, to settle for a warfare based upon self-interest (if buoyed by the alibi that my self-interest is ultimately also in the best interest of the other, but where the other is not consulted in this, or at least not without a certain paternalism), be that the warfare of rhetoric (insofar as rhetorical discourse, be it "philosophy," as we recall, solicits from the other his "yes" against his will—at once recognizing and corrupting the other's freedom), or be that the warfare lurking in, underwriting, the peace of the State (the pax Romana).

Nor is the negotiation of politics—the balancing of the rights of freedoms (still based upon "reciprocal" self-interest)—helpful here, if it is not recognized that such negotiation already presupposes apology, is already an inclining of myself before the other (in the very fact of speaking to him, in seeking the investiture of my freedom from the other). The possibility of such negotiation, of politics, rests, according to Levinas, upon my pre-original responsibility for the other, as does any ethics of mutuality, an ethics in which rights and responsibilities would be reciprocal (and which is, as such, already politics). Such a politics, such an ethics (as a system of rights and responsibilities), is indeed possible (and, in light of the third—already, as we have noted, present at the encounter with the other—necessary), and Levinas is not, we would argue, opposed to equality. But he claims that equality or mutuality is only possible based upon a prior asymmetrical responsibility of the one-for-the-other, that is, at a second step, when the terms of this mutuality have already been constituted between interlocutors based upon the gift of one to the other[60]—for if this step is omitted (or at least not remembered as having been necessary) we are returned to the problem with which we began: who will be permitted to govern the terms that govern the mutuality of rights and responsibilities when these terms are, in the problem of interparadigmatic dialogue, precisely that which is in dispute? For while in an organized society where the *logos* is entrenched in accepted social structures (where there is already consent among interlocutors as to protocols for truth and justice—which is already a society living, if unacknowledgingly, off the capital of, in the wake of, the one-for-the-other) I can appeal to the other for my rights as already delineated in an already constituted and common *logos,* where this appeal fails (where my appeal is not recognized, where the appeal to a *logos* does not meet with recognition on the part of the other—the precise situation we are describing as interparadigmatic) I must fall back into the ethical situation of asymmetry upon which any subsequent equality is to be founded, and accept my responsibility for the other outside of any demand for reciprocity, in the risk of sacrifice. Either that, or take the risk of war. The risk of peace or the risk of war: the other is always already there and cannot (with impunity) be ignored.

For a dialogue to be instituted, then, when there is no recognizable common *logos* to which effective appeal could be made, it is necessary that a *logos* be constituted in terms of the gift that one potential interlocutor would make to the other—and we have attempted to argue that the one called to offer that gift, in the uncertainty of a risk, is *me.* It is possible, of course, that the other will offer the gift to me (and there is precedent for this possibility in the feminine other who has already, in disturbing my enjoyment, invested my freedom with the gift of a home from out of which I can secure my enjoyment) but one cannot demand this (or for that matter, by definition, any) gift. My responsibility—in fact my very self—is to give: "Peace with the other is first of all my business" (OTB 139 [177]). For even if there might be "reason," in the precedent of the feminine, to have "faith" that my giving will be returned to me by the other (the faith in the "efficacy" of goodness to which many pacifistic traditions have recourse in their "arguments" for pacifism), in the end this "rationalization" (giving "reasons" to be good: "peace breeds peace," etc., where my peaceful gesture is reduced to a "means") is still founded in self-interest, and my duty, my responsibility, according to Levinas, is to take the risk of sacrifice to the other (which is to recognize myself as already sacrificed, *as* a sacrifice) for the sake of peace, but without the guarantee of peace, and Levinas therefore refers, in *Totality and Infinity,* to this sacrificial desire for the other as "against all good sense" (TI 47 [18]), and, in *Otherwise Than Being,* to "proximity" (a term describing my exposure to the other, my openness to the other), as "imprudent" (OTB 151 [192]). Indeed, without the guarantee of peace as an *outcome,* peace is in this gesture of peace, in my pacific gesture, and it is in such a gesture that the *hope* for dialogue is found. It takes two to make war; it takes one to make (a gesture of) peace.

Insofar as the *logos* of dialogue is founded in my generosity, in the gift that I make to the other in response to the other's poverty, the possibility of engendering dialogue in the situation we are describing as interparadigmatic requires of me,[61] therefore—and this, following Levinas, we present as our central thesis—that I be not more clever (more attentive to the *logos* as already constituted), but that I be "more good," ethically better (more attentive to the other to whom the constitution of the *logos* is already an appeal), offering myself to the other in a gesture of peace.[62]

To the *grand problème* of dialogue, then, put by Plato and, as we saw in our chapter 1, cited by Levinas (DVI 217), of how to lead to dialogue those beings opposed to it, and thus disposed to do violence to themselves, where a prior dialogue would need to be found in order to lead these to dialogue (and where the finding of such a dialogue is precisely the problem in the first place), Levinas would suggest that we need to reverse the priority of the terms. Levinas recasts the problem by asserting that it is not the *logos,* the true *logos,* that provides us with the possibility of contact with being—but the ethical relationship with the other. The other is not constituted or met through the *logos,* the *logos* is constituted in my relation with the other. Whereas the great problem of dialogue for the tradition presupposes that I am in possession (or at least potential possession) of the true *logos* that the other is in a position to recognize or refuse, for Levinas the *logos* is itself only in the recognition or refusal coming from the other in response to a gift that I offer to the other, which is itself already a response to the responsibility that I owe to the other qua other, qua face. Levinas's understanding offers a way past the impasse of interparadigmatic dialogue in tracing out a meaning that precedes and founds the ontological meanings that are in conflict in the situation of the impasse of dialogue, and thus a *point d'appui* outside of my closed hermeneutical circle—the possibility of a meaning that does not proceed from myself, and that as such is capable of breaking up (by calling into question) the categories of the same. It is this ethical meaning, my irremissible responsibility for the other, demanded by the face of the other, that breaks up the hegemony of the same and its powers of reduction, and puts me in contact, in a relation of discourse, with alterity: "The face opens the primordial discourse whose first word is obligation, which no 'interiority' permits avoiding. It is that discourse that obliges the entering into discourse, the commencement of discourse that rationalism prays for, a 'force' that convinces even 'the people who do not wish to listen' and thus founds the true universality of reason" (TI 201 [175]).

The possibility of interparadigmatic dialogue, the overcoming of the great problem of dialogue, depends, therefore, upon discourse, upon my responsibility to the point of the supreme risk of sacrifice, upon my generosity, my unilateral offering, my offering to the other "the bread out of my own mouth." This supreme risk is, however, as we have seen, "a beautiful risk to run," the condition of possibility for dialogue, the condition of possibility for peace. "Peace must be my peace, in a relation that starts from an I and goes to the other, in desire and goodness, where the I both maintains itself and exists without egoism" (TI 306 [283]).

Notes

1. Indeed, for Levinas, "the inequality [between myself and the other, and that is correlative with his ethical height with respect to me] *is* in this impossibility of the exterior point of view, which alone could abolish it" (TI 251 [229]).

2. This point, certainly implied in the notion of asymmetry (and we shall shortly analyze it), is put even more explicitly in Levinas's later *Otherwise Than Being,* where he writes, for example, "Obsession [my unavoidable responsibility for the other] as nonreciprocity itself does not relieve any possibility of suffering in common. It is a one-way irreversible being affected. . . . It is tied into an ego that states itself in the first person, escaping the concept of an ego in an ipseity—not in an ipseity in general, but in *me.* The knot of subjectivity consists in going to the other without concerning oneself with his movement toward me" (OTB 84 [106]).

3. Interestingly, Derrida, in a defense of Husserl in his "Violence and Metaphysics," perceives this alter-egoity of the other as the condition of possibility for his alterity. We will have to examine this claim later (see chapter 7). For now, it suffices to illustrate Levinas's view precisely by contrast to such a claim.

4. It is at this point that the severe language of *Otherwise Than Being* takes hold with all of its force, where the subject will be described as a "hostage," as "persecuted," as an "expiation" for the other, "obsessed" by the other, a self in "disposition" responsible even for the violence that the other commits against me: "to tend the cheek to the smiter and be filled with shame" (OTB 111 [141], from Lamentations 3:30).

5. Thus Levinas claims of *Totality and Infinity:* "One of the principle theses of this work is that the noesis-noema structure is not the primordial structure of intentionality" (TI 294 [271]). That is, as we shall see in this chapter, the structure of intentionality as knowledge (or any ex-

periences of "knowing" taken in the broad sense), rests upon a more primordial structure, or a more primordial "intentionality": that of discourse.

6. The *me voici* ("here I am," "see me here") is one of the ways in which Levinas describes the deepest meaning of the I, the self, in *Otherwise Than Being.* See, for example, "There is an assignation to an identity for the response of responsibility, where one cannot have oneself replaced without fault. To this command continually put forth only a 'here I am' [me voici] can answer, where the pronoun 'I' is put in the accusative, declined before any declension, possessed by the other, sick, identical" (OTB 142 [180–81]). More will need to be said about this reference to God, that Levinas suggests is implied in every *me voici,* in chapter 7 where we shall attempt to make a case for reading Levinas's texts as "prophetic," as a testimony to the God whose having passed by makes for, or is described by (across this essential ambiguity), responsibility.

7. "Transcendence is the transcendence of an I. Only an I can respond to the injunction of the face" (TI 305 [282]).

8. "To manifest oneself as a face is to *impose oneself* above and beyond the manifested and purely phenomenal form, to present oneself in a mode irreducible to manifestation, the very straightforwardness of the face to face, without the intermediary of any image, in one's nudity, that is, in one's destitution and hunger" (TI 200 [174]).

9. "For Plato true discourse can come to its own assistance: the content that is presented to me is inseparable from him who has thought it—which means the author of the discourse responds to questions. Thought, for Plato, is not reducible to an impersonal concatenation of true relations, but implies persons and interpersonal relations" (TI 71 [43]).

10. "In affirming truth to be a modality of the relation between the same and the other we do not oppose intellectualism, but rather ensure its fundamental aspiration, the respect for being illuminating the intellect" (TI 64 [35]).

11. "Man as other comes to us from the outside, a separated—or holy—face. His exteriority, that is, his appeal to me, is his truth. My response is not added as an accident to a 'nucleus' of his objectivity, but first *produces* his truth (which his 'point of view' upon me cannot nullify). This surplus of truth over being and over its idea, which we suggest by the metaphor of the 'curvature of intersubjective space,' signifies the divine intention of all truth. This 'curvature of space' is, perhaps, the very presence of God" (TI 291 [267]).

12. "This bond between expression and responsibility, this ethical condition or essence of language, *this function of language prior to all disclo-*

sure of being and its cold splendor, permits us to extract language from subjection to a pre-existent thought, where it would have but the servile function of translating that pre-existent thought on the outside, or of universalizing its interior movements. *The presentation of the face is not true* [at least qua ontological truth], for the true refers to the non-true, its eternal contemporary. . . . The presentation of being in the face does not leave any logical place for its contradictory" (TI 200–201 [175], our emphasis).

13. Levinas seems to maintain an ambiguous relationship to the Heideggerian notion of "letting be," in large measure, we believe, because for Heidegger "letting be" is largely a matter of ontology, of unconcealment, a letting the thing show itself from itself for what it is, founding a fundamental ontology in the space of which there is a certain ethical space, whereas for Levinas the "letting be" is first of all an ethical gesture, an ethics that opens up the possibility for ontology, for joining with the other in naming things in their being said: "To 'let him be' the relationship of discourse is required; pure 'disclosure,' where he is proposed as a theme, does not respect him enough for that" (TI 71 [43]). That is, Levinas wants to reject the idea of "letting be" insofar as it bears within it the idea of ontology as our primary possibility of contact with alterity ("Speaking, rather than 'letting be,' solicits the Other"; TI 195 [169]), but wants to maintain the idea of "letting be" as ethical "respect" for being, in which we constitute truth ("[M]etaphysics . . . leads to the transcendent as such, [where] transcendence means not appropriation of *what is*, but its respect. Truth as a respect for being is the meaning of metaphysical truth"; TI 302 [279]. "The aspiration to radical exteriority, thus called metaphysical, the respect for this metaphysical exteriority which, above all, we must 'let be,' constitutes truth"; TI 29 [XVII]).

14. This phrase appears on a number of occasions in *Otherwise Than Being* and illustrates graphically Levinas's claim that my responsibility for the other is to take root in the fullness of the economic order, that is, is a matter of flesh and blood (the other's and mine, and the other's before mine) and no mere matter of platitudes. It is, moreover, no mere giving from what is mine, but is a giving of "me" insofar—as we have seen in the previous chapter—as the goods that I take from the element are necessary to me, through nourishment "become" me. The first occurrence of the phrase appears in the context of the other's interruption of my enjoyment: "And to be torn from oneself despite oneself has meaning only as a being torn from the complacency in oneself characteristic of enjoyment, snatching the bread from one's mouth. Only a subject that eats can be for-the-other, or can signify" (OTB 74 [93]).

And two paragraphs later: "The immediacy of the sensible is the immediacy of enjoyment and its frustration. It is the gift painfully torn up, and in the tearing up, immediately spoiling this very enjoyment. It is not a gift of the heart, but of the bread from one's mouth, of one's own mouthful of bread. . . . The proximity of the other is the immediate opening up for the other the immediacy of enjoyment, the immediacy of taste, materialization of matter, altered by the immediacy of contact."

15. "The Other qua Other is situated in a dimension of height and of abasement—glorious abasement; he has the face of the poor, the stranger, the widow, and the orphan, and, at the same time, of the master called to invest and justify my freedom." And my response to the other, as desire, similarly reflects this double sense of the curvature of intersubjective space: "In *Desire* are conjoined the movements unto the Height and unto the Humility of the Other" (TI 200 [174]).

16. "Identification is kerygmatical. The said is not simply a sign or an expression of a meaning; it proclaims and establishes this as that. The surplus of this 'spontaneity' over the reflection which, in its reflection, thought involves, is not accurately suggested by the notion of *action* which is customarily opposed to the pure receptivity of the sensible. This surplus, situated between passivity and activity, is in the language that enters into a *hearsay,* an *already said,* a doxa, without which the identifying, naming language would not have been able to approach the sensible. In the doxa, the *already said,* tale, epos, the given is held in its theme" (OTB 35–36 [45–46]).

17. "The work of language [in opposition to disclosure] is entirely different: it consists in entering into relationship with a nudity disengaged from every form, but having meaning by itself, *kath'auto,* signifying before we have projected light upon it, appearing not as a privation on the ground of an ambivalence of values (as good or evil, as beautiful or ugly), but as an *always positive value.* Such a nudity is the face" (TI 74 [47]). Levinas's own emphasis here suits our point well.

18. "In distinguishing between the objectifying act and the metaphysical we are on our way not to the denunciation of intellectualism but to its very strict development—if it is true that the intellect desires being in itself" (TI 109 [81]).

19. Is Levinas not making a similar point later on when he writes: "When the subject commits itself in the order it contemplates, the truth of the significations it reads there is compromised. There is lacking the distance which guarantees that the spectacle not be troubled by the look itself" (OTB 190 [65])? Might I, a participant in the structures that I meditate upon as if from the outside, by means of my unacknowledged—un- or subconscious—desires, be the evil genius myself? Per-

haps one need not take at the letter Descartes's metaphorical extremes to take seriously the always possible evil genius, and the challenge to "the evidence of truth" that he poses.

20. Levinas rejects Descartes's starting point or principle for certainty, the *cogito* (which was also, in modified form, the principle, or principle of principles, for Husserl, the absoluteness of consciousness as consciousness of something: *cogito*-x), by claiming that Descartes did not allow his doubt to go far, or deeply, enough. For while, certainly, the *cogito* when doubted yields a *cogito* once again (the *cogito* that cannot doubt that it is doubting the doubting of the *cogito*), this does not guarantee that the *cogito* being affirmed in the doubting of the *cogito* is the same *cogito* that is being doubted, and that each subsequent *cogito* cannot in its turn also be doubted: "The truth of the second negation, then, is affirmed at a still deeper level—but, once again, one not impervious to negation." While, according to Levinas, "the distance traversed each time is not the same," that which saves Descartes from "purely and simply a Sisyphean labor [in this] movement of descent toward an ever more profound abyss which we elsewhere have called *there is,*" Descartes nevertheless "enters into a work of infinite negation . . . enters into a movement unto the abyss, vertiginously sweeping along the subject incapable of stopping itself" (TI 93 [65–66]). For Levinas, and according to Levinas for Descartes too, the "halting" of such recurrent doubt is only accomplished with the Third of Descartes's *Meditations*—which for Levinas is necessary to underwrite the first—when God (the Other in Cartesian terminology, according to Levinas) guarantees the *cogito* by providing it with a principle that comes to it from the outside—the idea of the Infinite: "But to possess the idea of infinity is to have already welcomed the Other" (TI 93 [66]).

21. This is why we cannot concur with Manning's view, in his *Interpreting Otherwise Than Heidegger* (see especially his chapter 3 on this point), that the ethical remains a function of the question of being for Levinas, even if it may have been prior to 1947. Ethical truth, for Levinas, makes even the truth of Being, the meaning of Being, possible, insofar as this ontological truth, be it of a fundamental ontology, is true or meaningful only in my saying it to an other—and as such is already founded in an ethical gesture (see Robert John Sheffler Manning, *Interpreting Otherwise Than Heidegger: Emmanuel Levinas's Ethics as First Philosophy* [Pittsburgh: Duquesne University Press, 1993]).

22. This "attendance" to his manifestation is what distinguishes the nonmanifestation of the other from the nonmanifestation of the evil genius, what permits the investment of truth to overcome the "anarchy of facts."

23. "Discourse conditions thought, for the first intelligible is not a concept, but an intelligence whose inviolable exteriority the face states in uttering the 'you shall not commit murder' " (TI 216 [191]).

24. And we shall argue later that the "fact" of this aspiration already testifies to the other as always already interior to my enjoyment itself.

25. Clearly, here, "being" must be interpreted as the pure, prereflective existence of enjoyment, rather than the structured, economic *ontos* of ontology, for "being" in this latter sense, for its very constitution, already presupposes a *logos*-directed, intersubjective concern for truth.

26. This tracing of the phrase to Hugo we have found in Theodore de Boer, "An Ethical Transcendental Philosophy," *Face to Face with Levinas,* p. 93.

27. "We think that existence *for itself* is not the ultimate meaning of knowing [as Levinas argues it is for the tradition], but rather the putting back into question of the self, the turning back to what is prior to oneself, in the presence of the Other. The presence of the Other, a privileged heteronomy, does not clash with freedom but invests it. The shame for oneself, the presence of and desire for the other are not the negation of knowing: knowing is their very articulation. The essence of reason consists not in securing for man a foundation and powers, but in calling him in question and in inviting him to justice" (TI 88 [60–61]).

28. "Theory, in which truth arises, is the attitude of a being that distrusts itself. Knowing becomes knowing of a fact only if it is at the same time critical, if it puts itself in question, goes back beyond its origin—in an unnatural movement to seek higher than one's own origin, a movement which evinces or describes a created freedom" (TI 82–83 [54]). Here Levinas is at his most un-Nietzschean: what is height for Levinas (the distrust of one's self) is base for Nietzsche, a movement that for Levinas leads to the truth of theory, and for Nietzsche to the decadence that is both religion and philosophy.

29. "If freedom were posited outside of this relation, every relation within multiplicity would enact but the *grasp* of one being by another or their common participation in reason, where no being looks at the face of the other, but all beings negate one another. Knowledge or violence would appear in the midst of the multiplicity as events that realize being. The common knowledge proceeds toward unity, either toward the apparition in the midst of a multiplicity of beings of a rational system in which these beings would be but objects, and in which they would find their being—or toward the brutal conquest of beings outside of every system by violence" (TI 302 [278–79]).

30. "The apology demands a judgment . . . in order to obtain justice.

. . . The will . . . seeks to place itself under a judgment, and to receive the truth from it upon its own witness" (TI 240 [217–18]).

31. "If, in contradistinction to the tradition of the primacy of freedom, taken as the measure of being, we contest vision its primacy in being, and contest the pretension of human emprise to gain access to the rank of *logos,* we take leave neither of rationalism, nor of the ideal of freedom. One is not an irrationalist nor a mystic nor a pragmatist for questioning the identification of power and *logos.* One is not against freedom if one seeks for it a justification. Reason and freedom seem to us to be founded on prior structures of being whose first articulations are delineated by the metaphysical movement, or respect, or justice—identical to truth. The terms of the conception making truth rest on freedom must be reversed" (TI 302–3 [279]).

32. Later, in chapter 6, this "ever and again" will be unfolded as "the eternal."

33. "If proximity ordered to me only the other alone, there would not have been any problem, in even the most general sense of the term. A question would not have been born, nor consciousness, nor self-consciousness. The responsibility for the other is an immediacy antecedent to questions, it is proximity. It is troubled and becomes a problem when a third party enters" (OTB 157 [200]).

34. "There is a betrayal of my anarchic relation with illeity, but also a new relationship with it: it is only thanks to God [grâce à dieu] that, as a subject incomparable with the other, I am approached as an other by the others, that is 'for myself.' 'Thanks to God' I am another for the others" (OTB 158 [201]).

35. The "personal" animates, for Levinas, ethics, and thus philosophy itself. Ethics is, for Levinas, a response to a person, and as such requires a personal response. Consequently, Levinas is "Against the Philosophy of the Neuter" (TI 298–99 [274]). It is the personal, we would argue, that permits Levinas to maintain the distinctions (despite the philosophical difficulties involved) between the *third* person and the neutral *third* term, and ultimately between *Ill*eity and the "il *y a.*"

36. "The ethical, beyond vision and certitude, delineates the structure of exteriority as such. Morality is not a branch of philosophy, but first philosophy" (TI 304 [281]).

37. "It is not that the entry of the third party would be an empirical fact, and that my responsibility for the other finds itself constrained to a calculus by the 'force of things.' In the proximity of the other, all the others than the other obsess me, and already this obsession cries out for justice, demands measure and knowing, is consciousness" (OTB 158 [201]).

38. And this is why the "if" of "If proximity ordered me to the other alone . . ." (see note 33 above) is precisely a hypothetical, delineates a structure that, while necessary to explicate the "real," is itself not real, *is* not: "Everything that takes place here [that is, in the consideration of the things of "mine" that the other makes a claim upon] 'between us' concerns everyone, the face that looks at it places itself in the full light of the public order, even if I draw back from it to seek with the interlocutor the complicity of a private relation and a clandestinity" (TI 212 [187]).

39. "The primordial positivity of enjoyment, perfectly innocent, is opposed to nothing and in this sense suffices to itself from the first. An instant or a standstill, it is the success of the *carpe diem,* the sovereignty of the 'after us the deluge.' These pretensions would be pure nonsense and not eternal temptations could not enjoyment tear itself absolutely from the disintegration characteristic of duration" (TI 145 [119]).

40. It is certain that I "need" other persons, with whom to work, to befriend, with whom to fall in love, with whom to relieve my loneliness, with whom to share enjoyments in order to make them whole, that is, that other persons are integral to the fulfillment of my needs as needs, are an integral part of my egoistic need structure. The other *as other,* on the contrary, does not correlate to my needs but disturbs my egoistic need structure by introducing shame into my neediness, is "desired" not for what he can do for me, but for what I can do for him.

41. This notion is perhaps even more important to *Otherwise Than Being:* "*Se passer*—to come to pass—is for us a precious expression in which the self figures [se dessine] as in a past that bypasses itself [qui *se* passe], as in aging [la sénescence] without 'active synthesis' " (OTB 14 [18]).

42. Time as the other, the time of the other, is thematized as an unanticipatable future in *Totality and Infinity,* and as an irrecuperable past in *Otherwise Than Being.* For an exposition of these thematizations, see Manning's *Interpreting Otherwise Than Heidegger,* chapter 2. We will undertake our own analyses of these, and other, temporal structures according to Levinas in chapter 6.

43. "Possession is accomplished in taking-possession or labor, the destiny of the hand. The hand is the organ of grasping and taking, the first and blind grasping in the teeming mass: it relates to me, to my egoist ends, things drawn from the element, which, beginningless and endless, bathes and inundates the separated being" (TI 159 [132]).

44. "The recollection necessary for nature to be able to be represented and worked over, for it to first take form as a world, is accomplished as the home" (TI 152 [125]).

45. Levinas adds, interestingly (for it helps us to situate Levinas's thought in relation to Buber's), that "The I-Thou in which Buber sees the category of the interhuman relationship is the relation not with the interlocutor but with feminine alterity."

46. This suggestion is sure to meet with some resistance, especially given the descriptions of "the feminine" in the analyses of the structures "Beyond the Face" found later in *Totality and Infinity*. There the feminine is described in terms of "the beloved," an "extreme frailty," or "vulnerability," where love "aims at him in his frailty [faiblesse]" (TI 256 [233]), as a "virginity, forever inviolate," "essentially violable and inviolable," (TI 258 [236]), where the feminine is "the simultaneity or the equivocation of this fragility and this weight of non-signifyingness," (TI 257 [234]), and where "the beloved, returned to the stage of infancy without responsibility—this coquettish head, this youth, this pure life 'a bit silly'—has quit her status as a person" to be played with "as with a young animal" (TI 263 [241]). Here the identification of "the feminine" with the *amante* (although the pronouns used there of the loved one are most often masculine—which at least keeps this structure from being directly identified with "woman" biologically qualified) seems straightforward. But it is not unusual, or such is our argument, for Levinas to describe different modalities of one and the same structure or term. Is the use of the term "other" to describe both the feminine other and the other as face a term that describes a similarity between two very distinct others, or do the feminine and the face describe different modalities of one and the same other? We are here attempting to develop a reading that answers affirmatively to the second of these interpretive options, and we shall attempt to gather textual evidence for such as we proceed. Indeed, the other, qua face, is alternately described as my master and, across structures we shall investigate, my equal, exposing different modalities of the other that few (if any) readers would dispute were modalities of one and the same other. We would argue that the same possibilities for delineating diverse modalities exist also for the feminine. What, on our reading, holds these modalities together, that makes them modalities of the same structure, is Levinas's consistent correlation of the descriptive term "feminine" with "the regime of the tender," and what distinguishes the diverse modalities of the feminine is its diverse functions within this regime. Thus, on our reading, the (motherly) feminine that welcomes me into the home, that protects my fragility, as the mediatresse of the "gentleness that spreads over the face of things," is the one who brings the regime of the tender to me, whereas the (wifely, lover) feminine, the eternal virgin, the one who demands my protection in her fragility, is the one who demands of me that I mediate to her the

regime of the tender (or that, in the couple, the "dual egoism" (TI 266 [244]), shares this regime with me (TI 265 [243])). So while nothing prohibits, and much recommends, that the other qua feminine and the other qua face are one and the same other (in different, if concurrent, modalities: "Equivocation constitutes the epiphany of the feminine—at the same time interlocutor, collaborator and master superiorly intelligent . . . and woman having to be treated as a woman"; TI 264 [241]), and nothing prohibits the other qua face and the other qua equal from being one and the same other (in different, if concurrent, modalities), so nothing prohibits the feminine other qua maternal and the feminine other qua lover from being one and the same feminine other (in different, if concurrent, modalities).

47. We are hesitant to endorse any reading of "Levinas as sexist" on this basis, a reading offered by certain feminists (and others, such as Derrida, who sees Levinas as emphasizing ethical difference at the expense of sexual difference in "At This Very Moment in This Work Here I Am," in *Re-reading Levinas*) from the time of Simone de Beauvoir to the present. We are hesitant to make this charge (though not altogether closed to the possibility that it could or even should be made—as Levinas himself would want his work to be called into question by his other, in which he would see, as we have recounted, its only hope of being "true") not only because there are also sympathetic feminist readings of Levinas, and because the problem of gender essentialism still persists in feminist thought itself (thirty-five years after the publication of *Totality and Infinity*), but above all because that which is at issue in these descriptions, that bear feminine names, or the name of the feminine, are not at all degraded or reserved for those of the empirical feminine sex. So while one might be tempted to conclude that the feminine other of *Totality and Infinity,* as "discrete," as "silent," lacks the fully human (male?) voice of the other that speaks to me and calls me into ethical question (and the pronouns designating the other coming from an ethical height and that speaks to me *are* consistently masculine ones), this feminine other (as we shall shortly see) "includes all the possibilities of the transcendent relationship with the Other" (TI 155 [129]) that does come from an ethical height, and is thus not (or so we shall argue) a less than fully human other, but the other—of either empirical gender—in the *mode* of the feminine. It is, moreover, difficult to take the feminine as less than fully human when one of the most powerful metaphors that Levinas employs to describe the very humanity of the self, in *Otherwise Than Being or Beyond Essence,* is "maternity," the self as sensible vulnerability to the other in the same for whom it is responsible, as "bearing [responsibility] par excellence" (OTB 75 [95]). Indeed, the

subject, even in *Totality and Infinity,* at its deepest level, precisely plays the role with respect to the other that the feminine here plays with respect to the egoism—as welcoming it into the home: "The subject is a host" (TI 299 [276]). Far from being less than fully human, the feminine here, as "maternity," as "host," is humanity itself.

48. Even, perhaps, from before the womb, if, as the analyses of the "Beyond the Face" in *Totality and Infinity* indicate, the "son" is already an always nonpresent future in the very caress of lovers.

49. And this, we shall later argue, is why Levinas claims that the arrival of the third is not an empirical event.

50. And, to anticipate, is it not this same "grace of God" that I am defined as being to the other in the figure of the self as "maternity" (the other in the same) that is central to the analyses of *Otherwise Than Being*: Me voici, au nom de dieu? We shall develop this thesis as we proceed.

51. This quotation continues: "but also capable of welcoming this face of infinity with all the resources of its egoism: economically."

52. Levinas characterizes this unquestioned allegiance to one's own justified freedom, taking here the voice of the tradition, in the following phrase: "If I could have freely chosen my own existence everything would be justified" (TI 83 [55]).

53. "An order common to the interlocutors is established by the positive act of the one *giving* the world, his possession, to the other, or by the positive act of the one justifying himself in his freedom before the other, that is, by apology" (TI 252 [229]).

54. "The other is maintained and confirmed in his heterogeneity as soon as one calls upon him, be it only to say to him that one cannot speak to him, to classify him as sick, to announce to him his death sentence; at the same time as grasped, wounded, outraged, he is 'respected' " (TI 69 [41]).

55. "Rhetoric . . . approaches the other not to face him, but obliquely—not, to be sure, as a thing, *since rhetoric remains conversation,* and across all its artifices goes unto the Other, solicits his yes. But the specific nature of rhetoric (of propaganda, flattery, diplomacy, etc.) consists in corrupting this freedom" (TI 70 [42], emphasis ours).

56. "The 'communication' of ideas, the reciprocity of dialogue, already hide the profound essence of language. It resides in the irreversibility of the relation between me and the other, in the Mastery of the Master coinciding with his position as other and as exterior. For language can be spoken only if the interlocutor is the commencement of his discourse, if, consequently, he remains beyond the system, if he is not *on the same plane* as myself. The interlocutor is not a Thou, he is a You; he reveals himself in lordship" (TI 101 [75]).

57. We shall have to say more on Levinas's idea of subjectivity in our chapters 4 and 5.

58. This violence and contradiction remain a temptation for us, at least in part, one would think, due to what Levinas refers to as the "hypocrisy" of "a world attached to both the philosophers and the prophets" (TI 24 [XII]).

59. Indeed, for Levinas, "what counts" for phenomenology "is the idea of the overflowing of objective thought by a *forgotten* experience from which it lives" (TI 28 [XVII], emphasis ours). We shall trace in chapter 7 the status of this re-membering description, this "phenomenology," and argue that since it cannot take the form of an a priori, objective truth without contradicting its own claim that the objective is only in the gift made to the other, it is rather best taken as a testimony, as a prophetic appeal made to an other, a pacific offering of a vision of peace that seeks from the other an investiture.

60. "In this welcoming of the face (which is already my responsibility in his regard, and where accordingly he approaches me from a dimension of height and dominates me), equality is founded. Equality is produced where the other commands the same and reveals himself to the same in responsibility; otherwise it is but an abstract idea and a word" (TI 214 [189]).

61. This condition is here stated not as a general rule, as an appeal to an "us"—for this these analyses themselves would seem to call into question—but in terms of "I." To what extent this condition can be stated as a general rule, that is, as a condition for anyone wishing to find the condition for engendering an interparadigmatic dialogue, will have to be discussed at some length. Can such a statement be taken as more than a statement of my own recognition of a personal, nongeneralizable obligation? We shall argue that such a claim, indeed, the discourse of Levinas as a whole, is justified only to the extent that it, and its statement of conditions such as this, in the end, be taken as "prophetic" rather than legislative. We will examine the possibility and status of such a prophetic voice in our chapter 7.

62. While this suggestion might well help me to engender a pacific interparadigmatic dialogue (or at least give it a chance) with the other insofar as I am one of the parties involved in the dialogue (and thus can offer what is mine to the other as gift), it does not help to engender a dialogue in a situation where I am called to play the role of mediator between others, since to demand the kind of giving of an other or of the others that I can demand of myself is, in Levinas's words, "to preach human sacrifice" (OTB 126 [162]), and we hope to have said enough to this point to show why this would be the case. We believe that Levinas's

discourse does have something to say about how I might proceed in such a mediatory task, but this can only be elaborated after we have examined (again, in our chapter 7) the status of Levinas's own discourse as "prophetic," and we shall therefore have to attempt to address it in our chapter 8.

PART II
The Possible Impossibility

INTRODUCTION TO PART II

I. Conditions of possibility and impossibility

In the previous chapter, we argued, following Levinas, that the condition of possibility of dialogue (of any dialogue, although our particular interest is in the possibility of interparadigmatic dialogue) is discourse—a non-allergic, ethical relationship with alterity (re)productive[1] of a meaning capable of founding communal meaning. In this second part of our work we shall put forth the thesis that the idea of discourse itself is well described as *a possible impossibility*. In order to work toward this thesis, in order to justify our recourse to this peculiar and at least seemingly oxymoronic description—and keeping to the transcendental-phenomenological language that we are (for reasons that will be clarified)[2] here employing—we will need, therefore, to delineate both the *conditions of possibility* of discourse (which we have already argued is itself the condition of possibility of dialogue) and the *conditions of impossibility* of discourse, and to lay out the interrelationships Levinas perceives between these diverse sets of conditions, or, to put it in terms whose meanings will emerge, to lay out the diverse modalities of language that articulate these conditions qua conditions. We will attempt to accomplish this by turning our attentions from a primary concentration on the analyses and vocabulary of Levinas's *Totality and Infinity* (1961) and to the more mature and more linguistically nuanced (that is, more nuanced both in its analyses of language and in its own use of language) analyses of his later *Otherwise Than Being or Beyond Essence* (1974). What will occupy us predominantly here will be Levinas's description of what might be thought of as two aspects, or modalities, of language, and that he refers to as "the saying" (*le dire*) and the "the said" (*le dit*). Our thesis for this part of our work will be that "the saying" (which in its deepest articulation will be revealed as my "substitution" or "expiation" for the other) does indeed provide us with a description of the condition of possibility for discourse (even if, in *Otherwise Than Being,* the term "discourse" in this technical sense—of a non-allergic, ethical relationship with alterity—will, for reasons that will emerge shortly, be eclipsed), and that "the said" (which will be revealed as the ontological regime of language, that is, a system of signifiers in the milieu of which monstration, as the exhibition of being, is "performed") will—as a noncontingent or necessary linguistic ancillary to the saying—provide us with a description of the conditions of impossibility of discourse, that is, with a description of a regime in terms of which discourse qua discourse would be precisely impossible. But this thesis, introduced in this opening paragraph still far too abstractly, is yet a long way off, on the other side of several analyses needed to explain and support it.

We shall proceed with these analyses by, first of all, providing under the rubric "From 'discourse' to 'the saying' " a brief account of Levinas's own perception of the transition and continuity between the works from which and to which we now turn—*Totality and Infinity* and *Otherwise Than Being*—in order to justify our reading of the latter work as a continuation and deepening of the project begun in the former, and thereby to illustrate the continuity between our foregoing and present theses. We shall then turn, in chapter 4, to an analysis of Levinas's descriptions of "The Two Aspects of Language: 'The Saying' and 'the Said,' " before proceeding with a description of their interrelationship in chapter 5, "The Two Directions in Language: The Reductive and the Re-constructive." It is across this interrelationship, at the point of crossing or intersection of these two aspects of language, the saying and the said (articulating respectively, we shall argue, the conditions of possibility and impossibility of discourse), that discourse will be revealed as a possible impossibility. We shall then proceed, in chapter 6, "The Moment of Responsibility: Time and Eternity," to refine the preceding analyses—across a study of Levinas's analyses of time—by bringing to this point of intersection, to the designation of the possible impossibility, a temporal articulation, which we shall argue Levinas himself does with his phrase "in this very moment." The implications of this notion of the possible impossibility for our understanding of and hope for dialogue as a means toward the promotion of peace—the motivating concern of this study—while implicit throughout these chapters, will be discussed more directly in our concluding chapter, "The Im/possibility of Peace."

II. From "Discourse" to "the Saying"

The meaning of the difference between the analyses of Levinas's 1961 *Totality and Infinity* (upon which we have predominantly focused so far) and those of his 1974 *Otherwise Than Being or Beyond Essence* (to the analyses of which we now turn) can be, and has been, interpreted in any number of ways, according to a vast array of differing criteria.[3] We shall begin our own discussion of this issue by grounding our comments in what Levinas himself has to say about the transition between these texts in his 1987 preface to the German edition of *Totality and Infinity*[4] in order to provide some context for the change (which we shall read as an evolution) in problematics (and thereby vocabulary) that our own analyses will undergo as we follow Levinas from the analyses of the earlier work to those of the later (ones).[5] In addition to the general remark that "Certains thèmes du premier ouvrage sont repris ou renouvelés ou reviennent sous d'autres formes dans les deux derniers; certaines intentions y sont précisées," Levinas adds "deux points pour éviter les malentendus":[6]

> *Autrement qu'être ou au-delà de l'essence* évite déjà le langage ontologique—ou, plus exactement, éidétique—auquel *Totalité et Infini* ne cesse de recourir pour éviter que ses analyses mettant en question le *conatus essendi* de l'être ne passent pour reposer sur l'empirisme d'une psychologie. Le statut de nécessité de ces analyses reste, certes, à déterminer malgré son analogie avec celui de l'essentiel.—Il n'y a, d'autre part, aucune différence terminologique dans *Totalité et Infini* entre miséricorde ou charité, source d'un droit d'autrui passant avant le mien, d'une part, et la justice, d'autre part, où le droit d'autrui—mais obtenu après enquête et jugement—s'impose avant celui du tiers. La notion éthique générale de justice est évoquée dans les deux situations indifféremment. ("PEA" I, II)[7]

But what is perhaps of greatest interest for our purposes in this brief preface is Levinas's assertion, in correlation with the passages quoted, that "*Totalité et Infini—essai sur l'extériorité,* paru en

1961, ouvre un discours philosophique que prolongeaient *Autrement qu'être ou au-delà de l'essence,* en 1974, et *De Dieu qui vient à l'idée* en 1982. . . . Pour la teneur de ce discours ouvert il y a vingt-cinq ans et qui est un tout, ce sont des variations non contingentes et sans doute instructives, mais dont on ne saurait faire état dans les raccourcis d'une préface" ("PEA" I).[8] That is to say that for Levinas himself, at least, the two works, indeed the three, despite the variations, are of a piece, at least insofar as they are part of one and the same discourse, one and the same project, sustained over the course of a quarter of a century. We therefore reject any thesis that would read *Otherwise Than Being* with respect to *Totality and Infinity* as representing any kind of radical discontinuity, or *Kehre,*[9] in the thought of Levinas to the extent that this would imply a turning that would set Levinas off in a new direction. For while there are certainly "strategic" and "orientational" and "methodological" differences between the two works (and these differences are not without important philosophical implications),[10] that which undergoes a "turn" here is not, we would maintain, Levinas's general philosophical orientation, his project, but the "object" of his analyses after the sense of adumbrational theory where the same "subject matter" is approached, like in the unfolding of a perceptual series, from a different side, and where earlier analyses are augmented and refined, even "corrected" (in the sense of having been filled out in perhaps unexpected ways), by the later ("*repris,*" "*renouvelés,*" "*reviennent sur d'autre formes,*" "*précisés*"). Our exegetical strategy, that is to say, is to read the two works—at Levinas's prompting—as basically continuous,[11] or, more exactly, to read the later as a narrowing of focus that serves to fill out the analyses of the earlier work by providing an explication of some of the structures that there functioned less explicitly, and we are hopeful of supplying, in the course of this reading, textual and conceptual materials that will enrich such a reading.[12]

Our "synoptic" reading of these two texts will therefore proceed on the following theses: whereas *Totality and Infinity* describes the two modalities (precisely: totality and infinity) in terms of which the same (the subject and all that falls within the purview of its "immanence") relates to the other (the "transcendent"), describing in turn the relation (section I, "The Same and the

Other"), the same (section II, "Interiority and Economy"), and the face of the other (section III, "Exteriority and the Face"),[13] *Otherwise Than Being* undertakes to provide a description of the subjectivity of the subject (the "underside"—which will turn out to be the condition of possibility—of the immanent same) in a progressively deepening way (from intentionality to sensibility, to proximity as the meaning of sensibility, to substitution at the basis of proximity, and as the relation between the subject and the Infinite)[14] on its way to disengaging the subjectivity of the subject as "otherwise than being or beyond essence" (OTB 19 [23]); whereas *Totality and Infinity* focused on the *approach of the other* in the face, disrupting the same by evoking responsibility, *Otherwise Than Being* will focus on *my approach to the other* out of a pre-original responsibility (where the other has always already approached);[15] whereas *Totality and Infinity* begins with the ego in the present being interrupted by the face calling it to a responsible future, the possibility of this call affecting the ego is traced, in *Otherwise Than Being*, to a deep past in which the ego is already implicated.[16]

Along these lines, then, whereas Levinas in *Totality and Infinity* defines "discourse" as the non-allergic, ethical relationship with alterity (that must, to be sure, on ethical grounds, be taken up unilaterally by the same) productive of a meaning capable of founding communal meaning, he describes this relationship *as if* from other than the subjective perspective (and, as we have seen, he tells us why: in order to avoid an "empiricistic/psychologistic" reading of this text), in *Otherwise Than Being* (undertaken as a description of the subjectivity of the subject) Levinas will speak of this same relationship (the non-allergic, ethical relationship with alterity) from the perspective of the subject, and will refer to it, from out of this perspective, as "the saying."[17] In a certain sense, then, the analyses of *Otherwise Than Being* might be taken to play out in a more consistent way than *Totality and Infinity* one of the central theses of *Totality and Infinity* itself: "the radical impossibility of seeing oneself from the outside and of speaking in the same sense of oneself and of the others" (TI 53 [24]).[18]

Yet, if Levinas in *Otherwise Than Being* no longer employs the term "discourse" in the technical sense that it has in the text of *Totality and Infinity*,[19] is it not strange that we would attempt to read this term through the later text, or this later text as elaborating upon the term that it no longer employs? The initial strangeness of reading the structures of "the saying" and "the said" in the later text as respectively the delineation of the conditions of possibility and impossibility of "discourse" (as this term functions in the earlier) requires a reading in which the contiguity of the two texts is maintained, and maintained in something like the manner described in this section. The plausibility or lack thereof, the fruitfulness or lack thereof, of this approach, will have to be proven as part II proceeds.[20]

Notes

1. One of the functions of part II of this work will be to argue that this "productive" is, after the analyses of *Otherwise Than Being,* more precisely read as "re-productive," in a sense that will have to emerge.

2. For an analysis of Levinas's philosophical method, see chapter 7.

3. For instance, Robert John Sheffler Manning (in his *Interpreting Otherwise Than Heidegger,* p. 61) sees a difference in the temporal ecstasis that each of these works focuses upon: "In his very earliest works, and especially in *Existence and Existents,* he [Levinas] interprets the present. In his middle and more mature period, initiated by *Time and the Other* and culminating in *Totality and Infinity,* he analyzes the future. Lastly, in his most recent works, especially in *Otherwise Than Being,* he is chiefly concerned with the past." Robert Gibbs claims that *Otherwise Than Being* "redevelops many of the analyses of *Totality and Infinity,* but with a narrower focus. Levinas explores the moment of encounter with an other, the moment of responsibility. He shifts away from ontological language and moves to a richer and more paradoxical vocabulary of super-phenomenological terms. Levinas seeks to describe the rending of consciousness that occurs when the other approaches me, and he has become more aware of the problematic nature of describing that event in any language" (Robert Gibbs, *Correlations in Levinas and Rosenzweig* [Princeton: Princeton University Press, 1992], p. 9). Adriaan Peperzak (in addition to suspecting that *Otherwise Than Being* is at least in part a response to Derrida's "Violence and Metaphysics"—a point argued more concretely by Robert Bernasconi in his "Skepticism in the Face of Philosophy" in *Re-reading Levinas,* pp. 149–61) makes the observation that *Otherwise Than Being* "states the problem of *Totality and Infinity* in a different manner and develops these problems from other perspec-

tives," and specifies that "In *Totality and Infinity,* the central place was taken by the Other and its visage; in *Otherwise Than Being,* Levinas meditates on the 'position' and the meaning of the subject; of the self who meets the other. . . . Whereas *Totality and Infinity* attempted, with Plato, to think beyond the totality of all beings and closed with eschatological questions, *Otherwise Than Being* goes back to a sort of (under)ground: it attempts to trace down the underlying 'fundament' and subject of the various relations it describes" (*To the Other,* pp. 209, 212). The length of such a collection of observations and theories could be multiplied many times over. I have chosen, largely at random, just a few.

4. This preface, in French, is reprinted in the "Livre de Poche" edition of *Totalité et Infini* (Dordrecht: Kluwer Academic, Marinus Nijhoff, 1971). Page references to this text will appear in our text indicated by "PEA" ("Préface à l'édition allemande").

5. Levinas is including in his remarks his 1982 *De Dieu qui vient à l'idée,* as we shall see shortly.

6. "Certain themes of the first work are taken up again or renewed or come back under different forms in the last two; certain intentions are there made more precise"; "two points to avoid misunderstandings."

7. "*Otherwise Than Being or Beyond Essence* already avoids the ontological—or, more precisely, eidetic—language to which *Totality and Infinity*—in order to avoid that its analyses, putting in question the *conatus essendi* of being, be taken as resting upon the empiricism of a psychology—does not cease to appeal. The necessary status of these analyses remains, certainly, to be determined, despite its analogy with that of the essential. There is, moreover, no terminological difference in *Totality and Infinity* between mercy and charity, source of a right of the other that has priority over mine, on the one hand, and justice, on the other hand, where the right of the other—but obtained after inquiry and judgment—imposes itself before that of the third. The general ethical notion of justice is evoked indifferently in either situation."

8. "*Totality and Infinity: Essay on Exteriority,* appearing in 1961, opened a philosophical discourse that would be continued in *Otherwise Than Being or Beyond Essence,* 1974, and *De Dieu qui vient à l'idée,* 1982. . . . For the content of this discourse opened twenty-five years ago and which is a whole, there are non-contingent and no doubt instructive variations, but of them we are not able to make an inventory in the summary of a preface."

9. If there is a *Kehre* in Levinas's thought, it comes, on our view, in 1947 (the publication date of a work written somewhat earlier), when Levinas announces his desire to leave the climate of Heidegger's

thought: "If at the beginning our reflections are in large measure inspired by the philosophy of Martin Heidegger, where we find the concept of ontology and of the relationship which man sustains with Being, they are also governed by a profound need to leave the climate of that philosophy, and by the conviction that we cannot leave it for a philosophy that would be pre-Heideggerian" (Emmanuel Levinas, *Existence and Existents,* p. 19). This also, however, must be qualified, for in 1935, in his article "On Evasion" ("De l'évasion"), Levinas already "asks how thinking can escape an all-penetrating dominion of Being" (Peperzak, *To the Other,* p. 12).

10. Indeed, as Levinas notes: "there are no details in architecture, according to Valéry's profound dictum, which is eminently valid for philosophical construction, where the details alone prevent the collapse" (OTB 129 [166]).

11. This does not mean that there might not be fruit to be picked in attempting to read the transition from *Totality and Infinity* to *Otherwise Than Being* as a turn of whatever sort, or that this could not be successfully done. Indeed, an author is not always the best interpreter of his or her own work, and Levinas's own evaluations of the relationship between these two texts (which themselves are of course always open to interpretation) can always be nuanced or even opposed.

12. It is our thesis—to use a contemporary analogy (that like all analogies can only be pushed so far)—that the text of *Otherwise Than Being* is the result of Levinas "double clicking" on the idea of "subjectivity" in *Totality and Infinity,* opening up a screen upon that which lies below and supports this idea as it appears in the earlier text. The previous "window" recedes from sight, from our focus, but that which it revealed continues to function as a part of the overall program. Our project in this part of our work, if you like, is to "double click" on the idea of "discourse" in *Totality and Infinity,* which we propose opens up upon the underlying screens, explicated in *Otherwise Than Being* as "the saying" and "the said."

13. We have yet to deal in this work with section IV, "Beyond the Face," even if some of the ideas that are at work in that section will come into play in the analyses of this chapter. Readers less familiar with the work of Levinas can find an analysis of this section (specifically, an analysis of the temporal structures therein exposed) in our chapter 6, section I, "From Simultaneity to Postponement."

14. This reading, wherein the text of *Otherwise Than Being* is read as an analysis of ever deepening structures of subjectivity—each being read as the condition of possibility of the former (which is the reading we are advocating)—is at once recognized and qualified by Adriaan Peperzak,

who cites in this regard not the listing from "The Itinerary" of *Otherwise Than Being* (which we have followed in our text), but two other descriptions of such a "deepening" in that book: "Sometimes Levinas announces a sequence that signifies a deepening, for example in OTB 184 [232], where he says that signification is analyzed as *proximity,* proximity as *responsibility* for the Other, responsibility as *substitution.* Precisely the same order of these three characteristics is found in OTB 182 [229], where the relation between them is indicated by the expression 'is only possible as' (ne se peut comme): 'The proximity of the Other . . . is possible only as responsibility for the Other, and responsibility is possible only as substitution for the Other.' " He then asks a question that raises a problem for the simple adoption of this program: "Is this a question of the relation between a reality and the conditions of its possibility? But *how* then does the one fit together into the other? Similar difficulties are presented by such formulations as 'a signification, which is possible only as embodiment (*incarnation*)' (OTB 69 [87]) and 'Only a subject which can eat can possibly be for the Other or signify' (OTB 76–77 [96–97]). In both cases, corporeity is 'deduced' from significance, which was previously described as a relation of the One-for-the-Other" (*To the Other,* pp. 219–20). The problem for Peperzak, it would seem, is that significance seems to be the condition of possibility for corporeity, and yet corporeity seems at once to be the condition of possibility for significance, which would throw any straightforward "deepening" schema into disarray. Peperzak then chalks up the "deepening" schema to Levinas's need for a philosophical architechtonic in order to make the thought—which exceeds any ontology—ontologically sensible, arguing that "[m]ost of the time, however, the various 'moments' are placed next to one another, seemingly without allowing a definite order among them" (*To the Other,* p. 220), and quotes Levinas in support of this: "The different concepts that come up in the attempt to state transcendence echo one another. The necessities of thematization in which they are said ordain a division into chapters, although the themes in which these concepts present themselves do not lend themselves to linear exposition, and cannot really be isolated from one another without projecting their shadows and their reflections on one another" (OTB 19 [23]). Briefly, our comments: (1) The fact that these concepts do not lend themselves to linear exposition (that they are inextricably interrelated) does not mean, necessarily, that there is not an "order" to them. (2) The quotation from Levinas warning against any straightforward division of these concepts immediately precedes one of his own statements of their ordering on a "deepening" schema (that of "The Itinerary"), and would thus seem to qualify rather than negate such a scheme. (3) Regarding Peperzak's earlier question/difficulty: It is not a strange thing for a condition of possibility to be "possible only" in and through that for which it is a condition, unless one believes in some or other version of Platonic forms. Having extension is a condition of possibility of physical objects, but there is no "having extension" outside of the objects so extended. We shall argue in what follows that "the good" and "justice" in Levinas follow precisely this model. That is, we are arguing that Peperzak's "seemingly" be taken perhaps more seriously than he would seem to take it himself.

15. We shall attempt to show that this focus was already implicitly present in *Totality and Infinity* in the analyses of the "the feminine."

16. We shall attempt to show, in chapter 6, how these divers temporal orientations come together in what Levinas refers to as "this very moment."

17. One is tempted to see any number of terms in *Otherwise Than Being* as the "replacement" for the "discourse" of *Totality and Infinity*, and chief among these perhaps "proximity." From our perspective and for our purposes, the most useful "substitute" is "the saying," as it is, like discourse, linguistically qualified, and thus more directly leads to an understanding of the production of ontological meaning, that is, to the production of the *logos* of *dia-logos*. Moreover, the saying, on our view, is the linguistically qualified term used to describe the whole sequence of sensibility, proximity, substitution, relation to Infinity, and so includes (or is a particular way of framing), all of these other "structures."

18. Does this mean that the analyses of *Otherwise Than Being* will be susceptible to a "psychologistic" reading, or that Levinas has ceased to concern himself with this? Indeed, by 1987, at least, Levinas was in a position to call into question the necessity of his anti-psychologistic emphases in *Totality and Infinity:* "The necessary status of these analyses remains, certainly, to be determined" ("PEA" II). But Levinas is clear that he does not intend, in *Otherwise Than Being*, to offer analyses of the subject that would be reducible to a psychological/naturalistic/empirical subject in the world. In speaking of proximity, for example, Levinas claims that this relationship that "throws me outside of the objectivity characteristic of relations . . . is not simply a passage to a subjective point of view" (OTB 82 [104]). That is, the "perspective of the subject" is not merely a "subjective perspective" because the perspective of the subject, indeed, the subject itself, is already founded in structures that precede it and make it possible. Its perspective "guards a trace" (to employ language whose meaning will emerge in the course of these next chapters) of the beyond of its subjective as psychological perspective.

19. When the term appears in the later text it is quite consistently

used in a manner that would link it to "the said" rather than to "the saying," in either the general sense of an ongoing conversation about something (e.g., "the discourse of science and philosophy" (OTB 160 [203]), "*the* [Western] philosophical discourse" (OTB 169 [215]), or to the active saying of the "said" of such a discourse ("the thematizing, the kerygmatic discourse"; OTB 160 [204]). In at least one place, however, the fact that every such "discourse" rests upon its being said to an other ("discourse qua discourse") shows that every discourse in the sense of conversation about something (the predominant sense of "discourse" in *Otherwise Than Being*) actually rests upon or goes back to discourse as an ethical relation with the other (the sense of "discourse" in *Totality and Infinity*): "This reference to an interlocutor permanently breaks through the text that the discourse claims to weave in thematizing and enveloping all things. In totalizing being, discourse qua discourse thus belies the very claim to totalize" (OTB 170 [217]). In this "qua discourse" the use of the word in *Otherwise Than Being* is borne back to, without being transformed into, its use in *Totality and Infinity.*

20. We thus set out in part II to accomplish three interrelated objectives: first, and primarily, to continue our investigation of the idea of discourse and the possibility of dialogue in Levinas as these ideas are deepened through the analyses of *Otherwise Than Being;* secondly and thirdly, and subordinately but to this end, to promote a reading of *Otherwise Than Being* that indicates its continuity with *Totality and Infinity,* and to continue (now in a more concerted and explicit manner) our arguments for a "transcendental" reading of Levinas, these latter two objectives making way for our reading of *Otherwise Than Being* as delineating the conditions of im/possibility for the relationship of discourse as this term is employed in *Totality and Infinity.*

4

The Two Aspects of Language: The Saying and the Said

I. Language As the Said

Let us begin our analysis of the saying and the said by analyzing a linguistic event, an event central to the possibility of dialogue, and attempting to sort out, on a Levinasian reading, the modes of meaning operative in it. *I say something to an other.* We propose that what Levinas refers to as "the saying" will come to the fore when we analyze the conditions of possibility for the "*I say* something *to an other*" aspect of the event, and "the said" in the aspect highlighted by the conditions of possibility for the "I say *something* to another," even as it is stressed that we are speaking all along of one and the same linguistic event.

So if "the said" has to do with the fact that in speaking to an other I am thereby—whether implicitly or explicitly—making reference to "something" (to a being [an entity], or the essence of a being insofar as it can be nominalized, or to an interrelated cluster of entities [up to, and perhaps always at least implicitly including, "being" as a whole], or an event, an action of—or a relationship between—beings, be that the generality of "eventfulness" [up to and including the "being of beings" or "essence"]) that can be identified by an other as the "subject matter" of my/our speaking, how are we to account for this possibility? What makes this shared reference to common "somethings" (and thus speech as the saying of *something* to someone) possible?

A preparatory answer to this question has already been provided in the foregoing chapter where we focused upon Levinas's analyses, in *Totality and Infinity,* of the relationship of discourse to argue that it is this ethical relationship that is the condition of possibility for dialogue, an analysis that Levinas (we are arguing) does not abandon but deepens in his *Otherwise Than Being* (and deepens precisely [or such is our claim] by providing us [although this is perhaps not the primary focus or even intention of the work] with an account of the conditions of possibility, and the conditions of impossibility, of discourse itself). In those analyses the common entity, and thus the possibility of a subject matter for dialogue, was shown to derive its shared (ontological) sense insofar as it was detached from, torn out of, the element as my "economy" of *jouissance*, or my *jouissance* exercised economically, by the interruption of the face of the other—by the face that represents, or, better, that is, the need and vulnerability of the other that demands of me the giving of my goods, and where such goods become thereby objects of shared reference, around which and in terms of which is constituted an ancillary rational order, the *logos* of *dia-logos*.

But this analysis could be, prima facie, misleading—albeit only if Levinas's philosophical method (at least on our reading) is misunderstood, if the results of the "(radicalized-) phenomenological method"[1] he employs—the search for and description of conditions of possibility for . . . , the search for the "originary" (or, as we shall see, for the "*pre*-originary," if origins are already the stuff of an ontology derived from "deeper" structures)—are taken as genetic descriptions, that is, as an account of "origins." For I no more re-make language (as a system of interdependent signs, as a "positive" language)[2] each time that I encounter a new interlocutor than I actually "once upon a time" lived in a pure state of *jouissance*, interrupted only *later* by the face. Rather, I am always already social, en-cultur-ated (my *jouissance* always already interrupted by the face),[3] and to say *something* to an other is always already to make an appeal or reference to—indeed, to make an appeal or reference in terms of—the ontological meanings borne by, or that together constitute, a linguistic system. I say *something* to an other in English, or French, or Dutch, and to the extent that the said something is successfully communicative, to the extent that some meaning content is communicated, the appeal to a common positive language is presupposed. That is, in order for the saying of *something* to an other, the something said, to be meaningful, I need make appeal to meanings that transcend the particular speech situation in which I say something now to a particular other.[4] Ontological meanings, meanings that delineate beings and actions and their interrelationships, are, in other words, dependent for their meaningfulness qua communicative upon a certain universality (where universality means accessibility to anyone who would learn the language in terms of which these meanings are communicated), depend upon a sense that transcends the particular situation of my saying something to an other (for the language in which I speak, in all likelihood, and at least in some form, preceded my birth and will survive my death), depend upon a universality and transcendence that would appear to run at counter-current to the meaningfulness of my responsibility in the face of the singular other—the purported "origin" (according to the analyses of *Totality and Infinity*, and a claim that will be reaffirmed in *Otherwise Than Being*) of all ontological sense.

Levinas's analyses of "the saying" and "the said" in *Otherwise Than Being* are, on our reading, and among other things, an attempt to give an account of how, at once, my ethical relationship with the other, the "singular" other, *is* the basis of all meaningfulness, and the fact that I do not re-make language (in the sense already prescribed) each time I encounter a new interlocutor, but participate, even in my responsibility for the other in his or her singularity, in a "universal" system of meanings. That is, these analyses could be read as being Levinas's attempt to account for (while withholding unqualified affirmation of, as we saw in chapter 1) the truth *in* (rather than *of*) the Heideggerian claim (and accepted as valid by most of his philosophical progeny) that I do not so much speak language as language speaks me—*die Sprache spricht*—a doctrine that reaches its apogee, perhaps, in Heidegger's famous dictum that language is the house of Being. Levinas, we would argue, does not so much dispute this claim as he would add to it what is for him the essential caveat (a caveat to essence) that questions in and of Being—the distinction between being and nonbeing,[5] the distinction between Being and beings[6]—are not the most important, or even the most "fundamental," questions that one can ask. For a meaningful saying of *something* to an other *does* presuppose universality, *does* presuppose an appeal to a meaningful system of interrelated signs (whose very meaningfulness refers, as we shall see, to these interrelationships), to a positive language. We shall argue, then, that *one* of the meanings of Levinas's "le dit," one of the meanings constitutive of the regime delineated by this term, is precisely "a positive language," the said as system, a necessary, but not the only, aspect of language as experientially spoken.[7] But we will begin by tracing out another though related meaning of "the said" in *Otherwise Than Being,* one that is closer to our starting point, the analysis of "I say something to an other": the said as the identification of the this as this or this as that—the saying of *some-thing.*

I.1. The Said As Identificatory

The saying of *something,* the identification in speech of something that can be identified (analyzed in relative isolation from *my* saying of this something *to an other,* abstracted from that concrete situation [from which the abstraction qua abstraction abstracts—and thus implicitly, as we shall see, retains]), is the identification of a being as the same being through the passage of time. It is to identify a certain endurance, a however brief constancy (or, as especially in the case of "events," a certain capacity for re-evocation, a certain reiterability that constitutes the identical), that is made to stand out across the flow of experience. And this temporality, this flow of experience over against which the identification qua identification stands out, imposes itself upon thought, according to Levinas, in the very saying of a said.

For what is the saying of a said, the identification of a something, but a reference to something that *is,* namely, the exhibition of being? Can we (in our interest in the possibility of dialogue, and a dialogue not necessary—at least not explicitly—mediated by "philosophical" discourse) extrapolate to a more general theory of saying something (expression) from what Levinas says, in opening the exposition of *Otherwise Than Being,* about the philosophical saying of something? "A philosopher seeks, and expresses, truth. Truth, before characterizing a statement or a judgment, consists in the exhibition of being" (OTB 23 [29]). For if the philosopher, after this description (which will not be Levinas's final evaluation of the role of philosophy), majors in the expression of "truth" as first of all the exhibition of being, is not any and anyone's saying of something not equally, if perhaps less self-consciously, before statement or judgment,[8] the exhibition of being, or at least a statement or judgment (or whatever other mode of discourse) that presupposes the exhibition of being?[9] For the saying of something is always a saying of *something,* a more or less explicit reference to that which *is,* to the "real," to something that exists, even if it only exists as a "real" mental construct, for instance. And if we may be permitted this extrapolation, then we may further, perhaps, follow Levinas in asking: "But what shows itself, in truth, under the name of being? And who looks?" (OTB 23 [29]).

Let us leave aside for the moment the amphibology of being and entities (the fact that, in the very reference to "being," there is a question as to whether we are referring to a nominalized being-substance or the verbal being-essence of that being) that resounds already, Levinas informs us in what immediately follows upon the queries stated above, in the question of the "what?" of the exhibition of being (an amphibology that will impose itself upon our analyses as we proceed), and inquire, for the moment, after the "who looks?" To whom does being exhibit itself in exhibition? While other ways of approaching this question will emerge in the course of Levinas's analyses (and are implicit within these opening analyses themselves, as we shall see), Levinas contends that so long as this question is posed as an *ontological* question, the answer to the "who looks?" question of exhibition can only be: another being. Indeed, onto-logy, as the *logos of being,* inquires after the being of . . . , is the very privilege of the question "what?" "The question ['What shows itself (in truth)?'] enunciates a 'what?' 'what is it?' 'what is it that it is?' Concerning what is it wants to know *what* it is. The 'what?' is already wholly enveloped with being, has eyes only for being, and already sinks into being" (OTB 24 [30]).[10] The question of the "who?" of "who looks?" posed ontologically, then, not so much converts the question "who?" into a "what?" as it translates the "who?" as "what?"—it "has eyes only" for quiddity. Thus, "the question 'who is looking?' is also ontological" (OTB 27 [34]); exhibition is the showing of being to a being.

The exhibition of being, truth, ontologically considered, is thus the exhibition of being to a being, wherein, at one and the same time, "the manifestation of being to itself would imply a separation in being" (OTB 28 [36]), and where "[t]ruth is rediscovery, recall, reminiscence, reuniting under the unity of apperception" (OTB 29 [36]). But a question/problem is immediately posed when it is acknowledged that in order for exhibition to issue in truth, being must reveal itself *as it is* (for to show itself otherwise would be untruth), must show itself not partially, but fully.[11] And if the exhibition of being is to be full, if truth is to be true, one must therefore take into account, in the exhibition of being, the being of the being who looks, to whom being reveals itself in exhibition:

> It is then necessary, in order that truth come about, that in one way or another this ex-ception of inwardness be recuperated, that the exception enter under the rule, that within the being exposed be found the subject of knowledge, and the pulsation and respiration of the "soul" belong to or come back to being as a whole. Truth can consist only in the exposition of being to itself, in self-consciousness. The upsurge of a subjectivity, a soul, a "who," remains correlative with being, that is, simultaneous and one with it. The mutation of the exhibition into knowledge has to be interpretable as a certain inflexion of this exhibition. (OTB 28 [35])

Exhibition as the revelation of being must be inflexive (if it is to be true); exhibition must be the revelation of being to being, of being to itself. And when this observation is coupled with the not unrelated ontological doctrine of the unity (totality) of being, exhibition of being as truth (qua truth) comes down to the revelation of being (as a whole) to being (as a whole). The exhibition of being to itself, "truth," philosophy as ontology, when thought through, is, for Levinas, Hegelianism.[12]

But what are we to make of the break in being that is the separation of being from itself necessitating the recovery or mending that is truth? Why would being in its fullness separate itself from itself, exhibit itself to itself, rather than resting in the still silence of its integrality? For even if being is not consciousness per se (*Geist* as reality—as some in the tradition maintain), there is at least consciousness in being—by dint of human being. And even if we were to maintain that that is "just the way it is," that the separation within being and the recuperation that is truth is integral to being, that being is its manifestation, we may still wonder with Levinas why this self-revelation (enacted by way of human being) is a problem, or a question for human being, in what Levinas refers to as "the question of the question." "Why does research take the form of a question? How is it that the 'what?', already steeped in being so to open it up the more, becomes a demand and a prayer, a special language inserting into the 'communication' of the given an appeal for help, for aid addressed to another?" (OTB 24 [31]). Could it be that the question "what?" is not the only question required to account for quiddity? Could it be that being cannot answer for itself? Could it be that being could not even pose, for itself, the question? And are these questions not already implicitly answered in Levinas's claim, in *Totality and Infinity,* that "Without separation there would not have been truth; there would have been only being" (TI 60 [31])? Does the trace of what Levinas will call the "otherwise than being" impose itself upon us already? We shall have to give attention to these questions that here foreshadow another line of questioning. For the present, let us merely ask: what are we to make, within the purview of ontology, of this reflexive loop that is exhibition? Does it belong to being or is it the introduction of (or a recourse to) an outside?

On the one hand, it would appear that this inflexive loop would have to belong to being, for if truth is to be true, if it can leave nothing outside (as an outside would compromise the fullness of truth, and thus its very truthfulness), this inflexive loop as constitutive of the truth of being would have to be included in this truth, would have to constitute part of the being revealing itself to itself. Truth could be complete only (could only be true) in subsuming its own production, its own exhibition, to itself.

But, on the other hand, if the break in being were to be recuperated, if the separation of being from itself that permits of exhibition were to be subsumed into being as unified, if the inflexive loop were part of being itself, there would be no more exhibition and therefore no more truth as the exhibition of being. The completion, the fullness, of truth (the coincidence of being with itself) would be the end of truth (as exhibition, for exhibition requires a break in being from itself). The consummation of truth (the recovery of being's break from itself), would be the destruction of truth (as the "act" of this recovery). "But if exposition implies a partition of the totality of being, exposition cannot be completed without extinguishing itself" (OTB 29 [37]).[13] And if the act of revealing itself to itself were to be read as constitutive of being (that is, if the exhibition of being were taken as part and parcel of the being of being—as Levinas claims is the case for Heidegger), if exhibition were itself to be part of the truth, would we not require a further break in being—one that did not already belong to being—if this truth were to be true, lest the same dynamics (of staticity) be set off (or put to rest)? Indeed, for the truth of exhibition to itself be true, would not another break in being be necessary to exhibit this belonging, this truth, that in turn would have to be appropriated to the truth for the truth to be true, the truth of which would require another break in being, . . . ad infinitum?[14] That is, if truth is to be true, we would require a break in being—a separation of being from itself—that precisely is not yet (that is, at least "temporarily," at least for the "present"—and these "temporal" designations are most telling) recuperated, even as truth itself names this recuperation.[15] This break, this separation, is, Levinas tells us, time: "The manifestation cannot occur as a fulguration in which the totality of being shows itself to the totality of being, for this 'showing itself to' indicates a getting out of phase which is precisely time, that astonishing divergence of the identical from itself!" (OTB 28 [36]).

This time, this "astonishing divergence of the identical from itself" (OTB 28 [36]), this getting out of phase (*déphasage*) with itself of being, is to be distinguished, however, from the time of history, of physics, of everyday "common sense," or any "subjective"—or "lived"—time, as the condition of possibility for the "constitution" of these diverse temporalities.[16] Levinas describes this primordial "time," this pre-original "diastasis of the punctual, this lapse" (OTB 30 [38]) or "the temporalization of time," as "a modification without change" (OTB 34 [44]), as the vibration of being, where being reverberates in its verbality in the verb "to be," as "essence"—the active "be-ing" of being.[17] Levinas, moreover, discovers this *déphasage* in the very flow of sensation, arguing that it shows itself (as we above indicated that it would), though enigmatically, in the very saying of a said, by means of the amphibology of being and entities that indwells any said, in the exhibition of what "is." For in saying that something "is" (in making an at least implicit reference to its "being" in the saying of this *something* to an other), what am I saying about it? Am I identifying a substance-entity, a nominalized "thing" that in its substantiality *is* indifferent to the time through which it persists, or is the *is* a reference to the *manner of being* of the entity so identified as it vibrates in the temporalization of time, the being (where "being" is verbal, or adverbial) of this entity, its essence?[18] It is Levinas's claim that these senses—and, precisely, across the "is"[19]—interrelate, that they slide into one another as the flow of "being-essence" is gathered up (as we shall shortly see) into "substance-being," but a substance always on the edge of dissipating once again into the flow from which it was gathered, and upon which it is constituted. What counts here is that across the amphibology of being and entities—that accompanies the exhibition of being that is truth—the being of beings, or essence, reverberates, and reverberates as the reverberation that essence is, the modification without change that is the temporalization of time. It is this separation, this being out of phase, that will make possible the recuperations of truth, and thus Levinas refers to it as the "original light" or "openness" (OTB 30 [38]). And while this temporalization of time can itself be named (as it is here and in Levinas's discourse), can itself be gathered up into the truth of a recuperation, it is nevertheless the case that in order for that operation to be possible essence must first vibrate "beneath" the level of truth, as truth's condition of possibility, a vibration vibrating "beneath" the truth that would name the vibration, an "original light," as it were, in which the light of truth could be manifest. We shall pursue the "signification" of this "beneath" in short order, but first back to the problem of saying *something.*

The identification of an entity, the saying of a said (our saying *something* to someone) is precisely the recuperation of this break in being, a recuperation of time across time:

> Denomination designates or constitutes identities in the verbal flow of sensation. Through the opening that temporalization works in the sensible, disclosing it by its very passing, assembling it by retention and memory (an assembling that Kant caught sight of in the diverse synthesis of the imagination, before every idealization of the sensible), the word identifies "this *as* that," states the ideality of the same in the diverse. This identification is a supplying with

meaning: "this as that." In their meaning entities show themselves to be identical unities. (OTB 35 [44–45])

The identification of an entity, the saying of a said, the delineation of the *something* in our "I say something to an other," is thus the gathering of the flux of sensation, the gathering of the temporalization of time, into a present: the "some-thing" made present to consciousness, brought into a present that is the correlation between a consciousness and its intended correlate, an identification that is articulated in the structure of subject-object.

Levinas stresses two points regarding this identification of an entity. The first of these is that "[i]dentification is kerygmatical. The said is not simply a sign or an expression of a meaning; it proclaims and establishes this as that" (OTB 35 [45]); that is, it is in the very saying of the said that the identification of the entity occurs, and that the meaning that the identity bears qua identified, qua said, resides. The saying of the said is not a response to, a saying of, a meaning that the identity bore prior to its being said, and that the said would merely reflect or put into language, nor is the meaning an addendum to the thematization. Identity, thematization, and meaning, are of a piece: "The 'identical unities' are not given and thematized first, and then receive a meaning; they are given through this meaning" (OTB 35 [45]). The meaning of an entity is inseparable from its being said.

Secondly, claims Levinas: "Identification is understood [*s'entend,* italicized in the French text] on the basis of a mysterious schematism, of the already said [*un déjà dit*], an antecedent *doxa* which every relationship between the universal and individual presupposes. For this relationship evidently can not be based on resemblance" (OTB 35 [45]). That is to say that the identification of an entity, entirely in the kerygma of the said (that is, not a response that would merely identify an entity that existed prior to a said that would merely recognize that meaning), is nevertheless not capricious, not purely subjective, is not "anything that I would like," because it is a response to an "already said." The entity that I identify in the said across the flow of experience, in stabilizing the lability of temporalization, is identified as what it is, not on the basis of some meaning prior to the said, but on the basis of its having already been said, on the basis of which any said is already a response to an already said. In reference to "the surplus of this 'spontaneity' [the saying of a said] over the reflexion which, in its reflection, thought involves" in the kerygmatical identification mentioned above, Levinas expands on the function of the *déjà dit:*

> This surplus, situated between passivity and activity, is in the language that enters into a *hearsay* [*un ouï-dire*], an *already said,* a doxa, without which the identifying, naming language would not have been able to approach the sensible. In the doxa, the *already said,* tale, epos, the given is held in its theme. . . . A word is a nomination, as much as a denomination, a consecrating of the "this as this," or "this as that" by a saying which is also *understanding* and *listening,* absorbed in the said. It is an obedience in the midst of the will ("I hear this or that said"), a kerygma at the bottom of a *fiat.* Before all receptivity an *already said* before languages exposes or, in all the sense of the term, signifies (proposes and orders) experience. (OTB 35–36 [45–46])

This reference to an already said, that which grants to identification a point of contact with the sensible, is not only, then, a rejection of a strict empiricism ("this relationship evidently can not be based on resemblance"), but also a rejection of idealism, for this identification is not merely the imposition of an a priori, rational or transcendental category upon reality in the form of a word, but already the response to another word, a said in response to an already said that already holds the given in its theme.

But if the identification of a said is possible only by reference to an already said, are we not immediately led to ask: *Who* has already said the already said? There is a temptation to believe that we are here already in the realm of positive languages, that the "doxa, the *already said,* tale, epos" by which the given is held in its theme is "the said" as a positive language, my enculturated context for giving meaning to the identifications I make across my experience, referring them to a stock of references that would precisely permit of a "this as this," or "this as that," as the this and the that must already be meaningful for the as-structure of identification to succeed. Now, while such an explanation would indeed move us closer to an account of the universal aspect of language we are attempting to account for, we are not to find Levinas's account of it here. We find, rather, that for Levinas the *déjà dit* cannot be equated with a positive language because it is precisely in terms of the *déjà dit,* in response to such, that positive languages are constituted, as we see when we continue the inset quotation above: "Before all receptivity an *already said* before languages exposes or, in all the sense of the term, signifies (produces and orders) experience, giving to historical languages spoken by peoples a locus, enabling them to orient or polarize the diversity of the thematized as they choose" (OTB 36 [46]). The already said, *before* languages, clearly cannot be equated with the languages it precedes and, as the orienting point of such languages, makes possible.

So, if in response to the question "Who has already said the already said?" we are not able to respond, "Those who have gone before and who have enculturated me into the language that they speak," we are left with this question, and to it we must add another: "And in what language (since it clearly cannot be any positive language—a language dependent upon this 'other' language, whatever it might be) is the already said said?" Mysterious schematism, indeed. We shall have to return to these questions.

I.2. The Said As System

While it is clear that the *déjà dit* to which Levinas refers *le dit* as the identification of an entity is not a positive language, it is nevertheless the case that, according to his analyses, the act of identification does, in language as spoken, participate in, and interact with, a positive language as the milieu of ontological sense, and that such a language (the said as system) is one of the senses (along with the said as identificatory) of "the said" in *Otherwise Than Being.*

For is not the identifying of an entity precisely described as an identification of "this as this," or "this as that," and does not the reference of this to this or this to that not presuppose that in language as spoken there is already, before the said as identification can be effectuated, a more or less fixed stock of meanings in terms of which the identificatory project would be able to fix the meaning of a this in terms of a this or in terms of a that, to fix something *as* . . . ? It is true, of course, that the identification of an entity will, as we are in the course of indicating, ultimately refer to an already said (that will provide the warrant for its meaningfulness) that is prior to the positive languages oriented with respect to it (and that awaits articulation). But, insofar as the identification of this as this or this as that occurs in everyday speech (and where else would it occur?—as prominent among our theses is that for Levinas there is no "world behind the world" or "nether spaces" in which events or anything else might transpire), the this or that to which the this being identified is referred cannot but be a reference (even if this is not the ultimate horizon of its meaning) to the system of signs that constitute the positive language in which my everyday speech is transacted. As an English speaker, I identify the large organism with the green leaves that I see out my window *as* "a tree," and not as "*un arbre,*" as I would most likely were I a francophone, and the meaning of this identification is meaningful insofar as the entity so identified is taken *as* related to similar other entities also so identified (this is a tree *as* that is a tree), and *as* related to other entities as dissimilar (this is a tree where*as* that is a bush): this as this (as similarity) or this as that (in contrast to another this).

If, therefore, as we saw above, in the saying of a said, in the saying of something (in the amphibology of being and entities already present in that [whether more or less explicit] reference to being), language could be seen to reverberate with the being of beings, also, and with equal right: "Language qua said can then be conceived as a system of nouns identifying entities, and then as a system of signs doubling up the beings, designating substances, events and relations by substantives or other parts of speech derived from substantives, designating identities—in sum, *designating*" (OTB 40 [51]).

This system of signs—the said as system—meaningful by dint of their interrelationships, is thus founded upon a synchronization: is the extreme synchrony of a language awaiting to be spoken, all of the signs equally co-present, forming a system, like in a dictionary. And this sense cannot be separated from the epos, the epic, the tale and the fable, in terms of which history is synchronized into a present, in terms of which history is itself constituted.[20] The said as a system of signs, the collection into the present of a system of signifiers, collected into the epos of an identificatory said, is, we would argue, a fundamental meaning of the said in *Otherwise*

Than Being: and such a system is a positive language—with its history, tradition, its meaningfulness—constituted in a meaningful present, the embodiment of the *logos* of *onto-logos,* and making for *dia-logos.*

So Levinas does not contest that meaning, ontological meaning, even properly ethical meaning (or least its trace, as we shall see), is *borne* in the said as a positive language. What he does contest is that it is in the said that meaning is *born,* that the said is the beginning and end of meaning, that the said is able to generate and justify meaning. The generation and justification of meaning refers, rather, as we have seen, to an already said.

I.3. The Said As Response to the Already Said

What we hope to have shown in the previous section is that kerygmatic identification, the delineation of this as this or that, participates in (constitutes even as it is constituted in terms of) language as a system: a positive language.

The identification of the this as this or the this as that (the condition of possibility of saying *something*) has, therefore, a dual reference that corresponds to these two senses of the said in the text of *Otherwise Than Being.* It is first of all a reference to the identification of an entity as the same entity across time that emerges as a picking out of an identity across the lability of time (the vibrating of essence) in a kerygmatic said, in a said in which the essence of being (as the lability of time that is stilled by a said) already and still vibrates. The saying of a said is a consecration of this as this or this as that—not the naming or identifying of an identity that pre-dated its identification, but the identity in the identification itself. But it is also, as a kerygmatic identification of this *as* this or this *as* that, already a reference to a system of signifiers that identify (that have already identified) other identities, for to kerygmatically declare that this is this is to distinguish this from that, and to identify this as that is to equate it with some other similar this—in either case the identification presupposes prior identifications, already constituted as a system of interrelated signs, meaningful by dint of their mutual interdependence.

This would seem to leave us in a logical circle: the identification of a particular entity in a said is dependent upon a preexistent system of signifieds, and a system of signifieds is dependent upon the identification of particular beings in terms of which a system might be constituted. Now, this problem of the relative priority of "the whole" and "the parts" with respect to an understanding that requires both in concert is not a problem that haunts (or would particularly haunt) Levinas alone. But in the search for originary or transcendental structures for meaning one is perhaps not being inappropriately troublesome in pressing the question, for it is precisely this sort of problem—the need to ground one's contact with reality in a structure that presupposes this same contact—that leads to the skepticism with respect to a purportedly self-grounded knowledge that we have already discussed in chapter 3, and that led Levinas to "guarantee" knowledge by reference to the face that calls it into question (and that can, as such, also "consecrate" or "invest" it). So, Levinas does not, in *Otherwise Than Being,* leave the dual and interdependent senses of the said (identification and system) to battle it out over which has priority over the other, nor does he attempt to integrate them by means of a hermeneutic circle, that, à la Heidegger, would already be grounded in being, nor does he—and this is the problem, for how would one "know" which?—leave them floating above being in an epistemological tornado that never touches down.[21] Rather, he refers the said (in both of its interrelated senses) to what he refers to as "the already said," a "*déjà dit,*" which, as we stress again, is not a reference to the positive languages that are instead oriented with respect to it. The saying *of something* is conceived of as always already a response to a call, a saying of something *to someone,* who has already spoken in the already said to which every said is already a response, and that provides language as system in terms of which one says something with its *point d'attache.*

But *who* has already said the already said? And in what language? For if the *déjà dit* is prelinguistic in the sense of calling for language (as the saying of something, as the saying of a said), that to which my saying of a said is already a response, and that in terms of which positive languages are constituted, it can itself be said in neither of the senses we are here in the course of exposing: neither in a positive language, nor as the ontological identification of an entity.

It cannot, as the language before language that evokes language, but be the face of the other that calls me to offer to it, in its vulnerability, the world (my world, myself!) in speech, and in more than speech. It cannot be but the claim that the other has already made upon the goods of my world of enjoyment "before" I have ever enjoyed them.[22] Here language as the saying of *something* meaningful is shown to rest for its meaning (its ultimate signification) upon the saying of this something *to the other,* meaningful as the offering of a gift (as we have already seen) to the other, an other who calls such meanings forth in a meaning that precedes meaning ontologically conceived, language as the language before language that is the vulnerable but unimpeachable (unimpeachable because vulnerable) language of the other calling me (before the communication of any content) to responsibility (and to saying) in its regard, or, as Levinas put it earlier on: "the language of the eyes, impossible to dissemble."[23] It is to an analysis of my saying to an other, in response to this *déjà dit,* that we will now turn our attention.

II. Language As the Saying

II.1. The Saying of the Said

If the saying of *something* is always (and implicitly even in soliloquy, or monologue)[24] saying this something *to someone* (and not only because language as communication would be superfluous without a recipient of such communication, but also because the very identification of this *something* already refers to an other whose claim upon it tears it from the anonymity of the element), it is nonetheless the case that this *to someone* can be "forgotten," can be subordinated to, or lost in, the ontological pursuit of truth that it motivates. For the pursuit of ontological truth is a legitimate and necessary consequence of the fact that saying something is always a saying of it to an other—as we shall shortly see. The subject (the *I* of the "I say something to an other") gets caught up in its legitimate (but not primary) task of revealing being (in the amphibology of being and entities), and it is not so much that it forgets the other entirely, forgets that it is a saying of something to an other, as this forgetting is a subordinating of the other to this process of revelation: the other becomes another being (like me; a *co-équippeur,* a *Mitsein*) to be revealed and to whom I may reveal my truth (our truth, *the* truth), a co-being in terms of which, or by way of which, being *se revèle* (is revealed, or reveals itself). The other here is not entirely forgotten; what is forgotten is the alterity, the very otherness, of the other, an alterity that would be capable of calling into question my very being, my *way* of being as revealing being.

Subordinated to the process of revealing the truth of being, my saying is here correlative—even in being a saying to an other (who is here incidental except that his being must be included in this telling of the truth qua truth)—with what is said, counts only as that which opens up being, its meaning equivalent with its role as revelatory, its role as a teller (sayer, revealer, or conduit) of the truth. Here the subject is correlative with an object;[25] its meaning consists in this correlation—as an active intending of an object that in the truth, that for the truth, must be made present in a present wherein everything (if truth is to be true) must be gathered: extreme synchrony. We have examined this making present, this presencing, the saying in correlation with a said, in our previous sections.

What is "forgotten" in this (legitimate and necessary) process, in this activity of the subject as consciousness (as conscious being, as the consciousness of ["of" in both senses, as a subjective and as an objective genitive] being), is the diachrony that reverberates already in the language of being in the amphibology of being and entities, of which, in terms of which, the synchronization of presencing is a synchronization. Might, Levinas asks, this diachrony resist synchronization, and might it then signify otherwise than as subordinate to the synchronization that is the saying of a said? Might the "to an other" that (at least tacitly) accompanies any saying of something signify, across this diachrony, a meaning of my saying that is not reducible to that which it says, "the said," and that can be shown to make this very saying *of something* itself possible?

II.2. The Saying As Passivity

If the saying as the act of identification, the saying of a said, can be subordinated to the ontological process as the active subject correlative with in intending an intended object—that is, itself subsumed to the system of signification that it activates in saying *something* to someone—Levinas also delineates a purely passive (under)side of the saying ("on the hither side [*en deçà*]" of the amphibology of being and entities; OTB 45–46 [58]), a side that will turn out to be—as the ethical motivation or inspiration for the identification of objects—the very condition of possibility for saying as an activity, for saying as the saying *of something to someone.* That is, whereas Levinas clearly does speak of the saying in correlation with the said, he also speaks of "the saying without the said" (OTB 45 [58]). "Saying states and thematizes the said, but signifies it to the other, a neighbor, with a signification that has to be distinguished from that borne by words in the said" (OTB 46 [58]). It is this sense of the saying—wherein "[s]aying signifies otherwise than as an apparitor presenting essence and entities" (OTB 46 [59]), that is, otherwise than as an apparitor presenting essence and entities to the other (which is implied in their being spoken)—that, we shall contend, is the deepest or primordial sense (in the sense of being the condition of possibility for any other sense) of "the saying" in *Otherwise Than Being.* In this section we shall attempt to trace out this signification, linking it to our earlier discussions of the analyses of *Totality and Infinity,* and preparing to read this sense of the saying as the condition of possibility of discourse.

II.2.i. Why Say? We have already seen, in our previous chapter, that for Levinas the *logos* of the identification of objects is a production of the ethical act of offering the goods of my joyous economy to the other who, in his neediness as face, calls upon me to give them. From that analysis we saw that the identification of an object-thing (the saying of *something*) is irrevocably linked to my responsibility for the other (the saying of something *to an other*). Indeed, the saying *of something* is always the saying of something *to someone* (the very raison d'être of speech). An act of saying has an ethical motivation (either directly as offering, or by way of the indirect offering of apology in an offering of reasons for, perhaps, not offering my goods to the other—but inclining itself before the other nevertheless).

But why would I give something to an other who calls upon me to give it, especially when my giving to the other is a giving away—a disturbance and a breaking down (in what is less a diminution than a "conversion," for what was once mine is now the other's)—of my *jouissance?* And this is true, in all of its *renversement,* even in the seemingly innocuous act of offering a "mere" word (as over against, for instance, food) to the other, for even in identifying an object for the sake of denying it to the other ("Don't touch, that's my pen!") I have already at least implicitly acknowledged (in refusing) the claim that the other makes on it—my naïve possession of the world and its nourishments being, already in the offering of a word that creates common places/objects, called into question (and this is why Levinas is able to trace the ethical gesture back through speech). So, why speak? Why give? Why would I not simply ignore the other and take the face as yet another nourishment, perhaps even using speech (if need be)[26] to assume and consume the other like I use my hands and mouth and digestive system to take and appropriate a fruit, converting its energy into my own, converting even its resistance into my own strength, in accordance with the "nature" of the egoism? Indeed, from a certain perspective, from the perspective of a free, separated ego, from an ego alone in and joyful of its enjoyment, Levinas admits that my responsibility for the other, and the vulnerability that this entails, would be an imprudence, and more than that, "folly," even "psychosis."[27] So why would I enter into an act of saying?

In short, why obligation? Or perhaps better, why does the other obligate *me* (*le moi,* the ego in its egoity)? In a certain sense there is no answering this question. Levinas claims, for example, that "[i]n an approach I am first a servant of the neighbor . . . [w]ithout asking myself: What then is it to me? Where does he get his right to command? What have I done to be from the start in debt?" (OTB 87 [110])[28] Indeed, there is, on Levinas's accounting, in a certain sense, no *reason* why,[29] as my responsibility for the other precedes reasons, and, as we have seen, gives to reasons and reasonings the only sense (reason) of which they permit. The face is, as the origin of reasons, as we have seen, its own reason, does not require a rational context but is the very context (the [ethical] reason before reasons) for rationality. And Levinas claims that the call that issues from the face, that the call that the face issues, is ineluctable. The face calls me into a relationship of discourse that I cannot, ethically, refuse. But why not? In a certain sense, of course, to ask the question "why not?" with respect to the ignoring of obligation is simply to beg the question of the "why?" of obligation, to ask for an answer to a question that in principle (as it precedes and makes possible any principle) cannot be answered. As (quasi- or radicalized) phenomenological descriptions of structures required to make sense of experience, enjoyment and obligation as *descriptions* can be contra-dicted ("But in my experience . . ."); one cannot ask for *explanations* for them as if they were *deduced* from principles. And yet, given these descriptions qua descriptions, one cannot but wonder (in attempting to understand their relationship to each other and to "life-world-experience," [the only experience we have!]) why—as a being originally unconstrained by any other who would call my joyous consumption of the element into question, as enclosed within the circle of ipseity ("life as the love of life")—I do not, in my enjoyment, simply refuse the interruption of the other (that is, if I could hear an exterior call at all)? Why would I not simply ignore (if not just be ignorant of) the interruption? Levinas's answer—his "because" to this "why?" or "why not?"—is not, cannot be, on the level of an appeal to a principle or a reason that would follow only upon (or that would be made possible by) that which the description describes, but proceeds by way of a deepening, or a making more precise (in the sense of relating this structure to others also operative in the description of experience), of the description. That is, across these deepening descriptions, the "without why" of obligation returns, but at a deeper level of understanding (be that at a deeper level of understanding why we cannot understand).

That is, if in *Totality and Infinity* Levinas argues that the call issuing from the face of the other is ineluctable, in *Otherwise Than Being* he affirms his earlier assertion and tells us why this is the case—provides in the later work, one might say, the condition of possibility for the assertion of the former, and does this through a shift in his analyses from an emphasis on the face of the other that interrupts the ego in its joyous economy of sameness, to an emphasis on proximity wherein this same is always already disrupted by the other from within. If the analysis of the face described an interruption of the same *by an outside* that I am incapable of appropriating to the same, and that as such must remain always and ever on the outside, the analysis of proximity explains why I cannot simply ignore that outside in its descriptions of the interruption of the same *from the inside,* by showing that the outside that must always remain outside is, in a certain sense, already internal to the same (which will turn out to be the result of the fact that the same is itself already, qua itself, "constituted" in response to, or graced as responsiveness to, an other, a trace of which it retains even in its separated sameness). Proximity describes this relation, the relation with the other whereby the face in its transcendence always already disturbs the ego from within its very immanence. Proximity is a description of, in Levinas's phrase, "the other in the same."

II.2.ii. The Passivity of Passivity Proximity articulates a closeness, a nearness to the other wherein, nevertheless, the separation of the subject and the other (which we traced through the analyses of *Totality and Infinity* in our chapter 2) is assiduously maintained. A nearness that goes beyond tangency, that is not first of all qualified as a spatial relation, in proximity I have—in what can only be taken in a *partially* metaphorical sense, because being bodily is essential to being in proximity (as we shall see)—the other "under my skin." That is, proximity describes a relation with the other that is the erasing of, and that which precedes, the "safe" distanciation that consciousness establishes with its object in order to "fix" it as "there," at arm's length, the distance necessary for perception, for conceptualization, for the appropriating grasp. Proximity describes the too far to be grasped of transcendence as a too near to be grasped. The other, the radically transcendent, is *in* the same, eliminating the possibilities of both fight and flight with respect to the other except as a betrayal of myself, except as a fleeing from or a combat with myself.

Levinas's discussion of proximity in *Otherwise Than Being* emerges at the point where intentionality has given way to sensibility[30]—where sensation is analyzed no longer as it functions in "intuition,"[31] as already on the way to being meaningful in the correlation between the sensate being and the "stuff," the "raw material," of meaning constitution fashioned by the consciousness into this or that, but is revealed in its proper and primordial meaning: as the passive exposure of the subject to alterity.[32] In this context, proximity is described as a species or a specification of sensibility,[33] as my exposure to the other, specifically the human other, and exposure of a particular kind—an exposure to responsibility. The other affects me in proximity by making an ethical claim upon me as I am affected across or in my physical sensibility, where the meaning of my being affected is not mediated across intentional structures that would provide the context for my being affected (although this may be done after the fact without negating, even if obscuring, the meaning of affectivity qua affectivity), but imposes itself *immediately*. Struck by a blow I did not see coming, I collapse *in pain* before I have a chance to constitute the experience *as painful*, or, perhaps better, before I have a chance to constitute the pain as an experience[34]—a constitution that already gives me a certain distance from the trauma by providing it with a context, by translating its meaning into a foreign language.

Proximity names the immediacy of my exposure to the other for whom I am responsible, my affectability, my having always already been affected by my responsibility for the other even before I constitute responsibility as an experience,[35] and thus names the fact that I cannot distance myself from this responsibility. That is, I cannot *ethically* distance myself from the other. For while I may well (and must, for reasons that will emerge—for "reason") translate this trauma into a rational-moral context, bring it into a said, I cannot do so without betraying the ethical trauma qua ethical, and can do so only on the basis of the ethical trauma of proximity underlying—and living on as a trace of itself in—its being brought to "experience." Moreover, while I may well be able (through the ever resuming exercise of consciousness) to constitute a meaningful context for my physical sensibility (e.g., my suffering teaches me to keep out of harm's way), there can be no reason given for the trauma of proximity (my responsibility for the physical suffering—that I had no part in effectuating—of the other),[36] as the responsibility that it signifies is, for Levinas, as we have shown, (at) the very origin of reason itself. Levinas argues that it is proximity, the fact that there is in proximity a passivity of responsibility that cannot be subsumed to any "project" of the self (as my personal suffering qua personal can, e.g., "no pain, no gain," "what doesn't kill me makes me stronger"), that therefore underlies sensibility as the sensibility of sensibility, that makes sensibility qua sensibility meaningful outside of meaning constitution.[37] That is, the meaning of sensibility as passivity can maintain itself in its passivity only if it is ultimately inconvertible into an activity, and this for Levinas is possible only when the "by" [*par*] the other of sensibility/proximity is transformed into (or derives its meaning from) the "for" [*pour*] the other of responsibility (which remains a "by" the other—is also a suffering), undergone in a patience more patient than any undergoing that could be welcomed could be.[38] That is, proximity instigates a permanent *défi* with respect to consciousness insofar as here the subject is faced with a face for which it must now answer but which it can nowise encompass, the meaning of which comes to the subject from outside of the subject (be that across the very immanence of subjectivity). In the irremissible grasp of the other who grasps me before I can grasp him, I am, in Levinas's term, persecuted by the other. Moreover, pain can affect me *as pain,* ultimately, because I am in proximity to the other, because my *body* is always already for the other,[39] prohibiting any ultimate sublimation of sensitivity to intentionality, leaving me in passivity—disinterestedness—even with respect to my own pain.[40] Proximity articulates the meaning of sensibility.[41] "The immediacy of the sensibility is the for-the-other of one's own materiality; it is the immediate opening up for the other of the immediacy of enjoyment, the immediacy of taste, materialization of matter, altered by the immediacy of contact" (OTB 74 [94]).

In one further move, Levinas deepens this passivity once again in describing the meaning kernel of proximity as "substitution"—my passivity qua responsibility for the other only irremissibly passive when I substitute myself for (or rather, when I am already substitution for) the other, responsible, that is to say, even for the responsibility of the other, responsible (culpable) for that which the other has done, that for which I am in no sense responsible (or culpable), thus "accused in innocence," but expiating for the other, wherein my unicity qua subject is ultimately "the very fact of bearing the fault of another" (OTB 112 [143]):

> This passivity deserves the epithet of complete or absolute only if the persecuted one is liable to answer for the persecutor. The face of the neighbor in its persecuting hatred can by this very malice obsess as something pitiful. This equivocation or enigma only the persecuted one who does not evade it, but is without any references, any recourse or help (that is its uniqueness or its identity as unique!) is able to endure. To undergo from the other is an absolute patience only if by this from-the-other [*par autrui*] is already for-the-other [*pour autrui*]. This transfer, other than interested, "otherwise than essence," is subjectivity itself. "To tend the cheek to the smiter and to be filled with shame," to demand suffering in the suffering undergone (without producing the act that would be the exposing of the other cheek) is not to draw from suffering some kind of magical redemptive virtue. In the trauma of persecution it is to pass from the outrage undergone to the responsibility for the persecutor, and, in this sense from suffering to expiation for the other. (OTB 111 [141])

From intentionality to sensitivity, to proximity as persecution, to substitution as expiation,[42] the text of *Otherwise Than Being* follows through ever deepening articulations of passivity, ever deepening articulations of the subjectivity of the subject, or self, qua *subjectum*:[43] "Soi . . . une passivité à mort!" (OTB 124 [159]).

II.2.iii. The Passivity of Saying What the saying signifies to the other before anything else is precisely this passivity, my responsibility for the other (to the point of my substitution for the other), a signification that is the presentation of no content signified, but the very signification of signification, the dealing of significance to the other in the context of which my signification of a content can be significant:[44] "To say is to approach a neighbor, 'dealing him signifyingness' [lui "bailler signifiance"]. This is not exhausted in 'ascriptions of meaning,' which are inscribed, as tales, in the said. Saying taken strictly is a 'signifyingness dealt to the other,' prior to all objectification; it does not consist in giving signs" (OTB 48 [61]). The saying, then, in its sense as the signification of signification, far from being merely or even primarily the active offering of signs to an other (signs signifying meanings that would have first been "in me"), is perhaps well thought of as the linguistically qualified description of the relationship of proximity. Indeed, according to Levinas, the saying, "[t]his signification to the other ["which signifies prior to essence" (OTB 45 [58]), "distinguished from that borne by words" (OTB 46 [58])] occurs in proximity" (OTB 46 [58]). To say is thus the ex-pression or exposure of myself in speech to the other as already exposed to the other, as already responsible to the other, the linguistic expression of this exposure and responsibility, a finding of myself already expressed and exposed to the other in speech.

According to Levinas's description, therefore, I do not, in fact, choose to give myself or not to give myself to the other in responsibility; I do not open myself to the other in an act of saying from out of an already established enclosure in terms of which such an act might be undertaken.[45] Rather, it is the other that chooses me (or "the good,"[46] or God, that chooses me on the other's behalf) before there is any question of my opening myself up or closing myself off. My responsibility for the other is prior to my choice, not mine to choose or not to choose, and, in fact, in choosing the good (in choosing to be responsible), I am already too late and guilty for so being;[47] I have already been chosen. I am elected (where this term has the religious resonance of "the chosen one") to the good prior to having anything to say in the matter (and where my saying is precisely a response to this having been chosen), chosen, despite myself (despite any will that I might try and exert over this election), to the service of the other, in "an assignation to answer without evasions, which assigns the self to be a self" (OTB 106 [134]). And it is in this context of nonchoice, and inescapability (for I cannot choose even after the fact to reject my having been elected—that which would presuppose a freedom with respect to my election), that the description of the subject as "hostage" comes to Levinas's pen: "The condition of being a hostage is not chosen; if there had been a choice, the subject would have kept his as-for-me, and the exits found in inner life. But this subjectivity, this very psyche, is for the other, his very bearing independence consists in supporting the other, expiating for him" (OTB 136 [173–74]).

That is, this election that makes of me a hostage is my deepest as pre-original identity (my "having been identified"[48] before I assume this identity, that in response to which self-identification is possible), my "identity prior to the for-itself" (OTB 106 [135]).

My having been elected is who I am "before" I "am" (before I assume a position in being among beings that "are";[49] the person, from the perspective of being, is "*personne*" (OTB 106 [135]). The self, my subjectivity, my very psyche, is a "passion" (OTB 117 [149]), a suffering by the other, a burning for the other, "one and unique, in passivity from the start" (OTB 105 [134]). Why would I give myself? I do not. I am already given. Why would I open myself in speech? I do not. I have already been spoken (for).[50] What Levinas is claiming, on our reading, is that obligation obligates me because I *am* (and the use of the copula here is, of course, already a kind of betrayal, a conveying in a said that which is not susceptible to being said in that it is what makes for the said, is the condition of possibility of the said),[51] before (or more primordially than) anything else, responsibility for the other.[52] That is, I am susceptible to being obligated because I am not first (or foremost) an enjoying/constituting/economical ego who is only later (or secondarily) called upon to give, or to be responsible for the other, for such an ego—independent and primordially autonomous—would have the freedom to refuse the call, and refuse it not simply in the sense of a negative modality of response ("I hear you, but I am saying 'no,' "—an empirical possibility that does not refute, in implicitly acknowledging, the ethical impossibility of refusing the call), but to refuse it outright—beyond a hearing and deciding not to hear—in a "constitution" (which would have to be pre-ontological) of the other as not other, or simply a not hearing at all.[53] An ego in *jouissance,* if this *jouissance* were not always already interrupted by exteriority, would be ethically deaf, and ontologically mute. (We begin already to trace the trace that ethics leaves in the ontological structures that it makes possible, here in the very phenomenon of language—a tracing that will occupy us more pointedly in the next chapter.)

In the analyses of our previous chapter we attempted to show that even in *Totality and Infinity,* in which the economy of the same is given extended treatment, Levinas argues for no such independent and autonomous ego, despite all of the talk there of such in its descriptions of the structure of *jouissance,* despite all of the talk of "separation."[54] In that text, as we attempted to show, the ego in enjoyment is always already disturbed, even in the description of the enjoying ego in a moment of isolated presence,[55] by a certain "care for the morrow," against which, as we have seen, it withdraws into a home, but where this domiciling itself is made possible only due to the *prior* (discrete) presence of the (feminine) other. In the very independence of *jouissance* the other disturbs me (driving me to seek the security of a home), even as she welcomes me (into that home). In my very being shut up at home with myself, the other dwells with me, even if this dwelling with me creates the possibility of living as an independent, self-only-concerned, self-constituted, economic *ipseity* in "forgetting" that my powers as an economic agent are due to the other, due to the home that (s)he welcomed me into, a home now disturbed by the other in the mode of the face who calls upon me to give of the goods collected in that home to feed his/her hungers, and to give the home itself in hospitality to protect him/her from the cold.[56] And it is in this context (in light of the constitution of the home made possible by the gracious welcome of the feminine other) that the metaphor of maternity for the subjectivity of the subject in *Otherwise Than Being*—"the other in the same" par excellence—takes on special meaning across the analyses of the two texts, as we shall see in our next chapter. Indeed, the whole analysis of "separation" in *Totality and Infinity* (which we examined in our chapter 2) is to be read in the context of the idea of "creation,"[57] as are all references to a free and self-referential ego in *Otherwise Than Being*.[58] My being created (by God), my being born (to the [feminine] other), means that the separation that I effect qua ego is dependent upon, is possible only in the context of, a "prior" relationship, the relationship established across creation or birth.[59] Separation is not some primordial state of affairs, but an accomplishment, and an accomplishment made possible in terms of an intrigue that precedes it, a participation in which is the very condition of possibility of breaking with participation, the condition of my nonconditionality. My freedom, my separation, is, from the first, before I have a "first," already invested by the other, is possible as freedom or as separation only as so invested, such that my freedom does not precede my relationship with the other, but is already the gift of the other, does not make relationship possible except that it is itself made possible by the relationship that invests it—but that invests it *as* free, as separate, so that my relationship to the other might be ethical (like the one that invests it), and not an ontological relationship within a totality that would preclude its "being," in its deepest meaning, responsible.[60]

In *Otherwise Than Being,* where the interruption of my interiority by the exteriority of the face is displaced (while simultaneously retained, for *Otherwise Than Being* still speaks of the face) by the vocabulary of "proximity," this point is made all the more clearly (that is, without requiring our interpretation that the feminine other and the other as face are one and the same other in different modalities).[61] In this text, the descriptions of interiority and economy (that made up over a quarter of *Totality and Infinity*) are largely dropped (although there is still a short section on "Enjoyment" (OTB 72–74 [91–94])), and the emphasis is on how, always already, the subject is confronted with, and awakened to itself as, "the-other-in-the-same."[62] Proximity means that I do not reach out to the other in saying from out of an enclosure that I would be first of all[63]—rather, I am (before I "am") that saying.[64] The other is always already interior to me. I do not *become* hostage to the other, I *am* hostage to the other (and it is precisely the structures built upon my being always already hostage that make my forgetting of this (in)condition possible, that permit me to empirically refuse the call that ethically I cannot refuse): "The ego is not an entity 'capable' of expiating for the others: it is this original expiation. This expiation is involuntary,[65] for it is prior to the will's initiative (prior to the origin). It is as though the unity and uniqueness of the ego were already the hold on itself of the gravity of the other" (OTB 118 [151]).

Rather than positing an original freedom that is only later interrupted by the face of the other (which was not, we maintain, the argument even in *Totality and Infinity*), Levinas shows here in a heightened way—through the idea of proximity—that while I may well be free *from the beginning,* from *before the beginning* I was obligated (by a pre-original call), and that the freedom that I have (by way of a pre-original gift) is only possible as freedom invested by the other[66]—an investment that, to be sure, I can squander on myself in forgetting that my freedom is an invested freedom (freedom from and for the other), but not without fault,[67] not without forgetting who I am, not without alienating myself from my self (and thus even from my ego, which is a derivative, if necessary and important, modality of my self). It is only in the context of this "forgetting" that the self hardens itself into an egoistic ego, distancing itself from itself and the other already in it, even if this forgetting will turn out to be necessary to an ethically inspired justice.

It is this always already of the-other-in-the-same that explains my susceptibility to obligation, that explains why I simply cannot refuse (in the sense of simply not hearing) the call of the other who calls me to responsibility, and why, as Levinas repeatedly claims, this responsibility is irremissible. Thus, if my saying *something* (the identification of entities) is always a saying of something to *someone* (this dative the raison d'être and condition of possibility of the accusative of identification), my *active* saying of something to an other is itself made possible and necessary by the fact that, before being able to decide for or against conversation, I am always already called to respond by virtue of my susceptibility to the call of the other—by virtue of my *passivity* with respect to this other-in-the-same, by virtue of the fact that I *am* the saying, elected to signifyingness, obsessed with my responsibility: "The passivity of exposure responds to an assignation that identifies me as the unique one. . . . The saying signifies this passivity; in the saying this passivity signifies, becomes signifyingness, exposure in response to . . ." (OTB 49 [63]). Moreover, I am not only *susceptible to* obligation as if I possessed a prior transcendental forestructure capable of receiving the call (for this still presupposes a self behind the being called), but I *am* (before I ontologically speaking "am") obligated, I *am* responsible, I *am* this passivity and this susceptibility. The subject of "I say . . ." is not "I" alone, an "I" who would *then* say something, but "I say," where the very subjectivity of the subject is already expression: "The subject of saying does not give signs, it becomes a sign, turns into an allegiance" (OTB 49 [63]). It is this extreme passivity, this susceptibility, this "giving a sign of its very signifyingness"[68]—that which makes possible and necessary my active saying of something to someone (but where "speaking" remains "exposing one's very exposedness," where "[t]he act of speaking is the passivity in passivity" (OTB 92 [117]))—that Levinas describes in *Otherwise Than Being* as "the saying," not the saying of a said, correlative with a said (even if its condition of possibility), but "the saying without a said," the pre-original exposure/response to the ethical call of the other that I *am* and that makes language (as active saying, as correlative with a said) possible (insofar as the I is already language, already the signification of signification).

So the saying of something to someone has as its condition of possibility the saying in its primordial and deepest sense, the sense that permits of sense: the signification of myself as signification, the signification of signification:

> Saying is communication, to be sure, but as a condition for all communication, as exposure. . . . The unblocking of communication, irreducible to the circulation of information which presupposes it, is accomplished in saying. It is not due to the contents that are inscribed in the said and transmitted to the interpretation and decoding done by the other. It is in the risky uncovering of oneself, in sincerity, the breaking up of inwardness and the abandon of all shelter, exposure to traumas, vulnerability. (OTB 48 [61–62])

We have come across this "risk" before, at the end of our chapter 3, as the risk necessary to discourse, the non-allergic, ethical relation with alterity (re)productive of a meaning capable of founding communal meaning. What the analyses of *Otherwise Than Being* add to the foregoing ones is a description of the (de)-structure of subjectivity, in proximity, as substitution, that describes why and how is it possible, even necessary, for the ego to enter into the relationship of discourse, for the ego to take the risk of exposure to the other, in showing that the subject (which is the subject of the ego) is already so exposed, is already responsible for the other, is, in its very subjectivity, the saying.

And that is why the saying at the deepest level is irreducible to the active saying of something to an other that would be the focus of speech act theory, which remains a saying in correlation with a said. The saying at the deepest level is not an activity at all, but a passivity, an "ethical" passivity on this side of, or "before," the alternative between activity and passivity as normally conceived[69] (i.e., where even passivity is conceived of as the "act" of being passive as opposed to the act of acting, where passivity articulates an undergoing welcomed, received, consented to, submitted to), an undergoing that does not even have yet enough of itself to assume its undergoing, the passivity of passivity, passivity as, ultimately (as we hope to have shown), the "pure" passivity of substitution as expiation[70]—such that the *to* the other of *saying something to the other* that is the active giving of a said is founded upon, made possible by, the *for* the other of allegiance, which is a having been elected to allegiance and not the act of allegiance.[71]

But the saying in its extreme passivity articulates, also, an activity, the saying of *something* to an other,[72] but an activity that, strangely, "remains, in its activity, a passivity."[73] The absolute passivity of proximity (of the saying as exposure) can turn into, or be reconciled or correlated with, the activity of saying (exposing myself in the saying of something) only if that activity is inscribed in the passivity itself as a kind of reflex in response to it—passive to the point of being driven perpetually back upon and beyond itself (the (in)condition of the subject) that produces a kind of perpetual motion (what we will refer to in our chapter 6 as the "recurrence" of the subject), back beyond myself (as substance, as in a place of rest, in *stasis*) to myself *as* being driven back itself, the distance between myself as otherwise than being (as responsible for being(s)) and my *being* as responsible (where this distance is the difference of nonindifference) seemingly creating, in a kind of elasticized tension, the motion, the act toward the other (the approach) from out of pure passivity (my having always already been approached), and a certain kind of freedom:

> In this most passive passivity, the self liberates itself ethically from every other and from itself. Its responsibility for the other, the proximity of the neighbor, does not signify a submission to the non-ego; it means an openness in which being's essence is surpassed in inspiration. It is an openness of which respiration is a modality or a foretaste, or, more exactly, of which it retains the aftertaste. Outside of any mysticism, in this respiration, the possibility of every sacrifice for the other, activity and passivity coincide. (OTB 115 [146])

At this point: respiration, where the pure passivity of inspiration engenders as its reflex expiration, expi(r)ation. In passivity I am in-spired by the other to ex-pire for him. This more "positive" metaphor (and is it a metaphor, or the first "truth" upon which the biotic process of breathing is constituted as meaningful?) of *inspiration* to describe my relationship to the other (as over against being his hostage, or being persecuted, for example) bespeaks the possibility of describing the relationship (of proximity or the saying) not from the perspective of an already constituted ego who has to be stripped of its *conatus,* stripped of its identity qua ipseity in egoistic enjoyment (and already set up in an economy) in order to find its identity qua the elected one, but from the perspective of a subject that is already for-the-other before it is for-itself, and who thus finds in the other not an imposition, but an inspiration, who inspires it to *be* itself, who ordains it, who invests it as a freedom free to be for the other.[74]

Here a whole collection of "negative" or "negating" terms that describe the subject as assailed in its self-sameness (*pour soi*) by the other (either from without or within)—persecution, hostage, alienation, inquietude, vulnerability, exposition, victimization, de-position, de-situation, susceptibility, traumatism, psychosis, being ordered—are transformed[75] into "positive" or "affirming" terms that describe the pre-original other-directedness (*pour autrui*) of the subjectivity of the subject—inspiration, animation, election, investiture, expiation, exaltation, elevation, ordination.[76] And we begin to glimpse here the redemption of this negativity, my being (before I "am") expiation for the other in terms of a pre-original expiation, across an "intrigue" in which the name of God will come to human speech. We will turn to an investigation of the necessity of this dual description, and to an "exposition" of this intrigue (that cannot properly be exposed) in the chapters to follow.

I respond actively to the other—I say something to the other—because I *am* responsibility for the other, that is, through (in terms of) my passivity as responsibility, in my passivity as responsibility, I am. I say, because I am (before I "am," as the condition of possibility of my "being") saying.

Notes

1. For a more extensive account of our analysis of Levinas's philosophical method, and what we shall call, after de Boer, his "ethical transcendentalism," see chapter 7.

2. Although I do, or so we shall maintain, re-make language as signifyingness each time that I encounter an other, which permits of either the re-affirmation or a re-constitution of the prevailing ontological sense. We shall return to this later in the chapter when we argue that the construction of a said is always, in fact, a re-construction.

3. That is, we are arguing that Levinas's analyses always begin in media res, and "return" us—across an analysis of the structures *for* this experience—to life-world experience. The tracing out these (pre)originary structures, that are taken to condition the "reality" in which I find myself, have no existence of their own (Levinas is not an idealist), but are precisely delineated as "conditions for . . ." Thus while enjoyment is described in *Totality and Infinity as if* there were a pure state of enjoyment possible, it is described *also* as always already disturbed by the other. There is no enjoyment that is not always already disturbed, but there is no disturbing of enjoyment without enjoyment. Enjoyment is thus described in *Totality and Infinity as if* there were, at the origin of experience, an undisturbed enjoyment only later disturbed by the face. But this structure (*jouissance*) is, on our claim, to be read not as original, but originary—as a structure that conditions experience and makes it possible (and that leaves its trace, certainly, on experience), but that is never itself—and never was—"experienced" in any straightforward way. Experience is always already miscegenated—conditioned by this and *other* conditions simultaneously. In a like manner, the other in the mode of the feminine that makes the economy of the home *possible* as graciousness is also, simultaneously, or so we are arguing, the other in the mode of "the face" (that breaks up—that has always already disturbed—my *jouissance*) that makes the security of the home *necessary* in the first place. That is, in media res, I find myself always already graced by the other with a home (protected from the alien) even as I am disturbed in my home by the other—called to give of my holdings, called to welcome the alien into my home. The other is, in the miscegenation of life, both within and without, sustaining and disturbing, and the description of its modes (as "feminine," as "other" proper), together with the descriptions of the structures of *jouissance*, dwelling, economy, etc., are all descriptions of the conditions of possibility of life as lived. But properly speaking they *are* not, and never *were,* except as they have a life in everyday life, in that which they condition.

4. We add the qualification "now" because it is conceivable (though highly unlikely) that I could develop a language along with a singular interlocutor that would be spoken only by the two of us. But such a language would still have to exhibit all of the qualities that accompany universality, like (i) accessibility to anyone who would learn the lan-

guage, and (ii) some sort of consistency over time (i.e., meaningful only if the word "rock," for example, meant the same thing now that it meant five minutes ago, and not now meaning "water").

5. "To be or not to be is not the question where transcendence is concerned" (OTB 3 [4]).

6. "But to hear a God not contaminated by Being is a human possibility no less important and no less precarious than to bring Being out of the oblivion in which it is said to have fallen in metaphysics and onto-theology" (OTB xlii [X]).

7. The other aspect of language, "the saying" (that will be described in II.2 of this chapter), will have to do with ex-pression, with the giving, or the "having already been given"-ness, of the self—not "the saying" in correlation with "the said," the saying of *something*, but the "saying without the said"—the *expression* of my responsibility to the other in proximity, which will turn out to be the other condition of possibility of saying something to someone.

8. This "before" is, of course, again the before of the originary, and not a chronological designation. One does not exhibit being first, and then state it or make a judgment upon it (as we shall shortly see), even if any statement or judgment presupposes (requires) the exhibition of being.

9. As does, for instance, a lie or an imagining, that must presuppose the truth in order to have their meaning as a lie or an imagining.

10. This quotation continues: "The question—even 'what is being?'—then questions with respect to being, with respect to what is precisely in question. The answer required is from the start in terms of being, whether one understands by it *entity* or *being of entities,* entity or being's *essence.* The question 'what?' is thus correlative of what it wishes to discover, and already has recourse to it. Its quest occurs entirely within being, in the midst of what it is seeking. It is ontology, and at the same time has a part in the effectuation of the very being it seeks to understand. If the question 'what?' in its adherence to being is at the origin of all thought (can it be otherwise, as long as thought proceeds by determinate terms?), all research and all philosophy go back to ontology, to the understanding of the being of entities, the understanding of essence" (OTB 23–24 [30]).

11. This remains the case even if it is acknowledged that our "little truth" (our piece of the truth) is never fully true insofar as we never see "the whole" (whether through matters of impracticality or "in principle" prohibitions). The whole truth remains the goal, even if unrealizable (and this unrealizability of truth will play a major role in these analyses). It thus remains the case always that "[t]ruth is something

promised. Always promised, always future, always loved, truth lies in the promise of the love of wisdom, even if it is not forbidden to catch sight, in the time of disclosure, of the structured work of history and of a progression in the successive up to the limits of non-philosophy" (OTB 29 [37]).

12. Under this regime, "The soul would live only for the disclosure of being which arouses it or provokes it; it would be a moment of the life of the Spirit, that is, of Being-totality, leaving nothing outside of itself, the same finding again the same" (OTB 28 [35–36]). This "result" holds for Levinas—is the argument of these analyses beyond the clearly Hegelian reference in the above quotation—despite the fact that in the opening pages of *Otherwise Than Being* it is the fundamental ontology of Heidegger rather than the phenomenology of Spirit of Hegel that would seem to be the predominant antagonist. It is helpful at this juncture to note Robert Gibbs's perceptive and helpful observation that "In a brazen shorthand, Levinas reads Husserl as Fichte and Heidegger as Hegel. Levinas views Husserl's egology as, despite itself, too close to Fichte's philosophy of the 'I'; while Heidegger's resurrection of ontology is seen as parallel to the totalizing system in Hegel. Indeed, Heidegger surpasses Hegel, because his totality of ontology dispenses with the mechanistic dialectics of history and rests ultimately on the anonymity of Being itself" (Gibbs, *Correlations,* p. 8).

13. We have translated Levinas's "sans s'éteindre" as "without extinguishing itself" in place of Lingis's flatter "without being put out."

14. And does this "to infinity" leave us with a trace, within ontology itself, of the Infinite? Does this "to infinity" open a(n always enigmatic, as we shall see) way "to Infinity?"

15. And thus, as Levinas tells us, truth is always promised, always future. Why? Because the consummation of truth is the end of truth as truth.

16. We provide a more comprehensive look at this temporalization in the context of a study of time in and across *Totality and Infinity* and *Otherwise Than Being* in chapter 6. There is, therefore, a brief but unavoidable overlap between this analysis and that one.

17. "*Essence* does not first designate the edges of solids or the moving line of acts in which a light glimmers; it designates this 'modification' without alteration or transition, independent of all qualitative determination. . . . This modification by which the same comes unstuck or parts with itself, . . . and thus is disclosed, . . . becomes a phenomenon—is the *esse* of every being. Being's essence designates nothing that could be a nameable content, a thing, event or action; it names this mobility of the immobile, this multiplication of the identical, this diastasis of the punctual, this lapse" (OTB 29–30 [37–38]).

18. "The verb *to be* tells the flowing of time as though language were not unequivocally equivalent to denomination, as though in *to be* the verb first came to function as a verb, and as though this function refers to the teeming and mute itching of that modification without change that time operates. . . . Essence, temporalization, is the verbalness of the verb. . . . Temporalization is the verb form to be. Language issued from the verbalness of the verb would then not only consist in making being understood, but also in making its essence vibrate" (OTB 34–35 [44]).

19. "In the copula *is* scintillates or sparkles an ambiguousness between the essence and the nominalized relation, . . . the logos enters into the amphibology in which being and entities can be understood and identified, in which a noun can resound as a verb and a verb of an apophansis can be nominalized" (OTB 41–42 [53–54]).

20. Thus "narrative" does not serve to disrupt the moment of absolute presence, but to extend this moment into the past and the future—does not, as is thought in certain circles, break down the moment of pure intuition by forcing upon it *historical* consciousness, but broadens the domain of presence in giving us historical *consciousness.*

21. That is, does the specter of the evil genius not also haunt the house of being?

22. This "before" is, of course, of the transcendental kind, a before of an irrecuperable diachrony irreducible to "time" (as constituted), and that will come to our attention in the next section. That is to say, the said as system comes to me with my mother's milk, is the gift of enculturation, the being welcomed into the home by the feminine other, while this other qua other already calls into question (as she provides for) my joyous possession of the world—calls upon me to give (to the other) of what I have been given (by the [feminine] other [or the other in the mode of the feminine]). These two simultaneous structures (welcome and disturbance, gift and call) that, while not being contradictory, move in opposite directions, nevertheless both (in their integrality) refer to an other—to a *déjà dit*—to the face of the other that in its diverse modalities both gives and makes a claim upon that which is given. (Here, possession, what has been given to me to give, is quite rightly stewardship.) A claim is made upon my "in the moment" (caring naught for but for the moment) enjoyment from out of a deep past—which is why my enjoyment is always already disturbed, why enjoyment is open always already (opened from the inside—as a disturbance as "care for the morrow") to an outside—to concern itself with the other, which is why, on Levinas's schema, enjoyment is open to and requires a home.

23. "The face speaks. The manifestation of the face is already discourse. . . . The eyes break through the mask—the language of the

eyes, impossible to dissemble. The eye does not shine; it speaks" (TI 66 [37]).

24. "The silent coming and going from question to response, with which Plato characterized thought, already refers to a plot [*intrigue*] in which is tied up the node of subjectivity, by the other commanding the same" (OTB 25 [31]).

25. "In correlation with the said (in which saying runs the risk of being absorbed as soon as the said is formulated), the saying itself is indeed thematized, exposes in essence even what is on the *hither side of ontology,* and flows into the temporalization of essence. And this thematization of saying does indeed bring out in it the characteristics of consciousness: in the correlation of saying and said the said is understood as a noema of an intentional act, language contracts into thought, into thought which conditions speaking, thought that in the said shows itself to be an act supported by a subject, an *entity* as it were put in the 'nominative,' in a proposition. The saying and the said in their correlation delineate the subject-object structure" (OTB 46 [59]).

26. The fact that I can use speech like a tool, to pry what I desire from the other, the fact that speech can be rhetoric, already indicates, for Levinas, my acknowledgment of the other's freedom, as "the specific nature of rhetoric consists in corrupting this freedom." Already the other is not a mere thing ("an inertia"), even if in rhetoric I "apply a category" to "a freedom, which, precisely as freedom, should be incorruptible" (TI 70 [42]).

27. "The psyche, the one-for-the-other, can be a possession and a psychosis; the soul is already a seed of folly" (OTB 191, n.3 [86]).

28. Levinas illustrates the perversity of asking these questions by way of two literary allusions, one from Shakespeare and the other from the Bible: "Why does the other concern me? What is Hecuba to me? Am I my brother's keeper? These questions have meaning only if one has already supposed that the ego is concerned only with itself, is only a concern for itself" (OTB 117 [150]).

29. John D. Caputo stresses this "without why" of obligation in his *Against Ethics.*

30. Chapter 2 is entitled "De l'intentionnalité au sentir" (the movement of this "From intentionality to Sensing" lost in Lingis's translation, "Intentionality and Sensing"); chapter 3, "Sensibilité et proximité" (Sensibility and Proximity).

31. "As discovery and knowing, sensible intuition is already of the order of the said; it is an ideality" (OTB 62 [79]).

32. "The signification proper to the sensible has to be described in terms of enjoyment and wounding, which are . . . the terms of proximity" (OTB 62–63 [79]).

33. Even if the deepest meaning of sensibility qua physical will turn out to be founded in the responsibility of proximity, as we shall see.

34. "Sensibility, all the passivity of saying, cannot be reduced to an experience that a subject would have of it, even if it makes possible such an experience" (OTB 54 [70]).

35. "Contact is not an openness upon being, but an exposure to being [à l'être]. In this caress proximity signifies as proximity, and not as an experience of proximity" (OTB 80 [101]).

36. The suffering of the trauma of proximity is thus described by Levinas in a later article as "useless," not subsumed to any "use" or "end" (see Emmanuel Levinas, "Useless Suffering," in *The Provocation of Levinas: Rethinking the Other,* pp. 156–67).

37. One is tempted to believe that Levinas equivocates here: he is speaking of sensibility and, *voilà,* my susceptibility to wounding is my call to responsibility to the other. From the perspective of the already constituted ego, proximity seems to be described on analogy to sensibility—that is, like physical sensibility, proximity is given a constituted meaning only after the "fact." It is only when we follow a thought that runs from proximity to sensibility, rather than following out the one that runs from sensibility to proximity, that the actual relationship between proximity and sensibility is made clear, and sensibility is shown, in a manner of speaking, to depend upon proximity, to derive its meaning qua sensibility (as irreducible to constitutive sense) from the relationship of proximity, that is, when the analyses of the reduction (from the said to the saying) are given their fuller meaning in terms of the possibilities for re-construction (from the saying to the said). We will trace out this double movement in section III of this chapter.

38. "To undergo from the other is an absolute patience only if by this from-the-other [par autrui] is already for-the-other [pour autrui]" (OTB 111 [141]).

39. "The body is neither an obstacle opposed to the soul, nor a tomb that imprisons it, but that by which the self is susceptibility itself. Incarnation is an extreme passivity; to be exposed to sickness, suffering, death, is to be exposed to compassion, and, as a self, to the gift that costs" (OTB 195, n.12 [139]).

40. "The reverting of the ego into a self, the de-posing or de-situating of the ego, is the very modality of disinterestedness. It has the form of a corporeal life devoted to expression and to giving. It is devoted, and does not devote itself: it is as a self despite itself, in incarnation, where it is the very possibility of offering" (OTB 50 [65]).

41. "The passivity of the 'for-another' expresses a sense in it [the 'despite' of the 'despite oneself'] in which no reference, positive or nega-

tive, to a prior will enters. It is the living human corporeality, as a possibility of pain, a sensibility which of itself is the susceptibility to being hurt, a self uncovered, exposed and suffering in its skin. In its skin it is stuck in its skin, not having its skin to itself, a vulnerability. Pain is not simply a *symptom* of a frustrated will, its meaning is not adventitious. The painfulness of pain, the malady or malignity of illness (*mal*), and, in the pure state, the very patience of corporeality, the pain of labor and aging, are adversity itself, the against oneself that is in the self" (OTB 51 [65–66]). This "against oneself that is in the self" is, for Levinas, the other-in-the-same or proximity—the very possibility of pain.

42. "In responsibility for another subjectivity is only this unlimited passivity of an accusative which does not issue out of a declension it would have undergone starting with the nominative. This accusation can be reduced to the passivity of the self only as a persecution, but a persecution that turns into an expiation" (OTB 112 [143]).

43. "The self is a *sub-jectum;* it is under the weight of the universe, responsible for everything" (OTB 116 [147]).

44. Recall the discussion of the "dream-like" quality of a knowledge that is not in "contact" with an alterity that would ground it in "reality" (chapter 3).

45. "[Exposure as sensibility] is a having been offered without any holding back and not the generosity of offering oneself, which would be an act, and already presupposes the unlimited undergoing of the sensibility. In the having been offered without any holding back the past infinitive form underlines the nonpresent, the noncommencement, the noninitiative of the sensibility. This noninitiative is older than any present and is not a passivity contemporaneous with and counterpart of an act. It is the hither side of the free and the non-free, the anarchy of the Good" (OTB 75 [94]). But compare: "The subject in saying approaches a neighbor in expressing itself, in being expelled, in the literal sense of the term, out of any locus, no longer *dwelling*, not stomping any ground" (OTB 48–49 [62]). Does this mean that there was, first, a subject "stomping a ground" that was only later expelled from this locus? This "no longer" bespeaks, on our reading, a manner of speaking from the perspective of a subject already stomping a ground, which is but one descriptive option, but one that begins (as is necessary, as we hope to show in the next chapter) with derivative structures. We are in the course of discovering another, a description of the subject "before" it has stomped any ground, a description of the subject in its pre-original (in)-condition. These two "directions," and their interrelationships, will be explored in our next chapter.

46. "The present is a beginning in my freedom, whereas the Good is

not presented to freedom; it has chosen me before I have chosen it" (OTB 11 [13]). "The passivity of the one, its responsibility and its pain, do not begin in consciousness—that is, they do not begin. On the hither side of consciousness, they consist in this pre-original hold of the Good over it, always older than any present, any beginning" (OTB 57 [73]).

47. "In an approach I am first a servant of a neighbor, already late and guilty for being late" (OTB 87 [110]). "Extreme urgency . . . I do not have time to face it. . . . It [the face] reclaimed me before I came. The delay is irrecuperable. [Retard irrécupérable.] 'I opened . . . he had disappeared' [Canticle of Canticles, IV, 6]. My presence does not respond to the extreme urgency of the assignation. I am accused of having delayed [d'avoir tardé]" (OTB 88–89 [111–12]).

48. "Ipseity is not an abstract point, the center of a rotation, identifiable on the basis of the trajectory traced by this movement of consciousness, but a point already identified from the outside, not having to identify itself in the present nor state its identity, already older than the time of consciousness" (OTB 107 [135]).

49. "Already the position of the subject is a deposition, not a *conatus essendi*. It is from the first a substitution by a hostage expiating for the violence of the persecution itself" (OTB 127 [163]).

50. This having been spoken is not my passivity as a speaker before a language that speaks me rather than my speaking it, the passivity of *die Sprache spricht* (OTB 47 [61], 54 [70]), as for Levinas it is I who speak language rather than being spoken by it. But my speaking is already spoken (for) insofar as my speaking is not my own production, at least not mine alone, but a response to a face, to another who calls me to speak.

51. The problem of finding a language in which to articulate this deepest identification or meaning of the subjectivity of subject as "otherwise than being," as saying or responsibility, in ontological language (the only language we have) pushes Levinas to descriptive extremes that nevertheless implicate him, as he avows, in a certain betrayal, the recognition and tracing out of which is a textual strategy intended to reduce this betrayal and promote the possibility of a certain if always limited fidelity to that which is at issue. (We shall deal with these issues more extensively in the following two chapters.) Thus Levinas's own use of the copula in describing the subjectivity of the subject is (as ours must be) carefully qualified. He therefore writes (in a note commenting on substitution and the recurrence of the subject as on "the hither side of the act-passivity alternative"): "One could be tempted to take substitution to be the being of the entity that is the ego. And, to be sure, the hither side of the ego lends itself to our speaking only by referring to

being, from which it withdraws and which it undoes. The said of language always says being. But in the moment of an enigma language also breaks with its own conditions, as in a skeptical saying, and says a signification before the event, a before-being" (OTB 196, n.20 [149]). Levinas, with this admission and this caveat, does (and it would seem necessarily so) succumb to the temptation, employing the categories of being to describe the otherwise than being, despite titanic efforts to, as much as possible (by using qualifiers such as "as if," "as," "perhaps"), avoid doing so; e.g.: "This transfer, other than interested, 'otherwise than essence,' is subjectivity itself" (OTB 111 [141]). We, in our descriptions, also succumb. In attempting to describe the deepest meaning of the "otherwise than being" we say what it "is." We sin. But we hope to sin not boldly, but rather sheepishly.

52. "But in the 'pre-history' of the ego posited for itself speaks a responsibility. The self is through and through a hostage, older than the ego, prior to principles. What is at stake for the self, in its being, is not to be. Beyond egoism and altruism it is the religiosity of the self" (OTB 117 [150]). Before the "history" of the ego, the "prehistory" of responsibility; before egoity (enjoyment and separation) and altruism (giving of what I have), a binding together of myself and the other. We will begin to trace out the lineaments of this "religiosity" very shortly.

53. We thus take our distance from the reading provided by Robert Gibbs that suggests that there is such an ego prior to obligation, and as necessary for obligation: "The me who is looked at does not come into existence at the moment I am seen. In order for me to learn from the other, to speak to the other, to be hospitable to the other, I must already be someone. Were I created in the moment when the other looks at me, I would have no resources, no inner freedom with which to become responsible. Levinas develops the concept of *ipseity,* of my corporeal uniqueness, drawing heavily on phenomenological resources. The individual person, before meeting an other, is a self-constituted, corporeal, specific self; not a member of a species, but in many key ways a self-created person. The intensity that allows me to fashion my own world is needed to create the infinite responsibility I have in relation to the other" (Gibbs, *Correlations,* p. 28). We are arguing, on the contrary, that the someone that I am, my subjectivity qua subject, is the learner, the speaker, the hospitable one, and that the subject capable of these things is derivative of the subject called to be them. I have no inner freedom with which to become responsible, on our reading, but am responsible before freedom. Even my corporeal self, that is (it is true) "in many key ways a self-created person," this separated self of *ipseity,* is separated, as we hope to show, *for* responsibility. That is, on our reading, the intensity

of fashioning my own world does not create the infinite responsibility I have in relation to the other; rather, it is as derivative of, and in service to, my infinite responsibility for the other that the structures of my own world are fashioned. (We wonder, in an aside, whether this difference in reading, ours from that of Gibbs, is not a matter of Gibbs's reading of Levinas in correlation with Rosenzweig, and particularly with Rosenzweig's attention, in part I of *The Star of Redemption,* to the construction of independent elements, and our reading of Levinas outside of that context. Does our less Jewish reading of Levinas miss the context, and thus miss the point of Levinas's discussion, or does a reading of Levinas in this context overdetermine Levinas's discussion, causing Gibbs to miss Levinas's radicalization of what is without question its context? We are, given the absence of any reader who would be able to read from a position of pure neutrality, skeptical of any definitive answers to such a question, but the possibilities in it are perhaps instructive.)

54. That is, these descriptions, as we have argued, are to be read as descriptions of an underlying structure abstracted from the reality that they structure, and that have no reality themselves apart from that which they structure, neither ontologically nor as a chronologically prior reality. (Just as the mental processes of a human being can be described as conditioning human behavior—whether they in fact do or not is not our point—but there are no human mental processes apart from or prior to concrete bodily, behaving human being, so the structure of "enjoyment" conditions human existence as we find it, but neither preceded nor exists independently of such concrete, human existence.)

55. This claim is repeated in *Otherwise Than Being:* "Pain penetrates into the very heart of the for-oneself that beats in enjoyment, in the life that is complacent in itself, that lives of its life" (OTB 56 [72]). "The complacency of subjectivity, a complacency experienced for itself, is its very 'egoity,' its substantiality. But at the same time there is a coring out [dénucléation] of the imperfect happiness which is the murmur of sensibility. There is a non-coinciding of the ego with itself, restlessness, insomnia, beyond what is found again in the present" (OTB 64 [81]).

56. Again, we would at least feel compelled to qualify Gibbs's analyses: "In *Totality and Infinity,* Levinas creates a moment of enjoyment prior to the ethical. We live for the sake of the Same, for assimilating what is other into ourselves. Independent of others, we stake a claim and make a home. We enter the world from our home, and we go home when the day is through. Labor is acquiring what is other and transforming it into property, which can be stored at home. Labor now occurs in this pre-ethical world as my triumph over the resistance of matter, furnishing me with good things to eat, a house to be home in, clothes

to protect me from the elements, etc. The key moment is the making mine by labor, the bringing it home—economics, in an etymological sense.

"Levinas now locates this economic theory of labor and enjoyment as pre-ethical, prior to the experience of the face, in order to have the other break into my self-centered world. At that moment I must feed him with my food and bring him into my home. Without an an-ethical economic life, I would not be capable of hospitality, of receiving the other, of giving from myself" (*Correlations,* p. 236).

We are arguing that there is no "moment of enjoyment prior to the ethical" (in either *Totality and Infinity* or *Otherwise Than Being*), and that our living "for the sake of the Same, for assimilating" needs be thought of as not "first"—to be interrupted by ethics later—but as a necessary "moment" of an ethical intrigue in which this enjoyment/labor/economy is meaningful even as enjoyment and that which serves enjoyment. (And a tracing out of this intrigue will become an increasingly explicit focus of this work from this point forward.) We do not, we are arguing, "stake a claim and make a home" "independent of others." The disturbance of the other is what makes a home necessary in the first place, and a home for me is established by the gracious welcome of the other (in the mode of the feminine). The "pre-ethical world as my triumph over the resistance of matter" is, for us, post-ethical, and while it can "appear" to be pre-ethical from a certain perspective, and be legitimately described from that point of view, it is in fact a derivative structure, already a function of a larger, already ethical, intrigue. Enjoyment, separation, the "an-ethical," are necessary to that intrigue. And whereas for Gibbs, "without an an-ethical economic life, I would not be capable of hospitality," for us, without this an-ethical life being already grounded in and derivative of a pre-original ethical "life," I would not even be capable of being called to hospitality. Moreover, we would argue, for Levinas, what counts is not that I am "capable" of hospitality, but that I am *as* hospitality, whether I am capable of it or not.

57. Recall from that text: "It is certainly a great glory for the creator to have set up a being capable of atheism, a being which, without having been *causa sui,* has an independent view and word and is at home with itself. We name 'will' a being conditioned in such a way that without being *causa sui* it is first with respect to its cause" (TI 58–59 [30]). In *Otherwise Than Being,* Levinas is careful to distinguish his use of the idea of creation from both the philosophical/ontological employment of the term (OTB 110 [140], 113–14 [145]) and its related theological contexts (OTB 113–14 [145]).

58. "It is the obsession by the other, my neighbor, accusing me of a

fault which I have not committed freely, that reduces the ego to a self on the hither side of my identity, prior to all self-consciousness, and denudes me absolutely. Must we call creature status [*créaturialité*] this 'hither side,' which a being [*l'être*] retains no trace of, this hither side older than the plot [*intrigue*] of egoism woven in the *conatus* of being?" (OTB 92 [117]).

59. "The oneself cannot form itself; it is already formed with absolute passivity. In this sense it is the victim of a persecution that paralyzes any assumption that could awaken in it, so that it would posit itself *for* itself. This passivity is that of an attachment that has already been made, as something irreversibly past, prior to all memory and all recall. It was made in an irrecuperable time which the present, represented in recall, does not equal, in a time of birth or creation, of which nature or creation retains a trace, unconvertible into a memory. . . . The oneself is a creature, but an orphan by birth or an atheist no doubt ignorant of its Creator, for if it knew it it would again be taking up its commencement. The recurrence of oneself refers to the hither side of the present in which every identity identified in the said is constituted. It is already constituted when the act of constitution first originates" (OTB 104–5 [132–33]).

60. That is, my responsibility for the other, fraternity, is possible only in terms of a "conditioning" parentage, described as paternity in *Totality and Infinity,* and as maternity in *Otherwise Than Being.* We shall have to investigate this parentage more deeply in the chapters to follow.

61. This "other" need not be the "same" other (the same empirical person) in both cases to be "the other" in both cases. For whereas Levinas's descriptions of fecundity in *Totality and Infinity* are an attempt to show how the father lives in the hope of extending "the good" to the world also through his son, we are arguing that the same process is evoked already in the discourse on the home where the feminine other (the mother, on our reading, in place of the father in the discourse on fecundity), in welcoming me into the home, hopes to extend her "goodness" to the world through me (the son/daughter), who will in turn be called to extend that good to others (and through my son to still further others), that is, across an ethical, religio-familial intrigue the shape of which we are here beginning to trace.

62. We do not believe, as indicated in the Introduction to this part of the work, that there is, between the two texts, a change in the general structure of the thought, but only a change in focus, a change in which the structures of enjoyment and economy have not been jettisoned, but made marginal by the specific focus of the latter work. We thus maintain that what is claimed of "the subject" in the second book in a focused

way was true for the subject also in the first, even if we must look a little harder to find it there given that it was other concerns that were center stage.

63. "For the condition for, or the unconditionality of, the self does not begin in the auto-affection of a sovereign ego that would be, after the event, 'compassionate' for another. Quite the contrary: the uniqueness of the responsible ego is possible only *in* being obsessed by another, in the trauma suffered prior to any auto-identification, in an unrepresentable *before*" (OTB 123 [158]).

64. "The 'giving out of signs' would amount to a prior representation of these signs, as though speaking consisted in translating thoughts into words and consequently in having been first *for-oneself* and *at home with* oneself, like a substantial consistency. The relationship with the other would then extend forth as an intentionality, out of a subject posited in itself and for itself, disposed to play, sheltered from all ills and measuring by thought the being disclosed as the field of this play" (OTB 48 [61]). This is precisely what proximity denies to the subject. For the saying, there is no play; my responsibility to the other is seriousness itself: "Nothing is more grave, more august, than responsibility for the other, and saying, in which there is no play, has a gravity more grave than its own being or not being" (OTB 46 [58]).

65. We have corrected Lingis's translation of *involontaire* as "voluntary."

66. "But the absolute accusation, prior to freedom, constitutes freedom which, allied to the Good, situates beyond and outside of all essence" (OTB 118 [150]).

67. "A fraternity that cannot be abrogated, an unimpeachable assignation, proximity is an impossibility to move away without the torsion of a complex, without 'alienation' or fault" (OTB 87 [109–10]).

68. "Saying is a denuding of denuding, a giving a sign of its very signifyingness, an expression of exposure, a hyperbolic passivity" (OTB 49 [63]).

69. "The passivity prior to the passivity-activity alternative, more passive than any inertia, is described by the ethical terms accusation, persecution, and responsibility for the others" (OTB 121 [151]).

70. "Impassively undergoing the weight of the other, thereby called to uniqueness, subjectivity no longer belongs to the order where the alternative of activity and passivity retains its meaning. We have to speak here of expiation as uniting identity and alterity" (OTB 118 [151]). "The self as an expiation is prior to activity and passivity" (OTB 116 [148]).

71. "In this analysis we do not mean to reduce an entity that would

be the ego to the act of substituting itself that would be the being of this entity. Substitution is not an act; it is a passivity inconvertible into an act, the hither side of the act-passivity alternative, the exception that cannot be fitted into the grammatical categories of noun or verb, save in the said that thematizes them" (OTB 117 [149]).

72. "But this pre-original saying does move into language, in which saying and said are correlative of one another, and the saying is subordinated to its theme" (OTB 6 [7]).

73. "But this saying remains, in its activity, a passivity, more passive than all passivity, for it is a sacrifice without reserve, without holding back, and in this non-voluntary—the sacrifice of a hostage designated who has not chosen himself to be a hostage, but possibly elected by the Good, in an involuntary election not assumed by the elected one" (OTB 15 [18–19]).

74. We are arguing that this is precisely what the other in the mode of the feminine does for me.

75. Certain passages bespeak this transformation of descriptive perspective quite explicitly, e.g.: "This passivity undergone in proximity by the force of an alterity in me is the passivity of a recurrence to oneself which is not the alienation of an identity betrayed. What can it be but a substitution for the others? It is, however, not an alienation, because the other in the same is my substitution for the other through responsibility, for which, I am summoned as someone irreplaceable. I exist through the other and for the other, but without this being an alienation: I am inspired. This inspiration is the psyche" (OTB 114 [146]). "And the proximity of the neighbor in its trauma does not only strike up against me, but exalts and elevates me, and, in the literal sense of the term, inspires me. Inspiration, heteronomy, is the very pneuma of the psyche" (OTB 124 [160]). "Then there is produced in this vulnerability the reversal whereby the other inspires the same" (OTB 64 [81]). "The-one-for-the-other has the form of sensibility or vulnerability, pure passivity or sensibility, passive to the point of becoming an inspiration, that is, alterity in the same, the trope of the body animated by the soul, psyche in the form of a hand that gives even the bread taken from its own mouth" (OTB 67 [85]).

76. There are further the terms that, while permitting of a "negative" interpretation, are transformed, with this change in descriptive perspective, into "positive" ones: "obsession" shifting from being possibly pathological to being "positively" mad in its unremitting love; "giving" shifting from giving up or over to gifting; passion shifting from a suffering to a being inspired.

5

The Two Directions in Language: The Reductive and the Re-constructive

I. From the Saying to the Said: Reduction

I.1. The Reduction

Let us now examine rather more closely the claim we are developing that for Levinas there is no sense in which the conditions of possibility for . . . *exist* in the sense that they *present* themselves to us, that they are present to experience or as experienced. There is a double sense in which this is true of "the saying," which we are in the course of arguing here—albeit circuitously—is the condition of possibility for discourse (which is itself a condition of possibility of dialogue, and so here we are dealing with the complex matter of a condition of possibility for a condition of possibility for . . .).

On the one hand, we are faced with the simple problem that the conditions of possibility for experience cannot be part of that experience itself lest the experience of these conditions would require, qua experienced, yet further conditions of possibility for the experience of them, which, if experienced, would require yet further conditions of possibility for their appearance, ad infinitum, ad nauseam (if contact with a ground is the cure for nausea). The Husserlian project of eidetic reduction (the representation of the conditions of possibility for representation, and for intentions other than those of representation) is perhaps an infinite task (opening upon ever new horizons) for precisely this reason. But if Husserl's reductive thoughts are sometimes dizzying, he saves us from nausea in stilling the vertiginous descent with the anodyne of the assurance of "presence," that self-grounding moment of intuition (the presence of the present) wherein, at the end of the day, the conditions of possibility for experience are experienced as conditioning themselves, conditions and conditioned, subject and object, past, present, and future, here and there, being and the experience of being, all "present" (or at least presentable) at once. And here, for Levinas, Husserl represents the whole of the Western philosophical tradition in its proclivity to idealism: wherein being and the disclosure of being are of a piece. Being subsumes (or has already provided) its own conditions of possibility as constituting a part of itself, as it does the showing of itself to itself: presence, and thus truth. Western philosophy is the performance of overcoming the problem by which the conditions of possibility for experience cannot show themselves in experience. Western philosophy as ontology is the showing of being to itself, the coincidence of condition and conditioned in a synchronic present.

Given the impotence of this "formal" problem against the weight of the tradition that produced it (and that persists in enclosing even the conditions of possibility for being within the circle of the comprehension of being), Levinas has recourse to another, and more substantial (if less substanc-ial), prohibition to subsuming the conditions of possibility for experience into experience itself: the unrepresentable (because ethically rather than ontologically qualified) "otherwise than being." In *Otherwise Than Being,* as we have been attempting to show, this "mode"[1] of "otherwise than being" is the subject as saying, the subject that in its responsibility for the other is exposed to the other, is for-the-other before being for-itself, whose saying to the other, "before"[2] being the saying of something, is a saying of itself as saying, a signifying, not of a content, but of signification itself, an expression of its signifyingness, the expression of its expression: subjectivity. But this (active or quasi-active) signification of (the passivity of) signification (of my having always already been signified), that which makes the saying of contents and thus communication as the transfer of information possible, does not itself become a content or an information communicated, is not a "being" (be that as noun, or as verb), is not some-thing, identifiable in a said.

We cannot therefore hope to "experience" this condition of possibility in any straightforward way, reading it off from out of experience as one experience among experiences, as a privileged experience, even if there may be certain privileged experiences that allow us to catch a glimpse of the trace that it leaves in the said that it conditions. But, as there is no "hinter-world" into which we might retreat in order to experience this condition directly, it must therefore be possible to arrive at a description of it (if it can be at all described) from out of the experience of life as lived. Levinas refers to this "process," this "procedure," this "method," which takes place *within* philosophy, as "the reduction," in an obvious reference to the phenomenological reduction of his teacher, Husserl. But whereas the conditions of possibility for intentional objects could, for Husserl, in turn be converted into intentional objects, could be brought to presence, for Levinas—for the reasons we have been outlining—they cannot. For Levinas, the saying, that which makes the said possible, never appears in the said, is inconvertible into a said. But it does, he claims, as constitutive of the said, leave its trace upon the said that it makes possible. It leaves a trace not as nonpresence, as absence, pure and simple—for then it would still be defined (be that negatively) by presence, would not be the trace of an otherwise than being, but nonbeing, nothingness, that for Plato, as Levinas reminds us, "in a certain sense is" (OTB 8 [9]). Its trace in the said, its nonpresence as "otherwise than nothingness," rather, indicates an irreducible diachrony, a diachrony that, qua irreducible, is precisely its resistance to "presence," to being collected into a present in which it could be presented to consciousness as its object. The trace is, therefore, necessarily ambiguous, an enigma, since that of which it is a trace is never present(ed) in it. That of which the trace is a trace is no-thing. Is it therefore "nothing?" Or is it rather "something" irreducible to the mode of quiddity, the mode of thing-ness (if things are identified in a said), and thus "something" that—without being nothing—is not some-thing, but a something that cannot be said, a "something" that is outside of the discourse on somethings and nothings? The trace, in the language of saids (which is the only language there *is*), must remain caught in this ambiguity between being the trace of something otherwise than being, and being simply nothing.

The text of *Otherwise Than Being* can be read, then, in terms of its overall structure (whatever the complications of this approach),[3] as enacting this reduction, the reduction from the said to the saying, across ever deepening structures that either describe conditions of possibility for earlier structures or provide the ever deepening meaning of these conditions: from intentionality to sensibility, to proximity as the meaning of sensibility, and to substitution as the otherwise than being at the base of proximity, and as the relation between the subject and the Infinite (OTB 19 [23]). To trace the trace of the otherwise than being (the subjectivity as saying), we must rehearse the movement of this work—but with this caveat in mind: that the tracing of the trace is conducted, in this work, for as philosophy, in the realm of the said, where, for reasons that will emerge in the next section, everything must show itself, *even* that which cannot show itself. Strange business this. Perhaps impossible. Perhaps im/possible. Whatever be the status we might accord to such an *essai* (*raté?*), the reduction, the attempt to bring to light that which resists the light, the attempt to say the unsayable, must therefore proceed on the basis of its being always already a betrayal of that which it thematizes: the unthematizable. And the perpetual process of reducing ever and again in turn that which is said under the auspices of the reduction will be central to our argument that discourse be read as a possible impossibility. But more on that in due course.

I.2. The Reduction to the Saying

For the present, let us proceed with the reduction by picking up our discussion of the saying and the said at that point where, within the said, the word "being" was shown, in speech, to be suspended between the various conjugations of the verb "to be" (referring to "being" or the "being of being") and the declensions of its forms as nominalized (referring to "beings"); that is, let us return to the amphibology of being and entities. The question, we recall, goes as follows: starting out from speech as identification, by indicating that something *is* x, am I in fact identifying, first of all, an entity x that exists across time, or the fact of its existing, its x-ing, across time? Am I identifying an entity ("That is a chair"), or an essence ("The being of that thing is to be in a chair-ly manner")? That is to say that, for Levinas, the very saying of a said (saying something to someone), the delineation of what something *is,* enacts (or participates in) the amphibology of being and entities by placing itself in (or finding itself within) the temporalization of time—the divergence of the same from itself—that makes possible both the gathering of this time into a substance identified (a nominalization in the said, which is a stilling of this "flux") and an attunement to the vibration of being across this divergency (an ear for the verbality of being).

Even when everything is turned toward the ontological project of stilling the temporalization of time through identifications of the same made across it, Levinas maintains that the resultant saids nevertheless retain, for those with ears to hear ("the 'eye that listens' "; OTB 30 [38]), a trace of the temporalization out of which these identifications emerge. Temporalization that remains temporalization, that remains a flux not gatherable into a present (but, in fact, making for the gathering into presence), "shows" itself (though obliquely, in betrayal by the very fact that this un-(re)-present-able time is here (re)presented) across the phenomenon of senescence, across the inexorable slipping away of time that cannot be gathered up, but that is lost time, time as pure loss. Philosophy, as ontology, exhausts itself (ages!) in attempting to collect even this time, presenting it to itself by memory, or by history—to the point where philosophy can be characterized as the refusal of loss, or the denial of death.[4] But philosophy, like the aging philosophers engaged in it, and despite ever new intellectual facelifts, ages; it is not what it was and they not what they were, and death approaches.

The inability to gather up time, the passing of time, the lapse, is traceable not so much through thought (for in thinking the lapse one is already assembling it, correlating it to a present—that which the lapse qua lapse refuses) as through sensibility. Sensation is the body's attunement to the temporalization of time, the body's participation in the temporalization of time, my being caught in, already bathed in, the passing of time. Sensation signifies, before it signifies a constituted meaning, the passing of time and my passivity in the face of this passing. Pain is not first the awareness of pain, but being *in* pain. Sensation bears me along, before and independently of my taking up a position regarding it. It is vulnerability, susceptibility, affectivity, my being borne along by a temporality I have not yet had time to constitute.

It is, phenomenologically speaking, as a vulnerability, as a susceptibility, as an affectivity, moreover, that I am affected by the other as face. Among the "sensations" whose meaning is irreducible to my constitution of the experience of them is my responsibility for the other, a responsibility that comes to me precisely across a temporality that I have in no sense constituted, a temporality that does not await my constitution of it, but that has already "passed by" by the time I arrive. I am always already responsible for the other, before I would take up a position regarding him (and in terms of which I must take up a position); with respect to responsibility, I am always already *en retard*.[5] Levinas, as we have seen, calls "proximity" this "sensibility" with respect to the other, and we have seen too why this relationship, proximity, has a special, even privileged, place among the sensations—for here the "object" sensed resists being assimilated to my meanings as constituted meanings in a particular and a particularly powerful way: as an *ethical* prohibition. Not only can I not subsume this meaning in terms of constituted meanings, I *may* not do so—and whatever force the *cannot* is capable of sustaining against the ego as *je peux* derives from this *may not*. Against the ever returning and ever powerful proclivities of the intending consciousness that insists on making everything present, the face throws up a surd, an ethical refusal (across an irreducible diachrony) whose force qua resistant is purely ethical. And this is what makes the trace that is the face (the face that is not the trace of something else, but a trace of itself) of the other enigmatic. For I can, as with any sensation, assimilate it to the meanings I constitute, be this after the fact, after its purely sensational trauma has passed. But with the face, I *may not* do so. And it is this ethical may not that is the ever weak warrant for the cannot of the assimilation of sensation, not only as proximity, but for sensation *tout court*. If we alluded to this dependence (the dependence of sensation qua sensation on proximity) in the previous chapter, we may here understand why this is the case. I cannot reduce my suffering to my experience of suffering because my suffering, my affectivity, *is* the other in the same—an other that cannot, across the irreducible diachrony introduced by responsibility, be reduced to my "present" experience, that is, to my experience period. The other who calls me to responsibility from out of an irrecuperable past keeps sensation itself from being reduced to a meaning that would be in correlation with consciousness; the diachrony of responsibility founds the diachrony of senescence, even if it is across senescence that the diachrony of responsibility is, in the reduction, traced.

If, then, in the saying of a said, in saying something to an other, the "saying" of the said can be traced across the said by dint of its being said to an other, by dint of its being an appeal for investiture which shows that it is always already *for* the other, the condition of possibility for this situation—my subjectivity as saying, which does not show itself in the said that it says—must be traced across the deepening structures of my passivity, of my exposure *to* the other, my being affected *by* the other, arriving at the *for* the other of my subjectivity that is the condition of possibility of my susceptibility, in a reduction from the said to the saying.

II. Intermezzo: Between Movements

We have shown, in the second part of chapter 4, and in the opening section of the present chapter, respectively, the meaning, in its deepest sense, of the saying for Levinas, and how he arrives at a description of this meaning—always enigmatic—by means of the reduction from the said to the saying. But if the saying is taken as the condition of possibility for the said (which guards a trace of the saying that makes it possible—that which makes the reduction possible), we must still describe how the said is itself constituted as a response to that which conditions it, namely, as response to the saying (i.e., how the saying enters into correlation with the said, becomes the saying of the said, that which makes ontological language—the language that bears upon the question of being—possible, and, as we shall see, necessary). And so we must follow out the movement from the saying to the said.

It is true that, in the Levinasian corpus, this movement, from the saying to the said, receives, in relation to the movement from the said to the saying, relatively short shrift. It is, for example, given *specific* thematic attention for only a few pages in *Otherwise Than Being* (16 [19–20], 157–62 [200–207]), and also relatively little in *Totality and Infinity* (212–15 [187–90]).[6] Levinas's philosophical obsession, that which occupies his attentions and all but dominates his oeuvre, is clearly the movement from the said to the saying, is clearly with making a case that at the bottom—or at the heart—of life-world experience and of language, and as integral to such experience, there abides, as foundational to that experience, an ethical moment—my responsibility for the other as substitution for the other, my *self* as substitution. The argument that we are in the course of developing in this work is, however, that the proper context for an understanding of Levinas's preoccupation with the movement from the said to the saying is a concern with how the saying (myself as ethical responsibility for the other) makes possible a said (an ontologically qualified linguistic regime) that is yet ethically qualified (in the qualified manner to be described), that is spoken as yet animated by the ethical meaning that undergirds its very meaningfulness. That is, Levinas's concern is not with delineating the structures of some "hinter-world" into which we might escape as a refuge from being, but in delineating the structures *for* being itself (and he finds "ethics" constitutive of being, that is, he argues that being does not rest on itself). His preoccupation with the reduction from the said to the saying is in the interest of understanding the possibilities for *being* good, of seeking a warrant for the ethical imperatives[7] that must govern a society if that society is to be just. Robert Gibbs is right, we believe, to contend that "[t]he central issue in Levinas's thought is how we come into society,"[8] even if, we believe, following Levinas—and this is what we are here arguing—this central issue can (from a slightly adumbrated perspective) be reformulated more deeply as "how we justly work out the society we find ourselves in always already" (or "how we keep the discourse that animates dialogue alive"), or, even more radically, "how *I* work toward just social structures from out of my pre-original responsibility for the other(s)" (or "how the saying inspires the said").[9]

That the movement from the saying to the said is as central to Levinas's overall philosophical proposal as that from the said to the saying (despite the fact that this movement is not thematized nearly to the degree as is its sister movement) is evinced, we believe, by the plethora of references to, or anticipations of, this movement that litter the analyses of *Otherwise Than Being* before the point at which in that text this movement is explicitly thematized, appearing sometimes in the notes and sometimes in the text itself. The abiding context of the reduction to the saying and its descriptions, the necessary milieu in terms of which sense can be made of them, is, we would argue, the reverse movement from the saying to the said.[10] Levinas's thought in *Otherwise Than Being* (and his analyses of language as integral to that thought) if taken as a whole (and not partitioned into the discrete analyses in terms of which it necessarily—on Levinas's own judgment, deceptively—proceeds)[11] moves *simultaneously* in two directions: from the said to the saying as a propaedeutic for moving back—enriched—to the said, which can then be shown to have been possible in the first place only in terms of the saying, but a saying that (as we shall see) is necessarily betrayed in this "showing" of it (in this dragging it into the said), forcing us to seek *again* the inspiration for this said in a new saying, which is the saying of and for a new said, etc. Such a movement establishes what might better be conceived of as a pendulum motion than that of a circle or a spiral, a dual motion that in our next section will be revealed as inspired by the desire for, as tracing out of the production of, justice.

Theodore de Boer, consistent with what he calls an ethical transcendental reading of Levinas (the reading that we, too, are advocating),[12] refers to these two movements as "the way down" (from the said to the saying that is the said's condition of possibility), and "the way up" (from the saying as the condition to the said that it conditions).[13] Jacques Derrida's terms for these two Levinasian movements would seem to be, respectively, interruption and resumption.[14] Another tempting possibility, evoked by a vocabulary popularized by Derrida, would be to refer to these movements, respectively, as "the deconstructive" and the "reconstructive," terms that while they might prove in many ways illuminating nevertheless bear—in contemporary philosophical discourse—certain perhaps obfuscatory connotations.[15] For our part, we have settled on Levinas's own term, "the reductive," to describe the movement from the said to the saying and have concocted (as a kind of *bricoleur,* to name what we shall argue involves a kind of *bricolage*) the term "re-constructive" to describe the movement from the saying to the said, although some caution will have to be exercised in its use. Having already traced out the reduction in the preceding section, it is to an analysis of the latter movement that we now turn, attentive to the fact that the iterative "re-" of "re-constructive" will keep this movement from being considered as a "construction" in any straightforward sense.

III. From the Saying to the Said: Re-construction

Hostage to the other; I am already hostage to the others.

If there had been a singular singular other, there would have been no *problem:* "If proximity ordered me only to the other alone, there would not have been any problem, in even the most general sense of the term. A question would not have been born, nor consciousness, nor self-consciousness. The responsibility for the other is an immediacy antecedent to questions, it is proximity. It is troubled and becomes a problem when a third party enters" (OTB 157 [200]). That is, with the approach of a third party (*le tiers*), I am no longer[16] confronted with a singular singular other but also with another other, an other to the other,[17] and another other for me to whom I owe all of the allegiance that I owe to the first other. With the approach of the third there is, thus, a *problem:*[18] to whom do I give myself, my resources, the bread from my mouth when the demands upon it, upon me, are multiple? "The third party introduces a contradiction in the saying whose signification before the other until then went in one direction. It is of itself the limit of responsibility and the birth of the question: What do I have to do with justice?" (OTB 157 [200]).[19] Justice, wherein each is to be given his or her due, as a function of the relationship of proximity wherein I owe *everything* to *each* other, demands the impossible: "a comparison among incomparables" (OTB 16 [20], 158 [201–2]).

The matter of justice is therefore "a question of consciousness" (OTB 157 [200]), and a question for consciousness: "The act of consciousness is motivated by the presence of the third party alongside the neighbor approached" (OTB 16 [20]). In the face of the problem of multiple demands upon my responsibility, responsible to the demand of the problem of multiple faces, "Justice is necessary, that is, comparison, coexistence, contemporaneousness, assembling, order, thematization, the visibility of faces, and thus the intentionality and the intellect, and in intentionality and the intellect, the intelligibility of a system, and thence also co-presence on an equal footing as before a court of justice" (OTB 157 [200]). It is for justice—in light of my not yet "regulated" proximity to *all* others, to *each* other, and the unlimited and conflicting responsibilities this entails—that proximity, "the pure signification of saying, the anarchic one-for-the-other of beyond being, [would] revert to being or fall into being, into a conjunction of entities, into essence showing itself in the said" (OTB 157 [199]). The (re-)construction[20] of *being* (already "reduced" for its meaning to the signification of the *otherwise than being*), the movement from ethics to justice, the movement from the saying to the said, is motivated by the saying itself—the limit of my responsibility, paradoxically, motivated by my unlimited responsibilities. To trace this movement from the saying to the said is thus to trace the "latent birth of a question,"[21] the question of justice, from within the saying itself.[22]

Justice, required by the approach of the third, thus imposes itself—from within proximity, from within the saying—as the "incessant correction"[23] of proximity and saying. This "correction" produces a certain distancing within proximity itself which is precisely the lack of any distance (the impossibility of taking distance), allows for the spacing (that between subject and object) that constitutes consciousness, and, consequently, for the relationships that arise within it, that are made possible by it, and an extensive list of such relationships could be assembled from the text,[24] relationships that could be said to together make up the "domain of the said." Now, it is true that the technical details of *how* the said would arise from out of pure saying are decidedly sketchy in Levinas's text,[25] even if we are given the reason *why* this movement from the saying to the said is necessary. Could it be, however (and such is our ongoing argument), that this paucity in explanation need be the case, because the said does not *in fact* arise from the pure saying as if there were, at first, historically speaking, my absolute responsibility for the other, and then, the next day, an other other who would come to interrupt this party of two, even if Levinas's manner of speaking here suggests that it does? Might, rather, this manner of speaking serve other purposes: namely, to indicate a transcendental rather than a chronological priority, a reading of priority that complicates the picture (in making a linear description running from ethics to justice, from the saying to the said, impossible), but that would allow us, in the end, to read differently (otherwise?) the role of responsibility in this philosophy?

This argument is advanced, we believe, by examining Levinas's frequently repeated claim, in the passages regarding the entry of the third, that this entry is not to be read as an empirical event:[26] "It is not that the entry of the third party would be an empirical fact, and that my responsibility for the other finds itself constrained to a calculus by the 'force of things' " (OTB 158 [201]). The fracturing of my responsibility into multiple responsibilities is not a function of the occurrence that, in empirical-historical fact, a third party shows up demanding the same responsibility from me as the "first" other (le premier venu), but is already effectuated in my responsibility to "the first comer." "In the proximity of the other, all the others than the other obsess me, and already obsession cries out for justice, demands measure and knowing, is consciousness" (OTB 158 [201]).

How is this so? We would maintain that the face of the other other is not an empirical third, but a "structural" third, only if "society" is presupposed from the first, with the coming of the first other, as Levinas asserts: "The others concern me from the first." At the approach of the other, the other other (the third), if not already there, at least simultaneously approaches. Levinas follows this assertion with another in which—and we think not coincidentally—the metaphor employed is familial: "Here [where "all the others that obsess me do not affect me as examples of the same genus united with the neighbor by resemblance or common nature"] fraternity precedes the commonness of genus" (OTB 159 [202]).[27] So I am not responsible for the other (who as other is precisely the resistance to any a priori commonality with me or with the other other) on the basis of our shared genus (or any other commonality). But I *am* responsible for him. The fact of this responsibility is, according to Levinas, based upon a fraternity (where fraternity would seem to mean no more than the "fact" of this responsibility)[28] that precedes any commonality of kind. And this fraternity is important for justice, moreover, insofar as it is in terms of this fraternity that there can be justice also for me—without which justice cannot be just. So what, if not the commonness of genus, resemblance, or nature, is the basis of this fraternity, this fraternity that is the context of my concern for the others? On what is this "human family," that cannot rely upon the genus "human" to do the job, founded as a family?

This question is best addressed, we maintain, by considering these passages in concert with another which almost immediately precedes them (separated by a paragraph that brings the thoughts we are about to consider into the context of the necessity of representation for justice). Here, considering the "incessant correction of the asymmetry of proximity" through "weighing, thought, objectification":

> There is a betrayal of my anarchic relation with illeity, but also a new relationship with it: it is only thanks to God that, as a subject incomparable with the other, I am approached as an other by the others, that is, "for myself." "Thanks to God" [Grâce à Dieu] I am another for the others. God is not involved as an alleged interlocutor: the reciprocal relationship binds me to the other man in the trace of transcendence, in illeity. The passing of God, of whom I can speak only by reference to this aid or this grace, is precisely the reverting of the incomparable subject into a member of society. (OTB 158 [201–2])

My membership in society, justice for me, a human fraternity in which I am a (br)other to the other, is here attributed to the grace of God. There is a temptation to read this "grace of God" that makes me into a member of society along empirical lines: the other *may* (and thank God if this turns out to be the case, for over this I have no control, even if I have ultimate responsibility for it) take me for an other, and then there will be justice for me too. But the "if" is missing from the text, which does not read "thank God *if* I am another for the others," but " 'thanks to God' I *am* another for the others." Human fraternity, a fraternity that includes me, seems to be already in place as the new relationship with illeity [justice] comes to be. Indeed, as we read in the opening "Argument" ("Being and Beyond Being") of *Otherwise Than Being,* it is "[i]n the indirect ways of illeity, in the anarchical provocation that ordains me to the other, [that] is imposed the way which leads to thematization, and to an act of consciousness" (OTB 16 [19–20]). Might it be that the "*how?*" of thematization and consciousness from out of the approach of the third is obscure because it is already implicated in the indirect (and enigmatic) ways of illeity? Might this grace of God require a "transcendental" rather than "empirical" reading? For while I might well be able to arrive at a concept of justice for all the others, might well be able to arrive at the concept, from out of *my* responsibility for each as I am forced by an unlimited number of unlimited responsibilities to distribute *my* bread to the others in a just manner, I could not derive justice for me too from this. For that, the grace of God is required.[29] And what is more surprising is that this grace is already in place with the coming of the other, in an approach that implies the (either prior or coincidental) approach of the third (which means justice for me, without which justice could not be justice),[30] and that this grace is the very nourishment for my graciousness/responsibility for the other. For as Levinas claims (in the context of "having to unravel other intrigues of time than that of the simple succession of presents"): "Men have been able to be thankful [ont pu rendre grâce] for the very fact of finding themselves able to thank [en état de rendre grâce]; the present gratitude is grafted onto itself as onto an already antecedent gratitude" (OTB 10 [12]).[31] This context for my being able to render grace (to be responsible to the other), is a grace already rendered to me (from God, by way of the third), wherein my thinking (consciousness, cognition, rendering justice, . . . in short, "the said") is already a thanking (but in a sense that differs from Heidegger's), a thankfulness grafted on to an antecedent thankfulness.[32] It is this intrigue (from thankfulness to thankfulness, from grace to grace), that carries the question of justice, of a human fraternity that includes me, "beyond the face"—and beyond the faces—and into the realm of God's grace, in a reading that runs through *Totality and Infinity* and *Otherwise Than Being*, and that we are in the course of tracing.

So the very coming of the third, the introduction of justice in which there is already justice for me, the "transcendental" fact that the third approaches with the other, *is* the grace of God. The third party bears the grace of God to me, is the mediator of the indirect ways of illeity. And we have noted that the approach of the third party is not empirical because the third party is always already there at the approach of the other. But have we not already in this work (in the analyses of "Interiority and Economy" in *Totality and Infinity*) come across an other who is always already there at the coming of the other, whose discrete presence welcomed me into a home through which my *jouissance* (already disturbed by the other in becoming "care for the morrow") becomes economy, an economy built around my *jouissance,* that same economy in terms of which the goods stored up against the "care for the morrow" can be called into question by the other who requires them—the way that, after our earlier analyses, responsibility moved into rationality (the same move we are analyzing in *Otherwise Than Being* here)? That discrete other, we recall, is the feminine other, or the other in the mode of the feminine. And if we think (as we earlier suggested as an appropriate reading) this feminine other as a maternal presence, then the feminine other can be seen as serving (and from the first, from birth and before birth!) precisely the function of the mediator of God's grace that is the function, after the analyses of *Otherwise Than Being,* of the third. For the feminine other treats me, from the first, as her other, and this by welcoming me into a home from out of which my possession of the world can be established without (at least not in the same stroke)[33] calling this possession into question. Is the grace of God whereby I am approached as the other of the other not concretely instituted by the other in the mode of the feminine (thought as maternal) who from the first affirms my existence, confirms my egoity, feeds my *conatus,* justifies my freedom, who, before all else, before the beginning (birth), in hospitality (by making for me a home in the world, by making me at home in the world), shows me through her grace that "my lot is important" (OTB 161 [205]) too? Could not this grace be thought of as "the same in the other"? And does the feminine other not from the first welcome me into society (through education and enculturation), make me into a citizen, set me—before I have a say in the matter, in pure grace—upon an equal footing with the others? Does she not, then, institute justice for me, too? This, according to our reading of Levinas, is the grace of God in the concrete. Mothers (or mothering persons, for Levinas specifies that the biological gender of this person is not what is relevant) are (or are the mediators of) the grace of God. Thank God for mothers!

Is it not this "maternal" presence that is, as the instrument of the grace of God, up to the task of founding "fraternity?" Is not the "commonness of a father," that which founds human fraternity after the testimony of *Totality and Infinity,* and that Levinas links to the idea of monotheism,[34] a fraternity that (by grace) makes me the equal of my brother, not mediated—after the testimony to grace read across both *Totality and Infinity* and *Otherwise Than Being*—by the mother? And is it any coincidence, then, that Levinas chooses as one of the central metaphors for the-other-in-the-same of proximity "*maternité?*" In an intrigue[35] that runs from grace to grace, from thankfulness to thankfulness, am I not called to render grace to the other as grace has been rendered unto me, to be motherliness to the other as I have been mothered, to substitute myself for the other (that is, take responsibility for the other) as the other, in the mode of the feminine, has taken, always already, responsibility for me, bearing the other in myself as the (m)other has born(e) me within herself? The other is always already in the same because the same is always already in the other. Is it not this gracious intrigue (in which "God is not involved as an alleged interlocutor" (OTB 158 [201])—for the crux of this intrigue is the human[36]—but which "makes the word God be pronounced, without letting 'divinity' be said"; OTB 162 [206]) that animates both responsibility and justice: from responsibility to responsibility, from justice to justice?

That the other of the other (the third) approaches with the approach of the other is not an empirical fact, in other words, only if my responsibility is from grace to grace, a grace received (in the name of God) from the other (in the mode of the feminine) to become grace I grant ("Here I am, in the name of God"; OTB 149 [190]) to the other. The third party is not an empirical fact that breaks up the "party of two" wherein I would be able to effectuate my full allegiance to the other, because a third is always already "present" at this party in the form of the discrete presence of the feminine other whose antecedent responsibility to me (in welcoming me into a home at the very moment when my enjoyment is always already disturbed by the other) has made possible my responsibility (my capacity to give) to the other. This feminine other is not empirical but "structural" as it is only in terms of this grace *already* received (in the past) that I can be called upon to be gracious (in response to the deep past of the other) in the moment in the face of the singular other. In every encounter of the face, at every moment of responsibility, and as its condition of possibility, the (m)other has always already been; even faced (empirically) by an other alone, the third is there.

This reading becomes possible, this "explanation" of why the third is not merely an empirical other, is possible, we maintain, only if the analyses of *Otherwise Than Being* are read—and we have tried, in the introduction to this part of our work, to show that such was Levinas's intention—as a narrowing and refining in continuity with, rather than a departure from, the analyses of *Totality and Infinity*. That is, we are suggesting that the references to "from grace to grace" and to the idea of "maternity" in *Otherwise Than Being* are to be read as a deepening of the analyses of the "feminine other" and "paternity/fecundity" in *Totality and Infinity,* in terms of an intrigue that—while taking us "beyond the face"—has as its fulcrum, as we shall argue shortly, the face of the other for whom I am alone and fully responsible.[37]

Thanks to God I am already the other to the (feminine) other (conceived of as maternal). I am, moreover, as saying, as the other in the same of proximity, already "motherliness" to the other; I am (as already borne toward the good, born in goodness for goodness) from grace to grace, from motherliness to motherliness. I am the gift and call of grace. The good lies beyond the face (though it "appears" enigmatically, across justice, in my responsibility for the other), is a matter of fecundity, as Levinas, in the analyses of *Totality and Infinity,* has shown.[38] The good, grace, in justice, in society, in the said—thanks to God!

IV. The Saying in Justice: Inspiration and Betrayal

Thanks to God, with the help of God, there is justice—but this justice must, to be just, remain animated by the saying, by proximity. The (pre)structures (my goodness, my responsibility qua subjectivity as saying, my having always already been a recipient of grace, that which is the condition of possibility for my being responsible to the other through justice) "beyond the face," that bear me toward the face, do not efface the face (but converge in it), any more than do the structures that derive from it (that spread out from it): justice in the said.

That is, there *is* no goodness, no ethics, without justice. The good, my subjectivity as the saying, *is* not. The saying, the inspiration of the said, does not *exist.* Its only "appearance" is in the said, as an enigmatic trace, in the said in which everything is conveyed before us, and conveyed before us for justice, but (as we shall see) betrayed. That is, there *is* no pure ethics. It is true that Levinas phenomenologically describes "the saying without the said," but there *is* (as an empirical actuality) no saying without the said, and there cannot be—for the "actualization" of the saying (my giving to the singular other everything owed to this other, namely, everything) would be patently unjust, and thus most unethical (for it would rob the third of this "everything" which is precisely what I owe also to this third).[39] The only goodness that is actual goodness is the good realized in justice. Thus: "The pre-original, anarchic saying is proximity, contact, duty without end, a saying still indifferent to the said and saying itself without giving the said, the one-for-the-other, a substitution." And yet we read in the very next sentence: "It *requires* the signification of the thematizable, states the idealized said, weighs and judges in justice" (OTB 161 [205], our emphasis). The saying *requires* the said as a necessary or ancillary realm if it is going to see the light of day and not be a mere abstraction,[40] some ideal issuing from a nether world in which we do not live and cannot live, wistfully or disdainfully evoked, loved, dreamed of, perhaps, but ignored (or paternalistically "shelved") as impractical in the "real world." The saying is driven, of its own momentum, into the said, where it has a life, but where it only appears in the garb of justice. It is not justice, but makes for justice; it animates, is the spirit of, justice.

Conversely, there is no justice without goodness, without ethics, no said without the saying. To the extent that there *is* the ancillary realm of the said (the realm of being and beings—the only region in which anything *is*), this possibility already refers back to the saying.[41] Justice as the weighing of responsibilities requiring and thus producing thought (consciousness, calculus, philosophy), and the congealing in being of this weighing through the establishment of institutions (culminating in the State), this justice as an equality in which even I—asymmetrically responsible for the other—am ("thanks to God") given my rights, this *equality of justice* is nevertheless born of *inequality,* "born from the signifyingness of signification, the-one-for-the-other, signification" (OTB 159 [202]), and must, if it is to be just, continue to breath the air of signifyingness as the breath that inspires it: "The concern for justice, for the thematizing, the kerygmatic discourse bearing on the said, from the bottom of the saying without the said, the saying as contact, is the spirit[42] in society" (OTB 160 [204]). Justice is "a modality of proximity" (OTB 161 [205]). "Justice, society, the State and its institutions, exchanges and work are comprehensible out of proximity. This means that nothing is outside of the control of responsibility of the one for the other" (OTB 159 [202–3]).

It is important to Levinas to show that the saying incarnates the said as its animating spirit and its condition of possibility, for if it does not we are left with the self-interest of the *conatus essendi,* with the war of all against all where everything possible is permitted, and where "goodness" is just a name for a prudence born of a not sufficiently strong—but wily—selfishness, where patience is politics:[43]

> It is then not without importance to know if the egalitarian and just State in which man is fulfilled (and which is to be set up, and especially to be maintained) proceeds from a war of all against all, or from the irreducible responsibility of the one for all, and if it can do without friendships and faces. It is not without importance to know that war does not become the insaturation of a war in good conscience. (OTB 159–60 [203])[44]

That is, Levinas's point (as we stressed earlier) is not that I *should* be the saying,[45] and (as we are stressing here) that society *should* be animated by the good, but that *I am* (before I *am,* ontologically speaking) the saying, and that society—in whatever form I find it, even if it does not look very good—*is* (to whatever degree it is just, to whatever degree it is "human") animated by the good.[46] Levinas's philosophical work, that is to say, is not to be taken, first of all, as the issuing of an imperative, but as descriptive,[47] descriptive of the structures in terms of which moral imperatives, constituted in the said, themselves take on their "just" meanings.[48] And this is why it is important to Levinas to provide a description of what the "true" (ethical) basis of society is (rather than simply issuing—in a hortatory text—an ethical imperative to enact this—as if there were a freedom that would be in a position to be or not to be impelled to respond). For being, and the structures of the said including a just society, have a tendency to take on a life of their own,[49] to be uprooted from their source, cut off from their nourishment, and (without putting too much stock in this one metaphor) wilt ("It is important to recover all these forms beginning with proximity, in which being, totality, the State, politics, techniques, work are at every moment[50] on the point of having their center of gravitation in themselves, and weighing on their own account"; OTB 159 [203]), across what Levinas often refers to as "forgetting."[51]

What is more, this "forgetting" is necessary[52] in order that that which is thereby forgotten can have a life in that which the forgetting makes possible, as we have seen. It is necessary to "forget" my absolute responsibility to the singular other in order to attend to the third, in order to be just;[53] it is necessary to "forget" my absolute responsibility to the singular other lest my responsibility becomes the height of irresponsibility. But it is also necessary to "remember" my absolute responsibility to the singular other lest "justice" become the height of irresponsibility, become the hallow halls of justice emptied of persons,[54] law applied for the sake of the law, or just another name for an all too clever self-interest: "Justice is impossible without the one that renders it finding himself in proximity" (OTB 159 [202]).

My responsibility for the other is thus "realized" only in justice, where it already has to have forgotten itself, where it cannot responsibly *be* itself. Levinas thus speaks of the "betrayal" of the saying in the said.[55] But this "realization" remains dependent upon a certain "remembering," upon a responsibility for the singular other that animates, that inspires, that makes possible justice in the said, since responsibility to the others, "justice for all"—as opposed to "justice for each"—is justice for no one, for no "one." Justice (the said), the betrayal of obsession (its "incessant correction"), nevertheless requires obsession (the subjectivity as saying) for the singular other:

> In no way is justice a denigration of obsession, a denigration of the for-the-other, a diminution, a limitation of the anarchic responsi-

> bility, a neutralization of the glory of the Infinite, a denigration that would be produced in the measure that for empirical reasons the initial duo would become a trio. But the contemporaneousness of the multiple is tied about the diachrony of two: justice remains justice only, in a society where there is no distinction between those close and those far off, but in which there also remains the impossibility of passing by the closest. The equality of all is borne by my inequality, the surplus of my duties over my rights. The forgetting of self moves justice. (OTB 159 [203])

But does not this attending to the nearest, that which animates justice, but that cannot be just in itself without being unjust, betray justice in being actualized—that which Levinas seems to advocate here, and advocate precisely as constitutive of justice? Justice, it seems, the necessary "forgetting" of proximity, of the signification of the saying, seems at once to be a necessary "remembering"—and even "realization"—of this signification, where that which animates justice must continually break through its even surface to attend to the neighbor in a special, perhaps "unjust," or "more than just," way, in a justice surpassing itself in responsibility, surpassing itself in the very responsibility that justice requires I remember/forget: "Signification signifies in justice, but also, more ancient than itself and than the equality implied by it, justice passes justice in my responsibility for the other, in my inequality with respect to him for whom I am a hostage" (OTB 158 [201]).

It is here, perhaps, that we best understand Levinas's "redemption" of love, in his calling for a revisioning of philosophy, no longer as "the love of wisdom," but as "the wisdom of love at the service of love" (OTB 162 [207]). Philosophy as the wisdom of love does not cease to be love (justice is still response to the face), does not cease to respond to the singular other in a special way—remains "human" in Levinas's deep sense—but does so wisely. The neighbor (*le prochain,* the near one) cannot, in a justice inspired by philosophy as the wisdom of love, attract all of my attention at the expense of the third, but attending to the neighbor (the love of neighbor) is the lifeblood of justice, and of philosophy as constitutive of a just discourse. While it is not the case in our reading of Levinas that it is only "the stranger, the widow, and the orphan" (in an empirical sense) that are to be taken as the other (rather, each other is encountered as "the stranger, the widow, and the orphan"),[57] there may well be warrant in this thought—by means of philosophy as *wisdom,* but as the wisdom of love—for a "preferential treatment for the poor."[58] But even the wisdom of this "political" decision (which may very well be wise) can be just only if it is motivated by love, by the love of all of my neighbors, and not by ideological concerns. Philosophy, a just philosophy, demands of me the wisdom of a serpent, *and* the gentleness of a dove.

Philosophy needs, therefore, as a discourse in the said, as constitutive of the discourse on justice, as the rational administration of the comparison of incomparables, as the love of wisdom, to speak justly. But it can only speak justly *as love*—and it must therefore keep alive, as the condition of possibility for justice, as the inspiration of justice, as the wisdom *of love,* its responsibility to the singular other; it must therefore speak of the unspeakable, say the unsayable. It must convey the saying before us, treat of the saying in the said, and thus betray the saying qua saying—qua a singular (incomparable) responsibility for the singular (incomparable) other that is ungeneralizable, nonuniversalizable—by conveying it in universal language. And it must by turn, almost simultaneously (in the same moment),[59] reduce this betrayal of the saying in the said in the language of the said itself, in a reduction that at once yields to the universalizability of the said, but guards a trace in the said of the saying that cannot be said properly speaking, that cannot "appear" in speech properly speaking.

The problem of a just society, of a just discourse, is thus reflected in the problem of philosophical language itself. For philosophy as a universal discourse in the said is nevertheless spoken *to an other* (out of a pre-original responsibility to this other), and this other to whom the philosopher makes appeal in seeking his or her consent to, or investment of, the truth of the philosophical *propos* does not belong to that *propos* or its truth, even if he or she is its alleged "subject matter," for this *propos* is yet addressed to the other who rises up again (and ever again) behind the said that would attempt to capture him or her.[60] Philosophical speech is thus described by Levinas as operating within a movement of *dire–dédire–redire* [saying–un-saying–re-saying]. The pre-original saying (my singular subjectivity as signification to the singular other), in entering into correlation with a said (where alone it *is*, which is the origin of the origin), is betrayed by the necessary universality of the said and therefore must (if this deformation—itself made possible and necessary by the saying—is not to prevail, is not to dominate entirely the saying to the point of covering it over by forgetfulness) be unsaid (reduced). But this reduction (motivated itself by the saying) is itself another saying in correlation with a said, and as such is already a re-saying of the said (another saying bending toward the justice of the said) and will, consequently, in its turn, need also to be un-said, re-said, un-said, re-said, . . . to infinity. Or, perhaps, to Infinity.

We can see a reflection of this movement also at the level of society in the quest for justice, where the said of justice, already betraying the ethical saying that inspired it and made it possible, needs to be un-said (criticized) in face of the "one" necessarily forgotten by justice. But then the discourse of and on justice must resume, be re-said as re-animated by responsibility to the forgotten "ones" who must, in order to *make* this discourse just, be forgotten again, even as their recurring remembrance is required to *keep* this discourse just.

But the first *dire* (in either philosophy or society) is never "pure" (even if Levinas describes a pure moment in it, the ethical moment of pure exposure, my susceptibility to total critique) insofar as the saying (as an activity inspired by this passivity) is always already correlative with a said—and entering into the said already implicates the saying in all of the structures that make up the said. Even saying "Me voici (au nom de Dieu)" implicates me in systems of meaning that drag me away from the "purity" of the responsibility that animates the saying-said (as the saying has a life only in and through those systems): the French language, the Hebrew scriptures, monotheistic belief systems, etc. The movement from the saying to the said, in other words, is not direct, but rejoins a said already in place (which is not, we have shown, to be confused with the *déjà dit*), a system or systems that predate and will likely outlive me, and systems in which to ignore my participation would be foolishness—a foolishness that Levinas with his discourse on the "otherwise than being" does not, we are arguing, advocate.

Thus it becomes increasingly clear why, in our previous section, we referred to the movement from the saying to the said as *re*-construction, rather than merely construction. I do not start from scratch; my experience, my "life," is already culturally conditioned. I am always already enculturated into a said that is the gift/grace (thanks to God) of the other in the mode of the feminine, and that is already inspired by the good. But the face of the other ever and again calls this cultural discourse (that I have assimilated as it has assimilated me), this said, into question, calls it up short (for it always comes up short of singularity), demands its *re*-ad-*just*-ment, demanding that I (in my subjectivity as saying) say it again, say it better, more responsibly, more justly, ever and again.

V. Discourse: A Possible Impossibility

We have been proceeding in this part of our work on the hypothesis (a hypothesis we hope to have supported in the course of our readings) that the analyses of Levinas's 1974 *Otherwise Than Being or Beyond Essence* can be fruitfully read as a refinement and deepening—undertaken from a somewhat different perspective, which itself constitutes a part of this refinement and deepening—of, but in continuity with, the analyses undertaken in his 1961 *Totality and Infinity*. Specifically, we are proposing that the ideas of "the saying" and "the said" in *Otherwise Than Being* can be read as a refinement and deepening of the idea of "discourse" in *Totality and Infinity*, discourse being that relationship (a non-allergic, ethical relationship with alterity (re)productive of a meaning capable of founding communal meaning) that, as we argued in our chapter 3, is the condition of possibility of interparadigmatic dia-logue, and thus the condition of possibility for the dialogue in which we place so much of our hope for peace—that concern with which we began and to which we will (by way of the analyses that make up the greater part of this work), in the end, return. That is, we are hopeful that the analyses of the saying and the said can illuminate our study of discourse, the condition of possibility of dialogue, as, respectively, its (discourse's) condition of possibility and condition of impossibility—that which yields the strange locution that provides this section with its descriptive rubric for discourse: an impossible possibility.

Now, on the surface of things, this reading would appear to be unduly elliptical, would appear, at best, to be following the path of two sides of a triangle to cover the distance stretched along its third side, or, at worst, involving ourselves in an unnecessary muddle born of ignoring the obvious. For is not "the saying," more or less, and more or less straightforwardly, simply a synonym for "discourse" (as the language before language that is ethics) as "the said" is synonymous with "dialogue" (as the communication of a content in the ontological realm)—*mutatis mutandis* regarding the change in focus from *Totality and Infinity* to *Otherwise Than Being?* If this is the case, then the later analyses might well, in a reprise of its themes, go deeper than the earlier ones (as they might not), but they would not necessarily be a deepening *of* them, and it is the latter that is our claim. The question we must answer, then, is: What does the pair saying-said say that the pair discourse-dialogue does not, and how does that relate to our understanding of the relationship of discourse?

If we may call that which "discourse" and "proximity" both name "the relation" (the ethical relation between the same and the other in which I am responsible, unilaterally, for the other), we can see that proximity is a deepening of discourse in its redescription of the relation (which as discourse is a relation with the other as transcendent to the same) as a relation arising from within a radical immanence, wherein the extreme exteriority of the other is traced out as within my very interiority. Here, in proximity, the other is so interior to me that my very interiority qua the same, my "origin" qua ego, is constituted in terms of this "pre-original" interiority as the other in the same, an interiority that is always already "open" to the other, that "is" this openness, and where the exteriority of transcendence with respect to the same (that which appears to come first in *Totality and Infinity*)[61] is already an "inversion" of the pre-original structure of the other in the same. Levinas articulates the possibility/necessity of the relation articulated earlier as "discourse" in terms of this pre-original interiority of the other in the same, an interior space already hollowed out by the other (the recurrence of the "subjectivity of a bottomless passivity, made out of assignation, like the echo of a sound that would precede the resonance of this sound"; OTB 111 [141])—before this interiority has a chance to harden its shell and become an interiority in any conventional sense: the interiority of a *pour soi,* an interiority that would constitute itself as an interiority over against an exteriority (and thus be implicated in a totality born of dialectics). That is, in "splitting up," in *Otherwise Than Being,* the relationship of the saying—in a "splitting" that allows for the articulation of two sides of one and the same relationship—into a saying without a said (my pure passivity across sensibility, proximity, signification, and substitution) and a saying in correlation with a said (the active or performative expression—re-productive of ontological sense—of my saying qua passivity) Levinas shows us both the "why?" and the "how?" of the relation of discourse.

In describing the subjectivity *as* saying, and not merely the subjectivity (actively) saying (as if the subject might be something before it were signifyingness to the other, as if it might have a place from which to refuse the relation), Levinas describes the condition of possibility, indeed, the necessity, of the relation, of discourse. The impossibility of refusing the relation (because I am the saying) is the condition of possibility of the relation. The possibility of signifying rests upon a description of subjectivity as signification. So where *Totality and Infinity* tells us *that* this refusal is impossible, *Otherwise Than Being* tells us *why* this refusal is impossible. The description of the saying, beyond that of discourse, delineates the (in)condition of the subject (as passivity, as signification, as substitution) that would make the relationship of discourse (as a non-allergic, ethical relationship) possible.

Conversely, in describing the realm of the said (the context for dialogue, the context for the transmission of information) as inspired by the relation (from which it draws its significance) but wherein the relation "appears" only by betrayal, Levinas also articulates the condition of impossibility of discourse. For the relation (discourse, the saying) is not transacted elsewhere (there is no elsewhere), but in the world in which the *eon* of the said (or the *logos* of *dia-logos*) has always already taken hold, imposing itself upon the subject that always already finds itself within it. There *is* no non-allergic relationship, even if every relation that there *is* is animated by the relation as pure passivity (by the pre-ontological responsibility I am for the other that becomes—or already is, chronologically speaking—the post-ontological calling into question of my very being), is made possible by my pre-ontological (always already) subjectivity as saying, or substitution. The relation, discourse, is transacted in a "world" *tout fait,* even if it does not belong to that world (but makes that world possible as significant)[62]—even if the relation qua condition of possibility for the meaningfulness of the world is able to *tout défait,* albeit in a moment where the *refaire* of resumption as dis/continuous re/constitution is always already underway. But my implication in this world does mean that the relation, discourse, *in its purity* is impossible, even if across the structures of the world the relation, as the condition of possibility of those structures, always already imposes itself and is, in an enigmatic and always betrayed trace, "for the eye that listens" (OTB 30 [38]), perceptible. But in the world of the said, the world of being and beings, essences and existents (the only world there is), the relation of discourse is impossible: it cannot *be.*

That is, for Levinas (on the reading we are proposing), despite a language suggestive of chronological priority, despite descriptions that seem to require a linear progression (a language that, we have been arguing, signifies a "transcendental" rather than "chronological" priority), everything is, in a manner of speaking, *all at once.* All of the structures described—ethics and ontology, enjoyment and responsibility, the other and the third, the saying and the said—meet as already in place (even when they designate a lack of site) in "this very moment" (in a "now" which is *not a present*). There are not first ontological structures that are then interrupted by an ethical obligations; ontological structures are already constituted as a response to obligation. There is not first enjoyment, that would then develop into an economy of the household, that would then be interrupted by a call to responsibility; enjoyment is already exposed to the other (that which explains the need for the household), is already welcomed into a home by the (feminine) other, and these others, already "present" in the structures of enjoyment (in my "vulnerable" enjoyment), and in the home ("discretely" as welcoming grace), turn out (in the course of the analysis) to be the very "presence" of the other who calls into ethical question the very structures they "first" (primordially) make possible. There is not first the other and then (as an empirical event) the third; the third is already there in the approach of the other. There is not first a pure saying that would only later align itself with a said; the saying is always already the saying of a said, even if the ethical moment of this larger event can be isolated descriptively.[63] That is, I am born into a world already gifted to me in grace, *and* already in question. The structures of the world are either good or not so good, more or less faithful to their animating spirit, but they are not "goodness." Goodness does not exist, even if things or persons can be good. Goodness has a life, is possible, only in that which is good. The relation, discourse, signifyingness, does not exist (it is impossible), even if everything that exists owes its existence, its capacity to be signified, to the relation that as signification signifies everything that can be significant, such that signifyingness, the relation, discourse, has a life (is possible—and here alone) through the signifying of that which is signified. Discourse is a recurrent possibility, but only in and through its own impossibility. Discourse is an impossible possibility, or an im/possibility.

The implications of this im/possibility of discourse for our prevailing concern, the possibility of peace through dialogue, will have to await the exposition of our chapter 8. But first, let us examine in a more focused way, across a study of temporality in Levinas, the temporal structure of this possible impossibility, the "meeting point" of these conditions of possibility and impossibility, which Levinas refers to as "this very moment."

Notes

1. "Mode" of what? Not "of Being," certainly, and thus not "of existence." Again, as with our earlier, awkward claim that the subject *is* the saying before it *is*, we do not really have a language in which the otherwise than being can be properly said: "But one immediately wonders if in the formula 'otherwise than being' the adverb 'otherwise' does not inevitably refer to the verb to be, which simply has been avoided by an artificially elliptical turn of phrase. Then what is signified by the verb to be would be ineluctable in everything said, thought and felt. Our languages woven about the verb to be would not only reflect this undethronable royalty, stronger than that of the gods; they would be the very

purple of this royalty" (OTB 4 [4]). Lacking a language that would properly say the otherwise than being, a discourse that would name it (improperly) must use the verb "to be" against itself, so to speak. We shall examine the betrayal and trace, the betrayed trace, of the otherwise than being in "our languages" later in this chapter. For the present, we simply signal the problems in which we are already mired so as to stay attentive to the "to be qualified" nature of the discourse we are attempting to follow, and the one we are ourselves undertaking.

2. Once again, we read this "before" in terms of a (quasi-, or radicalized) transcendental priority, rather than as the delineation of a chronology.

3. See note 14 of the introduction to part II.

4. For an intriguing characterization of philosophy as the fear of death, see the section entitled "Death and Philosophy" in Robert Gibbs, *Correlations,* pp. 36–40: "The philosopher, the one who fears and thinks, refuses to face his own death. But in order to deny his death—that 'unthinkable annihilation' of himself which he can only fear—the philosopher insists that reality is identical with thought: what he cannot think (death) cannot be. In a grand evasion of his own fear, the philosopher denies the object of his fear: death is absolutely nothing."

5. For relevant quotations, see note 47 of chapter 4.

6. Of course, as the terms "the saying" and "the said" are not employed in *Totality and Infinity,* it could be said that this movement is not properly treated there at all, but we refer to the passages in that text dealing with the problem of the third, which is, for Levinas, the motivation for the movement from an encountering of the face toward ontological language.

7. Levinas has characterized as "the essential problem" the question: "Can we speak of an absolute command after Auschwitz? Can we speak of morality after the failure of morality?" (in Tamara Wright, Peter Hughes and Alison Ainsley, "The Paradox of Morality: An Interview with Emmanuel Levinas," p. 176).

8. Gibbs, *Correlations,* p. 230.

9. Gibbs's way of formulating the question seems to presuppose, that is, that it is a question of coming into society from a starting point outside of or independent of society, out of the auto*nomy* of enjoyment become eco*nomy*. Our argument is that my status as an autonomous/economous individual is most properly thought as derivative upon my always already having been in society with the other, that my freedom (wherein is founded my auto/eco/nomy) is invested, from the start, by an other who precedes it, and who *already* calls it into question. Our coming into society is thus dependent upon a prior having always al-

ready been in society, our being always already in relation, and where this "sociality" is described by Levinas as my responsibility for the other: the saying.

10. The extent to which this movement is thought to be thematized in *Otherwise Than Being* is greatly expanded if the descriptions of the said in that text are read (properly, we believe) as being dependent upon, read as being the outcome of (even if thematized in the text before this movement is explicitly thematized), the movement from the saying to the said—even if this reading requires that the text be read twice: once "forward," and once "backwards."

11. "The necessities of thematization . . . ordain a division into chapters, although the themes in which these concepts [that come up in the attempt to state transcendence] present themselves do not lend themselves to linear exposition, and cannot be really isolated from one another without projecting their shadows and their reflections on one another" (OTB 19 [23]).

12. A defense, and radicalization, of which we shall undertake in chapter 7.

13. Theodore de Boer, "An Ethical Transcendental Philosophy," especially p. 102.

14. Derrida, "At This Very Moment in This Work Here I Am," pp. 26–27.

15. The term "deconstruction," though currently popularized and bastardized in almost every conceivable way, is perhaps best left, lest we hop on this bandwagon ourselves, to the one who coined it: Jacques Derrida. There *is* in Levinas, we would maintain, a quite properly deconstructive moment in Derrida's sense of the term, as Derrida himself would seem to affirm, when, in asking how Levinas gives a place to the beyond being in the language of being, he writes: "Mustn't one reverse the question, at least in appearance, and ask oneself if that language is not *of itself unbound* and hence open to the wholly other, to its own beyond, in such a way that it is less a matter of exceeding that language than of treating it otherwise with its own possibilities. Treating it otherwise, in other words to calculate the transaction, negotiate the compromise that would leave the nonnegotiable intact, and to do this in such a way as to make the fault, which consists in inscribing the wholly other within the empire of the same, alter the same enough to absolve itself from itself. According to me that is his answer" (Jacques Derrida, "In This Very Moment in This Work Here I Am," pp. 16–17). If deconstruction (as justice, which is Derrida's assertion in his "Force of Law") is the philosophical exercise of destabilizing a philosophical discourse from within in order to make space for the "other" of that discourse sup-

pressed (and suffocating) within it, then Levinas participates in this exercise, but this moment constitutes only a part of what the reduction from the said to the saying entails—for Levinas also risks a philosophical articulation (that too will need to be reduced) of the trace of the other left upon philosophical discourse itself. Across the endless *deconstruction of* saids (the deconstruction of the said, the deconstruction of the said of that deconstruction, and of the said of that deconstruction, . . .), Levinas proposes a *reduction to* the saying, to a term that is and is not caught up in the allergy of saids. Regarding other of our concerns with nomenclature here: "construction," it must be admitted, sounds too foundationalist to suit Levinas's account of the move from the saying to the said. It is true that for Levinas ethics is the "foundation" of ontology, but not in any straightforward sense as something upon which one might stand and confidently build. Ethics is more like sinking sand than a firm foundation. "Re-construction," the term upon which we shall settle, has its own problems if it is linked with any kind of fundamentalist reconstructionism. Levinas does not believe that it is possible to build a just society on any traditional or revealed system of law. We shall attempt to salvage this term by qualifying it with the iterative "re-."

16. This "no longer" (as with our later: "not yet"), as with Levinas's "when," "until then," "antecedent," "birth," "revert," "latent," "more ancient," etc., in that which follows (these temporal designations indicating a certain antecedence or posteriority or the transition between these) are not, again, to be read, we maintain, as "chronological" but "transcendental" designations, for, as we shall see shortly, the third is always already there when I encounter the other.

17. "The third party is other than the neighbor, but also another neighbor, and also a neighbor of the other, and not simply his fellow. What then are the other and the third party for one another? What have they done to one another? Which passes before the other? The other stands in a relationship with the third party, for whom/which [*dont*] I cannot entirely answer, even if I alone answer, before any question, for my neighbor" (OTB 157 [200]). Under Lingis's translation, this is a curious saying in light of the doctrine of "substitution," wherein I am precisely responsible for the free initiatives of the other. Would I not thereby be also responsible for the free initiatives of the third, who is, after all, another neighbor? We are therefore disputing, here, Lingis's translation of "L'autre se tient dans une relation avec le tiers—dont je ne peux répondre entièrement." Lingis translates *dont* as "for whom," where *dont* is taken to refer to the third. We would argue that contextually (that is, in reading just prior to this line: "The third party is other than the neighbor, but also another neighbor," and just after it: "The

other and the third party, my neighbors") it makes no sense to claim that the third, another neighbor, would fall outside of my responsibility, such that *dont* must rather refer to the relationship between the other and the third, and it is this "for which" [*dont*] I cannot entirely answer.

18. "A problem is posited by proximity itself, which, as the immediate itself, is without problems" (OTB 161 [205]).

19. That is, Levinas sees justice not as a question of the external imposition of some ethics or ethical system, but as the delimitation of ethics as my absolute responsibility for the single/singular other.

20. If it is not already clear, we shall indicate in our next section why this is a "re-construction" and not a straightforward "construction." That is, the "re" of the just encountered "revert" ("*re*" of "*retournerait*") is not coincidental.

21. This "question" is thus linked to the question of "why is there a *question* in exhibition?" that, as we saw in the previous chapter, comes to the surface (be that in the enigma of the trace) from within the praxis of exhibition itself, and that opens the way to questioning as the questioning of "someone," of someone who stands outside of the subject matter in question (and thus outside of a Platonic dialogue or Gadamerian conversation where the interlocutors are subordinated to the question-response of thought, in turn subordinated to some "subject matter"), that would interrupt the nonproblematical/unquestioning event of being revealing itself to itself.

22. "We then have to follow in signification or proximity or saying the latent birth of cognition and essence, of the said, the latent birth of a question, in responsibility. . . . We have to follow down the latent birth of knowing in proximity" (OTB 157 [199–200]).

23. "The relationship with the third party is an incessant correction of the asymmetry of proximity in which the face is looked at" (OTB 158 [201]).

24. This list would include: comparison, synopsis, togetherness, contemporaneousness, thematization (OTB 16), conjuncture of entities, essence, cognition, contiguity, the intelligibility of systems (OTB 157), assembling, moderating, measuring, putting into relationship, judging, knowing, asking, representation (OTB 158), calculus, visibility, writing, assembling into a book, law, or science (OTB 159), ordering, appearing, phenomenality, synchronizing, structuring, totalizing, bringing into community (OTB 160), idealizing, weighing, proposing, concern for the truth, disclosure, seeing, recounting, the imposition of a rational order, controlling, the bringing to bear of principle, philosophizing (OTB 161) [19–20, 200–207].

25. "But once, God only knows how, we gain reason, we start to think

in terms of a society of three equals" (Gibbs, *Correlations,* p. 241). This evocation of God in Gibbs's text, in this context, is not gratuitous (the throwing up of the hands in a beleaguered or snide bewilderment to an omniscience that alone would be capable of working through the obscurities), but is well founded in the text of *Otherwise Than Being* itself, as we shall see.

26. Levinas makes much of this, mentioning it, within the six pages of *Otherwise Than Being* in which this movement is most closely followed out, three times: OTB 158 [201], 159 [203], 160 [204].

27. Cf. "The other is from the first the brother of all other men" (OTB 158 [201]). Levinas refers us here in a footnote to *Totality and Infinity,* pages 212 ff. [187 ff.], wherein the following are almost certainly among the passages intended by the reference: "It is my responsibility before the face looking at me as absolutely foreign . . . that constitutes the original fact of fraternity. . . . Human fraternity has then two aspects: it involves individualities whose logical status is not reducible to the status of ultimate differences in a genus, for their singularity consists in each referring to itself. . . . On the other hand, it involves the commonness of a father, as though the commonness of race would not bring together enough. Society must be a fraternal community. . . . Monotheism signifies this human kinship, this idea of a human race that refers back to the approach of the Other in the face, in a dimension of height, in responsibility for oneself and for the Other."

28. This apparent circularity is perhaps explained—and we are in the course of trying to show this—by the fact that this fraternity is only in my responsibility for the other, even as it transcends it.

29. Levinas repeats this requirement: "Synchronization is the act of consciousness which, through representation and the said, institutes 'with the help of God,' the original locus of justice, a terrain common to me and the others where I am counted among them, that is, where subjectivity is a citizen with all the duties and rights measured and measurable which the equilibrated ego involves, or equilibrating itself by the concourse of duties and the concurrence of rights" (OTB 160 [204]).

30. "But justice can be established only if I, always evaded from the concept of the ego, always desituated and divested of being, always in non-reciprocatable relationship with the other, always for the other, can become an other like the others" (OTB 160–61 [204–5]).

31. This continues: "In a prayer in which the worshipper asks that his petition be heard, the prayer as it were precedes or follows itself." And in a footnote a page later, a related thought: "The Good invests freedom—it loves me before I love it. Love is love in this antecedence [Par cette antériorité—l'amour est amour]" (OTB 187, n.8 [13]).

32. We are able moreover, on this reading, to explain the apparent contradiction between the description, in *Totality and Infinity,* of the birth of consciousness (thought, rationality, etc.) in a giving of what is mine to the other, a giving that would seem possible, and seem to be described (as we followed this out in our chapter 3), outside of the approach of the third, and the repeated claim in *Otherwise Than Being* to the effect that "Consciousness is born as the presence of a third party" (OTB 160 [203]). On our reading, the third is already present (as the feminine other who as discrete presence has already invited me into the home where my called into question goods are collected) at the coming of the other, such that, for consciousness, the third is required too in the analyses of *Totality and Infinity,* even if her/his presence in this birth is inscribed in that text discretely, indeed, as the discrete.

33. On our reading, the feminine other is fully other, so is entirely capable of calling my possession of the world into question, even if in the modality of the feminine she does not do so. Qua feminine, she already makes me her other, is always already responsibility for me in the sense that I am responsibility for the other, and where my responsibility for the other is itself "grafted on" to her responsibility for me.

34. See note 27.

35. As promised, we are attempting in an increasingly explicit way to trace out across Levinas's two major philosophical texts what we take to be a religio-familial intrigue that is, if we may speak this way, the condition of possibility for ethics itself, even if it is only across ethics (which is its "crux") that this intrigue emerges and is renewed: the intrigue of ethics (subjective *and* objective genitive). Lingis, in his translations, translates Levinas's "*intrigue*" into English correctly but unfortunately as "plot." The word "plot," suggesting narrative emplotment, loses all of the mystery and openness, all of the "drawing me in" and "keeping me on the edge" allure, of the English word "intrigue," which we are suggesting is a better translation for what Levinas's term suggests.

36. This is why this intrigue (or its trace in my responsibility for the other) does not become a narrative in the sense of a metanarrative (it is not "God's story"), even if it can only be recounted, in betraying it, narratively. Narratives are the stuff of the said, which the intrigue we are here tracing makes possible. It is an "intrigue," however, with and without continuity: my capacity for grace is the result of an antecedent graciousness, but that graciousness must come to a full halt, and begin entirely new again, in me, in the self who is fully and alone responsible for the other.

37. We are here suggesting that Gibbs's belief that the ideas in *Totality and Infinity* surrounding the family that he sees as an alternative form of

sociality (to the political) are not dropped (as Gibbs claims) in *Otherwise Than Being* ("Throughout *Otherwise than Being,* Levinas abandons the discussions of the family and its alternative sociality"; *Correlations,* p. 241), but are preserved there under different forms, are articulated from a different perspective. We do not believe, in the first place, that the section in *Totality and Infinity* describing the "Beyond the face" is a description of an alternative sociality. (Another (over?)reading of Levinas in the context of the problematics of Rosenzweig? See note 53 of chapter 4.) Rather, we read the "familial" relationships of the feminine other and paternity/fecundity in that text as an attempt to articulate that which animates the political, much as the "familial" relationships of maternity (the mediating relationship of the legacy of grace) and fraternity (the equality of all that flows from grace, and that calls for my perpetuating it) in *Otherwise Than Being* play the same role. In neither book is politics played over against the family, on our reading, but in each politics is thought in terms of the family, that is, made possible only in the context of human fraternity.

38. Again, we have yet to analyze the section of *Totality and Infinity* that takes us "Beyond the Face." We shall do so in the next chapter.

39. This is the basis of Levinas's original, though later modified, distancing of ethics from love, where love is conceived of as losing oneself in the "community of two" where the third is ignored.

40. "All human relations as human proceed from disinterestedness. The one for the other of proximity is not a deforming abstraction. In it justice is shown from the first" (OTB 159 [202]).

41. We thus find in the introductory argument to *Otherwise Than Being,* and where the word "just" can now (after we have reviewed its "origins") resound with its "just meaning": "It is on the basis of proximity that being takes on its just meaning. . . . [That is:] Being must be understood on the basis of *being's other.* To be on the ground of signification of an approach is to be *with another* for or against a third party, with the other and the third party against myself, in justice" (OTB 16 [19–20]).

42. The life of the spirit is lived in the everyday world, where all of the latter's meanings (economic, legal, physical, etc.) are animated by the spirit (whether acknowledged or forgotten), and is not an escape from the "real world"—is not what Levinas has called elsewhere (in commenting on the work of Buber) a "disdainful spiritualism" (TI 69 [40]).

43. Recall one of the five epigraphs to *Otherwise Than Being,* one of the two from Pascal's *Pensées:* "They have used concupiscence as best they could for the general good; but it is nothing but a pretense and a false image of charity; for at bottom it is simply a form of hatred."

44. Levinas continues: "It is also not without importance to know, as far as philosophy is concerned, if the rational necessity that coherent discourse transforms into sciences, and whose principle philosophy wishes to grasp, has thus the status of an origin, that is, origin of self, of a present, a contemporaneousness of the successive (the work of deduction), the manifestation of being—or if this necessity presupposes a hither side, a pre-original, a non-presentable, an invisible, and consequently a hither side not presupposed like a principle is presupposed by the consequence of which it is synchronous." Insofar as philosophy is "State philosophy," the thought of totality (as Levinas claims it has been predominantly in the Occident), this particular point is indeed not without importance, even for politics itself.

45. We have thus been opposing throughout any reading that would take Levinas's descriptions of "the ethical" as an "ideal," as for instance in the claim of Robert John Sheffler Manning that "Levinas's philosophy is based on a description of an ideal situation wherein responsibility for the Other is recognized." And while it is true that Sheffler Manning qualifies this claim with "Yet Levinas is no idealist. He knows that every intersubjective encounter is not one of realized responsibility and peace . . . that relations of violence and oppression are always in the background of Levinas's discourse," his reading (which is moreover not uncommon) still implies the "possibility" of this ideal as "realized" (*Interpreting Otherwise Than Heidegger*, p. 11). On our reading, Levinas's descriptions of the ethical are not at all of an ideal, of something that might be realized, but of the conditions of possibility, the "inspiration," of every realized situation.

46. "All human relations as human proceed from disinterestedness. . . . This means concretely or empirically that justice is not a legality regulating human masses, from which a technique of social equilibrium is drawn, harmonizing antagonistic forces. That would be a justification of the State delivered over to its own necessities" (OTB 159 [202]).

47. We thus again take our distance from a reading like that of Manning: "Levinas's philosophy . . . is trying to argue against something and to argue for something else. It is trying to get us to rearrange our priorities in a certain way, trying to compel us to commit ourselves to something—our ethical responsibility for the other person" (*Interpreting Otherwise Than Heidegger*, p. 10). On our reading, Levinas's philosophy is not hortatory, but descriptive, not trying to get us to commit ourselves to something, but a "reminder" of a commitment already made on my behalf, and, as we shall see in chapter 7, ultimately taking the form of a testimony to a having been committed that is in its deepest moment a testimony to a grace always already received.

48. This is why we have been at such pains, earlier in this chapter and throughout this work, to emphasize that "doing good" is not so much a response to an imperative, but a response out of who I (in a pre-original, pre-ontological way) *am,* that doing good is the self as saying, a response in and as responsibility, more a matter of "authenticity" (see our chapter 7 for a description of Levinas's philosophy as "heterautonomous") than a response to a *Sollen.* For if "ethics" (in Levinas's sense) were taken as an imperative, this would still imply a subject capable of taking up or refusing it, and thus an imperious subject behind the responsible subject, behind the passivity of proximity (which for Levinas is the very subjectivity of the subject qua *subjectum*). I cannot not be who I "am" (signification), but I can (and even must, in a certain sense to be specified) forget who I am.

49. "My lot is important. But it is still out of my responsibility that my salvation has meaning, despite the danger in which it puts this responsibility, which it may encompass and swallow up, just as the State issued from the proximity of the neighbor is always on the verge of integrating him into a we, which congeals both me and the neighbor" (OTB 161 [205]).

50. See our chapter 6 for an analysis of "the moment" in Levinas, as the juncture of time and eternity, the precise point at which, as this passage too indicates, the diachrony of the saying and the synchrony of the said can, across the enigma their intersection creates, pass over into one another.

51. This might be seen as the correlative of Heidegger's "fallenness," and more so because it is a structural necessity. But it is not "the fall" from the Garden. It is a fall "into being," but this is a good fall (a fall motivated by the goodness of the good; and a fall not from some original nonfallen state, but a having always already fallen), because it makes for justice.

52. This is particularly disturbing to some commentators for whom this necessary distancing from the good means the structuralization or ontologizing of evil. James Olthuis takes this position in his article "Face to Face: Ethical Asymmetry or the Symmetry of Mutuality?" in *Knowing Other-wise: Philosophy at the Threshold of Spirituality,* pp. 131–58.

53. "[Justice] is the *necessary interruption* of the Infinite being fixed in structures, community and totality" (OTB 160 [204], our emphasis).

54. "Justice is impossible without the one that renders it finding himself in proximity. His function is not limited to the 'function of judgment,' the subsuming of particular cases under a general rule. The judge is not outside the conflict, but the law is in the midst of proximity" (OTB 159 [202]). And later: "But, come out of signification, a modality

of proximity, justice, society and truth itself which they require, must not be taken for an anonymous law of the 'human forces' governing an impersonal totality" (OTB 161 [205–6]).

55. And the "philosophical" problem of tracing the saying in the said—the latter being the only language there is, a language in which the saying is already betrayed—is reflected in the "ethical/ontological" problem whereby the saying as responsibility is already betrayed in the said.

56. "My relationship with the other as neighbor gives meaning to my relations with all the others" (OTB 159 [202]).

57. Even the powerful one, the persecutor, my persecutor, is given, by Levinas, the status of "the other": "The face of the neighbor in its persecuting hatred can by this very malice obsess as something pitiful. . . . 'To tend the cheek to the smiter and to be filled with shame,' to demand suffering in the suffering undergone (without producing the act that would be the exposing of the other cheek) is not to draw from suffering some kind of magical redemptive virtue. In the trauma of persecution it is to pass from the outrage undergone to responsibility for the persecutor, and, in this sense from suffering to expiation for the other" (OTB 111 [141]).

58. And this is, perhaps, the source of Levinas's attractiveness to some liberation theologians.

59. Again, see chapter 6 for our analysis of "the moment" in Levinas.

60. "Already the comprehension of Being is said to the existent, who again arises behind the theme in which he is presented" (TI 47–48 [18]).

61. Despite the caveats in this earlier text itself that we have been stressing.

62. One might even be tempted to say that the relation is in the world, but not of the world.

63. Our reading can be clarified by again commenting upon certain passages from Robert Gibbs, who writes (in commenting on the ordering of "the major works" of Levinas): "First, there is economics as the pre-ethical manufacture of the same, then there is the face and its infinitizing responsibility, and finally, there is justice as a negotiation and a weighing of those infinite responsibilities due to the presence of the third." We concur, if by this "first, . . . then, . . . finally . . ." is indicated either the textual ordering of the descriptions or the delineation of certain transcendental priorities of that which is described (that is, always from a certain perspective), but we do not concur if implied in this ordering is some kind of chronological (qua historical) ordering of moments as "events" in that which is described. Gibbs shortly thereafter

resumes: "However, in *Otherwise Than Being* Levinas focuses on the middle moment, that of the approach of the other, to the point of almost excluding the other two moments. Not only is the third moment of justice pushed to the boundary, but the first pre-ethical moment all but disappears. Levinas narrows his perspective to the complexities of that moment of obligation, the meeting with the other as proximity. Although Levinas insists on the sociality of ethics, his focus draws ever more narrowly on the asymmetry and nonreciprocity of the face or proximity. But that is not itself a moment of justice, but rather a moment that precedes justice. Economics becomes a prior moment, and in so doing creates a permanent context for ethics and politics and religion—while justice becomes the desired result for Levinas, but not the question that most concerns him" (*Correlations,* pp. 236–37). On our reading the narrowing of perspective is read precisely as a narrowing of perspective (as a deepening of vision rather than as a revisioning), and if the first and third "moments" are pushed to the boundary in terms of the specific focus of the analyses, they are in no sense pushed to the boundary of the problematics under analysis, but remain their context, a forgetting of which deforms the analyses. We would contend that justice, economic justice, *is* what most concerns Levinas, and that the analyses of proximity need be read as in the service of that concern, as a delineation of the condition of possibility of justice, as what keeps justice just, its "precedence" of a transcendental, rather than chronological, kind. Economics, on this reading, becomes not a moment *prior* to ethics and justice, but a moment *of* ethics and justice, as integral to the intrigue that runs from grace to grace across the *oikos.*

6

The Moment of Responsibility: Time and Eternity

AT THE VERY END of the main text of *Totality and Infinity,* right before the conclusions (closing the subsection entitled "The Infinity of Time," of the section entitled "Beyond the Face"), we find the following paragraph, which contains an unanswered question:

> But infinite time is also the putting back into question of the truth it promises. The dream of a happy eternity, which subsists in man along with his happiness, is not a simple aberration. Truth requires both an infinite time and a time it will be able to seal, a completed time. The completion of time is not death, but messianic time, where the perpetual is converted into eternal. Messianic triumph is the pure triumph; it is secured against the revenge of evil whose return the infinite time does not prohibit. Is this eternity a new structure of time, or an extreme vigilance of the messianic consciousness? The problem exceeds the bounds of this book. (TI 284–85 [261])

We would like to propose by means of a tentative agenda in this chapter to inquire as to whether any answers, or any clues to answers, to the question posed by Levinas in this paragraph—"Is this eternity a new structure of time, or an extreme vigilance of the messianic consciousness?" and that Levinas claims exceeds the bounds of "this book"—can be gleaned from an examination of what his later work, *Otherwise Than Being or Beyond Essence,* has to say about time.

We say "tentative" agenda, because the inauguration of this inquiry must be accompanied by a caveat, that is, the possibility that a prior question, a question prior to our question regarding

Levinas's question, might need to be asked, namely, whether it would make any sense to seek an answer to Levinas's question at the end of *Totality and Infinity* in his later book or books, or for that matter in any book. A negative answer to this prior question, which might render our project moot, seems (and at once does not seem, as we shall see) to be offered by Derrida. In his second article on Levinas entitled "In This Very Moment in This Work Here I Am" (an article that will much interest us later as we make alternative, though not necessarily contradictory, use of the Levinasian phrase therein highlighted: "In this very moment"), after quoting a passage[1] from *Otherwise Than Being* that announces on what terms "signification" has been analyzed "in the present work," and with specific reference to the Levinasian claim that "[t]he problem overflows the framework of this book," upon which we are focusing here, Derrida writes:

> I interrupt for an instant; "*in the present work*" the impresentable has therefore presented itself, a relation with the Other (*Autre*) that defeats any gathering into presence, to the point where no "work" can be rebound or shut in upon its presence, nor plotted or enchained in order to form a book. The present work makes a present of what can only be given outside the book. And even outside the framework. (Atvm 31)

So, on this reading, wherein the "this" of "this book" [*ce livre*] slips into the "the" of "the book" [*le livre*], the "unanswered question" posed at the end of *Totality and Infinity* as beyond its frame becomes an "unanswerable question," unanswerable in "the book," in any book. And if the deferral of the question has been extended from beyond the book in which it is inscribed, beyond "this book" to "the book," to inscription in general, our tentative project of searching for an answer to it in a book, say, in *Otherwise Than Being or Beyond Essence,* would, of course, be in vain.

Still, two things mitigate against stopping up short our project in the face of this interpretation. First, and simplistically, Levinas does, indeed, write *ce livre,* this book, and this alone should give us some, even if short-lived, pause. And secondly, and more complicatedly, Levinas informs us in his *Otherwise Than Being* that everything, even the nonpresentable, can, and even must, be manifested,[2] be that by betrayal, and this irony is, ironically, precisely what Derrida, in reference to Levinas's irony, is in the course of ironically pointing out in the above quoted passage.[3] We shall have to return, with less irony, to this labyrinth later in the chapter. For now we simply raise a flag, and give our reasons for, perhaps imprudently, marching past it.

We shall proceed, then, in three steps: first, by examining the structures of time and temporality as these are described in *Totality and Infinity,* the text in which Levinas's question—"Is this eternity a new structure of time, or an extreme vigilance of the messianic consciousness?"—arises, but which does not claim to answer it; then by tracing Levinas's descriptions of time and temporality in his *Otherwise Than Being or Beyond Essence* and asking whether the analyses of the later work add anything to those of the former that might pass as an answer, or a clue to an answer, or the clue to a principled prohibition against any possible answer, to the question posed in the earlier work as beyond its bounds; and concluding by reprising some of the issues raised in the article by Derrida to which we have already been referring, specifically with respect to the temporal status of the phrase from Levinas—"in this very moment"—therein thematized.

I. From Simultaneity to Postponement

The final paragraph of the main text of *Totality and Infinity* outlines two conditions of possibility for what Levinas is here referring to as truth: "Truth requires both an infinite time and a time it will be able to seal, a completed time." By the text's own admission, a description of the second of these conditions, a completed, or messianic, time, "exceeds the bounds of this book," which does not necessarily mean that this condition is not operative in the analyses of *Totality and Infinity,* only, perhaps, not therein thematized as fully as it might be.[4] What *Totality and Infinity* does provide us with is a description of the first condition of truth: "infinite time."

It is to a description of this condition as it is exposed in *Totality and Infinity* that we therefore first turn, and shall do so by highlighting the paragraph that precedes the one that contains the question that provides us with our agenda, and that provides the references to "infinite time" in that paragraph with their immediate context. Here we read:

> Why is the beyond separated from the below? Why, to go unto the good, are evil, evolution, drama, separation necessary? Recommencement in discontinuous time brings youth, and thus the infinition of time. Time's infinite existing ensures the situation of judgment, condition of truth, behind the failure of the goodness of today. By fecundity I dispose of an infinite time, necessary for the truth to be told, necessary for the particularism of the apology to be converted into efficacious goodness, which maintains the I of the apology in its particularity, without history breaking and crushing this allegedly still subjective concordance. (TI 284 [261])

According to this paragraph, then, the reason why infinite time is necessary to truth is that truth requires judgment, and it is infinite time that "ensures the situation of judgment." It is, we read, by fecundity, moreover, that "I dispose of an infinite time." A chain of conditions-for is thus established running from fecundity to infinite time, to judgment, to truth, each subsequent term relying upon its antecedent for its condition of possibility. Can we trace this chain of conditions-for by examining the analyses and descriptions of the text of *Totality and Infinity* as these bear upon an understanding of these terms, with an eye toward arriving back at the text's closing question (a closing that, in the form of an unanswered question, creates an opening)? We should like to do so beginning with the most general description, in *Totality and Infinity,* of the temporalization of time, examining the two "directions" in which this temporalization can be taken, according to the text, and ending with the idea of fecundity, which will be revealed as the very infinition of time, and which will underwrite the notion of temporalization with which we shall begin, and the interpretative possibilities to which it lends itself.

I.1. Finitude

According to *Totality and Infinity,* then, time is opened up, is temporalized, in terms of the possibilities that yet remain to a being in the face of an always approaching and inexorable death that will put an end to any further possibility. Indeed, Levinas describes death not as the possibility of impossibility, as, at least on

Levinas's reading, is the case for Heidegger, where the nothingness of death need be appropriated by the authentic subject as its ownmost possibility, but as "the impossibility of every possibility, the stroke of a total passivity" (TI 235 [212]) in the face of that which dissipates all of the subject's powers, the approach of that which it cannot project, beyond every project. My death is always mysterious, always future, for I know not the hour, nor the "what" of death (TI 234 [211]). Death menaces as a violence coming always and relentlessly toward me, pursuing me, not as a natural phase in the evolving of an impersonal universe, but menacing, the threat of "murder in the night" (TI 233 [210]). Indeed, I am always already in its grasp; it is inscribed in my present as fear, "in the fear I can have for my being" (TI 233 [209]), and a prescient of it imposes itself in physical suffering, the "privileged situation where the ever future evil becomes present" (TI 238 [215]) (qualified, as is the coming of death, by the impossibility of escape)—but it is not yet upon me. Death menaces from out of an unanticipatable future in which all of my future possibilities will have been exhausted, congealed into actualities in an incorruptible past that Levinas refers to as "fate."

To have time, then, is precisely to have possibilities remaining in the face of one's approaching death, to not yet be equated with one's fate, that which one will have been and meant when all is said and done, and one can say and do no more (and where fate, consequently, does not, on this reading, precede, but follows upon, history; TI 228 [204]). Death is inevitable, but is "not yet" (*pas encore*) (TI 224 [199]). That is, time permits to the subject a "retreat" (TI 224 [199]), an "adjournment" (TI 224 [200]), a "reprieve" (*sursis*) (TI 229 [205]), a détente (TI 224 [200]), which, as marking the possibilities remaining against an approaching and certain death, is, precisely and literally, temporary. On this interpretation, time is possible only, therefore, for a mortal, or finite, being, a being at once exposed and opposed to the violence of death (TI 224 [199]), which, as mortal, is a being-toward-death, but also, at the same time, by means of time, or as temporal, a being-against-death (TI 235 [212])—simultaneously for and against death: finite, for-death, but not yet dead.

Not surprisingly, it is in terms of this overarching temporal structure that Levinas articulates, in *Totality and Infinity,* the further but related notions of the freedom of the will, of consciousness, and of corporeality. For it is precisely in this adjournment of violence by time (TI 224 [200]) that Levinas locates the space of a freedom, a time for a freedom to act against death, time *as* the freedom to act against, or in spite of, death, a time in which to act before death arrives. As such, freedom on this accounting is not the freedom of the *causa sui,* that ideal of freedom to which, according to Levinas, the tradition aspires,[5] but is a freedom "originally null," but where time permits to the subject a "détente or distension—postponement by virtue of which nothing is definitive yet, nothing consummated, skill which finds for itself a dimension of retreat there where the inexorable is imminent" (TI 224 [200]). Since "human freedom resides in the future . . . of its non-freedom" (TI 237 [214]), freedom is neither the absolute freedom of the *causa sui,* nor the problematic mix of freedom and nonfreedom that would have to be sorted out in the notion of a "finite freedom," although, with the notion of freedom as "necessity relaxed and postponed" (TI 224 [200]), we can begin to make sense of this notion in terms of the freedom yet open to a finite being, in short, in terms of time.[6] Likewise, for Levinas in this context, to be conscious is "to have a distance with regard to the present: to relate oneself to being as to a being to come, to maintain a distance with regard to being even while already coming under its grip" (TI 237 [214]), which means having the capacity for glimpsing the impending danger, and, at least for a time, by means of time itself, averting it: "Consciousness is resistance to violence, because it leaves the time necessary to forestall it. . . . To be conscious is to have time" (TI 237 [214]). Under another, and correlative, articulation, a being that can have time is described as a corporeal being. Under Levinas's description, "the originality of the body consists of the coinciding of two points of view. This is the paradox and the essence of time itself proceeding unto death, where the [incarnated] will is affected as a thing by the things—by the point of steel or the chemistry of the tissues . . . but gives itself a reprieve and postpones the contact by the against-death of postponement" (TI 229 [205]). In this sense, then, to be finite, to be mortal, to be corporeal, to will, to be free, to be conscious, to be subject (that is, "subject to" the violence of death, and the "subject of" actions to avert it), and to have time—are synonyms.

To have time requires, therefore, that "[a]cross this distance of time the definitive is not definitive; being, while being, is not yet, remains in suspense, and can at each instant commence" (TI 281 [257]). Time requires a being that is capable of taking up a distance from its own being, born, but not yet "stuck" to itself, to its identity, capable of a break with being through its own way of "being not yet fully," that is, capable of a commencement and recommencement, where "one instant does not link up with another to form a present," but where, rather, "the identity of the present splits up into an inexhaustible multiplicity of possibilities that suspend the instant" (TI 238 [215]). In time, the moments of time do not adhere to one another in a causal chain, but are discontinuous—the instant not flowing into the next by necessity, but opening up upon a field of possibilities, giving meaning to the notions of initiative, and of consolation.[7] A being with time is a being "created," that is, "not simply issued forth from the father, but . . . absolutely other than him" (TI 63 [35]), that is, "atheist," created with a will of its own, "a being conditioned in such a way that without being *causa sui* it is first with respect to its cause" (TI 59 [30]). A being with time is a being "created," and not a being "thrown," that is, not having one's subjectivity defined by one's "nature," by "the fatality of the non-chosen birth" (TI 237 [214]), by one's fixed identity, but a being that "has not yet reached its term, remains at a distance from itself, is still preparatory, in the vestibule of being" (TI 237 [214]).

Time, in short, is described, in *Totality and Infinity,* as the struggle of the subject against the congealing of his or her future possibilities into past actualities—against fate, which is sealed by death, the impossibility of possibility. Time is temporalized as the "resistance" (TI 237 [214]) that a *finit*-ude is capable of maintaining over against its approaching and inexorable de-*finit*-ude. Death, yes, but not yet—this is time.

I.2. The Definitive

But death *is* inexorable, and the will, carving out a space of freedom in the time that remains to it, is exposed, as mortal, to this "primordial fact" (TI 224 [200]). Death will come, and will put an end to the resistance that a finite being is able to oppose to its *de*-finitude, to its being *de*-fined in terms of the past it will have become as accomplished, as complete, as "congealed into definitive reality" (TI 281 [258]), as lacking further possibilities, gathered into "fate"—that is, reduced to the meaning that this being will be assigned in relation to all other past facts, a process that is, moreover, always already under way in the process of aging, the process whereby the range of possibilities open to a subject narrows with the passing of time, whereby future possibilities are, relentlessly across time, like arteries in the same process, hardened into past actualities.[8] That is, in the very life of the will as resistance to death, the will is exposed to death, is contraried by an other that menaces it. *Time passes.* And it is from the perspective of this exposure to the violence of death, from the perspective of the subject's eventual demise (that is, by means of the being-for-death side of its temporal being-for/against death), that is transacted, that the will is exposed to, what Levinas refers to as the judgment of history.

This judgment of history is made possible, Levinas claims, by the in principle and necessary detachability of the products of the will from the will itself, the very products produced by the will in its opposition to death, the fruit of the time that marked its opposition to violence. That is, the will does "not accompany its work up to the end," and "a separation [thus] opens between the producer and the product" (TI 227 [203]). This separation is produced in the inherent susceptibility of the subject's works to usages dictated by a foreign will, that is, their suitability as goods to the marketplace, to an anonymous economy that revalues them (against the values of the will that produced them) as merchandise: "The other can dispose me of my work, take it or buy it, and thus direct my very behavior; I am exposed to instigation. The work is destined to this alien *Sinngebung* from the moment of its origin in me" (TI 227 [202–3]).[9] And it is this susceptibility, this "way a will plays a role in history that it has not willed [that] marks the limits of interiority" (TI 227 [203]), and that inscribes the will by means of its products "in events that will appear only to the historian" (TI 227 [203]).

For the judgment of history is pronounced by the survivors, the winners, the inheritors of the products left by now dead souls. The judgment of history is a judgment of works that traces the history of the heritage that a will has left in terms of results, that is, in terms of "realized possibilities," and as such a history of the products of wills no longer willing.[10] By their fruits shall you know them. This judgment of history, always already operative in the imminence of death, therefore lives from the distance necessary to separate absolutely a will from its works, lives from the distance imposed by death that puts an end to any control a will might still be able to exercise over the use made of its products: "As long as the will, in a being that speaks, takes up again and defends his work against a foreign will, history lacks the distance it lives from. Its reign commences in the world of realities-results, the world of 'complete works,' the heritage of dead wills" (TI 228 [203]). As dead, the will itself is converted by the judgment of history into an appropriable work, an artifact among artifacts, the person converted into a historical *persona,* into the theatrical mask (become death mask) in terms of which an "actor" played a role on the world stage of history, to be interpreted only by his actions (TI 228 [203]). The judgment of history thus capitalizes on the exposure of the will to its other in and through its very willing. The will plays a role in history it has not willed, betrays itself in the very struggle against its betrayal, exposes itself to a violence in its very opposition, in living acts,[11] to violence, to an alien, to alienation. I am fated by and for history as I am for death.

So, despite the struggle that the finite opposes through time to its *de*-finition, death has its day. As future possibilities slip into past actualities, fate takes hold, and history wins out against the will that would oppose its judgment.[12] And this is the basis of both tragedy and comedy, or at least comedy as tragedy, where the will, overtaken by a foreign will, by fate, ends up serving what it did not will.[13] Fate laughs at freedom, has a joke at the expense of a will too weak to oppose it, and which, in the end, at its end, is not only too weak to oppose its fate, but, from the perspective of history, is nothing at all: "There is no inward ['purely interior'] history" (TI 231 [207], 227 [203]). With death comes the withering of the will to nothing "real,"[14] to an illusion, to a dream that dissipates from the very moment the will is no longer able to wake up and smell the coffee. Vanity, vanity, . . . , is all willing, all freedom that would struggle to oppose its fate, its *de*-finition by others, vanity? From the perspective of the judgment of history: yes.

I.3. The Infinite

But this judgment of history, of works and not of wills, "forgetting the life that struggles against slavery" (TI 228 [204]), which struggles against its own enslavement to history,[15] is "necessarily unjust for the subjectivity, inevitably cruel" (TI 243 [221]), insofar as the will that it judges is judged in its absence, is not called upon to speak, to defend itself, at its own trial, judged, rather, in terms of the mute products it has left in its wake, or after its wake—its sentence pronounced in absentia:[16] "It excludes the apology" (TI 243 [220]). By their fruits shall you misknow them.

Yet the will, of itself, calls out for judgment, for a judgment upon itself *as* will (and not as reduced to its fate, to the place and meaning bestowed upon it by others in a system of meanings that negate it as will), "seeks judgment in order to be confirmed against death" (TI 240–41 [218]), desires a judgment on the truth of its testimony (TI 240 [218]): "The inwardness of the will posits itself subject to a jurisdiction which scrutinizes its intentions, before which the meaning of its being coincides totally with its inward will" (TI 231 [207]). This desire is testified to, on Levinas's claim, in the phenomenon of apology (this presenting oneself to the other in direct speech coming to its own assistance), which is absent from no speech insofar as all speech, whatever else it might be or say, is a call on the behalf of the speaker for some or other kind of confirmation, or acknowledgement, for some kind of response that will give it some or other bearing with respect to that which transcends the speaker: an external judgment that will permit of both the distinction between truth and ideology,[17] and a judgment with respect to its justice.[18] To speak, then, is already to acknowledge an alterity, to recognize a multiplicity in being, for within a totality the same need not speak to the same. Speech, discourse, is already a response to alterity, in which the will wills to subject itself to a judgment upon its own truth as will, as a measure of its fidelity as will, a truth invisible to the judgment of history.[19] Such a call is, consequently, to already recognize a discord between the will and historical events; the will seeks to subject itself to a jurisdiction beyond that of history—and precisely, to a judgment of its "goodness," where goodness means no longer willing for oneself, but willing for the other: "taking up a position in being such that the other counts more than myself" (TI 247 [225]); "dreading murder more than death" (TI 246 [224]). The will seeks from this judgment an investiture or confirmation as will, and a pardon or release from the judgment of history or fate,[20] and Levinas refers to this judgment as the judgment of God.[21]

But why would the will seek a judgment upon its "goodness," upon the will not in the usual sense of "willful," but as "willing-for-the-other?" Because, according to Levinas, the subject subject to death lives in absurdity, banging its head against the wall, so long as it lives its life for itself, lives in the slipping away of life and its remaining possibilities in aging toward an inevitable death that, in the face of even the most heroically stoic life, or that of the most hearty bon vivant, has the last laugh. Epictetus and Epicurus are, after all, both quite dead. "The absurdity of the *fatum* foils the sovereign will" (TI 227 [202]). The will is judged true, is meaningful, only when in time, that is, in terms of the possibilities and powers it has left before death, it is directed away from an ultimately futile concern for the perpetuation of its own powers—away from the ego as *conatus essendi*—and turned toward responsibility for the other whose death is not concurrent with its own, such that the meaning, the "truth," of its life is no longer determined by its death: "The will, already betrayal and alienation of itself but postponing this betrayal, on the way to death but a death ever future, exposed to death but not *immediately*, has time to be for the Other, and thus recover meaning despite death" (TI 236 [213]).[22] The will transcends the ridicule of death (though without removing its sting—for it still dies), tears itself from the ultimacy of its fate, and lives its life as ultimately meaningful by living not for itself, over which death always holds sway, but—"liberated from the egoist gravitation" (TI 236 [213])—by living for the other, undergoing the menace not for its own sake (which would be a losing battle), but for the other, which is to say the same as (for this claim purports not to be theological—or at least not in the sense of being deduced from some theological dogma) under the judgment of God. Levinas calls "patience" this carrying on for the sake of the other under the menace of an always imminent death, which, he claims, could only be endured where the ego no longer puts the accent upon itself:

> Violence does not stop Discourse; all is not inexorable. Thus alone does violence remain endurable in patience. It is produced only in a world where I can die *as a result of someone* and *for someone.* This situates death in a new context and modifies its conception, empties it of the pathos that comes to it from the fact of its being my death. In other words, in patience the will breaks through the crust of its egoism and as it were displaces its center of gravity outside of itself, to will as Desire and Goodness limited by nothing. (TI 239 [216–17])

The judgment of God therefore gives to the will a "new orientation" (TI 246 [224]) wherein its destiny need not be tragic because "one can speak to the Other and desire him" (TI 230 [206]), and where there exists "the possibility for the I that is exposed to the alienation of its powers by death to not be for death" (TI 247 [225]).

But this judgment, and the truth it promises (though only promises, as we shall see), requires, Levinas claims, an infinite time—a time that cannot be closed, that cannot be gathered into a fait accompli and subjected to the judgment of history, a time, consequently, that is not correlative with my time, that is, with my finitude, nor, in the form of memories and anticipations, brought into correlation with my present, presented to me in a whole that would constitute a History, and behind which subjective truth, the truth of the will, would vanish, pulverized into the works (which would be the whole measure of the subject's "works") of the clock Universal. Truth requires, on the contrary, a transcendence, an other that can judge in truth, divide truth from ideology. Truth requires, in other words, not the "judgment of history," but the "judging of history." But there can be no transcendence if time is one, if the movement of time lends itself without remainder to the grasp of a synchronic present, if time is Time, if time could be gathered into an immobile Eternity, were that Eternity spread across ecstases emanating, in either direction, from out of a present. For were the next moment in time a mere extension of its foregoing moment in an unbreakable causal chain, there could be no room for possibility, only necessity, and thus only a semblance of time, or at least no meaningful time (no time open to meaningful decision), for all would be determined in advance: the beginning and the end, the first cause and final effect, joined in a totality structure posing as time, but, in effect, all at once, regardless of the "temporal effects" it might create in an eternal if extended present. And a time that would be capable of refusing such a collection into a present is, Levinas claims, necessarily an infinite time—a time that continues on after every gathering up of time, after every history is written, breaking up and revaluing even the past in a perpetual rewriting of history, that which, we have seen, is the condition of possibility of pardon. But this infinite time cannot, in its turn, be conceived of as a deeper but still coherent time, still susceptible to a comprehensive telling (be that in the mind of God),[23] and that is why Levinas claims, we take it, that "it does not suffice to give oneself an infinite line of time to realize this condition" (TI 247 [225])[24] ("this condition" being an infinite time—to be effectuated, as we shall shortly see, in fecundity—that permits of the judgment of God), insofar as a line of time, even infinitely long, were it still mediated from out of a present, would again lend itself to histories and teleologies: bookends of a time that can be delineated, of a time that could be enclosed in a book as the history of the System, or the System as History.

Rather, the infinition of time depends upon the discontinuity of time—upon the introduction into time of the genuinely new, upon the introduction of a cause into time that was not contained in any preceding effect, upon the introduction of that which could not have been anticipated in correlation with a memory, assimilated and given its meaning in terms of any present. "This discontinuity," Levinas claims, "must be emphasized" (TI 282 [258]). And that which, after the descriptions of Levinas, precisely forbids any such assimilation, any such correlation with my present, that which is never, strictly speaking, present, is the face of the other[25] that calls me not to knowledge (at least not first of all), but to responsibility. The infinition of time thus depends upon an encounter with the infinite, and Levinas therefore claims that it is the "asymmetrical relation with the other," with "infinity," that "opens time" (TI 225 [201]).

So, against the congealing of *finit*-ude into the de-*finit*-ive, the will turns for a measure of its truth as will to the in-*finite,* to a time that cannot be collected into a totality even after its death, to an infinite time. And the condition of possibility of such a time is, Levinas claims, fecundity.

I.4. Fecundity

In fecundity, my child is not my project, is not anticipatable (TI 267 [245]), but results from *eros,* the desire of no object, but the desire of desire. Phenomenologically, Levinas claims, my son is at once me, and not me. "My child is a stranger (Isaiah 49), but a stranger who is not only mine, for he *is* me. He is me a stranger to myself" (TI 267 [245]). In fecundity, I desire that which goes beyond my self, in a self that is at once myself and the other. In the son I transcend my death in the other, without personally transcending my death:[26] "A being capable of another fate than its own is a fecund being" (TI 282 [258]).

This generation of generations provides the infinite time[27] that truth requires, that is, the introduction of a time that is not my own, in taking time beyond the possibilities that remain to me as the same, and extending it to the possibilities that remain for my son, and his son, and his daughter, and so on. And it is upon this structure that Levinas sees the possibility for pardon that apology demands, a remission from my fate across time, in the possibility of re-doing time infinitely. It is not that my past is eliminated—I am always becoming and will become nothing but history when "I'm history" (as we say today)—but time will be relived,[28] over and again, providing the possibility of a break with the past that is not heavy with this past, of a recommencement in time, liberated, time and again, with each passing generation, from fate.[29] Across generations, better than in my eternal life (and possible only because of my death), there is remission, and pardon.[30] And, thus, the infinite time of fecundity also provides continuity to time in that my son, while being an other, is me—continuity in that in my desiring of the other, I am Desire desiring Desire, bequeath through my son the gift of giving the gift, am goodness engendering goodness.[31] And that is why, according to Levinas, pardon is "constitutive of time itself" (TI 283 [259]) as the very possibility of break and resumption, death and resurrection[32]—yielding a time in which I can turn from the weight of my past toward an infinite future.[33]

It is, therefore, in terms of this infinite time—the time of infinite possibilities—that my time as my personal time—the time open to me in which to act—is time, opening upon meaningful possibilities for my life insofar as my life can be discourse, giving to the other, and not merely the inevitable degeneration into a fate that ends by dominating any meaning I would attempt to sustain against it. It is as rooted in this infinite time that the time of the subject, opened up as possibilities between a pregnant but already decomposing present and my personal death, becomes possible, and becomes meaningful insofar as this "being/not yet being" need not only be for death, but can be for the other, freely appropriated into an infinite future, not in terms of its historical heritage (where it is already "dead"), but in terms of fecundity as the gift of the gift of giving—as goodness. In the break of the son with the father, across discontinuities, being is shown to be multiple. Here is alterity—and thus, across fecundity that produces the infinition of time, that *is* "the primary phenomenon of time in which the phenomenon of the 'not yet' is rooted" (TI 247 [225]), the possibility of judgment, and thus the possibility of truth, of my testimony being judged true, subject to the judgment of God.[34] By their fruits shall you judge them, if by fruits one means the fruits of one's loins, though in a sense that transcends that of the strictly biological (TI 277 [254]).

Recalling, then, the chain of conditions-for outlined earlier as drawn from the penultimate paragraph of the main text of *Totality and Infinity* (fecundity–infinite time–judgment–truth), it is in fecundity, in its continuity across discontinuity—better than the continuation of the Same for permitting of the absolute re-commencement that is pardon—that we find the essence of time as it is articulated in *Totality and Infinity,* a fecundity that produces infinite time across never ending (re-)generations, a time incapable of being gathered into a present, and that is therefore productive of the multiplicity in being that is necessary for the transcendence that permits of judgment, that is in turn a necessary condition of truth.

But it is important to note that this infinite time opened up in fecundity (and opening up the possibility for alterity, and thus for judgment, and thus for truth) is still and always conceived in *Totality and Infinity* after the manner of possibilities that remain to a subject[35] in a future, not as my possibilities or as my future as the same, to be sure, but nevertheless as my possibilities and my future insofar as I am my son, while also not being my son. That is to say that infinite time as a condition of possibility of truth is so on the premise that it is and remains an open time, a time that keeps time open. But Levinas maintains that infinite time, *a* condition of possibility for truth after the testimony of the final paragraph of the main text of *Totality and Infinity*, is not truth's sufficient condition. An infinite and indefinite future does not suffice for truth, even if truth requires it. Infinite time promises truth (that is, creates the opening across which truth could be judged true), but never delivers (never permits of the coincidence of being with itself that truth traditionally names). Under the regime of infinite time, truth is always postponed. For, in its in(de)finitude, it is as susceptible to making way, leaving time, as much for untruth as for truth. Truth therefore also requires, Levinas claims, as evidenced by the "dream of a happy eternity," "a time it will be able to seal, a completed time, . . . messianic time, . . . where the perpetual is converted into the eternal, . . . [a triumph] secured against the revenge of evil whose return the infinite time does not prohibit" (TI 284–85 [261]). But would not this "eternity," this "completed" time, this "sealed" time, that Levinas refers to as messianic, not negate the infinition of time? Is not time as eternal precisely that against which all of the descriptions of infinite time were intended to oppose? Are, then, the two conditions of possibility for truth identified in the paragraph with which we opened this chapter mutually exclusive? So much the worse for truth? Or might this "eternity" bear another meaning? At this point Levinas simply asks: "Is this eternity a new structure of time, or an extreme vigilance of the messianic consciousness? The problem exceeds the bounds of this book." Can we investigate this question by, at Levinas's prodding, and forewarned of the dangers, turning to another book?

II. From Postponement to Recurrence

II.1. The Essence of Time

If time is shown to be temporalized, in *Totality and Infinity,* in terms of the futurity of possibilities, in terms of a certain future (that is always, qua "possibility," *un*certain), Levinas in *Otherwise Than Being or Beyond Essence* will describe the ultimate temporalization of time in terms of a certain past. But it is necessary to work through certain other structures to arrive at its articulation.

Levinas opens the "expository" section of his *Otherwise Than Being* (in chapter 2, "From Intentionality to Sensibility," after having laid out the theses of his argument in the introductory first chapter) by arguing that if the notion of truth as manifestation (which is its original philosophical sense) is to be meaningful, then this manifestation, this truth, can be only a showing of being to being itself. But how would such a showing of being to itself be possible? Would the possibility of this showing not necessarily imply a break in being such that there would be a part of being that is being seen, and a part that is looking,[36] and would this break not impose itself even if being were in its totality manifesting itself to itself, adding a supplement to the being being manifested in the form of this reflexive loop? That would be the case, unless this reflexivity is part and parcel of being itself, that is, unless being *is* manifestation. What is clear is that if manifestation is to yield truth, if being is to manifest itself to itself in truth, as it *is,* this reflexivity cannot distort the identity of being. If there is to be truth, being must be capable of sustaining itself in its identity across the break in being that manifestation implies, being must, that is to say, find itself again as the same being, unchanged in its identity. Indeed, this possibility of the permanence of identity across being's self-manifestation is precisely the possibility of truth.[37]

And it is this break in being, this separation of being from itself, across which being finds itself again unchanged, that Levinas in *Otherwise Than Being* identifies as time: the "astonishing divergence of the identical from itself" (OTB 28 [36]). Time is temporalized, after these analyses, in terms of this "diastasis of the punctual," in terms of this "modification without change that time operates" (OTB 34 [44]), this "getting out of phase" (OTB 28 [36]) with itself of being that manifestation requires. Indeed, this temporalization is, Levinas claims, apophansis itself, "exposition, the phenomenality of being" (OTB 31 [39]), the "original light" or "openness" (OTB 30 [38]) in which manifestation as the identification of an entity is enacted.[38] Levinas reserves the word "essence" to designate this temporalization, to name this vibration of being, this "silent resonance" (OTB 40 [51]) of being as temporal, this "flow" (OTB 34 [43]) which is the temporalization of time.[39]

To speak a truth, to manifest or have something manifested to oneself, is, after this schema, to recapture an identity across the time that divides it from itself *as if* the identity preceded its temporalization (while in fact it is only across temporalization that identities emerge (OTB 37 [48])), to identify something *as* something. It is to pronounce that A is A, or that A is B, to, in short, say what something *is*.[40] Manifestation names a being in a predicative proposition. But does the predicative proposition name only? It is Levinas's claim, on the contrary, that in the "is" (in the verb "to be") that joins the terms of a predicative proposition, this verb also, as verb, signifies the temporalization of time in signifying not only what (as nominalized) a being is, but in signifying its *way* of being, its *essence*. Thus, A is A is not only tautological, and A is B is not only to identify A with respect to a system of references in which it becomes meaningful, but a description of the *manner* (*la façon*) or the *how* (*le comment*) of A. In A is A we have not only an identification, but—Levinas tells us, "for the 'listening eye' " (OTB 37 [48])—A A's, wherein the qualities of things, for the sensibility, resound adverbially ("and, more precisely, as adverbs of the verb to be"; OTB 35 [44]); the sound resounds, red reds, not as an event, nor a dynamism, nor an activity, nor alteration of red, a becoming red or becoming redder, not as a process "in which the massive turns into energy" (OTB 39 [50]) that would take place in time or across time, but wherein "the immediate coincidence of the nominalized adjective . . . with itself is abruptly diachronized [*se diachronise*]" (OTB 39 [50]). In the verb "to be" essence resounds, for instance, in poetry and song (OTB 40 [52]), irreducible to the meanings these yield regarding identities. Thus Levinas writes:

> The verb *to be* tells the flowing of time as though language were not unequivocally equivalent to denomination, as though in *to be* the verb first came to function as a verb, and as though this function refers to the teeming and mute itching of that modification without change that time operates. . . . Essence, temporalization, is the verbalness of the verb. . . . Temporalization is the verb form to be. Language issued from the verbalness of the verb would then not only consist in making being understood, but also in making its essence vibrate. (OTB 34–35 [44])

It is not, then, that there is first essence, the temporalization of time, that would then be named with a verb, where this verb would function as a noun naming a process (although that can be done), but that *in* the predicative proposition that names beings, the temporalization of time, essence, already resounds.[41] Or again, for Levinas, phenomenality does not precede, but is contemporaneous with, phenomenology.[42]

So language *is* a system of nouns that, across the predicative proposition, designates this as that. "But also," Levinas warns, "and with as much right, language can be conceived as the verb in a predicative proposition in which the substances break down into modes of being, modes of temporalization. Here language does not double up the being of entities, but exposes the silent resonance of the essence" (OTB 40 [51]). Language is therefore at once nominalized adverbs and nouns dissolving into modes of being[43]—and this amphibology in language between beings and being, between entities and essences, keeps alive in language two interpretative possibilities: manifestation and signification.

II.2. Manifestation

The nominalization of essences, the constitution of entities as identical entities, as idealities, is enacted, then, in the identification of the same entity as the same across the time that is essence, in a "recuperation in which nothing is lost" (OTB 28 [36]), where being, disengaged from its being in the dispersal of sensations that is the temporalization of time, is re-collected by the memory, gathered by "the unity of apperception" (OTB 29 [37]) into an identity, wherein the temporality of time, modification without change, is gathered into a present, that is, brought into correlation with a consciousness that identifies it as the same: "Across time, the same finds again the same modified. Such is consciousness" (OTB 36 [47]).

As such, "the identity of entities refers to a saying," and specifically:

> to a saying that would be *correlative* with the said, or that would idealize the identity of entities. This saying would thus constitute that identity, and recuperate the irreversible, coagulate the flow of time into a "something," thematize, ascribe a meaning. It would take up a position with regard to this "something," fixed in a present, re-present it to itself, and thus extract it from the labile character of time. (OTB 37 [47])

That is, the saying that identifies, or re-presents,[44] the entity as the same entity across time, immobilizing the flow, "assembling time . . . into a conjuncture" (OTB 42 [54]), is the saying of a "said"[45]—the constitution of a meaning that is already a response to an already said (*un déjà dit*), a doxa that corresponds to an Urdoxa (OTB 35–36 [45–46]), the activity of the constituting subject and its receptive (and thus still "active") passivity in the face of what is—in perfect correlation: "The saying extended toward the said and absorbed in it, correlative with it, names an entity" (OTB 37 [47]).

This manifestation of entities, this denomination designating or constituting identities, indicates that language can indeed be legitimately conceived of as "a system of signs doubling up beings and relations" (OTB 35 [44]), that is, as a system of nouns, even if, as we are in the course of arguing, for Levinas language is not reducible to this. And this capacity to gather time into the conjuncture of a present, by memory, the possibility of the correlation of lapse and memory that time as essence permits, does yield a particular temporality: that of history. That is, for Levinas: "An entity or a configuration of entities emerge thematized and are identified in the synchronism of denomination (or in the unity of a tale which cannot be out of phase). They become history, are delivered over to writing, to books, in which the time of the narrative, without being reversed, recommences" (OTB 42 [54]).

But if the time of history is interpreted as time per se, if all of the past is re-memorable and the future able to be anticipated, gathered into a history and a teleology in correlation with a present, then all that is, all that can have meaning, draws its meaning from the place that it occupies in this totality, including the subject who then is operated, even in its constitutive capacities, as a functionary of this totality ("bits of dust collected by its movement or drops of sweat glistening on its forehead because of the labor of the negative it will have accomplished, . . . forgettable moments of which what counts is only their identities due to their positions in the system, which are reabsorbed into the whole of the system" (OTB 104 [131–32]), as Levinas puts it). Here the subject is but a detour that Being/History/Totality makes, assimilating this detour itself in its dialectical *tour,* as it heads toward the perfect and final showing of itself to itself, a perfect correlation that would put an end, as superfluous, to all showing—and thus to all time—in the fusion of perfect unity: "Time, essence, essence as time, would be the absolute itself in the return to self" (OTB 103 [131]).

II.3. Signification

But this lapse and recuperation by memory, this constitution of a present in the perfect correlation of the saying and the said that permits of the constitution of historical time, does not exhaust, for Levinas, the whole significance of time: "For the lapse of time is also something irrecuperable, refractory to the simultaneity of the present, something unrepresentable, immemorial, pre-historical. Before the syntheses of apprehension and recognition, the absolutely passive "synthesis" of aging is effected. Through it time passes [*se passe*]" (OTB 38 [48]).[46]

So the time of manifestation, wherein everything shows itself and is identified in a saying as something said, is constituted upon, presupposes, the passive passing of time that is essence—the break in which being diverges from itself, modification without change—and thus cannot return to dominate this passively undergone passing of time. For, even if this passing were itself to be named in a said, nominalized as an event, this manifestation would in turn require, as its condition of possibility, a time that does not show itself, the verb in its verbality underlying the verb as noun:[47] "The verb understood as a noun designating an event, when applied to the temporalization of time, would make it resound as an event, whereas every event already presupposes time. Time's modification without change, the putting of the identical out of phase with itself, teems behind the transformations and the endurance, and, as aging, even within endurance" (OTB 34 [43–44]).

A senescence, a diachrony or a passing of time irreducible to memorable time, thus insinuates itself into the heart of manifestation, as its condition of possibility, such that

> the immemorial is not an effect of a weakness of memory, an incapacity to cross large intervals of time, to resuscitate pasts too deep. It is the impossibility of the dispersion of time to assemble itself in the present, the insurmountable diachrony of time, a beyond the said. It is diachrony that determines the immemorial; a weakness of memory does not constitute diachrony. (OTB 38 [48–49])

In this original diachrony (or pre-original, if origins are the stuff of historical accounts), in this pre-original senescence (a passing of time that precedes an active subject's "constitution" of time as passing, arrived at in this account in what Levinas refers to as a "reduction,"[48] a "phenomenological reduction" that works back from phenomena to their conditions of possibility), Levinas argues that we discover (in a "discovery" that can only be named in a certain betrayal that is necessitated by this nominalization of the verbality of the verb) "a past more ancient than any present, a past which was never present and whose anarchical antiquity was never given in the play of dissimulations and manifestations" (OTB 24 [31]). But this diachrony, is it then "characterizable only negatively? Is it pure loss? Has it no signification?" If it does have a signification, this would clearly have to be a signification *other* than that of manifestation, wherein time is synchronized in a said, that is, it would have to be a signification "forgotten in ontology." Levinas therefore asks: "If saying is not only the correlative of a said, if its signifyingness is not absorbed in the signification said, can we not find beyond or on the hither side of the saying that tells being the signifyingness of diachrony?" (OTB 38 [49]). It is this significance that we shall next attempt to trace by way of Levinas's notion of "recurrence," a notion by means of which, we shall propose, we can discover a temporality that precedes and makes possible, not only historical time, but also the time of essence itself.

II.4. Recurrence

The passivity of aging signifies in the incapacity of the subject to gather itself into a present, to re-present itself fully to itself, and as such signifies an exposure of the subject to its other—an exposure that it can in no sense recuperate insofar as it is presupposed by every recuperation. It signifies the absolute passivity of the subject with respect to this other, to this passing of time that precedes any constitution of time: "Temporalization as lapse, the loss of time, is neither an initiative of an ego, nor a movement toward some telos of action. The loss of time is not the work of a subject" (OTB 51 [66]).

And it is precisely "in the form of the *being* of this entity, the diachronic temporality of aging, that there is produced despite myself the response to an appeal, direct like a traumatizing blow. Such a response cannot be converted into an 'inward need' or a natural tendency. This response answers, but with no eroticism, to an absolutely heteronomous call" (OTB 53 [68]). The negative signification of the passivity of aging takes on a positive significance when the other to which the subject is exposed in the passive undergoing of the passing of time turns out to be the human other, *Autrui,* who calls me to responsibility by means of his approach as face. Indeed, the alterity of the other that calls me to responsibility turns out to be *the* introduction of the other into the same, the very introduction of an incommensurable time into the recuperable time of the same, from which the passivity of aging (the negative signification of the passing of time) parasitically lives:

> The temporalization of time, as it shows itself in the said, is indeed recuperated by an active ego which recalls through memory and reconstructs in historiography the past that is bygone, or through imagination and prevision anticipates the future, and, in writing,

> synchronizing the signs, assembles into a presence, that is, represents, even the time of responsibility for the other. But it is not possible that responsibility for another devolve from a *free* commitment, that is, a present; it exceeds every actual or represented present. It is thus in a time without beginning. (OTB 51 [66])

From out of a time without beginning, the other calls me to responsibility in his regard, exceeding every present, and *preceding* every present. Preceding, in that before the subject finds its feet as a constituting ego, it finds itself already in relation to that which calls to it from out of a profound past ("deep yore, never remote enough" (profond jadis, jadis jamais assez) (OTB 106 [134])), a past to which it is already in relation (in the ethical relation that Levinas refers to as proximity), and to which it is always already a response—before choosing to be so or not to be so—a response that *is* its subjectivity.

Always already called, constrained by a responsibility before being able to collect itself into a present, into a consciousness, that would be able to receive this call, the subject is "already formed [*déjà fait*] with absolute passivity" (OTB 104 [132–33])—or "a creature" ("but an orphan by birth or an atheist no doubt ignorant of its Creator, for if it knew it it would again be taking up its commencement"; OTB 105 [133])—responding to the other before capable of active response, like an echo that precedes the sound it echoes. The subject *is* (if the word "is" can still be used here—since this subjectivity precedes and makes possible the very constitution of being) this response, is reduced—by the call of the other that approaches from out of an un(re)presentable past—from Me (*le Moi,* the active, present, and self-presenting ego) to the Self (*le Soi*), to the hypostasis[49] that underlies, precedes, and makes possible the ego, but a hypostasis that is no stasis, no place to take a stand, no state of equilibrium, but "restlessness" (*inquiétude*) (OTB 45 [58]). No longer (or, in fact, not yet) in correlation with a said (taking its meaning from the place it would occupy in a system of references), the subject in its very subjectivity is reduced to its exposure to the other, reduced to pure saying, that is, reduced to signification.[50] Stripped to the core of itself in a stripping *of* the core of itself, "a fission of the nucleus opening the bottom of its punctual nuclearity" (OTB

49 [64–65]), stripped of its identity as ego, where its identity is but the lack of any such identity, reduced to responsibility ("*one* without identity, but unique in the unexceptionable requisition of responsibility"; OTB 53 [69]), stripped of the capacity to assume or welcome this stripping,[51] the description of the subjectivity of the subject, *le Soi,* proceeds hyperbolically: "a passivity more passive still than any passivity," "an exposedness always to be exposed the more" (OTB 50 [64]), the "denuding of denuding" (OTB 49 [63]), and ultimately, the responsibility even for the responsibility of the other—which is the very meaning, in Levinas, of substitution.[52]

As such, the self is, despite itself (for it had no choice in the matter of its being chosen), elected to responsibility, to the good, before it could assume its election, is equivalent to its election—the "me and not other," the "*me voici,*" of responsibility—an obedience that precedes the reception of the command. But an obedience "where revolt is brewing" (OTB 52 [67]). The self, we recall, can forget its call, can identify itself with the said of its saying, can forget its responsibility, its goodness, can forget what it is, or forget, rather, the hypostasis that allows it to *be,* and this must remain a structural possibility if the good is to be the good, the judge of history, and not simply what *is:* history itself. Ironically, if the subject were simply good, were this its natural condition, the subject would not be good, it would simply be. Goodness requires that the subject not be good of itself, but that its goodness be a response to a heteronomous call to goodness. Goodness requires the reduction of the subject to the self, that is never in-itself, but always already response, responsibility, but capable of taking itself up egoistically.

Consequently, the reduction of the *Moi* to the *Soi* has its own temporal structure, or at least lends itself to a temporally qualified description, in Levinas's notion of recurrence. For the reduction is not once and for all. When the ego is driven back upon itself, or as Levinas often hyperbolically puts it (in order to avoid the conclusion being drawn that the subject is capable of gathering itself up there as if in a site), driven back beyond itself, by the call of the other that comes from out of an unrepresentable past, the subject both ontologically does as ego, and ethically cannot as self, *assume* this stripping of its identity *as* its identity. The ego, taking up a stance in, or converting into a site, the nonsite, the *u-topia*, of identity as nonidentity, usurping to the *eon* of visible historicity, by its powers as ego, the invisible reign of the good or of God (OTB 52 [67]), this ego must be reduced—if it is to become good, if it is to become its *self*—ever and again, "incessantly."[53] And it is in this ever and again of the interruption of the ego by the other (Levinas calls it an "interminable recurrence"—*récurrence irrésiliable*),[54] in the re- or de-establishment of the identity of the self as nonidentity in and as responsibility, that the self recurs to itself in a nonassumable recurrence, and that is found the original hypostasis on the basis of which any subsequent assumption (self-identification of this self) is possible. Ever and again called to a responsibility in response to an un(re)presentable past, the self is identified across the vibrations of its recurring nonidentity,[55] its interminable exile,[56] its (re)iterative passivity.[57] Ever and again self, ever and more deeply self, never enough self, "always insufficiently divested" (OTB 57 [73]), the self is "identified" across, and against, the revolt that would identify this nonidentifiable identification.[58] Ever and again—a temporality that precedes time and that would make time possible,[59] a pre-temporal temporality: recurrence. But if a temporality (and Levinas is clear that by the "already done" of the oneself in recurrence he does not mean "a duration prior to duration"; OTB 107 [136]), then a temporality in two times,[60] or between times, a "dead time" between the immemorial past of the other and the present of the ego[61]—recurrence of the subjectivity as the hinge point between incommensurable times, signifying a pre-original diachrony, equivalent with this pre-original diachrony.[62] And it is in terms of this pre-original diachrony that even the time of essence (that, as we have seen, both lends itself to the recollection of memory, and signifies time as pure loss in aging) finds its bearing. Levinas thus writes:

> Over and beyond the thematization and the content exposed in it—entities and relations between entities shown in a theme—the apophansis signifies as a modality of the approach to another. It refers to a saying on the hither side of the amphibology of being and entities. This saying, in the form of responsibility for another, is bound to an irrecuperable, unrepresentable, past, temporalizing according to a time with separate epochs, in a diachrony. (OTB 47 [60])[63]

Here recurrence, my being driven back, ever and again, upon myself and beyond myself out of an ever resuming present in response to an unrepresentable past that demands my response in the form of responsibility, demands my passive undergoing for the sake of the other as patience, signifies as the very temporalization of time: "Here the temporality of time is an obedience" (OTB 52 [68]).

III. A Temporary Conclusion

So the structure of the expositions of time in *Totality and Infinity* and *Otherwise Than Being* are not dissimilar. In each case we discover an original articulation of the temporalization of time (as future possibilities in the face of death, or as the vibration of the verb "to be") that can be interpreted either (or indeed both) in the direction of objective historicality, that traced by philosophy as ontology, or (and) in the direction of the infinite, as signifying that which transcends and undermines the ultimacy of objective historicality while simultaneously making such an interpretation possible. And in each case the original articulation of the temporalization of time is shown to be a function of a more fundamental temporality: in *Totality and Infinity* time as future possibility rooted in the time of fecundity, and in *Otherwise Than Being* the time of essence rooted in the recurrence of the subjectivity as saying, that is, respectively, in terms of an infinite future transcending my future as personal identity, and in terms of an irrecuperable past, a past irreducible to any past that I could appropriate as my own, that is, relate to my present as an ecstasis flowing from this present.

But while this future and this past play similar roles in these respective works as founding the temporalization of time by introducing the infinite into the same (and thus opening up the transcendence that truth requires), they are not, we would maintain, equivalent notions, that is, are not, with respect to the present they disrupt and condition (or disrupt *as* condition), interchangeable temporalities, where either one or the other would do equally well to introduce the same infinity into the equation such that, with the imposition of the one or the other, truth might bloom. Or, put another way, these extremities of time—the infinite future and the irrecuperable past—are not correlatives. One cannot think, or so we would argue, these notions as the equal but opposite extremes of one and the same temporal spectrum as that which overflows the spectrum at either end, as parallel if differently oriented ecstases conceived of from out of relation to the same temporal present. For if the infinitude of time remains, as we have argued, the articulation of a future generated, across generations, from out of a present that is mine, even across and despite and thanks to the interruptions and resumptions made possible and necessary by this time being also the time of my son, who remains in a sense me but who is not me (that which keeps this future in a certain sense mine while not assimilating it to the realm of my projects), the recurrence of subjectivity that responds to an always past past is in no way generated from out of my present, but cuts across the line drawn by and of infinite time at every point from out of an incommensurable past, from out of a time that does not at any point, even across generations, join up with my own.[64]

Might this irrecuperable past, this other temporality, the temporality of the other, that interrupts infinite time at every point, driving the subject back upon and beyond itself recurrently, ever and again, be read as a reference to the messianic time that, according to the final paragraph of the main the text of *Totality and Infinity,* truth requires in addition to infinite time? Messianic time, we recall from that text, means (reflecting the non-aberrational "dream of a happy eternity") "the completion of time," "where the perpetual is converted into the eternal" (TI 285 [261]). But if this completion of time, this eternal time, which is to be "secured against the revenge of evil whose return the infinite time does not prohibit," is not to negate the infinitude of time (which is also necessary for truth), then must not this "eternal" be the "eternal" of an *always and again* rather than the "bad eternal" of the *forever and always* (as the immobility of being)? Indeed, is it not the *forever and always* sense of the "eternal" against which the analyses of the infinitude of time in *Totality and Infinity* fought so hard to avoid, in that such would negate time (and infinite time above all), and thus transcendence, and thus the possibility of judgment, and thus the truth that messianic time, along with infinite time, is supposed to make possible? And is not such an "always and again" precisely that which is described by the recurrence of subjectivity? Is not the subject as recurrent, in response to the irreconcilable past of the other, reduced to pure Saying, in proximity to the other, responsible for the other to the point of substitution, "secured against the revenge of evil" because, as recurrent, stripped down to this responsibility, stripped down to its goodness, its being for the other, as its very (in)condition? This sense of "eternal," as "eternal recurrence," yields an eternity that does not close time down, but—recurring—keeps time open, and seals it by the recurrence of the call to goodness, a goodness secured against the return of evil in that it is prior to any choice between, or constitution of, good and evil as terms between which a freedom might choose. After this conception, the apparent conflict of eternity and infinitude is avoided, and eternity and infinitude are able to collaborate in the production of truth not as contradictories operating on the same temporal plane, but as articulations of distinct and irreconcilable temporalities that nevertheless intersect at the truth.

So we are suggesting that the eternal recurrence of the subject in response to an other who approaches from out of an immemorial past, as described by Levinas in his *Otherwise Than Being,* might well provide us with some clues to the question posed at the end of *Totality and Infinity:* "Is this eternity a new structure of time, or an extreme vigilance of the messianic consciousness?"

IV. At This Very Moment

In order to risk a possible answer to this question, we shall turn to an examination of a peculiar but, we shall argue, pivotal (i.e., central, and pivotal in a sense yet to be delineated) phrase found not infrequently (though most often in chapter 5) in *Otherwise Than Being:* "at this very moment" (en ce moment même). This temporally qualified phrase (and its variants: "this moment," "the moment," etc.) serves an interesting function in Levinas's articulation of the structures of time and temporality, namely, we shall argue, as the temporal articulation of the recurrent intersection of the two "temporalities" ("the present" and "the irrecuperable past") that are thematized in *Otherwise Than Being,* an articulation that illuminates (even as it is illuminated by), moreover (and we shall have to show how), the discussions of temporality and time in *Totality and Infinity,* and thus, perhaps, can help us to approach the question about the (temporal/ethical) status of "eternity" as it comes to articulation in that text.

This Levinasian phrase has been analyzed before. Indeed, "at this very moment" is one of the three Levinasian phrases that are highlighted by Derrida in an article whose title is made up of an amalgam of these phrases: "At this very moment in this work here I am." As our purposes in highlighting this phrase differ somewhat from those of Derrida in his complex article (in which the analysis of "this very moment" makes up but a "moment"), and while we shall not, in consequence, attend to all of the details of this article, it may nevertheless prove instructive to begin our own analyses from within Derrida's discussion, and borrowing some of the insights found therein. Let us begin, then, by citing some of the same passages from *Otherwise Than Being,* which contain the phrase "at this very moment," cited by Derrida (the square brackets indicate our extended citing), before moving on to some of Derrida's observations regarding them:

> Every contestation and interruption of this power of discourse[65] is at once related and invested by discourse. It thus recommences as soon as one interrupts it. . . . This discourse will affirm itself to be coherent and one. In relating the interruption of the discourse or my being ravished into discourse I connect its thread. . . . [If the philosophical discourse is broken, withdraws from speech and murmurs, is spoken, it nonetheless speaks of that, and speaks of the discourse which a moment ago it was speaking and to which it returns to say its provisional retreat.] Are we not *at this very moment* in the process of barring the issue our whole essay attempts, and of encircling our position from all sides? The exceptional words by which the trace of the past and the extravagance of the approach are said—One, God—become terms, reenter into the vocabulary and are put at the disposition of philologists, instead of confounding philosophical language. Their very explosions are recounted. . . . Thus the ladder-proof equivocation that language weaves signifies. (OTB 169 [215], emphasis is Derrida's)

> The intervals are not recuperated. Does not the discourse that suppresses the interruptions of discourse by relating them maintain

> the discontinuity under the knots with which the thread is tied again?
>
> The interruptions of the discourse found again and recounted in the immanence of the said are conserved like knots in a thread tied again, the trace of a diachrony that does not enter into the present, that refuses simultaneity.
>
> And I still interrupt the ultimate discourse in which all the discourses are stated, in saying it to one that listens to it, and who is situated outside the said that the discourse says, outside all it includes. That is true of the discussion I am elaborating *at this very moment.* This reference to an interlocutor permanently breaks through the text that the discourse claims to weave in thematizing and enveloping all things. In totalizing being, discourse qua discourse[66] thus belies the very claim to totalize. (OTB 170 [216–17], emphasis is Derrida's)

Derrida's immediate comments upon these quotations, his delineation of the different functions of (the same) "at this very moment" in the two passages cited—the first of these comments inserted between the two as cited in his text, and the second comment following the second citation—are worth, for our purposes, quoting at length:

> Within the question just posed ("And are we not at this very moment . . ."), the "at this very moment" would constitute the enveloping form or web of a text resuming without end all its tears within itself. But two pages later, the same "at this very moment," otherwise said within the text, caught within another enchaining-unchaining, says something wholly other, namely, that "at this very moment" the interruptive breakthrough has taken place, ineluctable *at this very moment* when the discursive relation, the philosophical *récit,* pretends to reappropriate for itself the tear within the continuum of its texture. (Atvm 21)
>
> At a two-page interval, an interval which neither can nor should be reduced, that here constitutes an absolutely singular seriality, the same "at this very moment" seems to repeat itself only to be disloged without return. The "same" "very" (*le "même" du "même"*) of the "at this very moment" has remarked upon its own alternation, one which will have ever since opened it up to the other. The "first" one, which formed the element of reappropriation in the continuum, will have been *obligated* by the "second," the other one, the one of interruption, even before being produced, and in order

> to be produced. It will have constituted the text and context with the other, but only within a series where the text coheres with its own (if this may still be said) tear. The "at this very moment" only coheres to itself by means of an immeasurable anachrony incommensurable with itself. The singular textuality of this "series" does not enclose the Other but on the contrary opens itself up to it from out of irreducible difference, the past before any present, before any present moment, before anything we think we understand when we say "at this very moment." (Atvm 22)

Derrida (or at least the—probably "male"—textual voice that speaks this part),[67] in these commentaries, is interested in "this very moment" as it recurs in Levinas's text(s), in the textual effect that this recurrence produces, as he attempts to trace out how, in the work of Levinas, Levinas allows the Work (the passing of Infinity) to work, allows the Relation with the Other, irreducible to the said, to come to expression in a philosophical said, or how Levinas calculates or negotiates, in his text, that which is incalculable or nonnegotiable. His answer is that it is by means of a seriality, or recurrence, or repetition of terms—"there must be a *series*" (Atvm 24)[68]—within Levinas's text, wherein the previously "said" meanings conveyed by these terms are disrupted or displaced by later employments of the "same" terms.

We too are interested in "this very moment" and its recurrence, or in it, precisely, *as* recurrence, not so much (at least for our present purposes) with the textual effects of its recurrence, but with the place that the recurrence of the moment—the "same" moment recurring in its "double difference"—occupies in Levinas's thinking of temporality and time. That is, while we continue to follow Derrida here, it is with an eye toward the temporal status or function of the recurring "at this very moment" (and not to its recurrence "in the text"—even if its recurrence can be textually traced/produced) that we do so. Thus, Derrida: "You will have noticed that the two occurrences of 'at this moment' are inscribed and interpreted, drawn along according to two different gestures" (Atvm 23). That is, "this very moment" lends itself, in the first usage, to an interpretation that would subsume it into a "history" of moments, that would make it into a "present." (Derrida: "In the first case, the present moment is determined from the movement of a present thematization, a presentation that pretends to encompass within itself the Relation which yet exceeds it, pretends to exceed it, precede it, and overflow it. That first 'moment' makes the other return to the same"; Atvm 23–24.)[69] Conversely, "this very moment" lends itself, in the second usage, to the signification of another temporality: to an irrecuperable past, the time of the other incommensurable with my own. (Derrida: "But the other, the second 'moment,' if it is rendered possible by the excessive relation, is no longer nor shall it ever have been, a present 'same.' Its 'same' is (will have been) dislocated by the very same thing which will have (probably, perhaps) been its 'essence,' namely, the Relation"; Atvm 24.)[70] But, as Derrida notes (and we concur):[71]

> Between the two occurrences of "at this very moment," the link is not one of distinction. It is the "same" moment which is each time repeated and divided each time in its link to its own essence, in its link to the responsibility that makes it possible. . . . But although, between the two "moments," there is a chronological, logical, rhetorical, and even an ontological interval—to the extent that the first belongs to ontology while the second escapes it in making it possible—it is nevertheless the *same moment,* written and read in its difference, in its double difference, one belonging to dialectic and the other different from and deferring from (*différant*) the first, infinitely and in advance overflowing it. The second moment has an infinite advance on the first. And yet it is the same. (Atvm 24)

That is, *the same* "this very moment" lends itself, "at the same time!", to two interpretations, goes, from out of its sameness, in either of two different—and irreconcilable (or at least incommensurable)—directions. The moment, "this very moment," would thus seem, in the ambiguity of this enigma, to be the temporal articulation of the point at which the deep past (that brings responsibility to the present in interrupting this present) intersects or crosses the present (with its gathered ecstases of past, present, and future). The moment is the "now" of an "interrupted present" and is thus the moment of responsibility. If this is the case, then this very moment plays a pivotal role in the articulation of the diverse temporalities (the deep past, the extended present, and, as we will argue, my/not my future in the son) described in the foregoing analyses, or, precisely, the role of the pivot. This very moment is the time in which the subject begins always and ever again to gather itself into an ego, to tell its tale in correlation with its needs and its projects, *and* the time in which the ego is interrupted in its continuity by the other who comes to it from out of a past that does not belong to this continuity. The moment articulates a time, a non/present now (a "now" both belonging and not belonging to any present) in which these times collide or from which they emanate; the moment is a time between times, or the time of between times.

If we are then to imagine an horizontal line that would represent historical time, and a vertical line representing the deep past (an other temporality, the temporality of the other, a past or a pre-origin that is not the past—the past present—that would be conceived of as stretching along the space between the beginning of the horizontal line and the point on that line representing the present) that would cut across (and cut up, if Levinas's image of the broken thread is taken up) the horizontal one, the moment, "this very moment," would be the point at which these two lines would meet. "At this very moment" the subject in its present—in its "present history" comprising its remembered past, lived present, and anticipated future—is interrupted by a deep past irreducible to its present (calling it to a responsibility it has not assumed and cannot assume to its extended present), but "at this very *same* moment" history is resumed (the thread retied), and the moment has passed. Perhaps nothing happened; the trace of the deep past that has cut (across) this present, as enigmatic, lends itself to multiple interpretations. But I am in another, a new (different but always the same as always different—the eternal recurrence of difference in the same), moment; I am faced, again, with the face, "at this very moment," recurrently. Derrida is right; for this, too (where "this" is the moment as the time between times), "there must be a *series*." For if there were only one moment, history would sub-sume it in re-suming. "This very moment" depends, therefore, upon its recurrence, upon the "ever and again" of its eternal recurrence, without this eternity ever being (ultimately) susceptible to being collected into a history of "these very moments." (Such a history could be written—in fact *is* being written by Levinas "at this very moment" in his texts, but it is also, as he points out—we have seen this—in its being said *to an other,* "in this very moment" in the process of fission, exploding the enclosure of which historiography is the circumscription.) That is, "this very moment" qua "this very moment," qua the temporality of the recurrence of the subjectivity of the subject, needs be eternal in our sense of ever and again.

But the subject is not eternal. Even the I that is but the *me voici* will pass away. The eternity of the ever and again of recurrence would come to an end (and thus lose its eternity) if I alone were responsible. The eternal recurrence of the subjectivity of the subject must therefore refer to an "ever and again" of a recurrence that exceeds my own time (even "my time" as "this very moment" in which I find myself—already implying a beyond of "my time" as my personal history), must implicate me "in this very moment" in a past that preceded me, and in a future that will continue on without me—*and* where this past and this future are implicated in recurrence. But have we not already run across such structures in, in terms of the past, an other who (before me, from out of a deep past that is in no sense "mine") has always already been responsible for the other (i.e., for me) in the figure of the feminine other, or the other in the modality of the feminine, and, in terms of the future, an other who will be responsible into a future (that is not "mine") in the figure of the son? Could it be that eternity, the eternity of the ever and again of recurrence (as opposed to the eternity of the forever and always that imposes itself as a totality), is precisely eternal in being the recurrence of the moment beyond any moment that I personally will live? "This very moment," the very moment of my responsibility, implicates me in an "intrigue," an eternal (ever and again recurring) intrigue (but an intrigue irreducible to history, that does not become a history behind history, non-narratable), or an eternal emplotting-unplotting (Derrida's "enchaining-unchaining") that transcends, in a certain sense, "this very moment" that I personally live.

But such an eternity would, as such, in no way absolve me of my responsibility "at this very moment," for I am responsible, at this very moment, for the past moments of responsibility insofar as the legacy (and not the history) of love or grace comes to rest, in utter restlessness, upon me at this very moment. The graciousness that has always already come to me from out of the deep past (by way of the feminine other who in love gives to me a home in an already enculturated [just] world), like the good that inspires justice and has a life only in justice, has a life only as it inspires me to graciousness—*is* only "at this very moment" (my moment) upon which it depends even as it has always already made this moment possible. The subject is from grace to grace (from being graced to being called to graciousness), gifted and called by and to grace; the giftedness of this gracious moment is at once a call to pass on this grace to the other. The son must receive the gifted legacy of grace—with its gift/call character—*from me.* I am as graced graciousness, as loved love, the passing of the gift into a future that as such rests upon me "at this very moment." That is, I am "at this very moment," as responsible to the other who approaches from out of an irrecuperable past, responsible also for the historical future, for a historical future into which the legacy of grace must be passed (by way of the son) by me. And this is why Levinas's thought is in no sense an eschewing of history, nor an attempt to escape from time, but precisely a concern for guarding a trace of the deepest (and inspirational) meanings of history, those meanings that permit of a history that, while never encapsulating the good (while never *being* goodness itself), nevertheless responds to the good in justice. Indeed, inspired by love, the other in the mode of the feminine has already given to me the gift of society, the gift of institutions that (more or less effectively) protect my freedom, that guard a trace and a space for my responsibility to the other at this very moment. And it is this gracious gift, the gift of this grace, that I bear into the historical future as I attempt to re-construct just institutions, to build more and more just institutions in my responsibility for a future not mine that derives from my responsibility for that which comes from a past not mine.

But this concern for institutional justice is never straightforward (cannot go forth in a straight, unbroken line, even if it depends upon my *droiture*), is never "simple" (in this word's nonsimple sense: never "easy," and never "one thing"). For the subject "at this very moment," is at the crossroads of two temporalities ("le Moi est au carrefour"; OTB 197, n.12 [154]), is pulled simultaneously in two directions, is a participant, at one time, in two times. The subject is a two-timer: torn between the love of the other and the love of the other of the other, torn between the love of love and the love of justice (wherein there is love/justice—because there always already has been—for me too). I am a lover that just (in justice) cannot realize my love (and that remains therefore desire), or that can only just (in justice, through justice) realize my love, but inspired (like all lovers) by the fact that I just (in justice) cannot love enough (the other, or enough others).

The lover in the present straining toward the future is grabbed always already from behind, from a past (not its past) that will not let it "go," not in order to impede its forward progress, not to prohibit a Kierkegaardian "repetition," a repeating forward, but to "remind" this *force qui va* (whose progress depends upon its "forgetfulness") that its "repetition" (a repeating forward, a movement toward the future) rests upon its "recurrence" (a repeating backwards, a responsibility to the past), its being driven back upon and beyond itself in the absolute passivity of responsibility, of substitution. There can be no "purity of heart" (the willing of one thing) for this two-timing lover—the moment is too divided for that. Its movement forward bears the weight of a past not its own ("take my yoke upon you"), a weight that does not prohibit progress, but keeps (recurrently, eternally, ever and again) the *conatus* on its heels, reminding it that it need, in its surging in this very moment toward the future, be gracious with its lover(s)—"Gently" (*Doucement!*), "lovingly," "justly"—that it need tread lightly, that it not be too sure of its balance. Here history is checked, as it is inspired, by that which it must not dominate—ever and again, recurring "at this very moment."

Might eternity (as the ever and again of the recurrence of the subjectivity of the subject) be a new structure of time (new each "time") as the implication of the subject in the oldest structure of time (coming from an irretrievable past)—the ever and again time of responsibility—repeating from generation to (re)generation, the grace that *I am* grafted onto a grace received, but that nevertheless rests entirely upon me at this very moment, the time of its (re)naissance? "At this very moment" of graced graciousness is the renaissance of a gracious time, or time as graciousness, that gives birth to any other, and thus subsequent, structures of time, including the time of history itself through which the eternal has a life, but wherein it cannot be contained. I am responsible to that which comes to me from out of the deep past, a past I in no way effectuated (and that I cannot, as I can and do the historical past, reconstitute), as the "one" upon whom the heritage (but not the history, for the "story" of grace is rewritten with each one who receives and gives it)[72] and the future of grace rests. But does not this require, on my part, at this very moment, an extreme vigilance of the messianic consciousness, where I as the chosen one, elected to responsibility, *the* irreplaceable mediator of God's grace, must expire myself by breathing out and out of the goodness that inspires justice, that keeps justice just? Eternity requires a grace that depends upon me, but that neither began nor ends with me, the ever and again of grace: the response of responsibility, the Kingdom of God, the bread from my mouth, in my hands, at this very moment.

V. The Moment of Responsibility

"This very moment," we have been arguing, is, as the point of intersection between the deep past and the historical present of past-present-future, in two times without belonging to either. Can the same not be said of Levinas's own philosophical text, that, as we have seen, at once answers to the exigencies of synchronic discourse (is a "said"), *and* yet (at the same time, or, better, in the same "moment") remains an offering (in a testimonial "saying," in a saying that qua saying is already testimony to a substitution for the other) to an other across an ungatherable diachrony? My said is said *to* an other. Indeed, the "at this very moment . . . (the said)" . . . "at this very moment . . . (the saying)" that we have been reading for what it can teach us about the structure of Levinas's thinking of temporality and time has as its explicit context (each time) Levinas's own philosophical production, his own philosophical said. Levinas, moreover, would seem to confirm this in drawing our attention to the phenomenon of skepticism (which he will claim is sustained by its being, at once, at one and the same moment, in two times) within the history of philosophy, and drawing an analogy between this phenomenon and his own thought. Indeed, the quotations that appeared above containing the phrase "en ce moment même" were drawn from a section of *Otherwise Than Being* entitled "Skepticism and Reason," wherein what is at issue is the possibility of skepticism and, by analogy, the possibility of Levinas's own discourse.

The possibility of skepticism: what is the possibility of skepticism, are the possibilities for skepticism, when the skeptical said ("There is no truth") is not only easily refuted, but—and this is why it is so easily refuted—even refutes itself? If it is true it is not true. This is nothing more than a morsel before the voracious law of noncontradiction, which hardly need even swallow. But what fascinates Levinas about skepticism, despite the fact that it is powerless against the logic of philosophy, and that it is ever and again defeated, is that it returns ever and again, after each defeat, unabashed. Why is it not chased from the house of philosophy once and for all, rather than (as Levinas repeats three times) returning ever and again as "the legitimate child of philosophy?"[73]

The reason, Levinas claims, is that skepticism is (and this is what we have claimed for "the moment") in two times without belonging to either, that is, the making of the skeptical claim (skepticism's "saying") and that which is claimed in the claim (skepticism's "said") are not in the same time, are irreducible to one and the same temporal order, to the order and the time of the same. The skeptical claim is a "possible impossibility,"[74] logically impossible as a said, but ever and again possible as the saying of this said.

This possible saying of an impossible said is important to Levinas in that it presents us with a model, within philosophy, of something that internally disrupts the philosophical discourse, and disrupts it even as it rejoins this discourse, for the skeptical said remains "philosophical" (is a legitimate child of philosophy) in the sense that it presents, in the said, a "truth," be it the truth of the denial of truth.[75] Skepticism, in its passion regarding the truth, does not renounce its family ties, even if it rebels. But it is not the quarrel over truth that captures Levinas's attention here. Levinas is, in his analyses, neither advocating nor renouncing skepticism. It is rather the possible impossibility that skepticism represents with respect to philosophy (that is only interested in measuring possibilities) that intrigues Levinas, and that causes him to draw an analogy between skepticism and his own philosophical "saids." For Levinas's own philosophical discourse follows a path similar to that of skepticism: reduced to its said, synchronized in a said that names being, the "otherwise than being" is relegated to nothing in being made into a "something," to nonbeing in saying that it "is," disappears or is refuted as "otherwise than being" in its appearance in a text as something that *is* otherwise than being. But the fact that the saying of this said is not in the same time as that which is said in it is evinced by the very fact of the saying of it, a saying that does not rest in the silence of a once and for all, but is ex-pression, a going out from itself in response to an always already from which it awaits investiture; the very fact of saying a said demonstrates its uncertainty, the fact that it requires the investiture of the other. And this is why Levinas can say that "language is already skepticism" (OTB 170 [216]). The fact that something appears in discourse—is offered to the other—is a function of its being "in question," a being in *ethical* question that makes for the possibility of something being in *ontological* question.

But does this not bring us back to our thesis of chapter 5, and to the issue of a possible impossibility? Levinas's philosophical discourse qua discourse (encompassed within a said, closed up within a book, but offered to the other), we submit, partakes in or exemplifies the possible impossibility that is discourse. It is ever again possible as a testimony to grace offered to the other and awaiting his/her investiture; that is, it is ever and again possible as saying, but as such it is impossible as a said where the said would purport (as the said qua said must) to encompass even the addressee, to speak in generalities, in universal terms, to and of a general or universal "other." It is therefore an offering undertaken in extreme risk (for Levinas's philosophical said is as susceptible to totalization as any other, and even, qua said, is a necessary forgetting of the saying that inspires it), is a testimony to grace that—already called to be just, already a call to give again the grace it gives[76] (and thus a prophetic gesture)—rests nevertheless upon the remembering/forgetting of a graceful gesture that outside of its enigmatic trace can only be mis-taken, if it can be "taken" at all. Levinas's work is possible as a gesture of grace, but impossible as a conceptualization of grace, even if, qua philosophy, qua a discourse answering at once to the other and to justice, it cannot but be both in the possible impossibility of this very moment.

Notes

1. That passage reads: "Signification—one-for-the-other—relation with alterity—has already been analyzed *in the present work* as proximity, proximity as responsibility for the Other (*autrui*), and responsibility for the Other—as substitution: in its subjectivity, in its very bearing as separated substance, the subject has shown itself as expiation-for-the-other, condition or in-condition of hostage" (Jacques Derrida, "At This Very Moment in This Work Here I Am," in *Re-reading Levinas,* p. 31, Derrida's italics. Hereafter this work will be indicated by the short form Atvm).

2. Levinas makes this claim at several points, as for example: "It [he is speaking here of God, but the same applies to any "ineffable"] is nonthematizable, and even here is a theme only because in a said everything is conveyed before us, even the ineffable, at the price of a betrayal which philosophy is called upon to reduce" (OTB 162 [206]).

3. Derrida continues later in the paragraph: "But what overflows has just been announced—it is the very announcement, messianic consciousness—on the internal border of that utterance, *on the frame* of the book if not *in* it. And yet what is wrought and set to work in the present work only makes a work outside the book. The expression 'in the present work' mimics the thesis and the code of the university community; it is ironic. It has to be so as discretely as possible, for there would still be too great an assurance and too much glibness to break the code with a fracas. Effraction does not ridicule, it indeed makes a present of the 'present work' " (Atvm 31).

4. There will be some question, as we shall see, as to whether it could be properly "thematized" at all—and a consideration of this question will be necessary to an adequate accounting of the problem at hand.

5. "If I could have freely chosen my own existence everything would be justified" (TI 83 [55]).

6. Levinas discusses the problems surrounding the notion of "finite freedom" at TI 223 [198–99], and again at OTB 121–29 [156–66]).

7. "For how could one sole tear, though it be effaced, be forgotten, how could reparation have the least value, if it did not correct the instant itself, if it did not let it escape in its being, if the pain that glints in the tear did not exist 'pending,' if it did not exist with a still provisional being, if the present were consummated?" (TI 238 [215]).

8. "Infinition by way of *power* is limited in the return of power to the subject from which it emanates, and which it *ages* by forming the definitive" (TI 281 [258]).

9. Levinas adds: "It is to be emphasized that this destination of the work to a history that I cannot foresee—for I cannot see it—is inscribed

in the very essence of my power, and does not result from the contingent presence of other persons alongside of me."

10. "Historiography recounts the way the survivors appropriate the works of the dead wills to themselves; it rests on the usurpation carried out by the conquerors, that is, by the survivors; it recounts enslavement, forgetting the life that struggles against slavery" (TI 228 [204]).

11. "In my action, in the for itself of my will, I am exposed to a foreign will" (TI 236 [212]).

12. "In power the indetermination of the possible does not exclude the *reiteration* of the I, which in venturing toward this indeterminate future falls back on its feet, and, riveted to itself, acknowledges its transcendence to be merely illusory and its freedom to delineate but a fate" (TI 268 [246]).

13. Levinas discusses tragedy in this context at TI 226–27 [202], and at OTB 129 [165] links this to the comic in invoking the tragi-comic tale by Tolstoy of the dying man's order of a twenty-five-year supply of boots.

14. "Interiority as such is a 'nothing,' 'pure thought,' nothing but thought. In the time of the historiographer interiority is the non-being in which everything is possible, for in it nothing is impossible—the 'everything is possible' of madness" (TI 55 [26]).

15. Levinas refers to this struggle as "the essential of the will": "In history the will is congealed into a personage interpreted on the basis of his work, in which the essential of the will productive of things, dependent on things, but struggling against this dependence which delivers it to the Other, is obscured" (TI 228 [203]).

16. "The judgment of history is always pronounced in absentia. The will's absence from this judgment lies in the fact that it is present there only in the third person. It figures in this discourse as in an indirect discourse where it no longer bears unicity and commencement, where it has already lost its voice" (TI 242 [220]).

17. "Truth takes form in this response to a summons" (TI 244 [222]).

18. "The apology demands a judgment . . . in order to obtain justice" (TI 240 [217]).

19. "Under the visible that is history, there is the invisible that is judgment" (TI 246 [224]).

20. "Fidelity is won by repentance and prayer (a privileged word in which the will seeks its fidelity to itself); and the pardon which ensures it this fidelity comes to it from the outside. Hence the rights of the inward will, its certitude of being a misunderstood will, still reveal a relation with exteriority. The will awaits its investiture and pardon. It awaits them from an exterior will, but one from which it would experience no longer shock but judgment, an exteriority withdrawn from the antago-

nism of wills, withdrawn from history. This possibility of justification and pardon, as religious consciousness in which interiority tends to coincide with being, opens before the Other, to whom I can speak" (TI 231 [207–8]).

21. "To place oneself under the judgment of God is to exalt the subjectivity, called to moral overstepping beyond laws, which is henceforth in truth because it surpasses the limits of its being. The judgment of God that judges me at the same time confirms me. But it confirms me precisely in my interiority, whose justice is more severe than the judgment of history. Concretely to be an I presenting itself at a trial—which requires all the resources of subjectivity—means for it to be able to see, beyond the universal judgment of history, that offense of the offended which is inevitably produced in the very judgment issued from universal principles. What is above all invisible is the offense universal history inflicts on particulars. To be I and not only an incarnation of a reason is precisely to be capable of seeing the offense of the offended, or the face" (TI 246–47 [224–25]).

22. True, the other too dies, but (1) his death has a meaning separate from my own, and (2) the other can serve yet another, who serves another, ad infinitum, as we shall see shortly.

23. "To place oneself beyond the judgment of history, under the judgment of truth, is not to suppose behind the apparent history another history called judgment of God—but equally failing to recognize the subjectivity" (TI 246 [224]).

24. This is our own translation of Levinas's text. The corresponding text in Lingis's translation reads for "une ligne infinie du temps" "an infinite time." On our reading, an infinite time is here being distinguished from an infinite *line of* time (the latter being an insufficient condition of the former), so it does not do to translate the one term by the other.

25. "Such a distension in the tension of the instant can only come from an infinite dimension which separates me from the other, both present and still to come, a dimension opened by the face of the Other" (TI 225 [200]).

26. "Fecundity encloses a duality of the Identical. It does not denote all that I can grasp—my possibilities; it denotes my future, which is not a future of the same. . . . And yet it is my adventure still, and consequently my future in a very new sense, despite the discontinuity" (TI 268 [245]).

27. "The relation with the child—that is, the relation with the other that is not a power, but fecundity—establishes relationship with the absolute future, or infinite time" (TI 268 [246]).

28. "Reality is what it is, but will be once again, another time freely resumed and pardoned" (TI 284 [260]).

29. "The fact and the justification of time consist in the recommencement it makes possible in the resurrection, across fecundity, of all the compossibles sacrificed in the present" (TI 284 [261]).

30. "Fecundity continues history without producing old age. Infinite time does not bring an eternal life to an aging subject; it is *better* across the discontinuity of generations, punctuated by the inexhaustible youths of the child" (TI 268 [246]).

31. "Transcendence is time and goes unto the Other. But the Other is not a term: he does not stop the movement of Desire. The other that Desire desires is again Desire; transcendence transcends toward him who transcends—this is the true adventure of paternity, of the trans-substantiation which permits going beyond the simple renewal of the possible in the inevitable senescence of the subject. Transcendence, the for the Other, the goodness correlative of the face, founds a more profound relation: the goodness of goodness. Fecundity engendering fecundity accomplishes goodness: above and beyond the sacrifice that imposes a gift, the gift of the power of giving, the conception of the child" (TI 269 [247]).

32. "In continuation the instant meets its death, and resuscitates; death and resurrection constitute time. But such a formal structure presupposes the relation of the I with the Other and, at its basis, fecundity across the discontinuous which constitutes time" (TI 284 [261]).

33. "Thus true temporality, that in which the definitive is not definitive, presupposes the possibility not of grasping again all that one might have been, but of no longer regretting the lost occasions before the unlimited infinity of the future. It is not a question of complacency in some romanticism of possibles, but of escaping the crushing responsibility of existence that veers into fate, of resuming the adventure of existence so as to be to the infinite" (TI 282 [258]).

34. "Hence truth requires as its ultimate condition an infinite time, the condition for both goodness and the transcendence of the face. The fecundity of subjectivity, by which the I survives itself, is a condition required for the truth of subjectivity, the clandestine dimension of the judgment of God" (TI 247 [225]).

35. "Infinite being, that is, ever recommencing being—which could not bypass subjectivity, for it could not recommence without it—is produced in the guise of fecundity" (TI 268 [246]), or again, "To be infinitely—infinition—means to exist without limits, and thus in the form of an origin, a commencement, that is, again, as an existent. . . . Unless the origin had its identity of itself infinition would not be possible" (TI 281 [257]).

36. Thus the opening paragraph of the section in question: "A philosopher seeks, and expresses, truth. Truth, before characterizing a statement or a judgment, consists in the exhibition of being. But what shows itself, in truth, under the name of being? And who looks?" (OTB 23 [29]).

37. "There is the same as this aim and the same as discovered, only discovered and *amounting to the same*—truth" (OTB 28–29 [36]).

38. "The disclosure of all things depends on their insertion in this light, or this resonance, of the time of essence" (OTB 31 [39]).

39. "*Essence* does not first designate the edges of solids or the moving line of acts in which a light glimmers; it designates this 'modification' without alteration or transition, independent of all qualitative determination. . . . This modification by which the same comes unstuck or parts with itself and thus is disclosed, . . . becomes a phenomenon—is the *esse* of every being. Being's essence designates nothing that could be a nameable content, a thing, event or action; it names this mobility of the immobile, this multiplication of the identical, this diastasis of the punctual, this lapse" (OTB 29–30 [37–38]).

40. "Denomination designates or constitutes identities in the verbal or temporal flow of sensation. Through the opening that temporalization works in the sensible, disclosing it by its very passing, assembling it by retention and memory, . . . the word identifies 'this *as* that,' states the ideality of the same in the diverse" (OTB 35 [44–45]).

41. "Apophansis—the red reddens, or A *is* A—does not double up the real. In predication the essence of the red, or the reddening as an essence, becomes audible for the first time. The nominalized adjective is first understood as an essence, and a temporalization properly so called, in predication. *Essence* is not only conveyed in the said, is not only 'expressed' in it, but originally—though amphibologically—resounds in it qua essence. There is no essence or entity behind the said, behind the Logos. The said, as a verb, is the essence of essence. Essence is the very fact that there is a theme, exhibition, doxa or logos, and thus truth. Essence is not only conveyed, it is temporalized in a predicative statement" (OTB 39 [50–51]).

42. "The entity that appears *identical* in the light of time *is* its essence in the *already said*. The phenomenon itself is a phenomenology" (OTB 37 [48]).

43. "In the copula *is* scintillates or sparkles an ambiguousness between the essence and the nominalized relation. . . . [T]he logos enters into the amphibology in which being and entities can be understood and identified, in which a noun can resound as a verb and a verb of an apophansis can be nominalized" (OTB 41–42 [53–54]).

44. "There is remission of time and tension of the recapture, relaxation and tension without break, without a gap. There is not a pure distancing from the present, but precisely re-presentation, that is, a distancing in which the present of truth *is* already or *still is;* for a representation is a recommencement of the present which in its 'first time' is for the second time; it is a retention and protention, between forgetting and expecting, between memory and project" (OTB 29 [36]).

45. "It is only in the said, in the epos of saying, that the diachrony of time is synchronized into a time that is recallable, and becomes a theme" (OTB 37 [48]).

46. More specifically: "Time passes (*se passe*). This synthesis which occurs *patiently,* called with profundity passive synthesis, is aging. It breaks up under the weight of years, and is irreversibly removed from the present, that is, from re-presentation. In self-consciousness there is no longer a *presence* of self to self, but senescence. It is as senescence beyond the recuperation of memory that time, lost time that does not return, is a diachrony, and concerns me. . . . This diachrony of time is not due to the length of the interval, which representation would not be able to take in. It is a disjunction of identity where the same does not rejoin the same: there is non-synthesis, lassitude" (OTB 52 [67]).

47. "Is the light of essence which makes things seen itself seen? It can to be sure become a theme; essence can show itself, be spoken of and described. But then light presents itself in light, which latter is not thematic, but resounds for the 'eye that listens,' with a resonance unique in its kind, a resonance of silence" (OTB 30 [38]).

48. "Do we not in fact find the non-thematizable flow of time by *reduction* from the said?" (OTB 188, n.18 [43, n. 18]). Or again, "One has to go back to that hither side, starting from the trace retained by the said, in which everything shows itself. The movement back to the saying is the phenomenological reduction. In it the indescribable is described" (OTB 53 [69]).

49. "The oneself is exposed as a hypostasis, of which the being it is as an entity is but a mask" (OTB 106 [134–35]).

50. "But [*mais voici*] the reduction is reduction of the said to the saying beyond the logos, beyond being and non-being, beyond essence, beyond true and non-true. It is the reduction to signification, to the one-for-the-other involved in responsibility (or more exactly in substitution), to the locus or non-lieu, locus and non-lieu, the utopia of the human. It is the reduction to restlessness in the literal sense of the term, or to its diachrony, which, despite all the simultaneous forces in its union, being can not eternalize" (OTB 45 [58]).

51. "I am assigned without recourse, without fatherland, already sent

back to myself, but without being able to stay there, compelled before commencing" (OTB 103 [131]).

52. I am truly passive, irreversibly so, in being held responsible for that which I have not been involved in effectuating, when I am constrained, against my will, to have this responsibility upon myself. "Substitution" is the ultimate passivity.

53. "In the subject it [signification itself: the one-for-the-other] is precisely not an assembling, but an incessant alienation of the ego (isolated as inwardness) by the guest entrusted to it" (OTB 79 [99]).

54. Rendered by Lingis as "uncancellable" (OTB 104 [132]), a translation which, while correct, occludes the temporal sense we believe to be implied. This "ever and again" of the stripping of the ego of its identity as ego (or the reduction from *moi* to *soi*), which is the reading we are suggesting for "recurrence," is perhaps confirmed in a later text wherein Levinas is discussing "insomnia" as a kind of pre-conscious (ethical) attentiveness, and where consciousness is interpreted (as Levinas had consistently interpreted it at least since 1947), in the "*égalité*" or "*état*" it establishes between *cogitation* and *cogitatum,* as a kind of sleep in which the attentiveness without specific object of attention of insomnia is put to bed in the rest established in the *cogitation-cogitatum* correlation, even if it is only in terms of this pre-conscious attentiveness (or wakefulness) that consciousness as consciousness of the object becomes possible in breaking up the *éternel repos* of Being/Totality. Here, the wakefulness (*la veille*), slipping always toward sleep (consciousness of the object), needs be perpetually (*sans cesse*) re-awakened (*re-veillée*): "C'est là [in insomnia] la spiritualité de l'âme sans cesse réveillée de son état d'âme où le veiller lui-même déjà se ferme sur lui-même ou s'endort pour se reposer dans ses frontières d'état" (DVI 99). It is true that the constitution of presence also entails a *sans cesse:* "La présence ne se peut que comme une incessante reprise de la présence, comme une incessante re-présentation. Le sans-cesse de la présence est une répétition, sa reprise, son aperception de représentation" (DVI 100). This same point is made at TI 69 [41]: "This present is not made of instants mysteriously immobilized in duration, but of an *incessant* recapture of instants that flow by by a presence that comes to their assistance, that answers for them. This *incessance* produces the present, is the presentation, the life, of the present." But this *sans cesse* of thought as consciousness in its constitution of the structures of finitude/immanence clearly works in a direction that is reversed by the *re*-currence of the subject as a response (and a response before response) to the Infinite/transcendence: "L'infini à la fois affecte la pensée en la dévastant et l'appelle: à travers une '*re*mise à sa place', il la met en place. Il la *ré*veille" (DVI 109, emphasis

ours). In short, *re*-currence is not the *re*-petition of *re*-presentation, but its condition of possibility.

55. "The psyche is the form of a peculiar dephasing, a loosening up or unclamping of identity: the same prevented from coinciding with itself, at odds, torn up from its rest, between sleep and insomnia, panting, shivering" (OTB 68 [86]).

56. "It is a term not reducible to a relation, but yet in recurrence. The ego is in itself like a sound that would resound in its own echo, the node of a wave which is not once again consciousness. The term in recurrence . . . outside of being, and thus in itself as in exile" (OTB 103 [130]).

57. "In the passivity of the obsidional extradition this very extradition is delivered over to the other, before it could be established. This is the pre-reflexive iteration of the saying of this very saying, a statement of the 'here I am' which is identified with nothing but the voice that states and delivers itself, the voice that signifies" (OTB 143 [182]).

58. "Through the psyche proximity is my approaching of the other, the fact that the proximity of the same and the other is never close enough. The summoned one is the ego—me. I repel and send away the neighbor through my very identity, my occupying the arena of being; I then have always to reestablish peace" (OTB 137 [175]).

59. "If the return to self proper to cognition, the original truth of being, consciousness, can be realized, it is because a recurrence of ipseity has already been produced" (OTB 106–7 [135]).

60. "Neither conjuncture in being, nor reflection of this conjuncture in the unity of transcendental apperception, the proximity of me with the other is in two times, and thus is a transcendence. It temporalizes itself, but with a diachronic temporality" (OTB 85 [107]).

61. Thus when Levinas writes, "The expression 'in one's skin' is not a metaphor for the in-itself; it refers to a recurrence in dead time or the *meanwhile* which separates inspiration and expiration" (OTB 109 [138]), might this recurrence, this dead time, be precisely the time between the penetration of the same by an other out of the past (which Levinas refers to explicitly as an "inspiration") and the from the inside to the outside constitution of a present ("expiration"), and where this recurrence names the very regime of the body? "Dead time," whose "originality consists in being between two times," is also discussed at *Totality and Infinity,* p. 58 [29], as the "interval of discretion or of death," "a third notion between being and nothingness."

62. "This diachrony of the subject is not a metaphor. The subject said as properly as possible . . . is not in time, but is diachrony itself" (OTB 57 [73]).

63. Levinas later explains why this is so: "But in order that there be produced in the drawing out of essence, . . . a break in the same, the nostalgia for return, the hunt for the same and the recoveries, and the clarity in which consciousness plays, in order that this divergency from self and this recapture be produced, the retention and protention by which every present is a re-presentation—behind all the articulations of these movements there must be the recurrence of the oneself. The disclosure of being to itself lurks there. Otherwise essence, exonerated by itself, constituted in immanent time, will posit only indiscernible points, which would, to be sure, be together, but which would neither block nor fulfill any fate. Nothing would make itself. The breakup of 'eternal rest' by time, in which being becomes consciousness and self-consciousness by equaling itself after the breakup, presuppose the oneself" (OTB 105 [133]).

64. This temporality, while not thematized as such in *Totality and Infinity,* makes its appearance in that book, we would argue, under the guise of the idea of "the good," in the Desire for the other irreducible to need that, through *eros,* engenders the other, and is ultimatized as desire desiring desire: the good beyond being animating the being of being itself. Without this notion of the good that cuts across history and permits of the judgment of history, history would be left alone to judge history, and ideology—the same judging the same—would displace the possibility of truth.

65. Clearly, here, discourse is used in the sense of "the philosophical discourse," or "the discourse on . . . ," and is not the technical "discourse" of *Totality and Infinity.*

66. This second "discourse" (qua discourse), against the conventions of *Otherwise Than Being,* approaches the "discourse" of *Totality and Infinity,* or rather shows that every discourse in the sense of a conversation about something (the usual sense of discourse in *Otherwise Than Being*) actually rests upon or goes back to discourse as an ethical relation with the other (the technical sense of discourse in *Totality and Infinity*).

67. This is the very plausible interpretation put forth by Simon Critchley in an article in which a reading of this very strange Derridian text is offered: " 'Bois'—Derrida's Final Word on Levinas," in *Re-reading Levinas,* pp. 162–89.

68. "But there must be a *series,* a beginning of a series of that 'same' (at least two occurrences) in order for the writing that dislocates the Same toward the Relation to have a hold and a chance. E.L. would have been unable to make understandable the *probable* essence of language without that singular repetition, without that citation or recitation which makes the Same come (*venir*) to rather than returning (*revenir*) to the

Other" (Atvm 24). And a little later, more precisely why: "One sole interruption in a discourse does not do its work and thus allows itself to be immediately reappropriated. The hiatus must insist, whence the necessity of the *series*" (Atvm 28).

69. Or, again later: "In the first case, E.L. thematizes the thematization that envelops, covers up, and dissimulates the Relation" (Atvm 24).

70. Or, again a little later: "In the second case, E.L. thematizes the nonthematizable of a Relation that does not allow further envelopment within the tissue of the same" (Atvm 24).

71. The following quotation from Derrida, as those in the present paragraph, are specifically comments upon a passage from the end of Levinas's "Le Nom de Dieu d'après quelques textes talmudiques," in *Archivio di Filosofia* (Rome, 1969), pp. 155–67, but are equally applicable, on our view, to the passages from *Otherwise Than Being* cited in our text. The passage from "Le Nom de Dieu" (quoted from Berezdivin's translation of Atvm) reads: "It will of course be objected that if any other relation than thematisation may exist between the Soul and the Absolute, then would not the act of talking and thinking about it *at this very moment,* the fact of enveloping it in our dialectic, mean that language and dialectic are superior with respect to the Relation?

But the language of thematisation, which *at this very moment* we are using, has perhaps only been made possible itself by means of that Relation, and is only ancillary" (Atvm 23, Derrida's italics).

72. That is, I "participate" in an eternity that does not become a forever and always (our "bad eternal" from above) because in the ever and again of recurrence at this very moment, at each moment, the "history" of this recurrence is interrupted by a difference that demands of me that it can never be the same.

73. The three mentions of the phrase "*enfant légitime*" appear at OTB 7 [9], 183 [231], 192, n.18 [108]. In each case Lingis mistranslates it as, in the first instance, "illegitimate," and in the latter two, "bastard."

74. Robert Bernasconi, reversing the negative and positive of the adjective and the noun, also calls it such: "What, if I may put it this way, renders this impossibility possible?" ("Skepticism in the Face of Philosophy," p. 150).

75. Or, as Bernasconi puts it: "The question of skepticism is still construed as a question about truth" ("Skepticism in the Face of Philosophy," p. 160).

76. Derrida is therefore just in giving his discourse on this discourse to the "other," the "feminine," in his "At This Very Moment in This Work Here I Am," rather than giving it *back* to Levinas. Indeed, it is central to our reading that what we are calling "the intrigue of ethics"

is not seen as entailing a kind of quid pro quo, a kind of reciprocal exchange of graciousness wherein grace would be the tender in an economy of grace, which would give me good "economic" reasons for being gracious, and which would negate the madness [*folie*] of responsibility found in Levinas's descriptions. That is, we are not arguing that my responsibility to show grace to the other is "required" by the grace already shown to me, and that responsibility is thus grace repaying grace, and thus not gratuitous. Rather, in the intrigue of ethics my having been shown grace (and purely gratuitously) is the "condition of possibility" for my graciousness faced with the other—but it is this face that faces me that calls me to grace, not the grace received from the (m)other (which only makes my own graciousness possible). That my having been gifted with grace by the (m)other and my owing of grace to the other are distinct moments in a dis/continuous time breaks up the circularity of reasonable exchange (even if the (m)other and the other are the same person for me in diverse [but simultaneous] modalities), leaving me ("bathing") in the "element" of grace without this grace being the stuff of economic exchange, leaving me a member of an *oikos* wherein grace (received and owed) subtends any subsequent *nomos,* leaving me a member of a gracious eco-*a*-nomy. My (m)other did not love me "so that" I would love others, and I do not love my other "so that" he will love others in turn—still, "love is love in this antecedence."

PART III

Discourse, Philosophy, and Peace

7

Levinas's Philosophical Discourse

IN THE PREVIOUS CHAPTER we have, across an analysis of temporality, shown how Levinas's own philosophical discourse is, by its own testimony, caught up at every moment, "in this very moment," in the moment as the *carrefour* of two temporalities that at once demands the structuring and de-structuring of its philosophical said. But as itself caught up in the dual exigencies of ethical saying and the just said(s) that the saying inspires, what, more precisely, is the status of Levinas's philosophical discourse qua "philosophy," and qua "discourse" in the technical sense upon which we have been elaborating throughout this work? We hope to have provided already a preparatory answer to this question in following Levinas's translation/transmutation of philosophy from the love of wisdom into the wisdom of love. Philosophical discourse under this conversion is already "discourse" (a non-allergic, ethical relation with alterity productive of a meaning capable of founding communal meaning), that is, philosophy is already ethics, or at least inspired by ethics, first as apology (an appeal to the other to ordain the truth of my said—which bespeaks already his ethical priority in regards to truth [and the priority of ethics to truth]), and as a discourse concerning itself with justice (with the equitable distribution of responsibilities and goods—which requires "knowing" what "is," that is, both epistemology and ontology). And would not philosophy, on Levinas's terms—and despite the consciousness or lack thereof of this matter on the part of the philosophers who have constituted the discourse called philosophy—always have been so?

But this does seem to leave Levinas in a peculiar position with respect to "traditional" philosophy whose preoccupation with being and truth as the context for ethics and justice—and not, as in Levinas, the reverse—would seem to mean that philosophy—if it is the wisdom of love before the love of wisdom, if ethics is first philosophy and not philosophy first ethics—has always (or at least predominantly, for Levinas does recognize certain exceptions) suffered from a certain "false consciousness" or "bad faith." And there would at least seem to be (and we believe that there *is*) a certain contradiction in an accusation of this sort coming from Levinas, in that accusing an other (let alone [almost] all other Western philosophers) of "false consciousness" is to assume, and presume, a kind of position above the fray, purportedly taking up a position outside of the face-to-face relation and pronouncing upon the relation (or the details of its interworkings) as if from the outside—that which Levinas, as we have early on stressed, precisely prohibits and persists in prohibiting above all on ethical grounds. In such a schema, the other would lose all of his priority as regards to truth—be that the truth of philosophy or the ethical veracity that is its guarantee—for here the other's "truth" (or lack thereof) would be co-opted into more or less true approximations of Levinas's "true" account of how things at root are. The irony of reading Levinas's philosophy as a pronouncement on "the way it in fact is" over against the claims of others would be, we believe, just too great, "in-credible!"—even if this "is" were successfully purified of its ontological content and read as delineating a pre-originary, pre-ontological "is"—when the whole weight of Levinas's descriptions of ethics would oppose such a claim, where ethics would have already called such a claim into question, or would be precisely the calling of such a claim into question. The "truth" of Levinas's philosophical "saids" must, on his own terms, seek their investment as truth from the other, and cannot first dominate this other as an account of how things really are for this other, whether the other recognizes it or not. Philosophy as the wisdom of love is not (at least not in the first instance, and even in the second instance only in an ethically qualified sense) a pronouncement or even a judgment upon what is, but a giving of what is, a giving that produces what is, in love.

And yet, Levinas's philosophical discourse is very much—whatever else it might be—philosophy. He describes, argues, reasons, situates his discourse within the discourse identified as philosophical, comparing and contrasting his thoughts with others who have done likewise, thinking about and disputing its origins, meaning(s), and connotations. He can, even must, do so, legitimately, on his own terms, it seems to us, in the name of, for the sake of, the third, but he cannot consistent with his own discourse do so in a manner that eclipses his responsibility to the other qua other in terms of which alone the responsibility to the third qua third takes on meaning. Levinas's philosophical discourse qua discourse (qua a non-allergic, ethical relationship with alterity) must itself first of all be ethical and ethical before it can be true (its being ethical the condition of possibility of its being—potentially—true), must be a responsible response to the other (the reader) and to the other others (Levinas's and the reader's others). This philosophical discourse, be it philosophy, cannot, qua discourse, eclipse—if it is to be consistent with its own claims, if it is to be responsible—its own ethical gesture by its philosophical saids, but must subordinate these latter to the former. But in what sense then is it still philosophy where philosophy is the love of wisdom, a claim to "know" (or a claim to know—wisely and/or skeptically—that one does not know) what "is" the case? How, in entering into conversation with traditional philosophy, does Levinas reconcile the wisdom of love with a debate over the wisdom traditionally loved by philosophy without making a claim to a superior wisdom (perhaps fed by ethics) that would give him *the* perspective from which to mediate from an alleged superior position the dispute over the ultimate ground or meaning of philosophy, without making a presumptive and suspicious claim to that which his own philosophy prohibits?[1] Or again, how does Levinas's own philosophical discourse, as participating in the universal claims of philosophy (this necessary and ancillary modality of language demanded by ethics itself), keep itself subservient to ethics, as a relation of singularity to singularity, rather than returning to dominate that which inspires it? Or again, how does Levinas's philosophical discourse remain at once philosophical (a discourse on the being and truth of being(s)) and discourse (a non-allergic, ethical relationship with alterity)?

We propose to examine these questions in two steps, first, by examining what, according to its own terms, must characterize Levinas's philosophical discourse qua discourse, and, then, by examining how Levinas's philosophical discourse qua philosophy is put in the service of this discourse as a performative of a non-allergic, ethical relationship with alterity. The form of this performative, we shall argue in our Part I, "Levinas's Philosophy as Discourse" (by way of an analysis of the status of the "I" in Levinas's texts), will be revealed to be a testimony that is at once prophetic, offered in the form of philosophy. We shall then, in Part II, "Levinas's Discourse as Philosophy" (in giving attention to Levinas's philosophical "method"), show how what we shall call, after de Boer, Levinas's ethical transcendental philosophy (or Levinas's philosophy on an ethical transcendental reading) is consonant with, in being shown to be put in the service of, Levinas's philosophical discourse as first of all testimonial-prophetic. Or, more directly put, in Part I we shall argue that Levinas's philosophical discourse need be read as precisely "discourse," and in Part II we shall argue that Levinas adopts transcendental philosophy as a mode of philosophizing that permits him to sustain his philosophical discourse *as discourse,* even in the garb of philosophy.

I. Levinas's Philosophy As Discourse

I.1. Asymmetry and Universality

As we have seen, the metaphysical asymmetry producing the impossibility of ascending to a position of neutral governance above the relationship in which I participate as a term, and thus the impossibility of demanding of the other that which I can by right demand only of myself, is central to Levinas's perdurable and consistent opposition to the violence inherent in totality thought. Such asymmetry prohibits my thinking of myself and the other as reciprocal, as interchangeable terms in the ethical relationship we have been in the course of delineating (a prohibition necessary to the relationship as ethical); rather, in this relationship, I remain I in relation to the other as other. To conceive of the other as "another me," as an alter ego, to subsume the other under categories at my disposal, is to practice a form of vandalism, the defacing of the face. But does not such an insistence, rigorously maintained, require as a radical consequence that there can be, for Levinas, no such thing as an "I in general," such that the "I" of his philosophical discourse must be the singular I, the narrator of the discourse, and that the other, the one to whom the discourse is addressed, is not an I in his turn? That is, the other is not *a* subject because there is no such thing, if this path of thought is pursued to the end, as *a* subject, but only *the* subject, namely, me—the one speaking out of my subjectivity qua "saying," substituting myself for each other, and where no other can take my place, *sub-jectum: me voici.* A number of passages would appear to make this intention clear, and this consequence inevitable:

> The non-indifference, the saying, the responsibility, the approach, is the disengaging of the unique one responsible, me. The way I appear is a summons. I am put in the passivity of an undeclinable assignation, in the accusative, a self. Not as a particular case of the universal, an ego belonging to the concept of ego, but as I, said in the first person—I, unique in my genus. (OTB 139 [177])

But does not such a thesis—that there is, for Levinas, no such thing as an "I in general" (and which it is our intention to defend)—raise a number of not so insignificant problems?

To begin, and perhaps chiefly, who is this singular "I" as it appears in the context of Levinas's discussions? Emmanuel Levinas himself? But is this discourse not then autobiographical, rather than "philosophical"? Is "ethics," as Levinas describes it, his, Levinas's, own purely private affair? Is encountering the face a purely private adventure of Levinas? Is his "ethics" solipsistic? But there are a number of indications, internal to Levinas's texts, that would suggest that a reading of these texts as strictly "autobiographical" would not be *à propos.* For not only does Levinas present his work as "philosophical" (even if in a nontraditional sense, namely, as philosophy in the service of justice rather than as a quest, at least in the first instance, for truth; e.g., OTB 165 [210]), that is, as some kind of appeal to that which lies beyond my own, or in this case Levinas's own, private experience (Levinas opposes "philosophy" to "opinion" and, if this is the choice, takes the side of philosophy),[2] but what, moreover, is the value of the writing of ethics if this writing is for the writer alone? Are Levinas's texts, by his own account of language, not addressed to an other? Are they not already an appeal to an other, and, on their own terms, an appeal to the other to pronounce upon their truth? Levinas, indeed, claims for his work not only the status of philosophy, but also of a philosophy that is, in the particular sense we have already hinted at, and that we shall make more precise in the next part of this chapter, "transcendental." As such, Levinas utilizes in *Totality and Infinity,* as he tells us in the preface to the German edition, "ontological, or more exactly eidetic, language . . . for the purpose of avoiding that its analyses, putting in question the *conatus essendi* of being, be taken to rest upon the empiricism of a psychology."[3] That is to say that Levinas seeks, in *Totality and Infinity,* to describe, neither a "subjective, individualistic" experience of the ethical relation, nor the "naturalistic, psychologisitic" experiences of a psychological subject, but the ethical relation as it makes up a part, even the "foundation," of "being"—and even if this ontological-eidetic language was avoided after *Totality and Infinity,* it was not so in order to permit a slippage of the discourse back toward individualism or psychologism, but because the concern with (even if implicitly) affirming the problematic co-implication of "being" and "totality" became increasingly pressing. That is, Levinas intended, and continues in his later works to intend, to describe a "structure" of subjectivity, insofar as being in relation to alterity, and being in such relation in a particular way, can be called "structural." And are not structures, above all those of a "transcendental" kind, however carefully qualified by Levinas, of necessity general?

Another problem arising from the insistence upon a nongeneralizable "I" is raised by Derrida. For, in a philosophy dedicated to a radical nonviolence with respect to the other, is not the "subjectivity" of the other necessary, *pace* Levinas, to maintain such nonviolence? This would appear to be Derrida's concern when, responding on Husserl's behalf to Levinas's claim that "[t]he other, as other, is not only an alter ego" but "what I myself am not," he claims:

> If the other were not recognized as a transcendental alter *ego,* it would be entirely in the world and not, as ego, the origin of the world. To refuse to see in it an ego in this sense is, within the ethical order, the very gesture of all violence. If the other was not recognized as ego, its entire alterity would collapse. . . . The other as alter ego signifies the other as other, irreducible to *my* ego, precisely because it is an ego, because it has the form of the ego.[4]

In this defense of Husserl, is Derrida not pointing to a violence inhabiting Levinas's nonviolence, the danger that this thought threatens to become, in its persistence to maintain radical asymmetry, "the very gesture of all violence," and that by stripping the other of precisely that by which he would be capable of resisting my totalizing comprehension? On top of this, and perhaps most problematically, does Levinas not argue that every moral imperative or behavior, as, for that matter, every positive language, and every society, finds its condition of possibility in "ethics" as responsibility of the one for the other of saying,[5] and insofar as these ethical codes or behaviors, languages, and societies exist outside of myself, and historically precede me, would it not then be necessary that the other too is, or at least some others too are, "subject," ethical subjects, "I" in the sense described in Levinas's discourse?

Does not all of this mitigate against the thesis that Levinas means, can possibly mean, by his "I" the singular "I and no other" that dominates the descriptions of proximity, and that he rather *must* intend a "generalized I?" He seems, moreover, to do so explicitly, and not infrequently, in statements like the following: "But each individual . . . is virtually a chosen one, called to leave in his turn, or without awaiting his turn, the concept of the ego, its extension in his people, to respond with responsibility: *me,* that is, *here I am for the others,* to lose his place radically, or his shelter in being, to enter in ubiquity which is also a utopia" (OTB 185 [232–33]). If *each* individual is elect, and elected to respond with responsibility, is not *each* individual an "I," and an ethical I like me?

Is the "I" not, then, inescapably, by certain aspects of Levinas's own account, an "I in general," despite, on other accounts, Levinas's seeming claims to the contrary? For "I" too, Jeffrey Dudiak, am thinking "I" when I read "I" in Levinas's discourse, and am writing "I" here, in some sense from within Levinas's discourse, and do not mean thereby "Emmanuel Levinas." You, too, in reading Levinas's "I" do so, presumably, from your own position, as [*your name here*]. Is not the "I" that Levinas writes, then, interchangeable, representing Emmanuel Levinas, me, and you? (How personal can this, or any, personal pronoun really be?)[6] And if this is the case, then does the discourse not necessarily devolve into one wherein there must be posited, even presupposed, a "symmetry of asymmetry?" And would not such a symmetry of asymmetry dissolve, in governing, asymmetry itself? And is such not to institute again the violence (the totality wherein the other is another "me," the warrant to demand of the other that which, in ethics, I can demand only of myself) that the whole of Levinas's discourse is devoted to avoiding? And this problem would not be avoided by asserting that each "I" is to be "taken up" personally, that is, that "each" is elected, but elected differently, that each "self" is *a* self without being *my*-self. On the contrary, for Levinas, "the self is a *sub-jectum* . . . under the weight of the universe, responsible for everything" (OTB 116 [147]), is an election that, when applied to the other, "is criminal" (OTB 195, n.18 [144, n.18]). My responsibility for the other cannot be "generalized" without rendering it, at least in terms of the way that Levinas describes it, irresponsible.

How, then, can Levinas at once sustain the "principle" of asymmetry, that issues in an ethics that concerns "me and no other," and appeal, as he does, as he must, to the "subjectivity" of the other? In the first part of this chapter we shall argue that this situation must be approached, and understood, by way of an exposition of Levinas's employment of "prophetic discourse," a discourse in which I "call forth the interlocutor's responsibility to respond," a discourse concurrent with, though ancillary to, and ultimately dependent upon ethics (and we shall have to specify how it is at once concurrent, ancillary, and dependent), and as such a mode of discourse that must, we will argue, ultimately be distinguished from ethics, as it must, we will also argue, be distinguished from the discourse on justice, even if, in the end, the discourses concerning each of these will turn out themselves, as will Levinas's discourse as a whole, to be prophetic. In the remainder of this part of the chapter we shall, therefore, argue that prophetic discourse is, and must be conceived of as remaining, rooted in metaphysical asymmetry (section I.2), that prophetic discourse emerges in Levinas's thought as grounded in the idea of testimony (I.3), and that Levinas's entire philosophical discourse must ultimately, qua "discourse," be conceived of as testimonial/prophetic (I.4).

I.2. From Ethics to Justice to Prophecy

Prophecy in Levinas, according to Richard Cohen, "is all speech that calls forth the interlocutor's responsibility to respond."[7] I speak prophetically, then, according to this definition, when I appeal to the good in the other, that is, when I appeal to the other as already responsible, as "subject" to responsibility, as a subjectivity in the sense elaborated in Levinas's descriptions. But, as we are stressing, after the exigencies of ethical asymmetry that are integral to these same descriptions, goodness is precisely that which I am permitted to demand only of myself, in that any "goodness" I might demand of the other would always of necessity be my conception of "goodness" (implicated irremissibly in my interests, in my *inter-esse*). Demanding this of the other is thus to bring him under my category, to impose my sphere of sameness upon the other, upon the other whose very otherness is an ethical resistance to any such imposition. How, then, is prophetic discourse, in which I appeal to the goodness of the other, ethically possible?

In order to respond to this question we shall attempt to sort out three distinct but interrelated facets of Levinas's thought: ethics, wherein I am alone and irremissibly responsible for the other; justice, wherein my absolute responsibility to the other is transformed into a concern for all (including myself) in society; and prophecy, wherein I appeal to the goodness of the other. To do so we shall reprise (although this time more briefly) the discussions of the introduction of the third party into the relationship between the same and the other. We shall begin by quoting, at some length, sections of some of the pertinent passages from both *Totality and Infinity* and *Otherwise Than Being* in order to trace, within these, the movement from ethics to prophecy, by way of justice.

First, from the section entitled "The Other and the Others" from *Totality and Infinity*, we read:

> The poor one, the stranger, presents himself as an equal. His equality within his essential poverty consists in referring to the *third party*, thus present at the encounter, whom in the midst of his destitution the other already serves. He comes to join me. But he joins me to himself for service; he commands me as a Master. This command

> can concern me only inasmuch as I am Master myself; consequently this command commands me to command. The *thou* is posited in front of a *we*. . . . The presence of the face, the infinity of the other, is a destituteness, a presence of the third party (that is, of the whole of humanity that looks at us), and a command that commands commanding. This is why the relation with the Other, discourse, is not only the putting in question of my freedom, the appeal coming from the other to call me to responsibility, . . . but is also sermon, exhortation, and prophetic word. By essence the prophetic word responds to the epiphany of the face, doubles all discourse . . . as an irreducible moment of discourse which by essence is aroused by the epiphany of the face inasmuch as it attests the presence of the third party, the whole of humanity in the eyes that look at me. (TI 213 [188])

Secondly, in *Otherwise Than Being,* from the section entitled "From Saying to the Said, or the Wisdom of Desire," wherein the primary task is to demonstrate the necessity of philosophical discourse to justice, we read:

> The relationship with the third party is an incessant correction of the asymmetry of proximity in which the face is looked at. There is weighing, thought, objectification, and thus a decree in which my anarchic relationship with illeity is betrayed, but in which it is conveyed before us. There is betrayal of my anarchic relationship with illeity, but also a new relationship with it: it is only thanks to God that, as a subject incomparable with the other, I am approached as an other by the others, that is, "for myself." "Thanks to God" I am another for the others. God is not involved as an alleged interlocutor: the reciprocal relationship binds me to the other man in the trace of transcendence, in illeity. The passing of God, of whom I can speak only by reference to this aid or this grace, is precisely the reverting of the incomparable subject into a member of society. . . . Out of representation is produced the order of justice moderating or measuring the substitution of me for the other, and giving the self over to calculus. Justice requires contemporaneousness of representation. It is thus that the neighbor becomes visible, and, looked at, presents himself, and there is also justice for me. The saying is fixed in the said, is written, becomes a book, law and science. (OTB 158–59 [201–2])

Now, it is of paramount importance to recall that these quotations are drawn from works whose predominant stress is upon the philosophical priority of asymmetry, and that such asymmetry is carefully reaffirmed by Levinas after each of these quotations: "Like a shunt every social relation leads back to the presentation of the other to the same without the intermediary of any image or sign, solely by the expression of the face" (TI 213 [188]) and "All human relations as human proceed from disinterestedness" (OTB 159 [202]), following respectively, and almost immediately, upon the above citations. So we must be ever vigilant, in our exegesis of these passages, to avoid imputing to the other that responsibility that falls to me alone. We must begin, as it were,[8] in our understanding of these passages, and of these passages from ethics to justice and prophecy, in asymmetry, and with an asymmetry that while "corrected" and "betrayed" does not relinquish its priority, its "foundational" relationship to the structures that emerge out of its elaboration.

We have already traced, in chapter 5, the passage from ethics to justice, required by the presence of the third, on our way to arguing that Levinas's ethics be taken, not as *an* ethics, but as a kind of transcendental condition for ethics (or for any other theoretical discourse). There we discovered that the absolute responsibility that I owe to the other, the description of which provides the center of gravity for the whole of Levinas's work, is "compromised," "corrected" by a correlative absolute responsibility owed to the third, the neighbor of the neighbor, another other, and to each other other. The need to weigh out these diverse, conflicting, but equally impinging responsibilities, the need to undertake "a comparison of incomparables," leads, Levinas tells us, by way of the thematizing and rationality of philosophy that is just such a weighing, to justice, indeed to philosophy as justice (the love of wisdom become the wisdom of love, the wisdom governing the parceling out of desire in terms of justice),[9] and it is within justice, according to Levinas, where I too may, even must, care for myself, where I pass from being the responsible one to being a citizen among citizens, with the same rights and responsibilities as everyone else. In the name of justice, ethics is transformed into philosophy, but a philosophy rooted in ethics,[10] where, in Levinas's famous phrase, "Ethics is first philosophy."

So far, so good. Being equally if conflictually responsible for more than one other, I indeed need have recourse to a weighing out of such rights and responsibilities and institute, *for myself* (for it is a weighing out of *my* responsibilities that is at issue here), a regime of justice: "Peace, peace to the neighbor and the one far-off."[11] Responsible for the third as for the other, I would, under such a regime, in the name of the third, no doubt demand justice from the neighbor for the third, as I would demand justice for myself, as a citizen among citizens. But on the basis of what could such a demand be made? If justice is a parceling out of myself in term of *my* diverse responsibilities, a matter of not spending myself entirely on any particular other, and these responsibilities are mine alone, on what basis should the other, to whom I am ethically incapable of imputing my own responsibilities, be expected to respect justice, be expected to participate in the economy of justice that results from the administration of *my* variant responsibilities? If justice is to be justice in the sense of just relations among members of a community of equals, and not merely an economy based upon the wise distribution of *my* responsibilities, must not justice already involve the participation of the other, and the other to whose "goodness" I am capable of appealing? But it is (and need this be repeated?) precisely this "goodness of the other" that, according to ethics, I am not permitted to presuppose in the other, or demand of the other. Am I then left, in the face of the other, in defense of the third, and in defense of myself, with making some sort of appeal to an economy of justice founded upon the self-interest of this other, persuading him of the value for him of citizenry under the auspices of some or other sort of social contract?

But as Levinas has doubted whether the commonness of a genus is sufficiently strong to found human fraternity,[12] he has also always doubted whether a social contract based upon self-interest is sufficiently strong to found human society; in each case goodness, in the sense of responsibility to one another (and not just a mutually agreed upon restriction of immediate self-interest in the interest of long-term self-interest), is, on his view, required. And concordant with this, already in the above citations, wherein the third that interrupts my unidirectional responsibility for the other is introduced, justice, and above all justice for me, is linked to my being "approached as an other by the others," that is, to the other's being responsible for me, not simply in the sense of respecting the rights and demanding the responsibilities accorded me as a citizen within an economy of justice founded upon self-interest, but in the strong sense of being responsible for me in the same way that I am ethically responsible for him: absolutely, sacrificially. But demanding of the other that he respect the rights of another (be that me) weighed (economically) against his own rights, is of an entirely different order of expectation than that whereby the other is expected by me to be hostage to his other (be that me), to be responsible for him without reserve, to be expiation for him—that which Levinas in his discourse on ethics has expressly and repeatedly refused. The dissemination of my absolute responsibility in the face of the other follows, we are arguing, from the presence of the third, and the fourth, and so on, to the point where my responsibility for the one becomes, through philosophy, my concern with a justice for each and all, but there is, here, no warrant for my being capable of demanding of the other a concern for justice, let alone a responsibility correlative with my own. And yet, it is precisely to such a concern with justice, and to such a responsibility, *in the other,* that Levinas has recourse in his writings on justice and the third. Must we not then distinguish between justice as the just distribution of my resources in the face of a multiplicity of others, and justice in the fuller sense of just relations in a society of equals of which I am one?

But how, then, beginning in asymmetry, are we to arrive at a site from which the absolute responsibility *of the other for me,* excluded from asymmetry, can be broached? Is not some sort of leap required here? How can the chasm between my own responsibilities and those of the other—and thus the possibility of prophetic speech—be traversed?

Indeed, my being considered the other of the other is not, in fact, "deducible" from my asymmetrical relationship with the other, but requires, according to Levinas (and such could only be, at least from the perspective of a rational derivation beginning in asymmetry, an absurdity), the grace of God: "It is only thanks to God [grâce à Dieu] that, as a subject incomparable with the other, I am approached as an other by the others, that is, 'for myself.' 'Thanks to God' I am another for the others" (OTB 158

[201]). That is to say that the other's "goodness" to other others as to me is not within my control: "The other stands in a relationship with the third party, for which[13] I cannot entirely answer, even if I alone answer, before any question, for my neighbor" (OTB 157 [200]). This goodness of the other is not something that I, incomparable, am able to insist upon, or, from out of my responsibilities, count upon, but something that happens, *if* it happens, as a matter of grace. But it does happen. It has already happened! For my part, I am responsible for the other and the others regardless of the responsibility or lack thereof of the other, where "reciprocity is his affair," but the other does, beyond any coercion on my part, undertake reciprocity, does reveal himself to me as good: "The poor one, the stranger, presents himself as an equal. His equality within his essential poverty consists in referring to the *third party,* thus present at the encounter, whom in the midst of his destitution the other already serves. He comes to join me [Il se *joint* à moi]. But he joins me to himself for service" (TI 213 [188]). The other reveals his goodness to me in calling upon my goodness in the cause of the third, and "the *thou* is posited in front of a *we*" (TI 213 [188]). So while justice as a wise distribution of myself in the face of my responsibilities is "founded" in asymmetry, justice as a society of equals already presupposes the grace of God, that is, the other taking on responsibility for others as for me: "The passing of God, of whom I can speak only by reference to this aid or this grace, is precisely the reverting of the incomparable subject into a member of society" (OTB 158 [202]). Justice as a society of equals, wherein I too am a citizen, already presupposes this grace.

It is, therefore, out of this self-revelation of the other as good that prophetic discourse, wherein I appeal to the responsibility of the other, becomes possible. Beyond anything that I could ethically demand, the possibility of prophetic discourse is a result of the experience of grace, the experience of the other testifying that he too has been called into service, called to serve the other (to which service he enjoins me), and called to serve me. And more than a possibility, prophetic discourse, in the light of such a revelation, becomes obligatory. For in joining himself to me in service, the other, initially Master, commands me out of such mastery to recognize that I am his other, his master, and thus "commands me to command" (TI 213 [188]), commands me to speak up, and even speak out against him, in the name of the good, for the sake of the other, his other, including me. Prophetic discourse becomes possible only when the other *presents himself* to me as responsible for the other others and for me, which opens up the possibility for me to appeal to this self-proclaimed responsibility of the other, an appeal that would have been violent, ethically impossible, in ethics, in that it could not have been but a projection of my own responsibility onto the other. The other's prophetic[14] testimony to his own goodness permits of a change in the register of Levinas's discourse, which can thus undergo a transformation from being solely a description of *my* responsibilities to a description of *our* responsibilities. What is prohibited in ethics, is permitted, even required, as prophetic discourse.[15]

It is at this point that prophetic language as a language calling out to, pacifically soliciting, the goodness of the other can be spoken without violence, and without violence because it (and the "categories" it implies) is not imposed by me upon the other, but is called for by the other in his own voice, and this "testimony of the other" as it is formulated by me can always be refused by the other who remains, after asymmetry, my master, who retains the final authoritative word with respect to any interpretations I might make of his significations. Prophetic discourse remains rooted in asymmetry in that I can command only insofar as I have been commanded to command. I have to have heard the command of the other as *command* to command before I am capable of commanding myself, such that my capacity to command remains a function of my being commanded.

Levinas, in insisting upon the "I and no other" of asymmetry, does not, therefore, on our reading, *deny* "subjectivity" to the other, and thus promote the extreme violence that Derrida suggests, in his defense of Husserl, such a move would entail, but, rather, refuses to *impose* subjectivity on the other, a subjectivity that is always my conception of what a subject is or should be, reducing the alterity of the other to a function of my sphere of sameness.[16] The other remains—in that my responsibility to the other is not negated, but only transformed, by the reciprocity enacted by the other—free to take up or refuse his subjectivity (whatever that might mean to him) in whatever manner the other must, independent of my interference or my imposition. As such, Levinas does not exclude the possibility of a certain reciprocity, and even, insofar as language is always already prophetic (as we shall argue shortly), presupposes it, even while it cannot be insisted upon ethically. Levinas does not exclude the possibility of the other's being good (far from it—as my goodness itself depends upon the other's having always already been good to me, in the modality of the (m)other, as we are arguing here across several analyses), but suggests that this goodness of the other must come to me in such a fashion that it is neither a function of my own categories, nor imputed to the other as an extrapolation of my own election to goodness. Prophetic discourse is not such an imposition because it appeals not to my concept that, and how, the other should be good (based upon my experience of myself), but appeals to a goodness the other has already claimed for himself in terms of his own testimony, as he "joins himself to me for service."

It is therefore as prophetic discourse that we are proposing be read those statements in Levinas that appeal to "each individual" to "respond with responsibility" (OTB 185 [233]). We would argue that those statements in Levinas that appeal to the goodness in the other, that appeal to all others as if they were subjects "like me"—which appear to contravene the mandate that I do not attempt to escape my own position regarding the other and transcend the relationship—need to be read as prophetic discourse. Prophetic discourse is then neither the violence of the category imposed, nor an adherence coerced, but a pacific solicitation. It asks, in "eschatological"[17] hope, and in the experience of grace, "Are you not good?" or "Have you not already testified to your own goodness?" and expects a positive response—for its testimony is always "You have already been good"—but can never forsake this interrogative for either the indicative "You are called to be good" or the imperative "You must be good," or, at least, it cannot forsake it without violence. These latter statements can only be put in the first person singular. So when Levinas quotes *The Brothers Karamozov,* "Each of us is guilty before everyone for everyone, and I more than the others" (OTB 146 [186]), the first portion of this phrase is to be read as a prophetic expression, and the second portion reminds us that such an expression must remain rooted in *my* responsibility for the other. As such, the "I" of Levinas's discourse does not only mean Levinas, himself alone, but is a pacific solicitation arising from out of the testimony of the other. It is a description of the "structure" of any "I" who finds himself or herself in Levinas's descriptions of the subject, without being ethically permitted to presuppose that all others or even any given other will so find himself or herself, even while Levinas's discourse is itself possible only as an expression of the grace of having so found the others, and as trusting in this goodness.

I.3. Prophetic Speech As Grounded in Testimony

If, as we have been arguing so far, prophetic speech (as "all speech that calls for the interlocutor's responsibility to respond") was shown to be ethically possible across the command that commands commanding, it is interesting to note that in the exposition of prophecy contained in *Otherwise Than Being* (and in this text it is more pointedly thematized than it had been in *Totality and Infinity*) Levinas does not make reference to this command to command. The focus here, rather than being on the other's testimony to his own goodness as the warrant for prophecy, is on prophetic speech as growing out of my own testimony to my own call to goodness—indeed, as correlative to, and (almost) synonymous with, this testimony. Here we read, regarding prophecy, in a section entitled "The Glory of the Infinite": "We call prophecy this reverting in which the perception of an order coincides with the signification of this order made by [*faite par*][18] him that obeys it. Prophecy would thus be the very psyche in the soul: the other in the same, and all of man's spirituality would be prophetic" (OTB 149 [190]). If in analyzing "the command that commands commanding" of *Totality and Infinity* we were able to see how the possibility of a nonviolent prophetic speech was opened up across the testimony of the other, in *Otherwise Than Being* we shall see how the possibility of a nonviolent prophetic speech opens up across my testimony, and see the manner in which the two "testimonies," for Levinas, link up in the pre-original "glory of the Infinite," mediated across—or, in an essential ambiguity, equivalent to—the religio-familial, ethical intrigue that we have been arguing throughout is a kind of ground zero for the thought of Levinas—ground zero in being that which founds without being founded, and zero ground in being no ground, but a kind of glorious, or divine, *an-arché*, "*sans-commencement*" (OTB 140 [179]). But we have much ground to cover, and uncover, before we begin again to approach (and endlessly, as we shall see) that nonsite. We shall make our way by means of a reading of "The Glory of the Infinite."

Throughout his exposition of "The Glory of the Infinite," Levinas is occupied with describing—in terms already familiar to us (we have discussed these matters already at some length in our chapter 4)—the subjectivity of the subject as "saying" to the other, that is, where, stated "negatively" (that is, from the side of the imperious "ego" reduced to its "self" by finding itself ethically called into question by the other), the subject is described as persecuted by the other, under accusation (and thus, at the deepest level, in the accusative), as already *en retard* regarding the other and thus as already guilty, as hostage to the other, as being hollowed out (*dénucléation*) in its encounter with the face, deposed from its place as constituting subjectivity, and—conversely but correlatively—where, stated "positively" (that is, where the imperious ego is no longer the starting point for the description), the subject is described as animated by the encounter with the other, inspired, ordained, or elected to responsibility as its very subjectivity. Here, as "saying," the subjectivity of the subject is, across the passivity of passivity, across the exposition of exposition, described as being reduced to a pure sign offered to the other, that is, to the very sign of being offered as a sign, or the signification of signification, the very signification (meaning) of the subject its signifying itself as having been elected to responsibility for the other. The very subjectivity of the subject is here summed up in the signification, not that it makes (which would presuppose an activity behind its apparent passivity), but that it is (before it "is," ontologically speaking) to the other: "*me voici*"—that is, here I am, at your service.

But here is, potentially, a problem, for does this being "elected" not lead to a new "substantiality" of the subject, a new position of the de-posed, a new identity arising behind the calling into question of identity qua ego?

> But does not this exposure, this exile, this interdiction to remain in oneself revert into a position, and in pain itself, into complacency puffing itself up with substance and pride? This reverting signifies a residue of activity that cannot be absorbed into the subjective passivity, an ultimate substantiality of the ego even in the very vulnerability of sensibility, and at the same time, or in turn, ambiguously, the infinite path [le parcours infini] of the approach. The path does not remain simply asymptotic of the neighbor. Beyond the bad infinity of the *Sollen* it increases infinitely, living infinitely, an obligation more and more strict in the measure that obedience progresses and the distance to be crossed untraversable in the measure that one approaches. The giving then shows itself to be a parsimony, the exposure a reserve, and holiness guilt. It is life without death, the life of the Infinite or its glory, a life outside of essence and nothingness. (OTB 142 [181])

That is, that which ensures that the subjectivity "signify unreservedly," that "the passivity of its exposure to the other not be immediately inverted into activity, but expose itself in its turn," that the subject is "a passivity of passivity . . . from which an act could not be born anew" (OTB 142–43 [181–82]), is that constituent to the ethical "experience"[19] is the fact that my responsibility to the other does not, according to Levinas, take the form of a *Sollen,* is not asymptotic to the other (ever approaching an ideal, even if that ideal is never achieved), but precisely increases to the degree that it is assumed—thus, infinitely. Again, given the diverse perspectives from which a description of the subjectivity of the subject could be undertaken, this infinite augmentation of responsibility could be described (if the description is taken up from the side of the egoistic ego) as being more and more severe, or (where the subject is seen as animated or inspired by its responsibility for other) more and more . . . glorious! Indeed, this increase of responsibility outstripping every obedience of responsibility, this infinition of responsibility, is the manner in which the infinite imposes itself upon the subject—across *le parcours infini* of the responsibility of the subject. And the subject, qua saying, qua signifying its very signifyingness as responsibility for the other, qua "*me voici,*" of itself testifies to this glorious infinitude, to the glory of the infinite.

But immediately, though almost imperceptibly—we have seen

this already in the inset quotation above—the infinity (*l'infini*) that is the infinition of responsibility becomes, in Levinas's discourse, "the Infinite" (*l'Infini*) (capitalized), which in turn becomes, again almost imperceptibly (first across a quotation from Claudel—OTB 147 [187])—and shortly thereafter in Levinas's own words; OTB 149 [190]), "God." This movement indeed appears to mark a suspicious "slippage" in Levinas's text: the introduction of God (here at least) into *le dit* of the text across a subtle capitalization—a "slippage" that, moreover, goes in both directions, for the capitalized Infinite, once introduced, is not rigorously maintained, but becomes again the noncapitalized infinite, only to cede periodically again to the capitalized Infinite, and the movement between "God" and "the infinite/Infinite" is no less fluid. The Infinite, God, comes to expression here, then, across an ambiguity—an ambiguity that Levinas will, as we shall see, insist is an essential one—and an ambiguity that persists as the text proceeds. Is this mere trickery, a slipping of God into the discourse by way of the back door? Perhaps. But perhaps this is a good thing, in the deep sense of the good (as responsibility for the other) with which this word resounds in Levinas's philosophical discourse. For recall that my responsibility for the other is not something that I would have chosen (as an ego in egoistic enjoyment) for myself, such that my responsibility for the other would have been, beginning from myself, inexplicable. The Infinite, or God, thus makes its legitimate appearance in the discourse if this term means, at least in the first instance (and an instance that must qualify any future meanings), that which, beyond myself, despite myself, ordains me to responsibility for the other, infinitely, ordains me *as* responsibility for the other: "Does not the sense of sincerity refer to the glory of infinity, which calls for sincerity as for a saying?" (OTB 144 [183]). But across an essential ambiguity.

But why essential? The ambiguity arises and persists in that, as Levinas insists, the infinite cannot, without degrading its infinitude, be captured in a theme:

> This glory could not appear, for appearing and presence would belie it by circumscribing it as a theme, by assigning it a beginning in the present of representation, whereas, as infinition of infinity,

> it comes from a past more distant than that which is within the reach of memory, and is lined up on the present. It comes from a past that has never been represented, has never been present, and which consequently has not let a beginning germinate. Glory could not become a phenomenon without entering into conjunction with the very subject to which it would appear, without closing itself up in finitude and immanence. But without a principle, without a beginning, and anarchy, glory breaks up themes and, prior to the logos, signifies positively the extraditing of the subject that rests on itself, to what it has never assumed. For, out of an unrepresentable past, the subject has been sensitive to the provocation that has never presented itself, but has struck traumatically. (OTB 144 [183–84])

The glory of the infinite, or the Infinite, cannot enter into a theme because it imposes itself upon me in the ethical experience, which is the calling into question of every theme correlative with an active and meaning constituting subject, is a resistance, as Levinas repeats seven times in this section, to "the unity of transcendental apperception." "Glory is but the other face of the passivity of the subject. Substituting itself for the other, a responsibility ordered to the first one on the scene, a responsibility for the neighbor, inspired by the other, I, the same, am torn up from my beginning in myself, my equality with myself. The glory of the Infinite is glorified in this responsibility" (OTB 144 [184]). And more than glorified, at least in the sense that the glorification could be traced back, as from a sign to the signified,[20] to that "indicated" in this glorification: "The glory of the Infinite *is* the anarchic identity of the subject flushed out without being able to slip away. It is the ego led to sincerity, making signs to the other, for whom and before whom I am responsible, of this very giving of signs, of this responsibility: 'here I am.' The saying prior to anything said bears witness to glory" (OTB 144–45 [184], our emphasis). This "is," of course, cannot be taken to indicate any ontological identity between glory and my testimony to it (we are here in a domain prior to ontology), but indicates an inseparability of the two. There *is* no infinity, no Infinity, outside of my testimony to it.

And, a bit later on in the analyses, the same thing is said specifically with respect to God:

> The Infinite is not in front of its witness, but as it were outside, or on the "other side" of presence, already past, out of reach, a thought behind thoughts which is too lofty to push itself up front. "Here I am, in the name of God," without referring myself to his presence. "Here I am," just that! The word God is still absent from the phrase in which God is for the first time involved in words. It does not at all state "I believe in God." To bear witness to God is precisely not to state this extraordinary word, as though glory would be lodged in a theme and be posited as a thesis, or become being's essence. As a sign given to the other of this very signification, the "here I am" signifies me to the other in the name of God, at the service of the men who look at me, without having anything to identify myself with, but the sound of my voice or the figure of my gesture—the saying itself. (OTB 149 [190])

Too high to push itself to the first place, the Infinite defers its place of preeminence to the other, calls not first of all for its own glorification, but is glorified in the responsibility that I am for the other and to which it calls me, across which it calls to me. Ironically, or perhaps not so ironically, here is a God that in refusing to be at the forefront of glorification is glorified, and is worthy of glorification.

There are two important consequences that follow from this nonthematizability of the Infinite. In the first place, the divine "presence" is thoroughly humanized: "The refusal of presence is converted into my presence as present, that is, as a hostage delivered over as a gift to the other" (OTB 151 [193]). In lieu of its being present, either, Levinas tells us, in the form of a theme or of an alleged interlocutor, "[t]he Infinite then has glory only through subjectivity, in the human adventure of the approach of the other, through the substitution for the other, by the expiation for the other" (OTB 148 [188]). But God does not, thereby, keep silent, does not fall dumb and leave humanity to its own devices. Rather, "In proximity, in signification, in my giving of signs, already the Infinite speaks through the witness I bear of it, in my sincerity, in my saying without said, pre-originary saying which is said in the mouth of the very one that receives the witness" (OTB 151 [193]). While it is impossible, without entering into positive theology (and Levinas—for reasons that will be delineated shortly—does not), to know why, in the phrase of Claudel that

Levinas quotes, "God writes straight with crooked lines" (OTB 147 [187], from "Satin Slipper"), why God would choose the circuitous route of one human being as the conduit of his voice to another rather than opting for the direct approach, it is clear to Levinas that this is a good thing—in that this alone leaves open the possibility of the good.

For were God to appear on the scene directly, were to enter into evidence, were to enter directly into experience as a theme or as an interlocutor, overwhelming being with His Presence, humanity would be reduced to a mere functionary of this presence, without freedom, without dignity—caught up in the most oppressive totality, so "oppressive" in fact that, there being no taking distance from it, there could be no semblance of oppression, for there would be no semblance of a freedom to be oppressed. It is true, of course, that Levinas's descriptions of the subjectivity of the subject resemble, and strongly, this being caught up in an irremissible "oppression" (to the point of being a hostage!) before any question of freedom or nonfreedom and suggest that I am, despite myself, through the "despite myself," a mere pawn in the intrigue of ethics, a functionary of a(n albeit divine) totality—and Levinas is not unaware of this.[21] But, as we recall from elsewhere, "It is not I who resist the system . . . ; it is the other" (TI 40 [10]). That is, while my own resistance to the totality might well be suspect of being an expression of egotistical pride or caprice, I cannot ethically deny the oppression of the other, the dignity of the other who cries out in pain against the weight of the universe. The face, beyond introducing the problem of who will be permitted to mediate the truth of the totality to the rest of us (a problem that could not even arise were God present), ruptures the totality—even a divine one. And the withdrawal of the divine from presence is the commencement of my responsibility, the commencement of the good.

Of course, the Infinite can be thematized ("I can indeed state the meaning borne witness to as a said"; OTB 151 [192]), *is* being thematized in our discourse, as it is being thematized—as Levinas readily admits—in Levinas's own, "in this very moment" (OTB 151 [193]), and this thematization is, Levinas claims, "inevitable, so that signification itself show itself" (OTB 151 [193]). For while it is true that we read "[r]esponsibility for the other is extraordinary, and is not prevented from floating over the waters of ontology" (OTB 141 [180]), such statements are intended to free ethics from deriving its meaning from ontology, but are not intended to suggest a realm of ethics separate from a realm of being, as if ethics were not—in its essence (if it could be said to have an essence, and Levinas is not allergic to such language)—a matter of offering to the other the bread from my own mouth. Ethics does not carry on a life of its own outside of being, but is the meaning, or "metaphysical depth dimension" (as de Boer will put it),[22] of being, and this meaning is meaningful only to the extent that it is meaningful in and across (be that at countercurrent to) the structures of being. The glory of the Infinite, and my testimony to it, must be thematized (must be offered to the other) in a said if (as we have put it in our chapter 5) it is to have a life—even if in the said it is betrayed, finitized, brought as an object into correlation with a meaning constituting subject:

> Thematization is then inevitable, so that signification itself show itself, but does so in the sophism with which philosophy begins, in the betrayal which philosophy is called upon to reduce. This reduction always has to be attempted, because of the trace of sincerity which the words themselves bear and which they owe to saying as witness, even when the said dissimulates the saying in the correlation set up between the saying and the said. Saying always seeks to unsay that dissimulation, and this is its very veracity. In the play activating the cultural keyboard of language, sincerity or witness signifies by the very ambiguity of every said, where, in the midst of the information communicated to another there signifies also the sign that is given to him of this giving of signs. That is the resonance of every language "in the name of God," the inspiration or prophecy of all language. (OTB 151–52 [193–94])

It is in the recognition of this dissimulation of glory in the said and the ever recurring requirement of its reduction that distinguishes Levinas's thought from positive theology, that keeps his inevitable thematization of God from believing in its theme, its *theo-logos*. What theology forgets, according to Levinas, is that "the word God is still absent from the phrase in which God is for the first time involved in words," that the God concept does not come first, but depends for its life upon the subject saying itself to the other, the responsible subject that, qua responsibility, testifies to the glory of the Infinite. What theology forgets, in short, is the ambivalence across which the revelation of transcendence qua transcendent is possible:

> The infinite would be belied in the proof that the finite would like to give of its transcendence; entering into conjunction with the subject that would make it appear, it would lose its glory. Transcendence owes it to itself to interrupt its own demonstration. Its voice has to be silent as soon as one listens for the message. It is necessary that its pretension be exposed to derision and refutation, to the point of suspecting in the "here I am" that attests to it a cry or a slip of a sick subjectivity. But of a subjectivity responsible for the other! (OTB 152 [194])

It is only across the interruption of the said, of active consciousness in correlation with (that is, constituting) immanent objects, the regime of the *logos* and its theology, that the saying without a said, the saying that animates without being reduced to the said, testifies—across the passivity of passivity of responsibility, entirely while remaining in the world and caught up in its "influences" (OTB 152 [194]), and thus saying a said, but *saying it to the other*—to transcendence, to the glory of the infinite, and, without (necessarily) invoking the name,[23] testifies to God: "that is the enigma, the ambiguity, but also the order of transcendence, of the Infinite" (OTB 152 [194]).

But if this ambiguity, this ambivalence between the Infinite ordering me to the other and the infinition of this order testifying to—and thus giving the life that it is capable of to—the Infinite puts the brakes on a positive theology that would purport to derive responsibility from a divine presence, it also keeps the said—in the form of a nonsaid—of negative theology, that would purport to keep God at a distance from being in keeping being out of God, from taking definitive hold. For here, the Infinite, God, "not contaminated by Being" (OTB xlii [X]), is not glorified merely through the negation of concepts that would purport to attach themselves to God and bring God down to earth, but finds a certain "positivity," a certain tertiarity with respect to being and nonbeing through my responsibility, signifying by way of my testimony, "not entering by the signification of the-one-for-the-other into the being of a theme, but signifying and thus excluding itself from nothingness" (OTB 147 [187]): "This negation of the present and of representation finds its positive form in proximity, responsibility and substitution. This makes it different from the propositions of negative theology" (OTB 151 [193]). The transcendent God is not elsewhere. God is with us, claims Emmanuel. Not as presence, to be sure—except insofar as "this refusal of presence is converted into my presence as present" in responsibility for the other—but in and through the command by which I am commanded to the other, in and through "the pure trace of a 'wandering cause,' inscribed in me" (OTB 150 [192]). "Transcendence, the beyond essence which is also being-in-the-world, requires ambiguity, a blinking of meaning which is not only a chance certainty, but a frontier both ineffaceable and finer than the tracing of an ideal line" (OTB 152 [194]). Transcendence requires my responsibility for the other testifying to the glory of the Infinite—to glory, *tout court!* Transcendence requires the human, in its full humanity qua subjectivity, glorifying it as the human is called to responsibility. And yet: "The Infinite does not appear to him that bears witness to it. On the contrary the witness belongs to the glory of the Infinite" (OTB 146 [186]). Across this essential ambiguity—that God has a life in-the-world only across the response God has always already evoked—ethics is not only first philosophy, for Levinas, it is also first theology.

The second important consequence of the nonthematizability of the Infinite is the ascendancy, in the thought of Levinas, of the notion of conscience, the "reverting of heteronomy into autonomy." For in lieu of a God present in a theme, in lieu of a God engaging me as an interlocutor, the order by which the Infinite orders me to the other is not present to me either, but is perceptible only in my own voice, across my obedience to it, in my testimony to it: "Witness, this way for a command to sound in the mouth of the one that obeys, of being revealed before all appearing, before all presentation before a subject" (OTB 147 [187]). Here, then,

> Obedience precedes any hearing of the command. The possibility of finding, anachronously, the order in the obedience itself, and of receiving the order out of oneself, this reverting of heteronomy into autonomy, is the very way the Infinite passes itself [*se passe*].

> The metaphor of the inscription of the law in consciousness expresses this in a remarkable way, reconciling autonomy and heteronomy. It does so in an ambivalence, whose diachrony is the signification itself, an ambivalence which, in the present, is an ambiguity. The inscription of the order in the for-the-other of obedience is an anarchic being affected, which slips into me "like a thief" through the outstretched nets of consciousness. This trauma has surprised me completely; the order has never been represented, for it has never been presented, not even in the past coming to memory, to the point that it is I that only says, and after the event, this unheard-of obligation. This ambivalence is the exception and subjectivity of the subject, its very psyche, a possibility of inspiration. It is the possibility of being the author of what has been breathed in unbeknownst to me, of having received, one knows not from where, that of which I am the author. (OTB 148–49 [189])

This return of the notion of conscience in the philosophy of Levinas, this conciliation of autonomy and heteronomy in what might be called Levinas's "heterautonomy," this notion whereby "[t]he exteriority of the Infinite becomes somehow an inwardness in the sincerity of a witness borne" (OTB 147 [187]), is remarkable. Is not Levinas the philosopher of heteronomy par excellence? Is the opening and perdurable gesture of this philosophy not a distrust of myself, the calling into question of the naïve violence of my egoism, and of the categories in terms of which I order the world in accord with my interests? And yet, here is the necessity of trusting my own voice, the voice by which—albeit across an essential ambiguity—God speaks.

But, of course, that which is to be trusted here is the subjectivity in passivity, in extradition from itself, the subjectivity as saying, signifying its passivity to the other: "In the passivity of the obsidional extradition this very extradition is delivered over to the other, before it could be established. This is the pre-reflexive iteration of the saying of this very saying, a statement of the 'here I am' which is identified with nothing but the very voice that states and delivers itself, the voice that signifies" (OTB 143 [182]). It is across the saying, and not in what is said, that the Infinite speaks: "The saying prior to anything said bears witness to glory. This witness is true, but with a truth irreducible to the truth of disclosure, and does not narrate anything that shows itself" (OTB 145

[184]). *What* I say, my *dit,* is always called into question, is always suspect as correlative with my powers for interested involvement in the world; *that* I say, the subjectivity as *dire,* this allegiance to the other that is already obedience ("incessant signification, a restlessness for the other. The response is put forth for the other, without any 'taking up of attitudes.' This responsibility is like a cellular irritability; it is the impossibility of being silent, the scandal of sincerity"; OTB 143 [182])—this is what is to be trusted, must be trusted, for in lieu of God (thanks to God),[24] this is all I have, for "[i]t is by the voice of the witness that the glory of the Infinite is glorified" (OTB 146 [186]).

Correlatively, it is not in the said of the other that the order is to be found either—not in the said at all. For the said is present before me, and "[t]he order that orders me to the other does not show itself to me, save through the trace of its reclusion, as a face of a neighbor" (OTB 140 [179]). The order that orders me to the other is not correlative with what the other says, but orders me to the other in my very responsibility for the face, which does not justify an ignoring of what the other says (ethics cannot be ethical as paternalism), but does not tie me to it. This is at least in part, perhaps, why Levinas maintains that, despite the fact that I am hostage to the other, I am not a slave to the other (OTB 68 [86]). If I am a slave, it is to my own conscience by which God orders me to the other. And this is why it is not unethical to engage in philosophical dispute, to engage in a struggle with the other over truth, unless my opinion is equated with truth, unless my truth is imposed upon the other rather than being offered to him in an ethical offering that is, according to Levinas, as we have seen, the truthfulness of truth (*la véracité du vrai*).

In this, my own voice, I testify to the infinite across *my* subjectivity, across *my* responsibility, I testify to the way that the Infinite imposes itself upon *me,* or the me as so imposed upon—*me voici*—and in this context the idea of prophecy is introduced as (almost) synonymous with testimony, where prophecy is an inspired declaration of divine will or purpose, but where the responsibility for this will or purpose falls upon me—me, and not the other: "We call prophecy this reverting in which the perception of an order coincides with the signification of this order given to him that obeys it. Prophecy would thus be the very psyche of the soul: the other in the same, and all a man's spirituality would be prophetic" (OTB 149 [190]). Indeed, everywhere that the word prophecy appears in these analyses the term testimony could be substituted, or so is our wager, without any substantial variation in the meaning. Prophecy seems here my prophesying to God's call to me to goodness, that to which I testify in my saying, and not a matter of my calling, on behalf of God, to the other. What, then, is the relationship between prophecy as it is employed here and prophecy as that which calls upon the other to responsibly respond? And, moreover, why is prophecy here introduced across, or in the context of, the idea of testimony, and not in the context of the command that commands commanding, that which, in the previous section, was shown to be necessary to prophecy as a calling upon the goodness of the other?

I testify to the glory of the infinite that transcends me across my responsibility, to my being caught up in an intrigue that transcends me. But my responsibility itself is only possible because of the responsibility of the other: the other that in the mode of the feminine has welcomed me into a home and given me a self (ego), making space for me in-the-world by providing me with the conditions of possibility for participation in economic life, ordering me qua ego, even while—already at once, or *tour à tour*—the other qua other, calls my egoism into question, orders me to the other. My responsibility itself is possible only because the other, in its diverse modalities, graces me and calls me to grace. So if my responsibility testifies to an intrigue that transcends me, it does so only across the intrigue of the love of the (m)other that also transcends me. But are these intrigues not the same? Is the intrigue in terms of which I am graced not the same intrigue in terms of which I am called to be gracious? And does my testimony to the glory of the Infinite not presuppose the testimony of the other—in the mode of the feminine—who across her graciousness to me has already testified to the glory of the Infinite? Is my testimony not then always already, even as I testify to the infinite across my own responsibility, a testimony to the testimony of the other? My testimony to the Infinite through responsibility to the other is already a testimony to the other's responsibility for me, and thus to the other's involvement in the intrigue of transcendence.

This would indeed explain why the idea of prophecy can emerge in *Otherwise Than Being* across the analyses of testimony, and why the terms in that text can be read as (almost) synonymous. My testimony is already prophetic in that my testimony is already a testimony to the testimony of the other to the glory of the infinite, and thus a testimony to the allegiance to the good to which the other has already, in her own voice, testified, and can thus be a prophetic word, a call to the other to be responsible in accord with this allegiance, a pacific call that takes the form not of a command coming as if from above, but the form of a reminder, a command that commands only in being commanded to command. In this way—if we read both "versions" of prophecy in terms of the religio-familial intrigue that opens up as it grounds these diverse articulations—the testimony/prophecy of *Otherwise Than Being* links up with the prophetic word of *Totality and Infinity*.

We have been attempting to delineate this intrigue—this religio-familial intrigue that across the dis/continuity of generations runs from grace to grace—throughout this work, tracing it from the analyses of *Totality and Infinity* on the structures that are "Beyond the Face" through a continuation and elaboration of these themes in *Otherwise Than Being*, and we reinvoke it here at Levinas's prompting, for all of its elements—reference to familial relations, to religion, and to the passing on of grace received—are present in the analyses of "The Glory of the Infinite" and present as explicitly related to the idea of an intrigue in which I am caught up and to which I testify in my responsibility.

To begin with, we would argue that it is not insignificant that Levinas opens and closes his analyses of "The Glory of the Infinite" by making reference, in the very first and very last sentences of the section,[25] to fraternity, evoking this familial relationship to describe the relationship that holds between all human beings, the relationship between brothers metaphorically applied to the ethical bond between person and person. (Or, is the ethical relationship between human beings the fraternity in relation to which the bond between biological brothers is metaphorically called fraternity? Are we here before yet another Levinasian ambiguity?) We read:

> The assembling of being in the present, its synchronization by retention, memory and history, reminiscence, is representation; it does not integrate the responsibility for the separated entity. Representation does not integrate the responsibility for the other inscribed in human fraternity; human fraternity does not arise out of any commitment, any principle, that is, any recallable present. . . . [The rest of the section, then:] It [transcendence] needs the diachrony that breaks the unity of transcendental apperception, which does not succeed in assembling the time of modern humanity, in turn passing from prophecy to philology and transcending philology toward prophetic signification. For it is incapable of denying the fraternity of men. (OTB 140 [179], 152 [194])

Let us note here that for Levinas, as the quotation from the beginning of the section attests, it is in human fraternity that responsibility is inscribed. My responsibility is not first, is not the relationship in terms of which fraternity would be produced; rather, it is fraternity that is the "context," the "horizon," the "raison (d'être)" of responsibility, the "condition" of my responsibility, even if the relationship of fraternity is "perceptible" only across, is "realized" only as mediated through, my ethical responsibility for the other. Responsibility does not make fraternity possible, fraternity makes responsibility necessary. If, as Levinas claims, human equality emerges on the far side of my responsibility for the other, human fraternity is on the near side.

As the very context of responsibility, then, as transcending the subjectivity as saying, as that in which the responsible subject is caught up despite itself and that to which it as responsible testifies, does not fraternity here describe the intrigue of grace that we have been attempting to delineate in this work, an intrigue that is perceptible only across the trace it leaves upon me as responsible, but that is beyond me, beyond me even as responsible for evoking my responsibility? And is it by chance, then, that the other reference to fraternity in the section under question is linked to the idea of the intrigue of Ethics?

> That the glory of the Infinite is glorified only by the signification of the-one-for-the-other, as sincerity, that in my sincerity the Infinite passes the finite, that the Infinite comes to pass there, is what makes the plot of Ethics [l'intrigue de l'Ethique][26] primary, and what makes language irreducible to an act among acts. Before put-

ting itself at the service of life as an exchange of information through a linguistic system, saying is witness; it is saying without the said, a sign given to the other. Sign of what? Of complicity? Of a complicity for nothing, a fraternity, a proximity that is possible only as an openness of self, an imprudent exposure to the other, a passivity without reserve, to the point of substitution. (OTB 150–51 [192])

That the Infinite is glorified only by my sincerity of signification renders primordial the intrigue of Ethics and language, but my self-exposure, the sincere subject as sign, is a sign of . . . fraternity. Is this fraternity not, then, the intrigue of Ethics and language itself? The rare capitalization of Ethics (*l'Ethique*) here (the only such capitalization of this term in this section, we believe) would seem, moreover, to shift the focus from ethics as my responsibility to an Ethics that would be associated with a capitalized Infinite, to an Ethics to which ethics (as my responsibility) would testify as the infinition of my responsibility testifies to the Infinite, and thus to an intrigue that transcends me and in terms of which I am called to responsibility, that is not my responsibility but that leaves its trace upon it in ordaining it as responsible, but in a trace that qua trace has a life across the ambiguity of ethics/Ethics, infinity/Infinity, that is, across my testimony to it.

It is, further, across this ambiguity—where my bond with the Infinite is (in) my bond to the other—that the idea of religion, and the recognition of the intrigue as a *religio*-familial one, comes to expression in these passages:

The saying without[27] the said of the witness born signifies in a plot [*une intrigue*] other than that which is spread out in a theme, other than that which attaches a noesis to a noema, a cause to an effect, the memorable past to the present. This plot [*Intrigue*] connects to what detaches itself absolutely, to the Absolute. . . . One is tempted to call this plot [*Intrigue*] religious; it is not stated in terms of certainty or uncertainty, and does not rest on any positive theology. (OTB 147 [187–88])

The "*Dire sans Dit*" testifies here not only *to* but *by* an intrigue through which I am attached to the Absolute in being responsible for the other, my bond with God realized across my fraternal bond to the other—in a religio-familial intrigue that transcends me.

Finally, that this intrigue, traced across my responsibility, is the very intrigue that runs from grace to grace, that, as we have been attempting to show throughout much of this work, runs, for Levinas, from grace received to grace required, is evinced in that the very structure of gift and call that we have been arguing qualifies this intrigue is evoked in this section when Levinas describes "what is proper to all the relations" being here unfolded: "The fact that the return is sketched out in the going, the appeal is understood in the response, the 'provocation' coming from God is in my invocation, gratitude is already gratitude for this state of gratitude, which is at the same time or in turn a gift and a gratitude" (OTB 149 [190]). My gift to the other here, given in gratitude, is already, in itself, a gift received from the other, is a gratitude grafted onto a prior gratitude that precedes my gratitude (even if it is only "present" in my gratitude itself). My being in a state of gratitude testifies to a gift given to me always already by the other, as it testifies to my requirement to "gift" the other, across which my gratitude is realized. It is across this intrigue of giftedness/gifting, grace received/graciousness, testified to in my very own saying, that the responsibility that the other has always already been to me is traced, and that makes possible testimony not only as a testimony to my own responsibility, but testimony as at once prophetic word, "calling upon the goodness of the other."

I.4. Philosophy As Discourse

Levinas's discourse is philosophical, and is, consequently, an attempt, across the vocabulary and protocols of the discipline, to argue for, and to persuade its readers of, its thesis: that ethics—in the sense we have been attempting carefully to delineate throughout this work—is first philosophy. But, if it is to be consistent with its own tenets, must not Levinas's own philosophical *dit,* like every *dit,* be animated by an ethical *dire,* by Levinas's own responsibility to the other, an offering offered from out of the passivity of passivity across which the Infinite is glorified, that is, as "peace announced to the other" (OTB 148 [188–89])? Levinas's philosophy is, it is true, qua philosophy, an attempt to thematize this *dire,* but is also, again qua philosophy, an attempt to reduce the inevitable betrayal of this thematization in an attempt that while yet philosophical could not be motivated by philosophy itself, but only by love, that is, where philosophy as the love of wisdom is converted into the wisdom of love in the service of love. Levinas's philosophical discourse, then, before (where this before indicates an ethical priority rather than a chronological antecedence in calendar time—as we have argued) it congeals into a philosophical said, must—if Levinas believes his own testimony—be a performance of love, must be this peace offered to the other. And we suspect that it is self-consciously so.

As peace offered to the other, this philosophical discourse cannot then be a pronouncement—as if from above, as if from a position purporting to be outside of the face-to-face relation from which it could be viewed "objectively" (that which Levinas's discourse precisely forbids as the origin of oppressive totality structures)—upon the way things in fact are, are for Levinas and are for the other whether or not the other acquiesces to this truth, and of which the other, reserving such acquiescence, must be convinced by the evidence. As peace offered to the other, this philosophical discourse cannot be Levinas's truth imposed upon the other, but his exposure to the other in truth. As peace offered to the other, this philosophical discourse can only be Levinas's testimony to his own responsibility for the other, and the philosophical saids that it offers must remain subordinate to, as animated by, Levinas's saying of them to the other, and cannot, ethically, return to dominate this saying. And, indeed, Levinas's philosophical saids, the "truths" they propose and argue for, have, as their condition of possibility qua true, as their "context," the face-to-face relation: they are offered by Levinas to the other, and await, if they are to become true, the other's investiture. And it is across this offering, before truths could be true, that Levinas in his own discourse testifies to the glory of the Infinite, which is not to sneak another truth that would be true for everyone (and mediated to everyone else by Levinas), another totality (albeit a pre-ontological one), in by way of the back door, for the responsibility for this offering falls, and has to fall according to his own testimony, upon Levinas alone; his philosophical discourse is his testimony, his exposure/responsibility to the other, and even when he testifies to structures that are "beyond the face," this testimony is still an offering made to the other and cannot return to dominate or dictate to the face-to-face relation. So even when this testimony is prophetic (and we have argued that it always already is so), Levinas can call upon our (his readers') responsibility, can invite us to find ourselves in the I of his discourse, only across his own testimony to the glory of God, only across a testimony that testifies to our own testimonies (but that cannot demand them or dictate to them), commanding us to remember the responsibility we have already acknowledged in commanding him to command.

We are arguing, that is, that Levinas's philosophical discourse is—before it believes in its own said (and must be according to its own conditions for the saying of a said)—first of all Levinas's testimony to his own responsibility, his responsibility as a testimony to his responsibility, glorification, and prophecy, in short: itself a saying before a said. And while this saying clearly is said (as it must be, as we have seen), and while Levinas's discourse qua philosophy will be and must be judged according to the requirements for an effective philosophical discourse, it should also be remembered that this discourse is not only or even primarily that even according to its own said. That is, there is a huge epistemological and ethical chasm between a philosophical discourse that claims to delineate the structures of being (or even of pre-being) as they really are, and a philosophical discourse that claims rather to testify to the way things "are" for "me," the author, in a discourse that invites the other both to join and to judge it. Levinas's testimony is at once a prophetic but pacific word of invitation to the other to recognize his own responsibility, but this responsibility called for is one to which the other has already testified by his own testimony to his own uncircumventable responsibility, and for which he is ultimately responsible in the sense that with respect to it he—and not Levinas—guards the final word, in accord with his conscience. Levinas's discourse is thus a testimony that leaves to the other the first and last word with regard to his own truth, and the power to invest or not invest mine. Levinas's philosophical discourse is misread, we are claiming, if it is read outside of this chasm, outside of this ambiguity in which it is, we believe, self-consciously inscribed.

Indeed, Levinas's philosophical discourse qua philosophy (qua persuasive arguments) can only get so far, for philosophy betrays even as it preserves the saying that animates it and that it thematizes. Its real effective force is in the testimony that it offers to the glory of the infinite, in its testimony as saying (its persuasive force being in its exposure of exposure—the ethical force of vulnerability), in its pacific, prophetic invitation to us to find ourselves in the "I and no other" of the discourse, to find ourselves in the intrigue of grace that it performatively enacts. Levinas's philosophical discourse is, we are arguing, before it is a philosophical said, precisely discourse in the technical sense that Levinas gives to this term—is a performance of a non-allergic, ethical relation with alterity (which is to say: peace offered to the other), and it is out of this inspiration that is produced its ontological sense—and can only be well read as such.

II. Levinas's Discourse As Philosophy

If in the previous section we argued that Levinas's philosophical discourse qua discourse is to be read precisely as discourse, that is, as a performance of a non-allergic, ethical relationship with alterity across the modalities of testimony and prophecy, and that its status as philosophical discourse, qua philosophy, qua "knowledge" of what "is" (as a pacific offering through which the world is known and ordered) is founded upon these structures, what remains to be determined is the status of this philosophical discourse qua philosophy. More precisely, why does Levinas's discourse take the form of philosophy? And why does Levinas employ the particular form of philosophy that he does?

The first of these questions would seem to be able to be dispatched with relative economy given the foregoing, insofar as philosophy has been shown to be, for Levinas, the organon by which ethics is both betrayed and preserved in distributive justice,[28] which as a pleonasm can be reduced to justice *tout court*, and it is to justice (albeit always already necessarily inspired by ethics) that I am called in daily life as I attempt to respond to, as I attempt to concretize, the diverse and conflicting responsibilities that I encounter in the faces of the others. Why philosophize? For justice. But the seeming satisfaction of this answer needs to be seen in the light of its circularity if it is to be taken as an explanation of why Levinas chose philosophy as an occupation as over against, for instance, painting, or the civil service, or professional golf, insofar as the carefully articulated results of one's philosophical research cannot be taken as one's impetus to philosophize in the first place, even if they might—after the fact—explain or justify the choice. Indeed, the decision for philosophy is likely a very personal one in the case of any given philosopher (interest, chance, a sense of calling, or what have you) that does not likely admit (and of course could not in advance) of "philosophical" explanation. But having entered into philosophy, Levinas does philosophize about the meaning of the discipline, and the above explanation figures prominently in his reflections.[29]

The second question is more philosophically interesting insofar as prior to asking why Levinas employs the particular form(s) of philosophy he does, it is necessary to determine what form(s) of philosophy he does in fact employ, and any answer to this question is complicated (among other things)[30] by the fact that such a determination will always be colored by our reading of the purpose this philosophy is taken to serve. We have argued that for Levinas philosophy always has an ethical *sens* (meaning or direction), an ethical inspiration. So what form of philosophy does Levinas employ, and how does this form serve the purposes of keeping philosophy subservient to ethics? This is our question. Our thesis in this section of the chapter is that Levinas's philosophical discourse qua philosophy is best understood as an "ethical transcendentalism," insofar as this mode of philosophizing allows him to work back from within philosophy (that is, from within *la philosophie transmise*) to that which conditions philosophy as its eternal and inspirational other, that is, as a method in philosophy that allows Levinas to maintain his philosophical discourse qua discourse (with its modalities of testimony and prophecy) against the domination of the "philosophical" language in which it is (necessarily) borne and betrayed. This argument should ring familiar, as, indeed, it is such a reading of Levinas that we have been developing, and that has guided us, throughout this work, and indications of this interpretative choice will have been present—sometimes more explicitly, sometimes more implicitly—throughout what precedes. We will here attempt to justify this reading, and we shall begin to do so by entering into a discussion on Levinas's philosophical method across two articles: the first by Theodore de Boer ("An Ethical Transcendental Philosophy"),[31] an early advocate of the "transcendental" reading of Levinas, and the interpreter who coined the phrase "ethical transcendental philosophy," and the second by Robert Bernasconi ("Re-reading *Totality and Infinity*")[32] in which this reading is called into question.

II.1. An Ethical Transcendental Philosophy

In his article, on his way to arguing that Levinas's philosophy can be read as a reconciliation, by way of a radicalization, of the two opposing approaches in twentieth-century continental philosophy delineated by Michael Theunissen in his monumental *Der Andere*[33] as the transcendental and the dialogical, de Boer argues that Levinas's philosophy is well conceived, along these lines, as "an ethical transcendental philosophy." Affirmatively citing Dondeyne's observation[34] that the title of Levinas's book is *Totality* and *Infinity,* and not, for instance, *Totality* or *Infinity,* de Boer in his article carefully and consecutively delineates, as correlative to totality and infinity, the two "regions" operative in Levinas's thought—"ontology" and "metaphysics"—before turning to an account of how, for Levinas, metaphysics founds ontology, or of how, to have recourse to the language of transcendental thought—that which interests us here—the metaphysical provides the conditions of possibility for the ontological. As we have traced out already in this work the lineaments of this argument (and have indicated already those points at which our own reading would attempt to supplement or to shade differently the one provided in this article by de Boer), we will not follow it out in detail here, but will pick up certain aspects of it as we turn our attentions to de Boer's contribution to the matter at hand—the characterization of Levinas's philosophy as an ethical transcendental one—and thus to the final section of his essay that appears under the rubric "The Transcendental Method."

Indeed, having demonstrated in the previous section ("The Founding of Ontology by Metaphysics") how, after Levinas's "specific form of transcendental philosophy," "the other, in his concrete analysis, functions as the transcendental foundation of the same" in the realms of knowledge, labor,[35] and society, de Boer opens his section on transcendental method by asking: "To which type of transcendental philosophy does the philosophy of Levinas correspond?" (ETP 104). So, after citing, by way of a caveat, Levinas's comment that "I do not believe that transparency is possible in method, or that philosophy is possible as transparency" (ETP 104, from DVI 143), de Boer proceeds with the claim that "if it is true that prophetic philosophy has the task of 'translating Jewish wisdom into Greek,' the concern for method is legitimate" (given that "[r]ationality, which is a Greek invention, implies the ambition to justify our rational thinking rationally"), and with the observation that "reflection on method is by no means absent in the work of Levinas" (ETP 104). To determine, then, the type of transcendental philosophy to which the philosophy of Levinas corresponds, de Boer does three things, more or less concurrently: he shows what Levinas's philosophy shares with traditional transcendental thinking (which determines Levinas's thought as legitimately identified as some sort of transcendentalism); he shows how Levinas's philosophy departs from traditional transcendental philosophy (which determines it as a transcendentalism of a different sort); and he specifies the root (*radix*) from which this departure grows (which determines the type of transcendentalism Levinas employs).

What Levinas, according to de Boer, shares with transcendental thinking is the thesis (which phenomenology, at least in the Husserlian form, believes to have apodictically demonstrated) that "representative consciousness has a horizon," that is, the thesis that

> If we explore this horizon by intentional analyses, that is, by penetrating the implications of the object of representation, we discover that it is embedded in a nonobjectifying consciousness. Levinas writes that the strictly cognitive relation has "transcendental conditions." These conditions lie beneath and beyond representation—in corporate and cultural existence. The object of perception is determined not only by the objectifying act but also by the attitudes of the body—in walking, for instance, and also by language and history. (ETP 104)

According to de Boer, Levinas, in his "New Commentaries" appended to the 1967 second edition of his *En découvrant l'existence,* already finds "indications" of such a horizon to representative consciousness in Husserl himself (although, in order for Husserl's idealism to be overcome, "certain concepts" of Husserl's must be "radicalized"; ETP 104). Indeed, this is to go beyond the letter in interpreting Husserl (or, perhaps, against Husserl's stated intentions, precisely to stay with the letter), for whom, as Levinas indicates, that which conditions representation is in its turn a representation, and it is precisely this which establishes the idealistic character of his philosophy. To break with this idealism is to discover, behind representations, not more representations, but a nonrepresentative horizon, and if this horizon is only implicit in Husserl's analyses, it is made explicit in Husserl's "existentialist" followers: in, for instance, Merleau-Ponty, "who roots the transcendental ego in the body-subject," in Heidegger "in his exploration of the pre-objective areas of human existence and their implicit understanding of being," and in Ricoeur in whom, in "dealing with symbolism, interpretation, and narration, the conditions of knowledge *beyond* objectifying consciousness are analyzed in a more detailed manner" (ETP 105).

So if Levinas shares with the phenomenologists, both Husserl and the existential phenomenologists, the methodological practice of working back, through intentional analysis, from representational consciousness to the horizon(s) that condition it, even as he shares with the existential phenomenologists the aspiration to break with Husserl's idealism, Levinas departs from them all insofar as he, by means of this method, in de Boer's phrase, "digs more deeply and discloses a metaphysical depth dimension" (ETP 105)—that which justifies a particular qualification of Levinas's transcendentalism. Indeed, the "method of thinking outside of phenomenology" (ETP 106) that Levinas attempts is an effort "to transcend the realm of experience, to think outside of this evidence" (ETP 106), which is another way of saying that "Levinas's method is not the intuitive, explicating disclosure of the phenomenologists" (ETP 106). That is, for Levinas, the metaphysical depth dimension is revealed (as *révelation,* over against *dévoilement*—"which would restore the all-embracing comprehension of the same"; ETP 105) precisely as the calling into question of experience, and thus cannot be traced by tracing back intuitively from the experience of which it is the calling into question. "[H]ere," de Boer maintains, "the transcendental condition is not a phenomenon! . . . The condition for the possibility of experience is not experience itself" (ETP 105). So, de Boer asks: "Is this still phenomenology?" (ETP 105) Indeed, as de Boer further implies, is it still philosophy? For if, as Levinas himself maintains, "it is essential for philosophy to oppose opinions and illusions in the name of experience and evidence," does not Levinas's endeavor

> to transcend this realm of experience, to think outside this evidence, amount to a falling back into prephilosophical opinions and beliefs? This would be the case "unless philosophical evidence refers from itself to a situation that can no longer be stated in terms of totality. . . . We can proceed from the experience of totality back to a situation that conditions the totality itself." This means that in certain situations where it "breaks," ontology itself refers to transcendental conditions. "Such a situation is the gleam of exteriority or of transcendence in the face of the Other. The rigorously developed concept of this transcendence is expressed by the term infinity." Levinas calls this way of working back from the objective certitude of objectifying knowledge (the way down) "the transcendental method." (ETP 106, citing TI 24f [xiii])

Clearly, this "digging deeper," this break with intuition, takes on a different aspect with respect to Husserl than it does with respect to the existentialists, even if it is the same metaphysical "content" (ETP 106)—the face—that will serve to question and transform the method of both pure and existential phenomenology, that is, that will serve to call each into question.

So, if Levinas can be seen to concur with the existentialists in criticizing Husserl's idealism, his motivation for doing so is yet more radical—that is, concerns the *radix,* or root, of thought itself. For, according to de Boer, "Husserl views his transcendental reduction as a return to the absolute bottom or ground of the existent, to 'the root of all things' "(ETP 107), which for him is "absolute consciousness—and in particular the original source (*Urquelle*) of immanent time" (ETP 107). If going beyond this "makes no sense," as Husserl often declares,

> Levinas wants to pose this "senseless" question, for he is looking for a source beyond the source. When knowledge becomes critical, when it is unsettled, it moves back to what precedes its origin. It is a "tracing back from its condition to what precedes that condition." "To philosophize is to trace freedom back to what lies before it." The origin prior to the origin, which lies on this side of the origin (or "higher than the origin"), is the other. This shocking of the condition, this awakening, comes from the other. Levinas calls it an "unnatural movement." In other words, it is really the surmounting of the natural attitude! The hypercritical philosophy of Husserl, which opposes every form of dogmatism, is itself dogmatic. It belongs to the old tradition of philosophy that seeks a foundation in the self, in immanent perception, in the "for itself" (*pour soi*) of consciousness. Levinas calls this "egoism" or "narcissism." If the essence of philosophy is critique, it enjoys the prerogative of calling itself into question. The face of the other is the principle, and the commencement, of philosophy. (ETP 107, citing TI 83 [54], 84 ff. [57 ff.], 88 [60], and *En découvrant l'existence avec Husserl et Heidegger,* p. 178)

De Boer then asserts that, for Levinas, this critique applies equally to Husserl's existentialist followers, for while they abandon the idea of absolute consciousness and its concordant idealism by finding consciousness embedded in pre-reflexive areas of experience (that is, in a horizon that is not its product—rather, consciousness is the product of the horizon in which it is embedded), they do not question the value of an autonomous ego. For them, "autonomy is only limited; it is not called into question" (ETP 107). So while the freedom of the ego is for the existentialists degraded in being shown to embedded in a horizon, "[t]he exercise of freedom is never unmasked as injustice" (ETP 108).

And it is this calling into question, this accusation of autonomy—a calling into ethical question of the very consciousness that would constitute the face as an experience of being called into question (and that is thus beyond, or before, experience)—this ethical prohibition/demand, that is the encounter with the face, that is the before experience that makes experience possible. Again, "[t]he condition for the possibility of experience is not experience itself" (ETP 105). And this is why de Boer insists (and he makes this point repeatedly throughout the article)[36] in conclusion that "if we call this philosophy an ethical transcendentalism, the adjective *ethical* must be stressed. . . . The transcendental condition is not a necessary ontological structure that can be reconstructed from the empirical phenomena; it is rather an unrecoverable contingent or ontic incidence that intersects the ontological order. In the words of Levinas, this dimension is 'more ontological than ontology, more *sublime* than ontology' " (ETP 108–9).

De Boer does, and can, we believe, take some encouragement in his interpretation from his exchange with Levinas around this issue at Leiden in 1975, a question and response worth, for our purposes too, quoting here verbatim:

> *Lévinas:* Cela répond aussi à la question écrite que je lis: "En 1972—donc avant *Autrement qu'être ou au-delà de l'essence*—le professeur Th. de Boer a écrite un article sur votre oeuvre sous le titre de *Un transcendentalisme éthique.* Si la condition transcendentale est expliquée non pas comme un fait mais comme une valeur préalable—en hallandais *voor-waarde*—est-ce que vous consentez à cette caractéristique?" Eh bien je suis absolument d'accord avec cette formule, si transcendental signifie une certaine antériorité : sauf que l'éthique est avant l'ontologie. Elle est plus ontologique que l'ontologie, plus *sublime* que l'ontologie. C'est de là que vient une équivoque où elle semble plaquée sur, alors qu'elle est avant. C'est donc un transcendentalisme qui commence par l'éthique. (DVI 143)[37]

II.2. The Challenge of Empiricism, and Beyond

In "Re-reading *Totality and Infinity*" (1989), Robert Bernasconi attempts to call into question de Boer's "transcendental" reading of Levinas.[38] If Bernasconi begins this article by posing the question "What status is to be accorded the face-to-face relation?" and dividing Levinas interpretation along the divergent answers given to this question, calling "an empirical reading" that wherein "interpreters understand it as a concrete experience that we can recognize in our lives," and "the transcendental reading" the one wherein "commentators have understood the face-to-face relation to be the condition for the possibility of ethics and indeed of all economic existence and knowledge" (Rr 23), he will end (while confessing that in this paper he "will be unable to give a direct answer to the question" of the status of the face-to-face relation, but only lead us to "a position to understand how Levinas prepares his answer"; Rr 27) by claiming that a sufficient reading of Levinas can rest with neither of these interpretations, as it cannot be satisfied with their integration, but must arise from "employing both languages and drawing them into contradiction," as he claims Levinas himself does in the notion of "the anterior posteriori" (Rr 34):

> It seems to me that Levinas is using the language of transcendental philosophy and the language of empiricism not in order to draw them together into a transcendental empiricism, but in an effort to find a way between these twin options given to us by the philosophical—and nonphilosophical—language that we have inherited. . . . If the disputes among the readers of Levinas have largely been a matter of contesting which limb of the dichotomy should be uppermost—the transcendental or the empirical—then we are still a long way from negotiating this language, which operates by a displacement of their disjunction. Neither a transcendental nor an empirical discourse can be maintained in isolation from the other. (Rr 34)

That is, for Bernasconi, either a transcendental or an empirical reading of Levinas—if attempted in isolation from, or if proposed as predominant with respect to, the other—will be partial, one-sided, and will thus miss Levinas's attempt "to introduce us to a way of thinking that rests on neither" (Rr 34).

One such reading, on Bernasconi's account, is the transcendental reading proposed by de Boer. For Bernasconi, de Boer provides not only an exemplary, but perhaps the paradigmatic, example of an attempt to maintain a transcendental reading in his "important essay, 'An Ethical Transcendental Philosophy' " (Rr 26).[39] On our analysis, Bernasconi's critique of de Boer's "transcendental" reading rests upon three interrelated criticisms: first, on the fact that Levinas himself claims that his method *resembles* the transcendental method,[40] where Bernasconi takes this "resembles" as Levinas's attempt "to distance himself from the common conception of the transcendental method" (Rr 24); second, by criticizing de Boer's attempt "to model his account of the 'transcendental' relation of the same and the other on Levinas's reading of the Cartesian idea of infinity" (Rr 26, citing ETP 95), which Bernasconi will claim is inseparable, for Levinas, from the correlative Cartesian *ego cogito* that de Boer reads as a derivative structure (Rr 32); and third, by suggesting that de Boer's reading ends by being implicated in the ontic-ontological distinction that Levinas rejected because he saw in it (as in the correlative Heideggerian distinction between the existentiell and existential) "an insidious form of the impersonal neuter" (Rr 26–27, citing TI 272 [250]). We shall return to these points in greater detail as they emerge in the course of our review of Bernasconi's article.

Bernasconi, in his article, undertakes to argue his thesis (from which will flow his criticisms of de Boer's reading) by illustrating the way in which, on his reading, Levinas employs both transcendental and empirical language and conceives of their interrelationship by focusing his attention on the second part of *Totality and Infinity,* entitled "Interiority and Economy," a section of the book that, despite his differences from de Boer, he credits de Boer with having—against the more common practices of reading Levinas—not ignored. Asserting that this part of Levinas's text "is concerned with labor and objectifying thought as relations analogous to transcendence (TI 109 [81])" that yet "already imply the relation with the transcendent," Bernasconi follows out what he perceives to be Levinas's "twofold task of, first, showing the difference between transcendent relations and relations analogous to transcendence and, secondly, showing the former to be reflected within the latter" (Rr 27). He then claims, following Levinas, that this task can be accomplished by employing neither "the classical logic of non-contradiction" nor "dialectical logic" (for in either case "the transcendent relation cannot be maintained"), but only across "the 'interval of separation' "(Rr 27). Bernasconi is claiming that in this second section of Levinas's book, the understanding of relation is being reconceived:

> Whereas we ordinarily understand by relation "a simultaneity of distance between the terms and their union," in separation "the being that is in relation absolves itself from the relation, is absolute within the relationship" (TI 110 [82]). Separation as inner life, as psychism, the interiority of a presence at home with oneself, habitation and economy, already exhibits the distance that resists totalization. (Rr 27)

If the "foils" of Husserl ("characterized as being concerned primarily with the intentional relation as a thematic or objectifying relation with an object") and Heidegger ("understood primarily in terms of the account of Being-in-the-world to be found in the first division of *Being and Time*"; Rr 28) are knowingly reduced by Levinas in this section to the level of caricatures, it is with the polemical purpose (or so Bernasconi claims) of showing that the structures that they employ are not up to accounting "for what Levinas analyzes under the name of *vivre de* or 'living from' " (Rr 28). We have ourselves already[41] analyzed the structure of enjoyment as "living from," as "not something added on to life subsequently, like the addition of an attribute to a substance . . . [but wherein] . . . 'life is the love of life' (TI 112 [84]) . . . 'beyond ontology' (TI 112 [84]) . . . [wherein] . . . '[t]o be an I is to exist in such a way as to be already beyond being, in happiness' (TI 120 [92])" (Rr 28). And Bernasconi concludes his review of this structure by reminding us that for Levinas, "The unicity, solitude, isolation of happiness and need already rupture the totality (TI 118 [90]). Needs 'constitute a being independent of the world, a veritable subject' (TI 116 [89])" (Rr 28).

But it is only when the structures of enjoyment and representation are examined, first independently of each other, and then in order "to exhibit their interdependency" that this analysis of enjoyment is, according to Bernasconi, "put to work" (Rr 28–29)—and we head toward that which interests him, and us, in this matter. For if, in representation, "the exteriority of the object appears to be a meaning ascribed by the representing subject" and "[a]lterity disappears in the same . . . [b]y contrast, the intentionality of enjoyment maintains the exteriority that representation suspends" (Rr 29). So,

> Whereas in representation "the same is in relation with the other but in such a way that the other does not determine the same" (TI 124 [97]), in enjoyment "the same determines the other while being determined by it" (TI 128 [101]). Whereas representation conforms to the model of adequation, enjoyment overflows its meaning. The maintenance of exteriority characteristic of enjoyment is accomplished by the body, which is the reversion of representation into life. The needs of the body "affirm 'exteriority' as non-constituted, prior to all affirmation (TI 127 [100])." (Rr 29)

And the recognition of this other "intentionality" has important consequences for the reading of Levinas's reference to transcendental philosophy, or of reading Levinas's philosophy as transcendental:

> The structure of enjoyment is therefore an offense against the transcendental method, which in Levinas's mind is closely tied to representation. The language of transcendental conditions is turned upside down: "The aliment conditions the very thought that would think it as a condition" (TI 128 [101]). The constituted becomes the condition of the constituting. Corporeity as both affirmation of exteriority and position on the earth contests the transcendental method and its reliance on the universality of representation and the directionality of constitution. "The world I constitute nourishes me and bathes me. It is aliment and 'medium' ('*milieu*'). The intentionality aiming at the exterior changes direction in the course of its very aim by becoming interior to the exteriority it constitutes, somehow comes from the point to which it goes, recognizing itself past in its future, lives from what it thinks (TI 129 [102])." (Rr 29)

Thus representation, in intellectualism, with its "transcendental pretension" (TI 169 [143]), believes itself constitutive of that in which, from another perspective (or before—in making possible—perspective), it is "already implanted": "Representation performs a kind of reversal by accounting for that which in fact underlies it" (Rr 31), but this reversal is itself reversed as soon as I open my eyes, or as soon as I eat: "The 'turning' of the constituted into a condition is accomplished as soon as I open my eyes: I but open my eyes and already enjoy the spectacle" (TI 130 [103]). "In 'living from . . .' the process of constitution which comes into play wherever there is representation is reversed" (TI 128 [101]). "But," claims Bernasconi, "Levinas does not side with the body here against representation; rather he examines the structure to which they both give rise" (Rr 31). What, then, according to Bernasconi, is this structure?

It is, Bernasconi informs us, the structure of "the anterior posteriori"—which is possible only across "the interval of separation" in terms of which (unlike in "the Husserlian privileging of representation and the Heideggerian privileging of care") "the distance between the I and its object, their opposition," is maintained (Rr 31). It is thus in the interplay between representation and enjoyment that " '[t]he represented turns into a past that had not traversed the *present* of representation, as an absolute past not receiving its meaning from memory' (TI 130 [103]), . . . [and] . . . [t]he represented, the present, as a *fact,* already belongs to the past prior to its representation" (Rr 31). And it is in this interplay that Bernasconi reads the interplay in Levinas of the languages of transcendental philosophy and empiricism:

> The empirical and the transcendental have their place in Levinas's *Totality and Infinity* in the discussion of the intentionality of enjoyment and of representation. Transcendental thought is under investigation with representation, just as concretization (corresponding to empiricism) is at issue in the theme of enjoyment. Levinas does not choose between them or attempt to reconcile them. They remain irreducible moments of the logically absurd structure of the *anterior posteriori* (TI 170 [144]). The a priori constitution of the object as performed by the idealist subject takes place only after the event, that is to say, a posteriori (TI 153 [126]). (Rr 31–32)

It is Bernasconi's further claim that this idea of "an absolute past not receiving its meaning from memory" that defines, in Part II of *Totality and Infinity,* enjoyment with respect to representation, "anticipates the notion of the trace" (Rr 29) that will come, after *Totality and Infinity* (but where this structure is already operative in the text that precedes this nomenclature), to define the transcendent with respect to the *cogito* that, even in its "constitution" of transcendence, is called into question by it. So knowing and doing and labor—the "economic" structures analyzed in Part II of *Totality and Infinity*—"imply the relation of transcendence" (are analogous to transcendence) insofar as in analyzing them Levinas "continues the transcendental enterprise behind the I" (Rr 32), the same enterprise that "reveals" the Other by calling the I into question, but are nevertheless differentiated from it.[42] Thus for Bernasconi:

> This is the sense in which the method Levinas adopts "resembles" the transcendental method, but is nevertheless to be differentiated from it. Indeed, representation and enjoyment do not only imply transcendence, they are analogous to transcendence. They are analogous to transcendence in the sense that they also exhibit the

> anterior posteriori of the relation of the infinite to the cogito. The double origin of the I and the element from which it lives is analogous to the double origin of the I and the radically exterior other. The blind spot in most discussions of Levinas, whether Levinas's account of the face-to-face is given a transcendental or an empirical status, is that they maintain the absolute priority of the face-to-face, something which Levinas's analyses constantly question. What is "analogous to transcendence" in the discussion of "Interiority and Economy" is the double origin. Just as representation and enjoyment are each found to presuppose each other, "the alleged scandal of alterity presupposes the tranquil identity of the same" (TI 203 [178]), while at the same time making it possible. (Rr 32)

So if the way to navigate between the two languages, the transcendental and the empirical, is attentiveness to this double origin—representation-element, ego-other—we can see why Bernasconi insists, first, that Levinas's method is only analogous to the transcendental method (which presupposes the constitutive priority of the ego), and, second, why he rejects de Boer's transcendentalism (which he reads as wrongly presupposing—while rightly rejecting the priority of the constituting ego—the priority of the other). That is, Bernasconi's first objection to de Boer seems to be that while de Boer reads Levinas as attempting to *invert* the transcendental method (to substitute the other as constitutive of the ego for the ego as constitutive of the other—as in traditional transcendental philosophy—but retaining the structure of transcendentalism), Bernasconi reads Levinas as, through his employment of both transcendental and empirical language while resisting their integration, attempting to *subvert* the transcendental method.

Indeed, on this reading, de Boer's is a strange sort of transcendentalism, a kind of reverse or inverted transcendentalism, one in which the priority of the *cogito* is rightly undermined ("De Boer is on more solid ground when he explains that by an ethical transcendental philosophy he does not mean 'a universal, impersonal, and necessary structure that can be reconstructed out of the phenomena,' in line with traditional transcendental philosophy (ETP 100)"; Rr 26), but replaced by another mere term in the relation, insofar as this reading is based on the priority of infinity, or on the priority of the relation of the terms over the terms in relation, and thus maintains "the absolute priority of the face-to-face, something which Levinas's analyses constantly call into question" (Rr 32). That is, according to Bernasconi, if de Boer is to maintain a transcendental reading of Levinas, even an inverted transcendentalism, he must do so at the expense of suppressing the equi-primordiality of the empirical language that Levinas also employs (and that corresponds to the other term of the relation), and he appears to be attempting to bolster his point by showing (against the possibility of a consistent transcendental reading) that the empirical (in the form of the ontic, to which de Boer appeals)[43] rears its head "at the heart of de Boer's attempt to sustain the transcendental reading" (Rr27).

And it is in the light of this emphasis on the "interval of separation," and thus of the priority of the terms in the relation over the relation itself (that which for him keeps the relation from devolving into a totality), that we can clarify Bernasconi's criticism of de Boer's attempt to base his transcendental reading on the Cartesian idea of infinity to the exclusion of the Cartesian *cogito:* "In his attempt to secure a transcendental reading of Levinas, de Boer rejects reference to the Cartesian *cogito* (ETP 85) in favor of the model afforded by the Cartesian infinite, so that the other 'functions as the transcendental condition of the same' (ETP 95)" (Rr 32). Bernasconi, on the contrary, claims that the *cogito* is necessary to the idea of infinity, such that de Boer's suppression of its equi-primordiality with the infinite "is to neglect the way in which Levinas had insisted in the first part of *Totality and Infinity* that the *cogito* and the infinite are both absolute starting points for Descartes" (Rr 32). If traditional transcendental philosophy in prioritizing the *cogito* suppresses infinity, de Boer's transcendentalism in prioritizing the infinite suppresses the *cogito.* But in neither case can the idea of infinity (on the structure of the anterior [infinity] posteriori [idea]) be sustained, in neither case can the "way of thinking which rests on neither" transcendental nor empirical language be pursued.

Bernaconi's third criticism of de Boer is that de Boer gets stuck on the horns of the ontic-ontological distinction (expressed in Bernaconi's hesitation—which we share—before de Boer's assertion that the transcendental condition, rather than being "a necessary ontological structure that can be reconstituted from the empirical phenomena . . . is rather an unrecoverable contingent or ontic incidence that intersects the logical order"; ETP 108). And it is by way of this criticism that Bernasconi hints at what this other "way of thinking"—that rests on neither transcendental nor empirical language, and that Bernasconi finds in Levinas—might be. These interrelated issues are perhaps best approached by following Bernasconi through his interpretation of a "difficult" (Rr 33) passage "near the end of *Totality and Infinity* in which Levinas attempts to clarify the way in which he understands the transcendental and the empirical or concrete in their interrelation" (Rr 32):

> Our work in all its developments strives to free itself from the conception that seeks to unite events of existence affected with opposite signs in an ambivalent condition which alone would have ontological dignity, while the events themselves proceeding in one direction [*sens*] or in another would remain empirical, articulating nothing ontologically new. The method practiced here does indeed consist in seeking the condition of empirical situations, but it leaves to the developments called empirical, in which the conditioning possibility is accomplished—it leaves to the *concretization*—an ontological role that specifies the meaning [*sens*] of the fundamental possibility, a meaning invisible in that condition (TI 173 [148). (Rr 32)

Bernasconi begins his interpretation of this passage by claiming that any reading that finds here—as Bernasconi finds in de Boer's reference to the transcendental condition as "a contingent or ontic incidence"—"the return of the problem of the ontological versus the ontic" (Rr 31), or the existential versus the existentiell, must be rejected insofar as Levinas sees in this distinction, as Bernasconi reminded us earlier in the paper, "an insidious form of the impersonal neuter." Rather, "Levinas in this passage doubts the efficacy of a procedure that remains viable only so long as the existential is kept safe from contamination by the existentiell" (Rr 33). But this does not mean, Bernasconi claims further, that the second sentence of the paragraph should be understood to say that "the meaning given to the formal structures by concretization equip them with an irreducible cultural specificity," or that Levinas is denying "the possibility of attaining a realm of meaning prior to or independent of culture and history" (Rr 33). Then, playing upon the double meaning of the French *sens* (meaning or direction), Bernasconi writes: "The passage is rather Levinas's acknowledgment that although his method is transcendental (at least by resemblance), the sense of the fundamental possibility it reveals is given concretely. It is given not as an injunction imposing a specific ethical act, but as specifying a direction [*sens*], the ethical direction, which neutralization would have eradicated" (Rr 33).

Thus the *sens* of *sens* as ethical direction is opposed to the transcendental "formalism" of Descartes, and it would seem at least by association to de Boer, even while Bernasconi recognizes that de Boer "properly" acknowledges that it is a charge of "formalism" that Levinas brings against Buber's "I-Thou" (Rr 33). So "Levinas's transcendentalism may formally resemble that of Descartes, but in the latter, formal structures hold sway. Descartes's procedure, in common with all transcendental philosophy hitherto, renders invisible the *sens* of the condition it reveals by withdrawing from the empirical or concrete" (Rr 33).

If, then, Levinas occasionally calls the face "abstract," he does so, Bernasconi claims, "only in the sense that it is a disturbance which breaks with cultural meaning and calls into question the horizons of the world," for it is also "the most concrete in that the face cannot be approached with empty hands but only from within society" (Rr 33). But this "concretization" cannot, Bernasconi claims—reiterating his earlier point—be read as along the lines of a transcendental condition or "ultimate ground" (either abstractly, or concretely, as in an empirical transcendental), because it must be held in differentiation from another "concretization":

> "No face can be approached with empty hands and a closed home," is Levinas's way of saying that the relation with the absolutely Other who paralyzes possession presupposes economic existence and the Other who welcomes me in the home (TI 172 [147]). Thus in a moment parallel to that found in the account of representation and enjoyment, Levinas reverses the movement by which it seemed that the face of the Other was being made an ultimate ground. Hence the intimacy of the home is the "first concretization" (TI 53 [126]). (Rr 34)

II.3. Ethical Transcendental Philosophy and Its Radix

II.3.i. There's Empiricism, and Then There's Empiricism We have here, then, two accounts of Levinas's philosophy by two of his most credible interpreters, one in which Levinas's philosophy is read as "an ethical transcendentalism," and another that maintains that a transcendental reading serves to obscure, if not annihilate, the ethical meaning (*sens,* direction) of this philosophy. It seems to us, moreover, that each of these accounts, intricate each in its own way, demonstrate a fidelity to both the word and spirit of Levinas, and a perceptiveness won from long and intense familiarity with his work. Is it a question of asking who is right and who is wrong, or even of asking whose account is most convincing, or most helpful? Attention to the first major section of this chapter suggests that perhaps this is not the first question to be asked—or at least we would first have to clarify what would be meant by helpful (insightful? pacific?). But Levinas's discourse, his discourse on discourse, is, we are arguing, philosophy and is (at least on one set of criteria) to be judged and accounted for according to the canons of philosophical discursivity. So let us see if (within this context, within the context of context: within the context of that which is *with*—in interrupting and inspiring—the philosophical *text*) some progress can be made in sorting out the problem that these diverse readings present on our way to arguing that, on our view, Levinas's philosophy is indeed well read as an ethical transcendentalism, even if we shall, in proposing this thesis, attempt to nuance the reading offered by de Boer, as we account for the objections raised by Bernasconi.

Our sense is that if we are to productively sort through the intricacies of these respective readings and engage them, and Levinas, at the level of their disagreement, we would do well to begin by attempting to make and sustain a distinction that, while important to Levinas, is nevertheless confusing owing to the seemingly inherent philosophical difficulties in languaging the terms to be discussed—and this confusion is apparent in the very naming of these terms insofar as it is a matter of distinguishing between "experience" and "experience." It is our contention that this homonym and the confusion surrounding it affects, if not the articles here under review themselves, then at least Bernasconi's reading of de Boer, such that attention to it should help us to clarify, and perhaps to some extent even mediate, the differences encountered in the two seemingly incommensurable readings being recommended by these commentators.

If it is true that this matter of experience and experience is, at least in part, at the root of the (perceived?) differences between de Boer and Bernasconi, it is true at the same time that neither of these commentators are ignorant of the problem. On the very first page of Bernasconi's article, for instance, he quotes (in the context of showing how, in *Totality and Infinity,* "the application of the word *experience* is put into question"; Rr 23) a key passage from Levinas: "The relation with infinity cannot, to be sure, be stated in terms of experience, for infinity overflows the thought that thinks it . . . but if experience precisely means a relation with the absolutely other, that is, with what always overflows thought, the relation with infinity accomplishes experience in the fullest sense of the word" (TI 25 [xiii]). And on the next page, in his own words, Bernasconi writes: "Levinas made it clear when he designated the face-to-face as an experience that this was possible only because the face of the Other ruptures what is ordinarily called experience" (Rr 24). So Bernasconi is aware of the difference in Levinas between what he (Bernasconi) calls here "ordinary experience" and what he translates, from "l'expérience par excellence," as "experience in the fullest sense of the word." (But does he, we shall ask, particularly in his reading of de Boer, remember it?)

While de Boer is less explicit in highlighting this distinction (he makes reference to "l'expérience par excellence," translated into English here as "experience preeminently," only in a footnote; ETP 115, n.85), he nevertheless employs it throughout his analyses, and, we would argue, more consistently than does Bernasconi. For, on the one hand, de Boer makes it clear that the face, which on his reading is the condition of possibility for experience in the ordinary sense, is not itself experienced, is "not a phenomenon": "The face of the other is not disclosed by a phenomenological unveiling (*dévoilement*), which would restore the all embracing comprehension of the same. It is disclosed by revelation (*révélation*). The condition for the possibility of experience is not experience itself" (ETP 105). Neither, on this reading, is

Levinas's "transcendental method" based on experience: "In the final analysis . . . this analysis is not based on experience or self-evidence but on tracing back from every intuition or reason to an ethical condition that cannot be thematized" (ETP 108).[44] And yet de Boer speaks, at other junctures, of the ethical relation to the other qua face explicitly as an experience: "This is an expression of the ethical experience that responsibility increases in the measure that it is assumed" (ETP 93). "The question is . . . whether one accepts the phenomenon—or better, the revelation—of absolute exteriority as an experience *sui generis*" (ETP 95). Indeed, de Boer's hesitation before the word "phenomenon" in describing the face, and his preference for "revelation," is instructive and important. For if the word "experience" is reserved for that which enters into correlation with a subject constituting meanings, even the meanings that it actively welcomes as a passive receptivity (and this is its normal sense in phenomenology and in Levinas), then the face is clearly not experienced; the very meaning of the face is its meaning as a refusal of the meanings I would constitute in its regard against its will. But how then can de Boer still speak of the encounter with the face as an experience? How can Levinas, who, indeed, often speaks of it in these terms, even as experience *par excellence,* as Bernasconi notes?

Yet, if de Boer is less explicit in articulating the distinction in Levinas between experience and experience (but, we are arguing, consistent in the way he employs the distinction throughout his analyses), he is most clear on that which founds it—and it is this which drives his argument: "As we try to achieve a correct understanding of Levinas's effort to express the relation to the other, we must bear in mind that the terms are to be taken in an ethical sense" (ETP 93).[45] We have already gone to some pains in this work to stress this point ourselves, to show that the relationship with the other, or discourse, is in no way founded or qualified by a prior ontological reality, but is itself the foundation of, or that which qualifies, ontological reality, that which de Boer claims in writing: "The alterity of the other cannot be absorbed into my identity; it is an absolute alterity, an alterity that calls my freedom into question" (ETP 93). It would therefore be incorrect to accede to a simplistic empirical reading of Levinas where the face would be an object of "ordinary experience," and neither of our commentators do so. For if the face of the other is taken to mean this calling into question, and this is Levinas's sense, then the ethical "experience" is a calling into question of my very experience of being a free ego constituting meanings, is an "experience" of the calling into question of my experience—to the point that the "experience" of the calling into question of my experience could not properly be conceived of as an experience (in the ordinary sense) of experience being called into question, for here my experience of this challenge to experience would reassert experience as the final arbiter of the meaning of its being called into question. Ethical experience—or experience *par excellence*—cannot be an experience of the ethical. And that is why we followed Levinas closely earlier in analyzing how the ethical experience with respect to ordinary experience evinces a change in modality. As not the experience of the ethical, but the ethical calling into question of experience, experience par excellence indicates that moment when experience is set back on its heals, is thrown off balance, off course, is decentered, disoriented, is made unsure of itself, before experience has a chance, or the time, to fall back onto its feet, to recenter and assimilate this challenge (in betraying it) into its own experience of being called into question, this anarchy into its *arché*, which the ego always does in time (literally, across time), and which is, nevertheless, necessary to justice, as is, as we have seen, the ethical moment itself.

To still call this being called into question, this calling of experience into question, "experience" is to acknowledge that this does happen to me, that I really am, in my life in the "real world," confronted by the face of the other, the flesh and blood other who asks for the dollar with which I had intended to buy myself a coffee, who desires the time I had set aside to read, who requires the seat that I occupy on the streetcar. But to qualify this experience as an *ethical* experience—that which distinguishes it from ordinary experience and transports us into another modality (which is not to say another modality of experience if ordinary experience is permitted to dominate what counts as experience)—is to recognize in it the jolt to ordinary experience that is this call to responsibility, before the responsible me has time to withdraw into the I of freedom with its capacities for measure, for decision, for commitment (which is to say before the responsible one has time), before reflection, self-consciousness—or consciousness *tout court*—has time to regain its feet and bring its own meanings to bear upon this meaning that is, from the perspective of consciousness constituting meanings, nothing but the meaning of the interruption of all meaning. Ethical experience is a conversion—a turning of the ego from its course as *une force qui va,* an over-turning of ontological sense (and the ontical sense that is its correlate), and a turning-over (or a having already been turned over) of the ego to the other, a turning of the ego into a self, stripping it—momentarily—of its self(ish)ness qua ego, but, as we have seen, thereby calling it to its "self."

But immediately, in the same moment (for, recall, the moment is the interruption of the continuing continuity of time, the intersection of time and eternity qua recurrence)—consciousness! The presence, in the very face of the other, of the other of the other, the interruption of interruption, and thus distance, and measure, reflection, and thus not only the ethical experience but the experience of the ethical, and the putting into play of ethical principles as a response to the an-*arché* of the ethical. Immediately, in the same moment, there is a conversion of conversion, a turning back to consciousness, for the sake of justice, but a justice that would never be just were consciousness never interrupted by the ethical experience that inspires and animates it, and thus never just so long as the ethical is not betrayed/maintained in consciousness, that is, so long as it is not at once the ethical experience *and* the experience of the ethical. Two of de Boer's (in form, Kantian) formulations reflect this duality of "experience," the simultaneous implication of these two senses[46] of experience in Levinas's thought: "It is true that charity without social justice is void, but social justice without this dimension of goodness and hospitality may be blind" (ETP 103). "Ontology without metaphysics is blind; metaphysics without ontology is void" (ETP 110).

Thus, when Bernasconi objects to de Boer's characterization of Levinas's philosophy as an ethical transcendentalism, which he seems to equate with an empirical transcendentalism—on the grounds that this is to import the empirical back into transcendentalism (into its very heart), an empiricism that degrades the transcendental qua transcendental and can thus only reflect a play of two methodological languages, neither of which can be sustained as predominant, and thus reflect a beyond of both—we wonder whether he has taken the distinction (with which de Boer operates, and that Bernasconi himself recognizes in Levinas) between experience and experience seriously enough. For the experience at the heart of de Boer's reading of Levinas's philosophy as an ethical transcendentalism is not ordinary experience, but ethical experience, the "experience" of experience in question, where even the experience of experience in question is in question. So when Bernasconi wonders (Rr 27) how de Boer is able to maintain at once that "the transcendental condition is an ethical experience enacted in discourse" (ETP 97) and that "the condition for the possibility of experience is not experience itself" (ETP 105), we would respond (for our part, and, we believe, on de Boer's behalf) that the experience that conditions experience and the experience so conditioned are not the same experience. So the experience ("an empirical moment") "at the heart of de Boer's attempt to sustain the transcendental reading" of Levinas's philosophy is not ordinary experience but ethical experience, is not an ordinary empirical moment but "an ethical empirical"—the naked *ethical* "fact" of responsibility "before" (as cutting across and through) ontic-ontological factuality and the empiricism of objects. Thus de Boer does not, *contra* Bernasconi's reading of him, "hold back from the conclusion" to which his interpretation would appear to lead (i.e., that the empirical is at the heart of his transcendental reading), nor is it true that de Boer "having at one point hinted at the conjunction of the transcendental and empirical readings, leaves their interrelation unclear" (Rr 27). The ordinary empirical is not at the heart of de Boer's transcendental reading (at least not in the sense that Bernasconi supposes), and there is no hint of a conjunction in de Boer between the ordinary empirical and transcendental readings of Levinas. For de Boer, the ethical experience is consistently read as the condition for ordinary experience. That is, the conjunction that de Boer *does* hint at (and we would say more than hints at, as we in our subsequent analyses hope to show) is that between the ethical empirical and the transcendental, where, indeed, the ethical experience *functions* as a transcendental for Levinas, but this is *not* to reintroduce an empirical reading into the heart of things, at least not insofar as the empirical is understood in the conventional way.

But before pursuing that relationship (which will be our task in the next section), it must be confessed that de Boer is not without some fault in encouraging what we are taking to be Bernasconi's misunderstanding of him. For while Bernasconi can concede in analyzing de Boer's attempt at a transcendental reading (to the extent he can go along with this language) that de Boer is "on more solid ground" when he (de Boer) explains that "[t]he transcendental condition is not a necessary ontological structure that can be reconstructed from the empirical phenomena" (ETP 108)—or as he also put it earlier in his article, is not "a universal, impersonal, and necessary structure, which can be reconstructed out of the phenomena" (ETP 100)—he hesitates before de Boer's positive description of what this transcendental condition is: "It is rather an unrecoverable contingent or ontic incidence that intersects the ontological order" (ETP 108). Bernasconi, we believe, overstates his case here when he over- (and we believe mis-) reads de Boer in putting his hesitation thus: "But can the face *as the object of transcendental cognition* be designated 'an unrecoverable . . .'?" (Rr 26, our emphasis). De Boer does not (either here, or elsewhere as far as our search was able to determine) refer to the face as an "object of transcendental cognition." The ethical experience, on our reading—and we believe on de Boer's—is precisely that which calls into question cognition, transcendental or otherwise, and is thus in no sense its "object." But overcoming this misunderstanding (which we believe reflects Bernasconi's insensitivity to the distinction between experience and experience in de Boer, and perhaps in Levinas—despite his initial acknowledgment of it) does not negate Bernasconi's other (and on our view more substantial) hesitation before this positive description, insofar as "Levinas had always sought to distance himself from Heidegger's determination of the ontological difference . . . [as] . . . 'an insidious form of the impersonal neuter' " such that "[t]heir reintroduction here is therefore problematic" (Rr 26–27). But are they really reintroduced here? On the surface of things, certainly. And even if we are to go beyond the surface, which we believe the rest of de Boer's article demands, we can still sympathize with Bernasconi in recognizing in de Boer's formulation an unfortunate, and perhaps imprudent, choice of words.[47] But given the distinction—operative in de Boer's article, as it is operative in Levinas—between experience and experience, between the empirical and the empirical, are we not permitted to perceive here a correlative distinction (albeit one that, as far as we can make out, Levinas does not invoke—and thus our charge of possible imprudence) between the ontic and the ontic, between the ontic as the correlate of ontological categories and the ontic as "an ethical ontic"—an "ethical" empirical, "ethical" ontic experience that cuts across the ordinary empirical, the ordinary ontic, as it cuts across ordinary experience. And lest this reading be taken as overly generous to de Boer on our behalf, let us note that, with reference to this "dimension," de Boer, in his very next sentence, quotes Levinas in asserting that it is "more ontological than ontology, more *sublime* than ontology." And if this dimension that "intersects the ontological order" can be described as more ontological than ontology, is it really so very unlikely that it might also be legitimately described as being more ontic than the ontical (insofar as the ontic would be read as the experiential correlate of the ontological)—where this *more* indicates, as it clearly does for de Boer elsewhere,[48] not a quantitative augmentation, but a qualitative change, a change in modality. That is, if we read "ontic" here in the same manner that we read "experience" and "empirical" in the rest of the article, its employment in this formulation, while perhaps initially prone to misunderstanding (as are—to be fair to de Boer—the employment of the terms experience and empirical in Levinas's work itself), need not indicate recourse to the ontic-ontological distinction, and need not ultimately trouble us.

II.3.ii. There's Transcendentalism, and Then There's Transcendentalism If carefully maintaining the distinction between experience and experience helps us to read de Boer's account as other than an invocation of the ontological distinction that Bernasconi rightly reads Levinas as rejecting, but that he wrongly, we believe, attributes to de Boer, the maintenance of the distinction also helps us to answer, on de Boer's behalf but also on our own, Bernasconi's other criticisms of a transcendental reading of Levinas, namely, (1) his insistence that Levinas's philosophy only resembles a transcendental philosophy (over against Bernasconi's reading of de Boer that would seem to take the latter as attempting to maintain a reading of Levinas's thought as a true transcendental philosophy—or at least a reading that could still legitimately be called "transcendental"), and (2) his concern that reading Levinas as a transcendental philosopher where this transcendentalism is based on the idea of infinity overlooks the necessarily correlative idea of the finite (a criticism that we earlier reformulated as a concern that de Boer's transcendental reading inverts—in giving priority to the face of the other rather than to the ego, as in traditional transcendental philosophy—but does not subvert—as Bernasconi claims is Levinas's intent—the transcendental method) that, according to Bernasconi, finds expression in Levinas's "dual origin" of the ego and the other, that which makes it impossible to maintain the face-to-face as an absolute priority.

But if we maintain the distinction between experience and experience, it seems to us that de Boer's reading is indeed more radical (following Levinas to "the radix, or root, of his thought"; ETP 83, 107) with respect to transcendental philosophy than Bernasconi supposes. For the face of the other, as experience par excellence, does not simply function *within* a transcendental framework on this reading, even as its privileged term, but calls into question the transcendental method itself, as it does all of the products of consciousness, and consciousness too, and it can only do so insofar as this experience of the face, experience par excellence, is not read as an object of transcendental cognition, but as a radical *undermining* of transcendental cognition by calling it into ethical question (and consequently, as we shall see, as a radical *underwriting* of transcendental cognition as a response to this ethical call).

That is to say that under the *anarché* of the change in modality that the face of the other brings to transcendental consciousness—a change in modality that is a genuine subversion of transcendental consciousness—transcendental philosophy in Levinas, on de Boer's reading, does not undergo a simple inversion (where the terms would be read from right to left rather than from left to right as in a mirror image that would retain the formal qualities of its inverse, for example),[49] but a radical inversion (where the terms in relation would be read differently, as if seen from the inside out rather than from the outside in, for example),[50] an *ethical* conversion that with respect to conventional transcendental philosophy is a genuine subversion indeed. So if experience in Levinas's sense of experience par excellence, *ethical* experience, indicates in Levinas an empiricism that cannot be read as an empiricism in the ordinary sense, the *ethical* transcendental in de Boer's reading cannot be read as a transcendentalism in the ordinary sense, cannot be read as a transcendentalism that begins in intuition, but, as Levinas has confirmed, as "a transcendentalism that begins with ethics." Bernasconi is right, then, to argue that Levinas is dissatisfied with both the philosophical discourses of empiricism and transcendentalism, but in claiming that Levinas employs both in order, by way of the "displacement of their disjunction," "to introduce us to a way of thinking which rests on neither" (Rr 34), and to radicalize philosophy thereby by indicating the ethical *sens* therein implied, he misses the fact that these terms have already themselves been radicalized by Levinas. Levinas does not only employ the languages of empirical and transcendental philosophy to subsequently subvert them; his references to experience par excellence and to an ethical transcendental (or in *Totality and Infinity* his employment of transcendental language with respect to ethics)[51] are already a subversion of them, their *radical* inversion.[52]

And this is why (*contra* Bernasconi's claim that Levinas's philosophy cannot be rightly qualified as transcendental) de Boer exercises some caution here in not saying that the face *is* a transcendental (which would be too readily equated with a transcendental in the traditional sense), but in claiming that the face *functions* as a transcendental, even if he goes on to designate Levinas's thought as an ethical transcendentalism. Indeed, as we have noted in reviewing de Boer's article, what Levinas shares with transcendental phenomenology is the practice of working back from phenomena to that which conditions them—that which justifies the qualification of Levinas's thought as transcendental. But his thought is distinguished from traditional transcendental phenomenology in asserting that these conditions are not available to consciousness or to intuition, but are "revealed" across the interruption of consciousness in calling consciousness and its intuition into ethical question (as opposed to the degradation of consciousness for the phenomenological existentialists who find the ego embedded in a horizon, and thus in epistemological, but not in ethical, question)—that which justifies the qualification of Levinas's transcendentalism as an ethical or radicalized transcendentalism. That is, Levinas's transcendentalism on our reading of it, a reading that traverses de Boer's reading, needs be read as a radicalized transcendentalism insofar as the conditions for experience transcend experience in a double sense. In the first place, the condition cannot enter into experience, cannot be "met" by experience and thus be conceived of as an ontological condition of an ontic experience, insofar as in ethical "experience" the condition qua ethical recedes infinitely from the subject who would attempt to meet it insofar as, as de Boer notes, the responsibility for which I am responsible increases to the degree that I am responsible, the debt accrues to the degree it is acquitted (that which Levinas refers to as the infinition of responsibility), which is the flip side, as it were, of the ego being called, and incessantly, into ethical question. In the second place, the condition cannot be "met" by experience insofar as concurrent with the "ethical presentation" of the face—and structurally, not only empirically—is another face, the other of the other *also* incessantly calling for my obsessive responsibility. I cannot "meet" my responsibility (to the singular other) without failing to "meet" my responsibility (to the other others). It is, moreover, impossible to speculate as to whether, were I faced with a singular other alone, I would be able to meet that responsibility or whether the infinition of responsibility would apply in that case too, since for Levinas there is no such situation, even at the level of the prestructural structure of the face. What counts here is that the ethical qua condition of possibility cannot be ethically, let alone ontologically, concretized, and thus cannot enter into experience even as it evokes experience (necessary to mediating between the diverse responsibilities contained in the evocation). That is, I do not experience myself as being absolutely responsible to the other, but always already as responsible to all the others and to myself, even though this experience has as its condition of possibility my absolute responsibility to the singular other. And this is, moreover, no matter of my finitude (such that were I to have infinite resources I would be able to meet the demand), but a matter of the demand being ethical—more and more stringent in relation to my responsibility, the infinition of responsibility in relation to which finitude is finite.

When de Boer (and we after him) describes Levinas's philosophy as an ethical transcendentalism, it is to this radicalized sense of transcendental that the designation refers, to a condition that while clearly not a transcendental in the traditional sense (that can be traced back from experience across intuition to an intuition of the condition), nevertheless functions as a transcendental in conditioning experience: simultaneously conditioning and interrupting experience across the subversive radicality of an infinitely accruing ethical call. On this reading, Levinas's transcendentalism only *resembles* (as Bernasconi quotes Levinas as himself maintaining) the transcendental method if traditional transcendentalism is what is meant, but is legitimately called a transcendental philosophy if this transcendentalism is read as already radicalized, already ethical: "a transcendentalism that starts with ethics."

This situation, wherein the face functions as a transcendental without being a transcendental in the traditional sense, can be clarified in yet another way when we recognize that for Levinas—at least on the reading we are advocating—the empirical *is* (before ontology) the transcendental. In distinction from a traditional scheme whereby the condition (the ontological structure) conditions the conditioned (the ontic structure), on Levinas's radicalized transcendentalism it is the empirical in the sense of experience par excellence that is the "transcendental" condition for experience in the ordinary sense. What needs to be distinguished here, then, is not empirical reality and the abstract categories that structure it thus and so, but experience in the ordinary sense and the experience par excellence that calls for it. Here ethical experience does not structure ordinary experience, but ordinary experience is structured in response to ethical experience. And seeing things in this way helps us to respond (in part, at least, on de Boer's behalf too) to two of Bernasconi's concerns related to the description of Levinas's philosophy as transcendental: first, that Levinas himself claims that his philosophy is not a search for foundations; and, second, that Levinas does not attempt to reconcile transcendental and empirical language, but to push beyond a dependence on either, which—concretely—issues in Bernasconi's explicit rejection of the description of this thought as an "empirical transcendentalism."

So when Bernasconi claims that "in the same place that Levinas gives his positive answer to de Boer's question about an ethical transcendentalism, he questions its association with the search for foundations" and wonders in the light of this "what is to be made of his claim that the face-to-face is the foundation of ethics?" (Rr 24), we would answer that that which provides the condition for ethics (and for everything else that *is*), the ethical relationship with the face, is precisely not a foundation even as it "founds" the possibility of ethics, even if it founds the possibility of possibility. Ethics, though it founds ontology, is not foundational in any traditional sense—in any sense that is sure. The encounter with the face, as that which founds ontology, is not a new ontological *arché,* but—as we have seen—anarchic: withdrawing incessantly as the subject, as the one subject to its demand, approaches. Not a sure foundation, but a sinking sand, on the anarchic ground of ethics ontology (culture, morality, values, truths) must be perpetually rebuilt.[53] Ethics is an/archic—a grounding that is not a ground.

And when Bernasconi rejects the nomenclature of "transcendental empiricism"[54] with respect to Levinas (for recall, on his view, "Levinas is using the language of transcendental philosophy and the language of empiricism not in order to draw them together into a transcendental empiricism, but in an effort to find a way between these twin options"; Rr 34), he makes this rejection on the premise that Levinas is employing the languages of empiricism and transcendentalism in their conventional sense. But if the terms transcendental and empirical are taken in the radicalized sense that we are arguing Levinas gives to them, if it is recognized that the empirical in the sense of experience par excellence is the transcendental, that is, the ethical transcendental, then the descriptive phrase "empirical transcendentalism" is as *à propos* to Levinas's thought as is its synonym "ethical transcendentalism."

That is, Bernasconi rightly opposes both an empirical and a transcendental reading of Levinas insofar as these terms are taken in the conventional sense. What he fails to perceive (and that which causes him, on our view, to take issue with de Boer), and that de Boer does perceive, is that these terms have already undergone a transformation in Levinas's discourse, an ethical transformation. So to make an appeal to the experience par excellence of the face is no longer to make a claim for the positivity that founds an ordinary empiricism, but to recognize an ethical positivity (or what Richard Cohen calls an "ultrapositivity")[55] that founds an ethical empiricism. The conditioning performed by the ethical transcendental in Levinas does not found experience in the traditional sense of a transcendental (as a form or category for experience—the ontological structures for the ontic), but calls forth experience as always already ethical responsibility to the other in terms of which ontological and ontic structures—in correlation—can be meaningful. The "ethical" of Levinas's ethical transcendentalism does not merely qualify transcendentalism as the specification of a type (despite de Boer's question: "To which type of transcendental philosophy does the philosophy of Levinas correspond?" (ETP 104)), but transforms it.

II.3.iii. There's Ethical Transcendentalism, and Then There's Ethical Transcendentalism Still, we have yet to respond, from the position of an ethical transcendental reading of Levinas, to Bernasconi's charge that the idea of infinity, upon which de Boer bases his transcendental reading, cannot be maintained without the correlative idea of the finite. Bernasconi claims that Levinas himself makes no such attempt, but rather, across the "interval of separation," shows how the "dual origin" of same and other is necessary to the relation as ethical. Bernasconi's model for this relation is, as we have seen, the structure of the "anterior posteriori"—a structure that, we will recall, applies both to the ego-object/element and same-other relations, that which makes the "relation" of enjoyment analogous to the relation to transcendence. The insistence that the dual origin of the same and the other is necessary to the infinitude of the ethical relation and thus to Infinity (is, in effect, its condition of possibility) makes the premise that the other as infinite is the condition of possibility of the same impossible, that is, logically so. And on this hook Bernasconi hangs his subsequent claim that the face-to-face, against most readings of Levinas (including de Boer's), is not to be accorded absolute priority (Rr32).

Is this but another way of saying that the terms of the relation precede, at least in a certain sense, the relation itself? If not, it at least means that the terms in the relation as separated from the relation are equi-primordial with the relation of which they are the terms. And even if the latter scenario, this requires that the terms be capable of establishing themselves as being in and of themselves independent of any relation in which they might—either subsequently or simultaneously—find themselves, and it is this that for Bernasconi ensures that the ethical relation is a relation governed by neither dialectical logic nor the logic of noncontradiction—but is a "relation without relation," a relation across the "interval of separation" of separated terms. Bernasconi, as we have seen, argues for this original separation—that which justifies his reference to the "dual origin"—on the basis of Levinas's own description of the egoism in enjoyment in part 2 of *Totality and Infinity,* wherein Levinas does indeed describe the ego as separated in its enjoyment—as "setting itself up all by itself"—to the point of atheism, that is, to the point that the separated being exists as separate even from its creator. And if the thesis of the dual origin is to hold, a parallel but noncorrelative "existing as separation" would logically have to apply (even if this separation could not be described except across the relation—for from what other perspective could it be described?) for the other. And if this separation, that is, the terms as nondialectically separated the one from the other, is in a certain sense "first," or even "equiprimordial" with the ethical relation as constituent of or necessary to the relation as a relation between separated terms, then—we have already said it—the relation cannot be the condition of possibility of the separated same. And, indeed, Levinas would seem to straightforwardly confirm this reading when he writes, for example: "The idea of Infinity implies [*suppose*] the separation of the same with regard to the other" (TI 53 [23]).

But is there not already an ambiguity here? For the separation that the idea of Infinity implies (in the sense of "presupposes") is a separation *by relation to the other.* That is, is not separation here, rather than being the description of the "manner of being" of an entity where its being separate would be able to be described in abstraction from that which it is separated, not rather—as the word separation would seem to imply—separation from . . . ? Indeed, later in the same paragraph—a paragraph in which Levinas is about explaining why separation cannot be a matter of opposition or antithesis or correlation between the same and the other, for such a separation would be subject to the encompassing embrace of a totality and thus not constitute a real separation—we read:

> An absolute transcendence has to be produced as non-integratable. If separation then is necessitated by the production of Infinity overflowing its idea [Si donc la séparation est nécessitée par la production de l'Infini . . .] and therefore separated from the I inhabited by this idea (the preeminently inadequate idea), this separation must be accomplished in the I in a way that would not only be correlative and reciprocal to the transcendence in which the infinite maintains itself with respect to its idea in me, it must not only be the logical rejoinder of that transcendence; the separation of the I with regard to the other must result from a positive movement. (TI 53 [24])

Marking these words carefully we note that "separation is necessitated by the production of the Infinite overflowing its idea . . ." *Nécessitée par,* not *nécessitée pour:* it would seem, here at least, that separation is not so much the prerequisite for the idea of the Infinite, its *prior* condition of possibility, but itself a (necessary) production of the relation here named "the idea of the Infinite." And this reading whereby the separated same is not first with respect to, or even contemporaneous with, but rather setting itself up *as separate from* the other to which it relates, and where its very separation is a function of (necessitated by) the relation in which it is always already implicated (*before* it separates), is seemingly confirmed when Levinas goes on, in the next paragraph, to describe the "positive movement" from which separation results: "A separation of the I that is not the reciprocal of the transcendence of the other with regard to me is not an eventuality thought of only by quintessential abstractors. It imposes itself upon meditation in the name of a concrete moral experience: what I have the right to demand of myself is not comparable with what I have the right to demand of the other" (TI 53 [24]). Separation here is not, it seems, a prior state of affairs, a state of affairs that would make a subsequent relation as ethical possible, but a function of, or a response to, a "concrete moral experience." That is, separation is ethical, is itself demanded by the ethical relation, is a function of the ethical relation, and therefore (even qua separated) relational—whatever other structures it will subsequently, or simultaneously, become involved in as it concretely accomplishes this separation. And does not Levinas describe the separated ego, not as "separation and, then, separation in relation," but as "separation in relation"?

So, is the relation first, and separation a function of this relation, or is the ethical relation only the way a prior nonrelational separation "imposes itself upon meditation"? And if the ethical relation is first, who exactly enters into this relation, and would be capable of entering into it ethically except a previously separated being? And so a dilemma, or at least a semblance of a dilemma: in order to enter into the ethical relation qua ethical my prior separation from the relation is required—and thus the setting up of the ego for itself all by itself (as Levinas describes in section II of *Totality and Infinity* in the structure of enjoyment); and, at the same time, in order to separate I need to have been in a relationship from out of which separation as separation from . . . is conceivable (that which Levinas describes as an ethical relationship). Do we find ourselves here, then, asking after the "which comes first" of philosophical chickens and eggs? This dilemma, or at least apparent dilemma, can be addressed in at least two ways.

The first interpretative possibility would be to see the original separation, that which would make the entering into the ethical relationship qua ethical possible, as being not an ethical separation but a *kind* of ontological one, or, more precisely, a kind of pre-ontological or ontic or empirical (in the ordinary as opposed to "ethical" sense of these terms) separation articulated by Levinas in the pre-ontological enjoyment of the independent ego, wherein the terms are what they are prior to, or at least contemporaneous with, their being in relation, which are then "changed" or called to their true selves as they enter into a subsequent or contemporaneous relation with the other. On such a view, the concrete moral experience invoked above would not be the context or horizon or meaning of separation, but merely that relation by which separation "imposes itself upon meditation." And the "positive movement" that makes separation possible as other than a "logical rejoinder" would not, at root, be the ethical encounter but enjoyment qua enjoyment, from the first, qua enjoyment, independent of the other. That is, here there would be a being that would either precede or at least exist independently of any ethical relationships into which it might (or even might be forced later to) enter. And if in holding to this interpretation we would be able to be consistent with Levinas's claim that ethics precedes ontology, we would nevertheless have to be claiming that ethics does not precede the ontic. For here ethics is not, could not be (for the possibility of ethics would presuppose it), the depth structure of the *ontos,* but a meaning (or a *logos*) imposed upon a previously, or at least simultaneously, meaningless or neuter *ontos.* Here ethics could indeed be conceived of as the meaning of being, its *sens,* but being as *ontos* (prior to its logicization in ontology) is either prior to, or least contemporaneous with but apart from, ethics. That is, there is here a being, or a "manner of being," genuinely independent of ethics, and if not prior to it then at least contemporaneous with it. This reading would thus suggest that the movement goes from a pre-ontological ontic (as the realm of enjoyment) to the (subsequent or simultaneous) ethical encounter with the other (as a refusal of becoming a function of my enjoyment) producing its infinitude, to ontology (as the realm of the negotiation of spaces and objects between these previously entirely independent beings now in ethical relationship). That is, this reading solves the philosophical chicken and egg problem by arguing—in terms of the dual origin of the same and the other—that the ontic egg (one given, or origin) is sat upon by the ethical chicken (another origin, given with the givenness of another egg) hatching ontology.

That this is Bernasconi's reading, or at least the reading in terms of which he criticizes de Boer as founding a transcendental reading on the idea of infinity, should not surprise us, as his stress on the dual origin of the same and the other is central to his argument. We, at least, are then surprised that, at least at a certain level, this becomes de Boer's reading too. For in the penultimate paragraph of his article we read: "Becoming oneself by means of the other represents an investiture. What happens in the confrontation is there is a transformation from egoism to being-for-the-other, to goodness and hospitality. I am not 'constituted' by the other, for in my joyous existence I was already an independent being; rather, I am judged by the other and called to a new existence" (ETP 110).

But do not at least two problems remain for this reading? For, in the first place, why—not to mention *how*—would I, as a separated being, enjoying myself all by myself, enter into a relation with an other? And even if, as de Boer claims (in the sentence that follows those just quoted), "[t]he encounter with the other does not mean the limitation of my freedom but an awakening to responsibility," these questions are not answered. For on this view, I am not responsible for the other, I become responsible for the other. But would I not have to have been already responsible to be awakened to my responsibility, to be inspired to be (more and more) responsible?

The second problem is that such a reading reintroduces, albeit at a deeper level, the "impersonal neuter" that Bernasconi rightly reminds us was rejected by Levinas, which was Levinas's reason for rejecting the ontological distinction in Heidegger as *the* philosophical question, and one of Bernasconi's chief reasons for rejecting de Boer's transcendental reading when he [Bernasconi] believed to have found its "insidious form" being reintroduced there. Indeed, if enjoyment can be designated as an ontic structure (and Levinas does refer to it as a "manner of being"), and if the ontic in Levinas (qua experience and not experience par excellence) always correlates to the ontological, is not its reintroduction in this reading not precisely a different but still "insidious form of the impersonal neuter," and another way of invoking the ontological difference (although here it is my original manner of being that is ethically neutral and not Being)? De Boer, in showing how Levinas sides—on Theunissen's terms—with the dialogical school (at least in certain respects) over against the phenomenologists, puts the question we are here trying to raise here like this: "Is man primarily present to himself (*pour soi*) and secondarily directed towards the other (mediated by the world), or is he face to face with the other from the very beginning (in conversation, hospitality, and desire) and only in the second place (by abstraction) a self-consciousness?" (ETP 92). De Boer's whole argument is that Levinas answers affirmatively to the second formulation. But in claiming near the end of his article that the other does not "constitute" the same, "for in my joyous existence I was already an independent being," that "there is a transformation from egoism to being-for-the-other," does he really follow Levinas in his answer to this question all the way to the end, or does he back off and admit of an original *pour soi* after all? That is, does de Boer follow the "metaphysical depth dimension" of being that he finds in Levinas, and that permits him to read Levinas as an ethical transcendental philosopher, all the way down—that is, does he follow it down far enough?

The second interpretative option here (and the one we are advocating) would be to see separation not as an ontic or empirical separation that precedes or is at least contemporaneous with the ethical relation into which it enters, subsequently or simultaneously, but as itself a function of the ethical relation, such that the meaning of being is not imposed upon a neutral manner of being, either subsequently or simultaneously, from the outside, but infuses being always already with a meaning that is already ethical. On this reading, the separation of the ego is not an a priori ontic event accomplished by the ego outside of the ethical relation, but is precisely an *ethical* separation, accomplished *within* the ethical relation to the other. Here the separated being does not have an existence of its own independent of ethics, ethics supplies the meaning of separated existence qua separated.

Now, some caution must be exercised here, for we are in no sense denying the radicality—to the point of atheism—of the ego in separation, nor are we asserting that the descriptions of the ego in its independence of enjoyment that both de Boer and Bernasconi follow out in Levinas are not serious or are not (as far as they go, and from a certain perspective) entirely valid. What we are arguing is that the separation of the ego is not a "bare fact," is not a given without context, without—from another (and deeper) perspective—*une raison (d'être) separée, une raison éthique!* That is, on this (our) reading, the separation of the separated ego plays a role in ethics. The ego is "created" as separated—or as capable of separation—so that it may relate ethically to the other. Its atheism is not in the first instance an arbitrary *is* (be this before the *logos* of ontology has taken hold), but is, in the words of *Totality and Infinity, for* the greater glory of the creator (whose glory, as we saw earlier in this chapter in the analyses of *Otherwise Than*

Being, is in the responsibility that I have or even "am" for the other). I am created for the other, created to be goodness for the other. But for this goodness to be truly good (and not, as we have seen, the "goodness" of a mere functionary in a totalizing if divine economy), the ego's separation must be "real," must be a genuine separation—to the point that the creature, losing itself in its egoistic enjoyment (lived always already through the economic world as an extension of its enjoyment), can refuse, or "forget," that for which it was created, to the point that in its independence—while necessary to its goodness—it can isolate itself from the other for whose sake it exists as separated. But not without fault. Levinas calls this *le prix* (the price, the worth) of separation. Separation, and separation specifically as enjoyment, serves an ethical purpose, and is accomplished across this meaning (even if the accomplishment can turn against its purpose), for "only a being that eats can be for-the-other, or signify" (OTB 74 [93]).

Indeed, far from being ethically neutral and a priori, on Levinas's descriptions, as we have seen, the enjoying ego is disturbed from the start (and from within) with a "care for the morrow"; there is always already an other in the same even at the basest level of enjoyment. But at the same time, as contemporaneous with this disturbance, there is the feminine other who welcomes me into a home as a protection against the care for the morrow, investing my freedom by her graciousness to me (welcoming me into the world and society by making for me a home in it while not, in the modality of the feminine, calling this "place in the sun" that she makes for me, into which she has born(e) me and continues to bear me, into question)—even while the other qua alterity is already there, disturbing my enjoyment by calling it into question, as the mendicant standing on the stoop "calling me out" of my home, and out of myself. The other both qua gracious, feminine other investing my being in enjoyment and qua alterity disturbing my enjoyment in calling forth my graciousness in his regard are there from the start (before my start, for the one bears me into the world and the other has already accused me when I arrive) and are constituent of the ego even in enjoyment.

Thus the ego even at the level of enjoyment is already implicated in an ethical intrigue that transcends it, and that gives ethical meaning to its separation. We are describing this intrigue as the religio-familial intrigue that across the dis/continuity of generations goes from grace to grace, but the responsibility for which falls upon me alone—upon me who neither began nor chose this intrigue. Separation is not a *sui generis* structure any more than is the ego who separates (that is, who as "will" is "a being *conditioned* in such a way that without being *causa sui* it is first with respect to its cause"; TI 59 [30], our emphasis), but is built into this intrigue in that it is transacted from generation to generation—as is the binding (the *religare*) of ethics. The son both is and is not the father. The dis/continuity of this passage from generation to generation—and the capacity for ethical separation opened up across this discontinuity—is nevertheless inspired by an ethical *continuity;* separation has its meaning as a separation across which the binding binds.

It is, on our reading, this religio-familial intrigue that is for Levinas the ultimate horizon, or meaning, of experience, that articulates my ethical relation to the other as the condition of possibility of ordinary experience. So in response to Bernasconi's objection that the relation to the face cannot be the transcendental condition of the same because Levinas insists upon the "dual origin" of the same and the other, we have attempted to follow Levinas in tracing out the *pre*-origin of this dual origin, the pre-originary font from which the terms of the ethical relationship, the same and the other, flow as already implicated in this intrigue. So while Bernasconi expresses concern that most commentators have overlooked the importance of section II of *Totality and Infinity,* "Interiority and Economy" (which causes them to miss, claims Bernasconi, the dual origin of the terms in the face-to-face relation), our concern is that Bernasconi overlooks section IV of *Totality and Infinity* that delineates the structures that go "Beyond the Face." That is, on Bernasconi's reading, section II, with its delineation of the structure of the "anterior posteriori," seems to operate as foundational for his reading of the whole work—and the relation to the face is thus read as analogous to the relation of the ego to the element, implicated also in a "dual origin."[56] While Bernasconi's observations are not without considerable merit, on our reading the descriptions of the same as separated are not foundational to an understanding of the rest of the book, but are a piece of the puzzle that is *Totality and Infinity,* and a piece that when taken as a first piece or as an opening and founding gambit obstructs our capacity to see it as an important, no doubt, but mere piece in the puzzle, that obstructs our capacity to see the separated ego and its relation to the face as already meaningful only against that which is the context or condition for both enjoyment and the face-to-face relationship: the structures that take us beyond the face, and beyond the ego whose separation is (whatever other structures it, in the course of this separation, espouses) an ethical separation—a separation by and for the other.

Indeed, what, on our reading, is analogous between the relation to the element that is enjoyment and the relation to the other that is ethics is not (at least not principally) the structure of the anterior posteriori that each involve, but the fact that each of these relations are transcendental in the sense that each make for ordinary experience while not entering directly into that experience. In ordinary experience there is no pure enjoyment any more than there is the pure experience of the face. I *am* never alone in my enjoyment (even in separation, even if the structure of solitary enjoyment is necessary to the experience of enjoyment), and I *am* never confronted by a single singular other. In terms of experience, my enjoyment is always the enjoyment of this or that, this cultural object, or a separation directed toward that which already has a cultural reference, is the enjoyment of a moment already claimed by the other. And in terms of ethical experience, the encounter of the other is no less an abstraction than is the solitary ego of enjoyment. The face is always this face or that, embedded in a network of faces, this face that belongs to my circle of acquaintance, that face that is the face of a foreigner. Neither enjoyment nor the face of the other are ever "experienced" in the conventional sense of the term, but they make for experience, are conditions of possibility for life-world experience. But I cannot experience my enjoyment as always already disturbed by the other without enjoyment functioning as a structure for experience, and I cannot experience my responsibility for the others without the structure of the face of the other also conditioning experience. Neither enjoyment nor the face are "real," but neither are they "irreal" or "ideal." They are neither empirical nor transcendental in the traditional sense, but are transcendental conditions for experience insofar as they are constituent aspects of "ethics" as the transcendental condition for experience. That is, it seems to us that Bernasconi, in privileging the separation of terms as necessary to the ethical relation rather than seeing separation as a function of the intrigue wherein terms are already in ethical relation through the separation/relation of generational dis/continuity, gives a too "real," or too "empirical," reading to both enjoyment and the face of the other,[57] building the relation out of constituent parts rather than seeing the parts as already implicated in the relation that already lends to separation the only meaning that it can accrue, that is, where separation is only meaningful as separation from . . . Thus he is prejudiced against a transcendental reading from the start, and blind to the ethical intrigue that functions as *the* transcendental for Levinas—and that already gives meaning to the other, and subsidiary, transcendental structures operative in Levinas's thought: enjoyment and the face-to-face—that, as dually original, are nevertheless reconciled in the pre-originary intrigue of which they are constituents, reconciled in being already meaningful in terms of their ethical, or religio-familial context.

Finally, while we have in our reading of Levinas as an ethical transcendental philosopher been inspired by de Boer's reading, we believe that if this reading as inaugurated by de Boer is to be consistently followed through, we need to push beyond de Boer's particular articulation of it. That is, our reading is (at least in part) an attempt at discovering how de Boer's reading can be true to its own "heart" insofar as it maintains that the same is from the start (and we would say before the start) *pour autrui,* rather than leaving a fragment of my being that is not initially or structurally so.[58] We accomplish this in our reading by showing how the *pour soi* is itself in the service of the *pour autrui,* that its very meaning as "for itself" is a function of its meaning as "for the other." But this requires, in analyzing my relations to the other, a going beyond the face, a tracing out of the intrigue in which, for Levinas, my relation to the other is a relation to the other qua feminine and the other qua face—which we have earlier argued is the same other in different modalities: the other as gracious and the other to whom I am to be gracious (that which, as we saw earlier, makes prophetic speech, or speech as already prophetic, possible). To "complete" a reading of Levinas's philosophy as an ethical transcendental philosophy, it is necessary to radicalize yet again this radical reading, or this reading of the *radix,* and seek with Levinas the root of the face-to-face relationship itself: the religio-familial intrigue of grace borne across the dis/continuity of generations. On our reading, that which functions for Levinas as the ultimate transcendental (that grounds my being and my experience by invoking them, without itself being a ground), the ultimate meaning "horizon" for experience as ethical, is the relationship to the other in both of the modalities Levinas discloses in his tracing out of the intrigue, the intrigue that bears—though always enigmatically—a trace of the Infinite. And yet, there remains here nevertheless—and so de Boer's analyses retain (as far as they go) an inexpungible poignancy—a certain priority of the face-to-face insofar as the gracious intrigue in terms of which the face-to-face is itself produced is only "revealed" across the face-to-face itself. Though I did not invent grace, though grace did not begin with me (I am always already graced and called to graciousness), this grace nevertheless is revealed to me only across my own voice, across my own testimony to it, across my own obedience to the call to be gracious. The responsibility for responsibility, the responsibility for the gracious intrigue that is my condition of possibility, falls upon me alone—on me and no other.

We are suggesting, then, in this our radicalized, ethical transcendental reading of the philosophy of Levinas, that it is the relation to the other by whom I am graced and to whom I am called to be gracious, the relation to the Infinite who leaves a trace upon this intrigue, who leaves a trace of this intrigue upon my being always already responsible for the other (which thus is a trace of a trace), that is the ethical transcendental condition for the same as responsible and of which the ego in enjoyment is an essential constituent. I am, through and through, from first to last, and before my first and after my last (across the dis/continuity of generations), *pour autrui.*

II.4. Discourse As Philosophy

As the analyses of the second part of this chapter have attempted to show, Levinas adopts and adapts the transcendental method of philosophy, constructing his own radical, or ethical transcendental philosophy, as a philosophy that allows him to work back from experience to that which conditions experience, to a condition that is not susceptible to the grasp of philosophical intuition, but that nevertheless leaves its trace upon philosophy, namely, ethics. That is, Levinas employs his particular transcendental philosophy as a kind of philosophizing that allows him to consciously and conscientiously trace and preserve in philosophy, even as it is therein betrayed, that which inspires philosophy but that can nevertheless not be subsumed by it. In short, we hope to have justified our interpretation by illustrating that, and how, the ethical transcendental method allows Levinas to sustain a philosophical discourse that is itself principally "discourse," a philosophy that is itself a performance of a non-allergic, ethical relationship with the other, a testimony/prophecy to the glory of the infinite across Levinas's own responsibility to his other(s): peace announced to the other—"*me voici*"—in the form of philosophy.

Notes

1. Does not even this prohibition make a subtle a priori claim to such a superior wisdom, to the superior wisdom of knowing (when others apparently do not) that there is no such superior wisdom? Unless this prohibition is directed against his own philosophy—first and unrelentingly, including against this claim itself—and not necessarily the philosophy of the other. Indeed, this prohibition has an ethical rather than a "philosophical" motivation, and this ethical prohibition is directed to me, to me and no other, as we shall shortly see. That, after a manner, will be our argument.

2. "And is not philosophy itself after all defined as an endeavor to live a life beginning in evidence, opposing the opinion of one's fellowmen, the illusions and caprice of one's own subjectivity?" (TI 24 [XII]).

3. Emmanuel Levinas, "Préface à l'édition allemande, Janvier 1987," in *Totalité et Infini,* pp. I–II (our translation).

4. Jacques Derrida, "Violence and Metaphysics," in *Writing and Difference,* p. 125.

5. Levinas claims, for instance, that "The thematizing logos, the saying stating a said in monologue and dialogue and in the exchange of information, with all the cultural and historical dimensions it bears, pro-

ceeds from this pre-original saying. This saying is prior to all civilization and every beginning in the spoken speech that signifies. The unlocking of sincerity makes possible the dimension in which all communication and thematization will flow. The trace of signifyingness in the making of signs and in proximity is not thereby effaced, and marks every use of speech" (OTB 198, n.6 [182]).

6. "It is indeed true that this I has already become a universal in the present exposition itself" (OTB 139 [177]).

7. Richard A. Cohen, "Emmanuel Levinas," in *Interpreters of Judaism in the Late Twentieth Century,* ed. Steven T. Katz (Washington: B'nai B'rith Books, 1993), p. 222. The larger quotation reads: "Prophecy is not the words of the major and minor prophets recorded in nineteen books of the Bible, once and for all, sealed. These words are prophetic for Levinas, and he often quotes the biblical prophets, especially Isaiah, but so too is all speech that calls forth the interlocutor's responsibility to respond. Levinas finds prophetic speech in Dostoevsky, in Shakespeare, and in his contemporaries."

8. That is to say, for the purposes of tracing the "foundation" of social relations we must begin in asymmetry. In point of lived fact, we begin always already among the simultaneity of social structures *déjà accompli* (the said), and their always possible interruption by the ethical relation that founds and animates them (the saying).

9. Derrida correctly notes that for Levinas, and he concurs, "the law" (Levinas's "justice") is not fundamentally a matter of constraining evil, but of constraining the good, a check against my spending all of my goodness on any one or any one group of others to the exclusion of the other others.

10. Our point in chapter 5 was to argue that Levinas does not advocate, as an "ideal," a cutting down of the tree and a subterranean life among the roots. Rather, his project is to expose the roots, to show the dependence of the tree (of life) upon its hidden source of nourishment: my responsibility for the other.

11. As Levinas quotes Isaiah 57:19, in the course of his discussion of the third (OTB 157 [200]).

12. "Human fraternity thus has two aspects: it involves individualities whose logical status is not reducible to the status of ultimate differences in a genus, for their singularity consists in each referring to itself. (An individual having a common genus with another individual would not be removed enough from it.) On the other hand, it involves the commonness of a father, as though the commonness of race would not bring together enough" (TI 214 [189]).

13. For details of our deviation here from Lingis's translation, see note 17 of chapter 5.

14. The other's testimony is rightly called prophetic insofar as in joining himself to me for service the other calls upon my goodness.

15. Recall the first of five epigraphs from *Otherwise Than Being:* "Or if a righteous man turn from his righteousness and do what is wrong, and I make that the occasion for bringing about his downfall, he shall die; because you did not warn him, he shall die for his sin, and the righteous deeds which he has done shall not be remembered, but his blood will I require at your hands" (Ezekiel 3:20).

16. Derrida, as we have noted above, defends Husserl's notion of the transcendental ego as necessary to the other's being "outside of the world," that is, as the foundation of an alterity capable of resisting the violence of being included in and reduced to my world, that is, that the other must, to be other, be capable of constituting his own world. For Levinas, Husserl's "outside of the world" is not sufficiently outside, for as alter *ego* it is constituted for me on analogy to my own ego. For genuine alterity, Levinas insists, following Rosenzweig, rests upon the "solitude of the *Selbstheit*" (*l'ipséité*) over against "the individual (*l'individu*) belonging to the world," and where, in an obvious reference to Husserl, this "would be a matter of the isolation of the 'nothing in common with anyone or anything' and which does not have need, we mention in passing, of any 'transcendental reduction' in order to signify an 'outside the world' " (DVI 222, our translation).

17. For Levinas on "the eschatology of messianic peace" and its relation to "prophetic eschatology," see the "Preface" to *Totality and Infinity,* 22–24 [X–XII]: "Of peace there can be only an eschatology."

18. We depart in small measure from Lingis's translation here. Lingis has rendered "*faite par*" by "given to," but we would argue, beyond pure matters of translation (though here too Lingis's interpretive choice seems odd), that the signification in question here is not "given to" the one who obeys it, but "made by" the one who obeys it in "giving it" to the other.

19. We shall discuss the nature of this ethical "experience" in part II of this chapter.

20. "The witness is not reducible to the relationship that leads from an index to the indicated" (OTB 151 [192]).

21. In the section that follows the one upon which we are concentrating, Levinas acknowledges the "problem," and then seems to attribute it (qua problem) to the betrayal of the saying in the said: "a new dilemma. Responsibility without a prior commitment, without a present, without an origin, anarchic, is thus an infinite responsibility of the one for the other who is abandoned to me without anyone being able to take my place as the one responsible for him. Does this confer upon me a new

identity, that of being the unique chosen one? Or does this exclusive election, as signification of the Infinite, reduce me to the status of an articulation of its divine economy? Are we reduced to humanity as an extreme possibility in being, where the substantiality of 'supporting oneself' is desubstantialized in a 'supporting the other,' 'substituting oneself for him'? Or through this ipseity reduced to being irreplaceable hostage, is the self equivalent to the entry of the subject into the play or designs of the Infinite?

"But is this dilemma rather an ambivalence, and the alternative an enigma? The enigma of a God speaking in man and of man not counting on any god? It is a dilemma or an alternative if one sticks to the phenomena, to the said, where one passes, successively, without being able to stop, from the affirmation of the Infinite to its negation in me. But the question mark in the said, which, contrary to the univocal logos of the theologians, is alternating, is the very point of revelation, of its blinking light. It is experienced precisely by incessantly running up against it, and crossing over its own contestation. There is a dilemma in the said, but an ambivalence in the signification of saying, in subjectivity, the entity expelled outside of being into itself; saying enigmatically and diachronically signifies transcendence or the Infinite, the otherwise than being and the disinterestedness from essence" (OTB 153–54 [195–96]).

22. De Boer, "An Ethical Transcendental Philosophy," p. 105.

23. And when the word "God" is pronounced in a said, this said, though animated by the saying of it, because animated by the saying of it (that which keeps it from finally closing in around itself and congealing into an object), harbors the seeds of its own unsaying: "The word God is an overwhelming semantic event that subdues the subversion worked by illeity. The glory of the Infinite shuts itself up in a word and becomes a being. But it already undoes its dwelling and unsays itself without vanishing into nothingness. It invests being in the very copula with which it receives attributes. (It is receiving them at this very moment, when this semantic adventure is here being thematized.) A said unique in its kind, it does not narrowly espouse grammatical categories like a noun (neither proper nor common noun), and does not incline exactly to logical rules, like a meaning (being an excluded middle between being and nothingness). This said gets its meaning from the witness borne, which thematization does betray in theology which introduces it into the system of a language, in the order of the said. But this abusive statement is at once forbidden. The limits of the present in which infinity betrays itself break up" (OTB 151 [193]).

24. Recall that for Levinas, the "atheism" of the ego, its separation

from even God, is to the greater glory of the Creator: "It is certainly a great glory for the creator to have set up a being capable of atheism, a being which, without having been causa sui, has an independent view and world and is at home with itself" (TI 58–59 [30]).

25. At least in Levinas's text. The reference to fraternity is pushed to the second sentence in Lingis's translation.

26. We have departed from Lingis's translation here in preserving the capitalization of Ethics, which Lingis does not do, because we shall make something of this.

27. We have corrected Lingis's translation that supplies "in" here for "*sans.*"

28. Here philosophy seems to be a form of political theory, or even political practice. But if the essence of philosophy is critique, as Levinas asserts elsewhere, then the birth of philosophy is correlative with the meeting of the face that calls me into question. If the philosophical discourse, where discourse here means the dialogue among philosophers, is to be traced back to the administration of my diverse responsibilities (the wisdom of love), this philosophy in turn must be traced back to its essence: my being called to responsibility.

29. There are other aspects of Levinas's self-perceived relationship to philosophy that are more particular to him (and others like him, presumably), as when, for example, he asserts that he sees part of his philosophical task, qua prophetic philosophy, as "translating Jewish wisdom into Greek" (*Quatre lectures talmudiques* (Paris: Minuit, 1968), p. 24), but here we are more interested in philosophy in general, or with "universal" philosophy, or at least with Western philosophy's pretension to be universal.

30. Levinas himself complicates this issue when he claims "I do not believe that there is transparency possible in method nor that philosophy is possible as transparency. Those who have spent all of their lives on methodology have written many books instead of the more interesting books that they could have written. Too bad for the walk under the sun without shadow that philosophy would be" (DVI 143, our translation).

31. De Boer, "An Ethical Transcendental Philosophy" (1986); this article is a revised version of a chapter from de Boer, *Tussen filosofie en prophetie* (Baarn: Ambo, 1976). Hereafter we shall refer to this article with the short form ETP.

32. Hereafter we shall refer to Bernasconi's "Rereading *Totality and Infinity*" with the short form Rr.

33. Michael Theunissen, *The Other: Studies in the Social Ontology of Heidegger, Sartre, and Buber,* trans. C. Macann (Cambridge, Mass.: MIT Press, 1983).

34. A. Dondeyne, "Inleiding tot het denken van E. Levinas."

35. De Boer is much less clear regarding how the other functions as the transcendental foundation of the same when the issue at hand is an analysis of the structure of labor than he is regarding knowledge and society. We shall attempt to give an explanation for why this is the case in note 58 below.

36. This insistence that what is at issue here is to be read as "ethical" over against ontological can be found in "An Ethical Transcendental Philosophy" on pp. 93 (twice), 95 (twice), 97, 98, and 108.

37. "This [the foregoing] responds also to the written question that I read: 'In 1972—thus before *Otherwise Than Being or Beyond Essence*—Professor Th. de Boer wrote an article on your work entitled "An Ethical Transcendental Philosophy." If the transcendental condition is explained not as a fact but as a prior value—in Dutch '*voor-waarde*'—do you give your consent to this characterization?' Well, I agree absolutely with this formula if transcendental signifies a certain anteriority: that ethics is before ontology. It is more ontological than ontology, more *sublime* than ontology. It is from this that an equivocation arises in which it [ethics] seems stuck onto [ontology], although it is before. It is therefore a transcendentalism which begins with ethics."

38. For an article that supports Bernasconi's reading against de Boer, see John E. Drabinski, "Between Representation and Being: Levinas and Transcendental Thought," *Skepteon* I (fall 1993): 57–72.

39. Interestingly, not only does Bernasconi not discuss any exemplary figures representing an empirical reading, he does not mention any. See note 57 for a *possible* significance to this omission.

40. Bernasconi cites TI 25 [xiii]: "The way we are describing to work back and remain this side of objective certitude *resembles* what has come to be called the transcendental method" (emphasis Bernasconi's).

41. See our chapter 2, section III.

42. How? Bernasconi does not say, exactly, and this does not seem to be his interest. We wonder whether this is not perhaps his "blind spot"—that which keeps him (as we shall suggest shortly) from taking seriously enough, despite his seeming avowals of such, the qualitative or even modal difference between the "object" of enjoyment and the "object" that is the other in his interest to point out the "structural" similarities between these two nonrepresentative "intentionalities."

43. "But can the face as the object of transcendental cognition be designated 'an unrecoverable contingent or ontic incidence that intersects the ontological order,' as de Boer suggests (ETP 108)?" (Rr 26).

44. De Boer also employs the word experience in this ordinary sense when he writes: "essential for philosophy to oppose opinions and illu-

sions in the name of experience and evidence" (ETP 106); "The philosophies of Heidegger and Merleau-Ponty penetrate beneath the level of representational thinking to pre-reflexive areas of experience but do not call these areas of experience themselves into question" (ETP 107); "both these thinkers [Levinas and Heidegger] take their point of departure in a dimension that, while not experienced itself, is the foundation of experience" (ETP 107).

45. Assertions of this kind abound, moreover, throughout de Boer's analyses. See note 36.

46. It would not be correct here to say that these are two modalities or kinds of experience, as if experience were the genus of which ethical and ordinary experience were species.

47. Here, as elsewhere in de Boer's as in Levinas's language, there is a necessary betrayal in the necessity of languaging the pre-ontological singularity in the universal categories of ontology, a necessity/impossibility of and for which we are in the course, throughout this work, of giving some account.

48. For example: "The other is not infinite in a quantitative or ontological sense; he is an ethical authority" (ETP 95).

49. That is, where the other constitutes the same rather than the same constituting the other, as in traditional transcendental philosophy.

50. That is, read as ontologically related (or unrelated) on the basis of their pre-original ethical relatedness rather than as ethically related on the basis of an original ontological separation.

51. For the term "ethical transcendental" only surfaces later, in Levinas's 1975 response to de Boer at Leiden.

52. Levinas himself uses, and seemingly synonymously, both "subversion" and "inversion" with respect to the effect of, for example, obsession on identity, when he writes: "The defection of identity is a for-the-other in the midst of identity; it is the inversion of being into a sign, the subversion of essence that begins to signify before being, the disinterestedness of essence" (OTB 153 [195]). Insofar as Levinas's inversion is taken as a radical inversion, one should not make too much of the distinction between these terms.

53. De Boer: "Levinas lays a foundation—and at the same time some dynamite—under institutions" (ETP 103).

54. And this, he would seem to be asserting, would have to be de Boer's position if de Boer did not "hold back from the conclusion to which his interpretation appears to lead" insofar as, on Bernasconi's reading, there is "an empirical moment at the heart of de Boer's attempt to sustain the transcendental reading" (Rr 27).

55. Richard Cohen, "Absolute Positivity and Ultrapositivity: Husserl and Levinas," in *The Question of the Other*, pp. 35–43.

56. This "prejudice" (on our judgment) in Bernasconi's reading is evinced, for instance, in his claim that "What is 'analogous to transcendence' in the discussion of 'Interiority and Economy' is the double origin. Just as representation and enjoyment are found to presuppose each other, 'the alleged scandal of alterity presupposes the tranquil identity of the same' (TI 203 [178]), while at the same time making it possible" (Rr 32). But on our reading, there is no tranquil identity of the same (the egoism is always already disturbed from within), and the "scandal" of alterity is only alleged, that is, is only a scandal if the tranquil identity is presupposed (which for Levinas it is not). This "scandal" can be read alternatively, for instance, as inspiration.

57. And is this why he, despite his claim that Levinas is to be read neither empirically nor transcendentally, only "takes on" in his article a representative of the transcendental reading, because he himself harbors, in his own reading, a certain empiricism? Here we merely speculate.

58. It is this fragment left in de Boer's reading that we believe explains why, in his description of how the face-to-face is the condition of possibility for labor, de Boer's analysis devolves into ambiguity and inconclusiveness. We read there: "Could it be argued, regarding the economic process and the polity of labor, that the other has a constituting function there? Is labor not a manifestation of our egoism, of our attempt to secure our own joyous existence? As such, does it not testify to the absence of the other? In the course of his argument, Levinas sometimes says that the other is also the 'condition' of labor. When we look more closely, it appears that what he is thinking of is the presence of the 'discreet' other, that is, the woman who plays a dominant part in the dwelling. Dwelling is the condition for the possibility of work. It is by no means fortuitous that the other is here called 'discreet.' The discreetness consists in not calling the possession into question. Love is a dual egoism. 'It excludes the third party and remains intimacy, dual solitude.' This seems to be an affirmation that economic life is primarily egoistic in character. But in that case, what does it mean that the other is the 'condition of possibility' for economic life? Economic life is seemingly in no need of the presence of the other" (ETP 99–100). Then, after a digression to the previous section, and a suggestion that an offering of the goods of my own labor gives my giving a bite that speaking lacks, de Boer concludes by restating the question—"What does it mean when we call him [the other] the transcendental presupposition of economic life?"—but leaves the question unanswered. But if the feminine other is also the other in a certain modality, as we have argued, that is,

if the relation with the other is not limited to the face-to-face relationship, then it is as clear how the other is the condition of possibility for labor (the other is the condition of possibility of the dwelling, which is the condition of possibility for labor) as it is clear how the other is the condition of possibility of knowledge and society.

8

The Im/possibility of Peace

I. Incredulities

Over thirty years have passed since Jean-François Lyotard first characterized "the postmodern condition" as an incredulity toward meta-narratives, that is to say, as a loss in the belief that a Master Story (a comprehensive account of the truth of being and history used to legitimate the sciences) can effectively, and innocently, integrate and guide our communal existence,[1] and this characterization has, in the meantime, become increasingly plausible. For our age *is* marked by a widening recognition of the legitimacy of a variety of disparate discourses, each seemingly answering to its own parochial exigencies, and as such locked in an intractable struggle with the others due to their respective and (at least seemingly) incommensurable "interests." It is, of course, nothing new to find a variety of voices vying for cultural preeminence. What is new is a widespread suspicion (despite a powerful backlash arising from many domains) that no account of what is and should be *should* have preeminence, and that the ascendancy of any particular voice over the others is (at) the very root of violence. So where "modernists" saw the eventual conversion of all reasonable persons from their parochial prejudices to the one true, rational, objective view of things as our salvation, as the way to universal peace, justice, and prosperity, "postmoderns" perceive the modernist drive toward such unity as just one more competing meta-narrative, just one more prejudice among prejudices, one more dogmatism among dogmatisms.[2] Alasdair MacIntyre perspicaciously puts the postmodern question: "Whose justice? Which rationality?"[3] Now, while this condition has, thank God, begun to help to alleviate (or at least created a cultural and political climate sympathetic to the alleviation of) at least some societal oppression in taking the nasty edge off the oppressive hegemony of the "one true way,"[4] it does create a certain difficulty in generating enthusiasm for the hope that through an ongoing dialogue we might be able to pacifically resolve certain of our conflicts that threaten to degenerate into violent confrontations. And this "difficulty" should be of particular interest to any of us who are of the conviction that words, however harsh, are better than guns. For if we postmoderns[5] no longer believe in a unified truth, or in a universally accessible, human faculty in terms of which truth might be attained (which for the greater part of our occidental tradition—from Plato to Habermas—and for modernism in particular has been "reason," or the "*logos*"), what becomes of the possibility of dialogue (which is, etymologically, *dia-logos:* communication "through" the "word" or "reason")? That is, the problem with the recognition of competing and incommensurate rationalities and the diverse conceptions of justice that correlate to them (what we might technically call a multiplicity of "life-world, constitutional paradigms") is that we can no longer presuppose a common "point of appeal" on the basis of which a dialogue might be founded and proceed.[6] And this is not without serious repercussions. For while valuing differences is no doubt a good thing, we are still faced, both locally and globally, with working out just (consensual) solutions to common problems, and problems that very often do not admit of an "each to his or her own" kind of solution. But lacking the common point of appeal requisite to dialogue as *dia-logos,* on what basis, starting out from what, are we to speak to "others" and work toward such solutions?[7] How are we even to agree as to what a "just" solution might be? And is this not precisely the problem? Is dialogue, and the hope for peace we have long placed in it, another casualty of postmodernism? Are we inevitably faced with the violence of a deepening tribalism? Or are we better off attempting to return to the "violent peace" of modernism, the Pax Romana of "peaceful," if crushingly oppressive, hegemony?

II. Offerings

This work has been motivated by a belief that the analyses of Levinas, particularly his idea of discourse, have much to contribute to a philosophical analysis of the conditions of possibility for dialogue *within* the postmodern condition, that is, in a situation where the common *logos* that indwells *dia-logos* on the traditional philosophical model can no longer be presupposed. The current problem, as we read it, is this: How do we arrive at a common *logos* (i.e., a shared rationality) that would be capable of founding and sustaining dialogue (as *dia-logos*) as an organon of conflict resolution, without violently imposing upon others, under the pretence of neutrality, our own truth, our own world and life view, or a solution arising out of it?

That is, the common *logos* requisite for *dia-logos* cannot (without violence) be a function of the movement that runs from a self grounded in its truth (and which Levinas refers to as "the same") toward the other that would be an object of this experiencing self (in philosophical language, experienced in correlation with an a priori, or, in the language of phenomenology, Levinas's own philosophical idiom, in terms of transcendental forestructures), which is precisely the movement, the direction, that has dominated Western, philosophical discourse.[8] Levinas refers to this phenomenon of bringing all alterity into correlation with a pre-given and pre-justified subject, and the intellectual tradition that participates in it, as egology.[9] If the common *logos* is to be constituted as other than a perpetuation of *my* life-world, constitutional paradigm (a perpetuation that would make the distinction between truth and ideology impossible insofar as truth would be inseparable from my interests),[10] this constitution must begin with the de-position, the interruption, of my truth. That is, truth itself (in distinction from ideology) must be constituted as a calling into question of *my* truth. Truth ("metaphysical" truth—being in relation with an other who is not merely an extension of myself)[11] is possible only in the decentering of truth (as an adequation between my epistemic categories and that which these categories actively welcome). And for Levinas, this condition cannot be met on the epistemo-ontological plane, for the knowing ego is forever capable of assimilating the foreign, domesticating the strange, bringing it into line with its a priori categories. In fact, the knowing ego has as its meaning kernel (its "essence") this consumptivity, insofar as it can only encounter, only know, that which always already is subject to, and thus limited by, its categories. On this model, nothing can be "known" that does not correlate to a knower. The other that is not knowable does not (and never will) exist for me. "Experience" is always already a form of domination, a "welcome" that is the active (i.e., determined by the knower) side of receptivity. In order to de-center, rather than be received by and thus confirm, my truth, the other must disturb, disrupt, interrupt my truth, must throw it into confusion, must impose itself upon the self-same beyond the latter's capacity to receive. For Levinas, the condition of possibility of truth, the possibility of a *logos* that transcends my idiosyncratic particularity, as over against the violence of ideology, is the anarchic other. Levinas uses the term "encounter" (as distinguished from experience) to name this disruptive coming of the other beyond receptivity, beyond the a priori.

For Levinas, this interruption, this anarchy, this encounter, can only be ethical. It is the "face of the other" in its fleshy vulnerability, in its exposure to violence and outrage, in its indigence—and before its insertion into any interpretative (*logos*-regulated) matrix of meaning—that calls me out of myself (and my parochialism) and into an ethical relation of responsibility to the other,[12] a relationship that Levinas (technically, and rather idiosyncratically) refers to as "discourse," or, in his later works, as "proximity."[13] In this relationship, the face of the other does not await a meaning that would emanate from out of my pre-understanding of the world (and from out of which I would be capable of interpreting the other as friend or foe, as compatriot or stranger, as the one to be loved or feared, etc.), but is encountered (in its poverty and vulnerability qua face, as a face qua its poverty and vulnerability) as an ineluctable call to me to immediate responsibility in its regard. Across responsibility the other is revealed as neighbor, *le prochain* (the next), *der Nächste* (the near/next one), the one in "proximity." Only the vulnerable face of the other has the gentle force necessary to paralyze my interests,[14] to make me feel the violence of my subtle appropriations of the other and of his or her interests—my consumptive taking in and over of them, converting them into nourishments that feed me.

As such, the face of the other presents itself to me as intrinsically meaningful, as the "first" meaning, as the very origin of sense.[15] It calls me to a responsibility in its regard that, as coming from beyond and interrupting my "rational" categories,[16] is its own "reason."[17] The face of the other is a meaning that runs at counter-current to the vectors that flow from the same to the other in meaning constitution, a meaning that runs, rather, from the other to the same, that constitutes the self as the passive recipient of a responsibility for the neighbor.[18]

It is in terms of this my responsibility for the other (as prior to the constitution of anything shared) that, for Levinas, the common *logos* and the concomitant possibility of *dia-logos* is constituted. For my responsibility to the other requires of me, if I am to responsibly address his or her vulnerability and neediness, a giving[19] of what is mine to the other, up to and including my very self.[20] It is, for Levinas, in this giving to the other (in responsibility) of what is mine, of what had heretofore been mine alone, that a thing is torn from my egological economy and posed (in being named,[21] as claimed, by the needy face of the other) in the between space of a shared referentiality.

Here, the groundwork is laid for "objectivity,"[22] and for the truth of the *logos* (that constitutes a world in naming it) as a however complex system of signifiers in a language and logic that names and organizes the goods possessed and de-possessed.[23] On this conception, language (as system) is tied irrevocably to economics, and *logos,* rationality, is tied irrevocably to materiality (putting the lie to idealism as the ultimate source of meaning). Here, the possibility of logical truth thus lies in a prior allegiance to the good—in my giving, in my being always already given (avowed [avoué]) to the other. The logic of *logos* is founded in giving, in my generosity.[24]

Here, the constitution of a shared truth (that would not be ideological) requires a relaxation of my interest, an interruption, a détente, of the interpretive framework that functions as an assimilative "force on the move" (force qui va) (appropriating, domesticating alterity, which is its very function), a dis-interestedness[25] that considers (and prioritizes) the interests of the other as other (i.e., outside of, or across, any interpretative framework I would bring to an encounter with the other). For Levinas, the whole realm of meaning as universal that the *logos* names, and that opens the door to dialogue as *dia-logos,* is founded upon, requires as its necessary condition, the *ethical* meaning of the face of the other. The condition of possibility of *rational* dialogue is my *ethical* responsibility for the other. Or, on Levinas's own terms: ethics is first philosophy.[26] Put yet another way, as long as the other requires, as integral to his or her meaning, a place in my a priori framework of meaning, the other cannot be approached as "other," and dialogue cannot but be a more or less subtle form of coercion: polemics, be this, in place of a full-blown *polemos,* the more subtle form of polemics that is rhetoric,[27] but violence just the same.

Finally, the rational *dia-logos* that begins in my responsibility before the face of the other must, if it is to be an ethical dialogue, remain grounded in this goodness. That is, the objectivity and reasonable truth of the *logos* are not once and for all, but a temporary constitution and regulation of a world of things that exist between me and the other (in the space of an offering, or a refusal to give), to be reconstituted as new needs and new others call forth in me new responsibilities. A perpetual vigilance is thus required to address the oppression that accompanies any and every new concatenation of *logos,* this ever and again calling into question being as central to the good as the response to the face that called the *logos* into being in the first place.

III. Testimonies

The radicality of Levinas's thought is in its refusal to lapse back into yet another version of "the one true way," even implicitly, as, for instance, the final truth that there is no final truth. It is a radical refusal to be (ultimately)[28] lulled into laying claim to *a* truth that would purport to be *the* truth, that would be paraded (even in the name of peace) as a neutral third ("God," "reason," "justice") between myself and the other and that would, as such, govern our relations as if from above. It represents a radical refusal to be seduced into believing that any such recourse could be other than "political" in the derogatory and dangerous sense of that term, other than another (however subtle) power-play, another means of extending my influence and expanding my powers, in short, a matter of self-interest.[29] It is to relativize, in allowing to be called into question, any onto-theo-logical judgments about the general structure of things (being, God, truth) that I would make, called into question by the face of the other that qua face reveals to me the violence of my judgments, demanding to speak in its own voice, to interrupt my judgments by the ethical power of its empirical powerlessness (as susceptible to my judgments and vulnerable to my actions). My responsibility for the other as face precludes recourse to a purportedly neutral third that would mediate the relationship (i.e., that would claim to provide the reasons for *why* I should be responsible—a tactic that, paradoxically (if oh so logically!), opens the possibility for providing counter-reasons—*rational*-izations—for why I need not respond, especially when the neutral third to which I would be wont to appeal in such situations is in question—which is precisely the "postmodern" problem). And this cutting off of access to a neutral third term (which in truth cannot be extricated from my interests, and which as such is never really neutral) has two important consequences for our discussion, and that take up different emphases within the Levinasian claim that "peace is my responsibility."[30]

First, "peace is *my* responsibility." Since I am incapable of making appeal to a term that would tie the other to a responsibility for me that would correlate to my responsibility for him or her, my ethical responsibility for the other is unilateral, and Levinas thus refers to the relation of discourse as asymmetrical.[31] I cannot, that is, insist that the other be equivalently responsible for me or for yet another other without falling back into the violence of imposing the particularity of my interpretative framework upon the other, that which the face precisely prohibits. To insist that the other give him or herself to me or to another, that which the face demands of me, is, in Levinas's graphic description, "to preach human sacrifice" (OTB 126 [162]). Cut off from the myth of neutrality (the myth of justice),[32] peace (peace that is not the political peace of the social contract, but a matter of genuine "society") can be effectuated only in my unilateral gesture of peace, my offering of what is mine, down to my very self, to the other (in response to having already been passively offered), in response to the face that calls upon me to serve (that calls me forth as service), to be in its service, to be service to it. Peace, Levinas claims, begins in me: "Peace with the other is first of all my business" (OTB 139 [177]). For peace *imposed* (be it the purported peace of mutual subjection to a supposedly universal "*logos*," and that would claim to found the universal dialogue) is no peace, even if it is paraded about under that banner. Genuine peace is without guarantees, without the power to impose itself.

So, incapable of demanding for myself the same responsibility from the other that I owe to the other, my peaceful response to the other is taken in ultimate risk. The other might not return my service. The other might capitalize on my vulnerability and cut me down. This does not, of course, preclude the possibility of the other taking responsibility for me,[33] but I cannot (in lieu of the neutral third term in terms of which I would make such a claim) demand it. So, when this does happen, Levinas refers to it (without thereby evoking any theological content) as the grace of God.[34] God's grace to me is beyond my control. This risk is, of course, difficult, almost impossible, perhaps genuinely impossible. But the risk that peace requires is, according to Levinas's own testimony, always "a beautiful risk to run."[35] Indeed, perhaps it is the most beautiful. But the alternative is also "a supreme risk," and a less beautiful one: the risk of war.[36] I cannot live without risk, the only question is which risk I take. Dialogue, we are therefore suggesting, a pacific dialogue, a dialogue productive of genuine peace, requires *my* extreme risk as its condition of possibility, the risk of *unilateral* responsibility for the other. Peace is *my* responsibility.

If the first connotation of giving up on the illusion of a neutral third highlighted the mineness of the responsibility, the second highlights the "nature" of peace itself, and so we read "Peace *is* my responsibility." Peace, on this reading, is not a matter of "getting things right," of being in tune with (or in philosophy, in knowing and acting in accordance with) the truth of being. Peace cannot be effectuated by making an appeal to a neutral third term to which I *and* the other are to be mutually subjected, for the third term, as proffered by me, as we have seen, is always mine. Its purported neutrality is the veil of a myth that hides (and often even from myself) power relations. Justice is *my judgment* of justice, and I and my interests are fully involved in any of my judgments, and peace, conceived of as a purportedly neutral state of affairs, is subject to the same suspicion in being always my (or someone's) conception of peace: peace *for me*. Far from being the road to peace, an appeal to a "neutral" third is (even if unwittingly, even in the name of peace) a perpetuation of violence in propagating the clash of ideologies, triumphalism, and "war." In lieu of such a universal conception, peace can only be my offering of a peaceful gesture to the other, my testifying in my words and actions to the other who calls me to responsibility as face from out of the peace that I have received in grace. Peace is (in) this gesture. Peace is nothing outside of this gesture. Peace *is* my responsibility.[37]

Levinas's thought, if it is to be true to its deepest motivation, cannot itself, then, be an imperative, cannot be an ethics. Neither is it ultimately philosophy of the transcendental kind that purports to neutrally lay out conditions of possibility for . . . , although, as philosophy, it takes that form. Rather, it is most faithfully read (or this is our thesis, among the principle theses of this thesis) as a testimony to peace. It is a testimony to a grace already received, and a response to that grace which makes it possible, and as such a testimony to peace.[38] Levinas's thought testifies not to the way things in fact are (and are therefore for everyone), not even to the "truth" of his own claims (as, for instance, that ethics precedes ontology), but to a graciousness, a graciousness that cannot be imposed (for it would as such lose its graciousness), but only testified to. Can I (not "I" as the I of Levinas's discourse, but "I," Jeffrey Dudiak) join in the "I" of Levinas's discourse? Can I testify to peace? Levinas does not tell me I must (or even that I can), but invites me to challenge myself to make a gesture of peace in response to the grace I have received.[39] Levinas offers us, ultimately, a philosophy as "spiritual" autobiography, as testimony, as prophecy, as a gesture of peace.[40] Similarly, this work, if it is not to distort the spirit that inspires it, cannot but be our own testimony to peace, even if it takes, here, the form of a testimony to a testimony to peace, a testimony to a grace received through the work of Levinas, even if this be, ultimately, a testimony to a Work that does not belong to Levinas.[41]

If the way to go suggested by this reading of Levinas rings truly (that is, with ethico-spiritual rather than ontological-epistemological truth) in our ears and hearts, then we should perhaps consider what this might mean for the "practice" of peace hopeful of engendering peacefulness, including the practices of peace studies and peace activism. To begin, my research and praxis hopeful of engendering peace would need to be itself peaceful, would need to be, above all, a gesture of, and as such a testimony to, peace. On this model, peace studies and activism only fulfill their mandate of promoting peace by being performative, by themselves being offerings of what is mine to the other, as a putting of myself in the service of the other. Such research and praxis, on this perspective, would be futile, folly, even violence, if it were not first *itself* the running of the beautiful risk of peace,[42] if peace were to be conceived of as the result—the outcome—of these activities, and not first indigenous to them qua activities. Since I cannot demand this sacrifice of the other (which would be to impose *my* responsibility on the other), my advocacy of peace rests on my testimony to peace. My "appeal" to the other for the sake of the other others (for the sake of justice) as I attempt to mediate between others for the promotion of peace is reduced, in the end, to the strength and vulnerability (the strength through vulnerability) of my own "testimony" to peace, of my own pacific gesture to the other, is reduced, that is to say, to the testimony that, in the end, issues from my own responsibility for the other. There can be here no justification of means by ends—for peace is not an outcome, but a gesture, my gesture, of peacefulness. Peace is born(e) in my testimony to peace, meaningless (literally) without it. For peace, on this way, is not first of all the imposition upon persons or situations of whatever and however clever or well-intentioned models or paradigms for peace (including this one, and although such might well be contextually required), but the bringing into a situation a pacific testimony, an inspiration to others who alone must themselves decide whether or not to take the risk of peace. Here alone rests hope for autochthonous solutions to violent and potentially violent situations. Here alone is a genuinely ethical/pacific gesture—in risk, an offering of mine and of me to the other, peace as my responsible peacefulness, the condition of possibility of *logos,* in turn the condition of possibility of *dia-logos,* in turn the condition of possibility of a peaceful society, or, simply, of society.

Notes

1. Jean-François Lyotard, *The Postmodern Condition: A Report on Knowledge,* trans. G. Bennington and B. Massumi (Minneapolis: University of Minnesota Press, 1989), p. xxiv.

2. What distinguished Enlightenment rationalism from the dogmatisms it hoped to supplant was that its advocates believed it possible to rationally ground this very belief, which would effectuate its being removed from the realm of a belief and elevated to the level of a proven (or at least provable) "fact." The "fact" that the canons of proof were derived from the belief they were supposed to ground seems to have been lost on the Enlightenment philosophers, and this realization has had no small part to play in the loss of credulity regarding Enlightenment thought (along with the further "fact" that the Enlightenment thinkers—themselves the most reasonable of men [sic]—could not actually agree even among themselves as to what exactly those "clear and distinct," rational ideas were that were supposed to elicit the consent of all rational thinkers, the irony of which Alasdair MacIntyre takes some joy in pointing out in his *Whose Justice? Which Nationality?* [Notre Dame, Ind.: University of Notre Dame Press, 1988], p. 6).

3. See the previous note for bibliographic information. Of course, MacIntyre is not himself a "postmodern," but seeks to revive (as an antidote to modernism) a kind of premodern Aristotelianism.

4. There is a sense in which postmodernism is more liberal than even classical (modernist) liberalism, insofar as liberalism permitted of a plurality, but only on its own terms. On the postmodern view, there is no reason for one's idiosyncratic beliefs to be chased (and chastened) into a private sphere, leaving one with mere, "neutral" reason in the public sphere.

5. Is it fair to refer to our age as a postmodern one, and to us as postmoderns when so many among us would reject (and with some bitterness and scorn) the appellation? The belief that the one true way/one true story has in fact been, or is potentially to be, found is alive and well, and is, to tell the truth, extremely difficult to shake even for those who desire to do so. What is confessed by most, however, and even by those who bemoan the situation, is that there exist no accounts of the Truth that do, in fact, command the respectful adherence of the greater part of us. To say "we postmoderns" is not, therefore, to claim that there is among us anything that is "shared," but perhaps to signal precisely that there is not, to signal that "we postmoderns" are, to borrow a phrase from Alphonso Lingis, "the community of those that have no

community." That there are many among us who still believe in or seek a unifying story does not exclude these from the category, but serves to constitute it as a category whose unifying feature is this lack of unity regarding even the question of unity itself.

6. Postmodern thinkers are recognizing that "interests" are not merely an interpretive layer placed over a neutral and impassive truth, but constitutive of truth itself, the very condition of possibility of truth where truth is conceived of as a judgment, the very points of reference in terms of which a judgment—true/false, good/bad—could be made. We have been arguing throughout this work that there is possible a deeper sense of truth, truth as the good, a matter of relating truly, truth not as noun, but as adverb.

7. The "linguistic turn" in twentieth-century philosophy has made commonplace the recognition that language and thought are inseparable, although a shared positive language does not guarantee agreement between persons whose language/thoughts are conditioned by diverse sublanguages (down to one's "personal" language), and who thus could be said, for instance, across their different shadings and connotations of words, to not really share a vocabulary. Thus we say, in a situation with a same language speaker that does not promise understanding, "He does not speak my language."

8. There is, of course, a correlative stress upon "receptivity," but this receptivity is, precisely, "correlative" to an active aspect of knowing. Indeed, "receptivity" is at once passive and active, a bit like catching a ball is to actively receive.

9. "The relation with the other is here accomplished only through a third term which I find in myself. The ideal of Socratic truth thus rests on the essential self-sufficiency of the same, its identification in ipseity, its egoism. Philosophy is an egology" (TI 44 [14]). My encounter with a genuine alterity cannot, moreover, be an experience of the other as another *me,* another subject *like me,* for what is less other than the other as my identical term, but merely spatially displaced into an over there? Levinas thus rejects as a model for alterity the "alter-ego" of Husserlian phenomenology.

10. See, for example, Levinas's "Idéologie et idéalisme," (DVI 17–33).

11. Levinas's specific sense of "metaphysics," to be distinguished from the "metaphysics" of the now almost too popular (in postmodern circles) "history/deconstruction of metaphysics," is most readily outlined in the opening pages of section I of *Totality and Infinity,* pp. 33 ff. [3 ff.].

12. Here I am called out of myself as constituting ego, but to myself

in my deepest self, to my subjectivity, to my being "subject" to the other in responsibility.

13. The correlation between "discourse" in *Totality and Infinity* and "proximity" in *Otherwise Than Being or Beyond Essence* is not perfect (see introduction to part II). That is, these terms are not synonyms as the emphases of the descriptions of the respective works require differently shaded definitions, but the meanings are sufficiently close to be, for our present purposes, thought of together.

14. Thus, the face does not incite to battle (will against will), nor does it present itself as an obstacle to be overcome (will against a neutral inertia), but demands, qua face, to be respected and cared for, demands from me a responsibility prior to my assuming or rejecting of responsibilities in terms of my a priori categories (and as such is a will called to will for the other, called to be will for the other).

15. The first meaning is thus an ethical one, prior to any "truth" as a term that would reflect being: "The ethical relation, opposed to first philosophy which identifies freedom and power, is not contrary to truth; it goes unto being in its absolute exteriority, and accomplishes the very intention that animates the movement unto truth" (TI 47 [18]). We can glimpse here also the subtle connection in Levinas between sense (meaning) and sensibility (my susceptibility to the other, which reaches its apogee in responsibility conceived of as substitution).

16. These are the very categories in which my responsibility for the other threatens to be "lost" in gaining my first allegiance, in demanding to be that in terms of which my responsibility for the other must be legitimated.

17. Even if the "content" of this reason is nothing other than the interruption of "reasons": "The face brings a notion of truth which, in contradistinction to contemporary ontology, is not the disclosure of an impersonal Neuter, but *expression:* the existent breaks through all the envelopings and generalities of being to spread out in its 'form' the totality of its 'content,' finally abolishing the distinction between form and content. This is not achieved by some sort of modification of the knowledge that thematizes, but precisely by 'thematization' turning into conversation" (TI 51 [21–22]).

18. In order to emphasize the extreme passivity (a passivity incapable or reverting back into activity) involved in responsibility, in "subjectivity," Levinas has recourse here to hyperbolic language for the subject, describing it as "the passivity of passivity," "hostage," "already guilty," "ashamed," "obsessed" by the other, "substitution" for the other (which means responsible even for the other's responsibility), as the one called "to tend the cheek to the smiter and be filled with shame" (OTB

111 [141], from Lamentations 3:30). The use of hyperbole does *not* mean, however, that he is here exaggerating merely for rhetorical effect. Rather, it is Levinas's belief that it is in the superlative, rather than in negation, that the "system" of ontological thought is disturbed (which permits of a space for the other), and his use of hyperbole is aimed at effectuating this disruption (see, e.g., OTB 187, n.5 [8, n.4]).

19. "But Desire and goodness concretely presuppose a relationship in which the Desirable arrests the 'negativity' of the I that holds sway in the same—puts an end to power and emprise. This is positively produced as the possession of the world I can bestow as a gift on the Other—that is, as a presence before a face. For a presence before a face, my orientation toward the other, can lose the avidity proper to the gaze only by turning into generosity, incapable of approaching the other with empty hands" (TI 50 [21]).

20. Levinas expresses this most graphically—and grippingly, because implicating in it the devotion to the other of my very bodiliness—with the idea of feeding the other from out of my own nourishments, with the bread from out of my own mouth. One example of this usage: "And to be torn from oneself despite oneself has meaning only as a being torn from the complacency in oneself characteristic of enjoyment, snatching the bread from one's mouth" (OTB 74 [93]).

21. "Fixed by the word which gives them" (TI 139 [113]).

22. "Objectivity . . . is *posited* in discourse, in a *conversation* which proposes the world" (TI 95–96 [68]).

23. "To recognize the Other is therefore to come to him across the world of possessed things, but at the same time to establish, by gift, community and universality. Language is universal because it is the very passage from the individual to the general, because it offers things which are mine to the Other. To speak is to make the world common, to create commonplaces. Language does not refer to the generality of concepts, but lays the foundation for a possession in common. It abolishes the inalienable property of enjoyment. The world in discourse is no longer what it was in separation, in the being at home with oneself where everything is given to me; it is what I give: the communicable, the thought, the universal" (TI 76 [48–49]).

24. "The generality of the Object is correlative with the generosity of the subject going to the Other, beyond the egoist and solitary enjoyment, and hence making the community of goods of this world break forth from the exclusive property of enjoyment" (TI 76 [48]).

25. Levinas often makes this point by employing the word "non-indifference," where the double negative preserves the "difference" while indicating that my relationship to it is qualified ethically, that is, that I cannot be indifferent with respect to this difference.

26. "Morality is not a branch of philosophy, but first philosophy" (TI 304 [281]).

27. "Rhetoric . . . approaches the other not to face him, but obliquely—not, to be sure, as a things, since rhetoric remains conversation, and across all its artifices goes onto the Other, solicits his yes. But the specific nature of rhetoric (of propaganda, flattery, diplomacy, etc.) consists in corrupting this freedom" (TI 70 [42]).

28. To philosophize in the Occident is to enter into the idiom of truth claims, to make claims about what *is*. Levinas, in conducting a philosophical discourse that attempts to point beyond what "is" to the "otherwise than being," conducts, therefore, this discourse in a language that, by his own admission, cannot but betray itself.

29. The strength of this seduction is astounding. We need not be adherents of his views (and there are many "good" reasons not to be) to be stunned by Nietzsche's analyses that cast the lives and teachings of even Socrates and Jesus (the paradigmatic martyrs of "truth" and "the Kingdom of God" respectively) in terms of such self-interest, as, for instance, in his *Twilight of the Idols*.

30. We are not sure Levinas ever writes this phrase exactly, but using it as our basis here does allow us to highlight two important aspects of Levinas's thought regarding issues of peace. The closest articulation we have found, and one that, in many respects (as we shall see), sets the agenda for that which follows, is "Peace then is under my responsibility. I am a hostage, for I am alone to wage it, running a fine risk, dangerously" (OTB 167 [212]).

31. "The Other measures me with a gaze incomparable to the gaze by which I discover him. The dimension of height in which the Other is placed is as it were the primary curvature of being from which the privilege of the Other results, the gradient of transcendence" (TI 86–87 [59]). Levinas likes to express this asymmetry with a quotation from Dostoevsky's *The Brothers Karamozov:* "Everyone is responsible for everyone else, and I more than the others" (see, e.g., OTB 146 [186]).

32. That is, the myth that someone would be in a position to mete out desserts that would correspond to some objective, neutral standard.

33. In fact, the other has always already taken responsibility for me, which is the very "reason" why I am called to take responsibility for the other, as we have seen. But the other of the other who has always already taken responsibility for me (the other not in the modality of the feminine) may not, and my responsibility to him remains a risk, even if an always already "inspired" one.

34. "It is only thanks to God [*grâce à Dieu*] that, as a subject incomparable with the other, I am approached as an other by the others, that is,

'for myself.' 'Thanks to God' I am an other for the others" (OTB 158 [201]).

35. See note 30.

36. "War presupposes the transcendence of the antagonist; it is waged against man. It is surrounded with honors and pays the last honors; it aims at a presence that comes always from elsewhere, a being that appears in a face. It is neither the hunt nor the struggle with an element. The possibility, retained by the adversary, of thwarting the best laid calculations expresses the separation, the breach of totality, across which the adversaries approach one another. The warrior runs a risk; no logistics guarantees victory. The calculations that make possible the determination of the outcome of a play of forces within a totality do not decide war. It lies at the limit of a supreme confidence in oneself and a supreme risk" (TI 222–23 [198]).

37. "Peace must be my peace, in a relation that starts from an I and goes to the other, in desire and goodness, where the I both maintains itself and exists without egoism" (TI 306 [283]).

38. Thus Levinas writes, in a passage we take to be applicable to his own philosophical offerings, that "Men have been able to be thankful [rendre grâce] for the very fact of finding themselves able to thank [en état de rendre grâce]; the present gratitude is grafted onto itself as onto an already antecedent gratitude [sur une gratitude déjà préalble]" (OTB 10 [12]). In a similar vein, note my call to goodness or love in terms of a prior goodness or love with which I have been invested: "The good invests freedom—it loves me before I love it. Love is love in this antecedence" (OTB 187, n.8 [13, n.7]). On our reading, this antecedent grace, goodness, love, is given to me by means of the feminine other, or (as we prefer) the other in the mode of the feminine.

39. And clearly, some of us have received less, and can offer less, and my response to these should not be accusation, but an offering of further grace in accordance with my measure.

40. See chapter 7 for an exposition of the important but difficult sections of *Otherwise Than Being* that appear under the rubric of "The Glory of the Infinite" (OTB 140–52 [179–94]), wherein Levinas expounds upon the notions of "witness" and "prophecy" and on the way in which they function in his thought. Our thesis is that these terms need to be read as characterizing Levinas's thought—at least in its spirit—as a whole. We read, for example: "We call prophecy this reverting in which the perception of an order coincides with the signification of this order given to him that obeys it. Prophecy would thus be the very psyche of the soul: the other in the same, and all of man's spirituality would be prophetic" (OTB 149 [190]). Our suspicion is, that is, that Levinas's

own thought would be a product of, and participate in, this prophetic spirituality.

41. See Derrida's "At This Very Moment in This Work Here I Am" for an analysis of the relationship between Levinas's work and the Work that it permits to be put to work, or, in our terms, to which it testifies.

42. We (I personally) owe to (my friend) Nik Ansell the suggestion that a proper Christian response to violence is to interpose oneself between the combatants and, if necessary, take the brunt of the blows. This "testimony" to peace seems to us consonant with that of Levinas.

A BRIEF BIBLIOGRAPHY

Works Cited

Bernasconi, Robert. "Rereading *Totality and Infinity*," in *The Question of the Other*, ed. A. B. Dallery and C. E. Scott, pp. 23–34. Albany: State University of New York Press, 1989.

———. "Skepticism in the Face of Philosophy," in *Re-reading Levinas*, ed. R. Bernasconi and S. Critchley, pp. 149–61. Bloomington: Indiana University Press, 1991.

Boer, Theodore de. "An Ethical Transcendental Philosophy," in *Face to Face with Levinas*, ed. R. A. Cohen, pp. 83–115. Albany: State University of New York Press, 1986.

Caputo, John D. *Against Ethics: Contributions to a Poetics of Obligation with Constant Reference to Deconstruction.* Bloomington: Indiana University Press, 1993.

Cohen, Richard A. "Absolute Positivity and Ultrapositivity: Husserl and Levinas," in *The Question of the Other*, ed. A. B. Dallery and C. E. Scott, pp. 35–43. Albany: State University of New York Press, 1989.

———. "Emmanuel Levinas," in *Interpreters of Judaism in the Late Twentieth Century*, ed. Steven T. Katz, pp. 205–28. Washington, D.C.: B'nai B'rith Books, 1993.

Critchley, Simon. " 'Bois' ": Derrida's Final Word on Levinas," in *Re-reading Levinas*, ed. R. Bernasconi and S. Critchley, pp. 162–89. Bloomington: Indiana University Press, 1991.

———. *The Ethics of Deconstruction: Derrida and Levinas.* Oxford: Blackwell, 1992.

Derrida, Jacques. "At This Very Moment in This Work Here I Am," trans. R. Berezdivin, in *Re-reading Levinas*, ed. R. Bernasconi and S. Critchley, pp. 11–48. Bloomington: Indiana University Press, 1991. ("En ce moment même dans cet ouvrage me voici," in *Textes pour Emmanuel Lévinas*, ed. François Laruelle, pp. 21–60. Paris: Jean-Michel Place, 1980.)

———. "Violence and Metaphysics," in *Writing and Difference,* pp. 79–153. Chicago: University of Chicago Press, 1987.

Dondeyne, A. "Inleiding tot het denken van E. Levinas," *Tijdschrift voor Philosophie* 25 (1963).

Drabinski, John E. "Between Representation and Being: Levinas and Transcendental Thought," *Skepteon* 1 (fall 1993): 57–72.

Dudiak, Jeffrey. "Again Ethics: A Levinasian Reading of Caputo Reading Levinas," in *Knowing Other-wise,* ed. J. H. Olthuis, pp. 172–213. New York: Fordham University Press, 1997.

Gibbs, Robert. *Correlations in Rosenzweig and Levinas.* Princeton: Princeton University Press, 1992.

Heidegger, Martin. *Being and Time,* trans. J. Macquarrie and E. Robinson. San Francisco: Harper & Row, 1962.

Levinas, Emmanuel. *Quatre lectures talmudiques.* Paris: Minuit, 1968.

———. "Le Nom de Dieu d'après quelques textes talmudiques," in *Archivio di Filosofia,* pp. 155–67. Rome, 1969, pp. 155–67.

———. *Existence and Existents* (*De l'existence à l'existent*), trans. A. Lingis. The Hague: Martinus Nijhoff, 1978.

———. *Totality and Infinity: An Essay on Exteriority,* trans. Alphonso Lingis. The Hague: Martinus Nijhoff, 1979. (Emmanuel Levinas, *Totalité et Infini: Essai sur l'extériorité.* La Haye: Martinus Nijhoff, 1961.)

———. *Otherwise Than Being or Beyond Essence,* trans. Alphonso Lingis. The Hague: Martinus Nijhoff, 1981. (Emmanuel Levinas. *Autrement qu'être ou au-delà de l'essence.* La Haye: Martinus Nijhoff, 1974.)

———. *De dieu qui vient à l'idée.* Paris: Librairie philosophique J. Vrin, 1986.

———. "Le dialogue," in *De dieu qui vient à l'idée.* Paris: Librairie philosophique J. Vrin, 1986.

———. "Useless Suffering," trans. R. Cohen, in *The Provocation of Levinas,* ed. R. Bernasconi and D. Wood, pp. 156–67. New York: Routledge, 1988.

———. "Wholly Otherwise," trans. S. Critchley, in *Re-reading Levinas,* ed. R. Bernasconi and S. Critchley, pp. 3–10. Bloomington: Indiana University Press, 1991. (Emmanuel Levinas, "Tout autrement," in *L'Arc,* "Jacques Derrida" (special issue), pp. 33–37. Paris: Librairie Duponchelle, 1990.)

———. "Philosophy and the Idea of the Infinite (La Philosophie et l'idée de l'infini)," in A. Peperzak, *To the Other: An Introduction to the Philosophy of Emmanuel Levinas* (reprinted in English and French), pp. 88–119 [73–88]. West Lafayette, Ind.: Purdue University Press, 1993.

———, and Richard Kearney. "Dialogue with Emmanuel Levinas," in *Face to Face with Levinas,* ed. R. A. Cohen, pp. 13–33. Albany: State University of New York Press, 1986.

Llewelyn, John. "Am I Obsessed by Bobby? (Humanism of the Other Animal)," in *Re-reading Levinas,* ed. R. Bernasconi and S. Critchley, pp. 234–45. Bloomington: Indiana University Press, 1991.

Lyotard, Jean-François. *The Postmodern Condition: A Report on Knowledge,* trans. G. Bennington and B. Massumi. Minneapolis: University of Minnesota Press, 1989.

MacIntyre, Alasdair. *Whose Justice? Which Rationality?* Notre Dame, Ind.: University of Notre Dame Press, 1988.

Manning, Robert John Sheffler. *Interpreting Otherwise Than Heidegger: Emmanuel Levinas's Ethics as First Philosophy.* Pittsburgh: Duquesne University Press, 1993.

Nietzsche, Freidrich. *The Twilight of the Idols: Or How to Philosophize with a Hammer.* Harmondsworth: Penguin Books, 1987.

Olthuis, James. "Face to Face: Ethical Asymmetry or the Symmetry of Mutuality," in *Knowing Other-wise,* ed. J. H. Olthuis, pp. 131–58. New York: Fordham University Press, 1997.

Peperzak, Adriaan. *To the Other: An Introduction to the Philosophy of Emmanuel Levinas.* West Lafayette, Ind.: Purdue University Press, 1993.

Rolland, Jacques. "*Avertissement,*" to Emmanuel Levinas, *La Mort et le temps,* pp. 5–6. L'Herne (Le Livre de Poche), 1991.

Smith, Steven G. "Reason as One for Another: Moral and Theoretical Argument in the Philosophy of Emmanuel Levinas," in *Face to Face with Levinas,* ed. R. A. Cohen, pp. 53–71. Albany: State University of New York Press, 1986.

Theunissen, Michael. *The Other: Studies in the Social Ontology of Heidegger, Sartre, and Buber,* trans. C. Macann. Cambridge, Mass.: MIT Press, 1983.

Wright, Tamra, Peter Hughes, and Alison Ainley. "The Paradox of Morality: An Interview with Emmanuel Levinas," trans. A.

Benjamin and T. Wright, in *The Provocation of Levinas,* ed. R. Bernasconi and D. Wood, pp. 168–80. New York: Routledge, 1988.

Other Works Consulted

Ainley, Alison. "Amorous Discourses: 'The Phenomenology of Eros' and Love Stories," in *The Provocation of Levinas,* ed. R. Bernasconi and D. Wood, pp. 70–82. New York: Routledge, 1988.

Alvarez, Olmedo Gaviria. "L'Idée de création chez Levinas: une archéologie du sens," *Revue Philosophique de Louvain* (August 1974): 509–38.

Berezdivin, Ruben. "3 2 1 Contact: Textuality, the Other, Death," in *Re-reading Levinas,* ed. R. Bernasconi and S. Critchley, pp. 190–200. Bloomington: Indiana University Press, 1991.

Bernasconi, Robert. "Levinas and Derrida: The Question of the Closure of Metaphysics," in *Face to Face with Levinas,* ed. R. A. Cohen, pp. 181–202. Albany: State University of New York Press, 1986.

———. " 'Failure of Communication' as a Surplus: Dialogue and Lack of Dialogue between Buber and Levinas," in *The Provocation of Levinas,* ed. R. Bernasconi and D. Wood, pp. 100–135. New York: Routledge, 1988.

———. " 'Only the Persecuted . . . ': Language of the Oppressor, Language of the Oppressed," in *Ethics as First Philosophy,* ed. A. Peperzak, pp. 77–86. New York: Routledge, 1995.

Blanchot, Maurice. "Our Clandestine Companion," trans. D. B. Allison, in *Face to Face with Levinas,* ed. R. A. Cohen, pp. 41–50. Albany: State University of New York Press, 1986. ("Notre compagne clandestine," in *Textes pour Emmanuel Lévinas,* pp. 79–87 Paris: Jean-Michel Place, 1980.)

Boer, Theodore de. "Theology and Philosophy of Religion according to Levinas," in *Ethics as First Philosophy,* ed. A. Peperzak, pp. 161–71. New York: Routledge, 1995.

———. *The Rationality of Transcendence: Studies in the Philosophy of Emmanuel Levinas.* Amsterdam: J.C. Gieben, 1997.

Boothroyd, David. "Responding to Levinas," in *The Provocation of*

Levinas, ed. R. Bernasconi and D. Wood, pp. 15–31. New York: Routledge, 1988.

Burggraeve, Roger. *Emmanuel Levinas: The Ethical Basis for a Humane Society.* Leuven: Center for Metaphysics and Philosophy of God, Institute of Philosophy, 1981.

Chalier, Catherine. "Ethics and the Feminine," in *Re-reading Levinas,* ed. R. Bernasconi and S. Critchley, pp. 119–29. Bloomington: Indiana University Press, 1991.

———. "The Philosophy of Emmanuel Levinas and the Hebraic Tradition," in *Ethics as First Philosophy,* ed. A. Peperzak, pp. 3–12. New York: Routledge, 1995.

Chanter, Tina. "Feminism and the Other," in *The Provocation of Levinas,* ed. R. Bernasconi and D. Wood, pp. 32–56. New York: Routledge, 1988.

———. "Antigone's Dilemma," in *Re-reading Levinas,* ed. R. Bernasconi and S. Critchley, pp. 130–46. Bloomington: Indiana University Press, 1991.

Ciaramelli, Fabio. "Levinas's Ethical Discourse between Individuation and Universality," in *Re-reading Levinas,* ed. R. Bernasconi and S. Critchley, pp. 83–105. Bloomington: Indiana University Press, 1991.

———. "The Riddle of the Pre-original," in *Ethics as First Philosophy,* ed. A. Peperzak, pp. 87–94. New York: Routledge, 1995.

Cohen, Richard A. " 'Introduction' to Face to Face with Levinas," in *Face to Face with Levinas,* ed. R. A. Cohen, pp. 1–10. Albany: State University of New York Press, 1986.

Comay, Rebecca. "Facies Hippocratica," in *Ethics as First Philosophy,* ed. A. Peperzak, pp. 223–34. New York: Routledge, 1995.

Davies, Paul. "A Fine Risk: Reading Blanchot Reading Levinas," in *Re-reading Levinas,* ed. R. Bernasconi and S. Critchley, pp. 201–26. Bloomington: Indiana University Press, 1991.

———. "On Resorting to an Ethical Language," in *Ethics as First Philosophy,* ed. A. Peperzak, pp. 95–104. New York: Routledge, 1995.

Delhomme, Jeanne. "Savoir lire? Synchronie et diachronie," in *Textes pour Emmanuel Lévinas,* pp. 151–65. Paris: Jean-Michel Place, 1980.

Dudiak, Jeffrey. "Structures of Violence, Structures of Peace: Levinasian Reflections on Just War and Pacifism," in *Knowing Other-*

wise, ed. J. H. Olthuis, pp. 159–71. New York: Fordham University Press, 1997.

Dufrenne, Mikel. "Venir au jour," in *Textes pour Emmanuel Lévinas,* pp. 105–10. Paris: Jean-Michel Place, 1980.

Gans, Steven. "Levinas and Pontalis: Meeting the Other as in a Dream," in *The Provocation of Levinas,* ed. R. Bernasconi and D. Wood, pp. 83–90. New York: Routledge, 1988.

Gibbs, Robert. "Height and Nearness: Jewish Dimensions of Radical Ethics," in *Ethics as First Philosophy,* ed. A. Peperzak, pp. 13–23. New York: Routledge, 1995.

Greef, Jan de. "Ethique et religion chez Levinas," *Revue de Théologie et Philosophie* (1970) no. 1: 36–51.

———. "Skepticism and Reason," trans. D. White, in *Face to Face with Levinas,* ed. R. A. Cohen, pp. 159–79. Albany: State University of New York Press, 1986.

Greisch, Jean. "The Face and Reading: Immediacy and Mediation," trans. S. Critchley, in *Re-reading Levinas,* ed. R. Bernasconi and S. Critchley, pp. 67–82. Bloomington: Indiana University Press, 1991.

Halperin, Jean. "Liberté et responsabilité," in *Textes pour Emmanuel Lévinas,* pp. 61–69. Paris: Jean-Michel Place, 1980.

Hand, Sean. " 'Introduction' to *The Levinas Reader,*" in *The Levinas Reader,* ed. S. Hand, pp. 1–8. Oxford: Basil Blackwell, 1989.

Heaton, John. "The Other and Psychotherapy," in *The Provocation of Levinas,* ed. R. Bernasconi and D. Wood, pp. 5–14. New York: Routledge, 1988.

Howells, Christina. "Sartre and Levinas," in *The Provocation of Levinas,* ed. R. Bernasconi and D. Wood, pp. 91–99. New York: Routledge, 1988.

Irigaray, Luce. "The Fecundity of the Caress: A Reading of Levinas, *Totality and Infinity* section IV, B, 'The Phenomenology of Eros,' " trans. C. Burke, in *Face to Face with Levinas,* ed. R. A. Cohen, pp. 231–56. Albany: State University of New York Press, 1986.

———. "Questions to Emmanuel Levinas," trans. M. Whitford, in *Re-reading Levinas,* ed. R. Bernasconi and S. Critchley, pp. 109–18. Bloomington: Indiana University Press, 1991.

Jabès, Edmond. "Il n'y a de trace que dans le désert," in *Textes pour Emmanuel Lévinas,* ed. François Laruelle, pp. 15–20. Paris: Jean-Michel Place, 1980.

Laruelle, François. "Au-delà du pouvoir: Le concept transcendental de la diaspora," in *Textes pour Emmanuel Lévinas,* pp. 111–25. Paris: Jean-Michel Place, 1980.

———. "Irrécusable, irrecevable: Un essai de présentation," in *Textes pour Emmanuel Lévinas,* pp. 7–14. Paris: Jean-Michel Place, 1980.

Levinas, Emmanuel. *Humanisme de l'autre homme.* Montpellier: Fata Morgana, 1972.

———. *The Theory of Intuition in Husserl's Phenomenology.* Evanston: Northwestern University Press, 1973.

———. *Noms propre.* Paris: Fata Morgana, 1976.

———. *Le Temps et l'autre.* Paris: Quadrige, Presses Universitaires de France, 1979.

———. "The Ego and the Totality," trans. A. Lingis, in *Collected Philosophical Papers: Emmanuel Levinas,* ed. pp. 25–45. Dordrecht: Martinus Nijhoff, 1987.

———. "Freedom and Command," trans. A. Lingis, in *Collected Philosophical Papers: Emmanuel Levinas,* pp. 15–23. Dordrecht: Martinus Nijhoff, 1987.

———. "God and Philosophy," trans. A. Lingis, in *Collected Philosophical Papers: Emmanuel Levinas,* pp. 153–73. Dordrecht: Martinus Nijhoff, 1987.

———. "Meaning and Sense," trans. A. Lingis, in *Collected Philosophical Papers: Emmanuel Levinas,* pp. 75–107. Dordrecht: Martinus Nijhoff, 1987.

———. "Reality and Its Shadow," trans. A. Lingis, in *Collected Philosophical Papers: Emmanuel Levinas,* pp. 1–13. Dordrecht: Martinus Nijhoff, 1987.

———. "Transcendence and Evil," trans. A. Lingis, in *Collected Philosophical Papers: Emmanuel Levinas,* pp. 175–86. Dordrecht: Martinus Nijhoff, 1987.

———. *Autrement que savoir.* Paris: Osiris, 1988.

———. *En découvrant l'existence avec Husserl et Heidegger.* Paris: J. Vrin, 1988.

———. "Ethics and Politics," trans. J. Romney, in *The Levinas Reader,* ed. S. Hand, pp. 289–97. Oxford: Basil Blackwell, 1989.

———. "Ethics as First Philosophy," trans. A. Lingis, in *The Levi-*

nas Reader, ed. S. Hand, pp. 76–87. Oxford: Basil Blackwell, 1989.

———. "The Pact," trans. S. Richmond, in *The Levinas Reader,* ed. S. Hand, pp. 211–26. Oxford: Basil Blackwell, 1989.

———. "Prayer without Demand," trans. S. Richmond, in *The Levinas Reader,* ed. S. Hand, pp. 227–34. Oxford: Basil Blackwell, 1989.

———. "Revelation in the Jewish Tradition," trans. S. Richmond, in *The Levinas Reader,* ed. S. Hand, pp. 191–210. Oxford: Basil Blackwell, 1989.

———. "The Servant and Her Master," trans. M. Holland, in *The Levinas Reader,* ed. S. Hand, pp. 151–59. Oxford: Basil Blackwell, 1989.

———. "The Transcendence of Words," trans. S. Hand, in *The Levinas Reader,* ed. S. Hand, pp. 145–49. Oxford: Basil Blackwell, 1989.

———. *Entre nous: essais sur le penser-à-l'autre.* Paris: Bernard Grasset, 1991.

———. *La Mort et le temps.* L'Herne (Le Livre de Poche), 1991.

———. *Outside the Subject,* trans. M. B. Smith. Stanford: Stanford University Press, 1994.

———. "Is Ontology Fundamental?" trans. P. Atterton, trans. revised by S. Critchley and A. Peperzak, in *Emmanuel Levinas: Basic Philosophical Writings,* ed. A. Peperzak, S. Critchley, and R. Bernasconi, pp. 1–10. Bloomington: Indiana University Press, 1996.

———. "Peace and Proximity," trans. P. Atterton and S. Critchley, in *Emmanuel Levinas: Basic Philosophical Writings,* ed. A. Peperzak, S. Critchley, and R. Bernasconi, pp. 162–69. Bloomington: Indiana University Press, 1996.

———. "Substitution," trans. P. Atterton, S. Critchley, and G. Noctor, in *Emmanuel Levinas: Basic Philosophical Writings,* ed. A. Peperzak, S. Critchley, and R. Bernasconi, pp. 80–95. Bloomington: Indiana University Press, 1996.

———. "Transcendence and Height," trans. T. Chanter, S. Critchley, and N. Walker, trans. revised by A. Peperzak, in *Emmanuel Levinas: Basic Philosophical Writings,* ed. A. Peperzak, S. Critchley, and R. Bernasconi, pp. 11–31. Bloomington: Indiana University Press, 1996.

———. "Transcendence and Intelligibility," trans. S. Critchley and T. Wright, in *Emmanuel Levinas: Basic Philosophical Writings,* ed. A. Peperzak, S. Critchley, and R. Bernasconi, pp. 150–59. Bloomington: Indiana University Press, 1996.

Lingis, Alphonso. "The Sensuality and the Sensitivity," in *Face to Face with Levinas,* ed. R. A. Cohen, pp. 219–30. Albany: State University of New York Press, 1986.

Llewelyn, John. "Levinas, Derrida and Others: Vis-à-vis," in *The Provocation of Levinas,* ed. R. Bernasconi and D. Wood, pp. 136–55. New York: Routledge, 1988.

———. "Amen," in *Ethics as First Philosophy,* ed. A. Peperzak, pp. 199–209. New York: Routledge, 1995.

———. *The Genealogy of Ethics: Emmanuel Levinas.* New York: Routledge, 1995.

Lyotard, Jean-François. "Logique de Lévinas," in *Textes pour Emmanuel Lévinas,* pp. 127–50. Paris: Jean-Michel Place, 1980. ("Levinas' Logic," trans. I. McLeod, in *Face to Face with Levinas,* ed. R. A. Cohen, pp. 117–58. Albany: State University of New York Press, 1986.)

Malka, Salomon. *Lire Lévinas.* Paris: Les Editions du Cerf, 1989.

Miller, Hugh. "Reply to Bernhard Waldenfels, 'Response and Responsibility in Levinas,' " in *Ethics as First Philosophy,* ed. A. Peperzak, pp. 53–58. New York: Routledge, 1995.

O'Connor, Noreen. "The Personal Is Political: Discursive Practice of the Face-to-Face," in *The Provocation of Levinas,* ed. R. Bernasconi and D. Wood, pp. 57–69. New York: Routledge, 1988.

———. "Who Suffers?" in *Re-reading Levinas,* ed. R. Bernasconi and S. Critchley, pp. 229–33. Bloomington: Indiana University Press, 1991.

Peperzak, Adriaan. "Devenir autre," in *Textes pour Emmanuel Lévinas,* pp. 89–103. Paris: Jean-Michel Place, 1980.

———. "Some Remarks on Hegel, Kant, and Levinas," in *Face to Face with Levinas,* ed. R. A. Cohen, pp. 205–17. Albany: State University of New York Press, 1986.

———. "From Intentionality to Responsibility: On Levinas's Philosophy of Language," in *The Question of the Other,* ed. A. B. Dallery and C. E. Scott, pp. 3–21. Albany: State University of New York Press, 1989.

———. "Presentation" in *Re-reading Levinas,* ed. R. Bernasconi and S. Critchley, pp. 51–66. Bloomington: Indiana University Press, 1991.

———. "Transcendence," in *Ethics as First Philosophy,* ed. A. Peperzak, pp. 185–92. New York: Routledge, 1995.

Reed, Charles William. "Levinas' Question," in *Face to Face with Levinas,* ed. R. A. Cohen, pp. 73–82. Albany: State University of New York Press, 1986.

Richardson, William J. "The Irresponsible Subject," in *Ethics as First Philosophy,* ed. A. Peperzak, pp. 123–31. New York: Routledge, 1995.

Ricoeur, Paul. "L'Originaire et la question-en-retour dans le *krisis* de Husserl," in *Textes pour Emmanuel Lévinas,* pp. 167–77. Paris: Jean-Michel Place, 1980.

———. *Oneself as Another,* trans. K. Blamey. Chicago: University of Chicago Press, 1992.

Robbins, Jill. "Tracing Responsibility in Levinas's Ethical Thought," in *Ethics as First Philosophy,* ed. A. Peperzak, pp. 173–83. New York: Routledge, 1995.

Rolland, Jacques. *Dostoïevski: la question de l'autre.* Lagrasse: Editions Verdier, 1983.

Scott, Charles E. "A People's Witness beyond Politics," in *Ethics as First Philosophy,* ed. A. Peperzak, pp. 25–35. New York: Routledge, 1995.

Smith, Steven G. *The Argument to the Other: Reason beyond Reason in the Thought of Karl Barth and Emmanuel Levinas.* American Academy of Religion Academy Series no. 42. Chico, Calif.: Scholars Press, 1983.

Strasser, Stephan. "Antiphénoménologie et phénoménologie dans la philosophie d'Emmanuel Levinas," *Revue Philosophique de Louvain* (1977) no. 1: 101–25.

Tallon, Andrew. "Nonintentional Affectivity, Affective Intentionality, and the Ethical in Levinas's Philosophy," in *Ethics as First Philosophy,* ed. A. Peperzak, pp. 107–21. New York: Routledge, 1995.

Taylor, Mark C. "Infinity: Emmanuel Levinas," in *Altarity,* pp. 184–216. Chicago: University of Chicago Press, 1987.

Tracy, David. "Response to Adriaan Peperzak on Transcendence," in *Ethics as First Philosophy,* ed. A. Peperzak, pp. 193–98. New York: Routledge, 1995.

Valevicius, Andrius. *From the Other to the Totally Other.* New York: Peter Lang, 1988.

Vries, Hent de. "Adieu, à dieu, a-Dieu," in *Ethics as First Philosophy,* ed. A. Peperzak, pp. 211–20. New York: Routledge, 1995.

Waldenfels, Bernhard. "Response and Responsibility in Levinas," in *Ethics as First Philosophy,* ed. A. Peperzak, pp. 39–52. New York: Routledge, 1995.

Weber, Elizabeth. "The Notion of Persecution in Levinas's *Otherwise Than Being or Beyond Essence,*" trans. M. Saatjian, in *Ethics as First Philosophy,* ed. A. Peperzak, pp. 69–76. New York: Routledge, 1995.

Werhane, Patricia H. "Levinas's Ethics: A Normative Perspective without Metaethical Constraints," in *Ethics as First Philosophy,* ed. A. Peperzak, pp. 59–67. New York: Routledge, 1995.

Westphal, Merold. "Levinas's Teleological Suspension of the Religious," in *Ethics as First Philosophy,* ed. A. Peperzak, pp. 151–60. New York: Routledge, 1995.

Wyschogrod, Edith. "Doing before Hearing: On the Primacy of Touch," in *Textes pour Emmanuel Lévinas,* pp. 179–203. Paris: Jean-Michel Place, 1980.

———. *Saints and Postmodernism: Revisioning Moral Philosophy.* Chicago: University of Chicago Press, 1990.

———. "The Art in Ethics: Aesthetics, Objectivity, and Alterity in the Philosophy of Emmanuel Levinas," in *Ethics as First Philosophy,* ed. A. Peperzak, pp. 137–48. New York: Routledge, 1995.

INDEX

Abraham, 11
Ansell, Nik, 419
anterior posteriori, 360, 363–65, 382, 390–91
Aristotle, 45
asymmetry, xiii, 67, 96, 99, 110–11, 117, 129, 138, 144, 146, 149, 152, 236, 255, 262, 275, 320, 323–31, 395, 409, 417

Beauvoir, Simone de, 161
Berezdivin, Ruben, 312
Berkeley, George, 13, 49
Bernasconi, Robert, 45, 172, 312, 354, 359–93, 398–401
betrayal, 148, 158, 198, 203, 217, 227–28, 236, 243, 245, 249, 252, 264, 271, 273, 284, 303, 326, 340, 350, 396, 400
Binswanger, Ludwig, 52
Boer, Theodore de, 105, 157, 209, 232, 252, 320, 340, 354–61, 365–93, 397, 398–401
Buber, Martin, xv, 160, 258, 368

Caputo, John D., 50, 54–55, 69–71, 74–75, 86, 99–100, 102, 214
Cassirer, Ernst, 52
Claudel, Paul, 336, 338
Cohen, Richard A., 325, 382, 395, 400
communication, xiii, 4, 21–26, 31–34, 39–40, 42, 52–55, 62, 80, 86, 90, 147, 162, 184, 193, 207, 225, 248, 395, 404
conversation, 23–25, 34, 52, 104, 117, 119, 121, 126, 129, 162, 177, 206, 255, 311, 319, 387, 415–17
creation, 120, 204, 220–21
Critchley, Simon, 102, 311

death, 76, 85, 103, 113, 143, 162, 180, 215, 228, 252, 263, 266–77, 289, 305–6, 310, 335
Derrida, Jacques, 45, 48, 69, 70, 75, 99, 102, 116, 152, 161, 172, 232, 253, 264–65, 292–97, 303, 311, 312, 322–23, 331, 394, 395, 396, 419
Descartes, René, 10, 15, 45, 48, 75, 76–78, 84, 97, 103, 123, 125, 143, 156, 366, 368
dialogue, xi–xiii, xv, xvii, 3–6, 16, 20–44, 50–62, 67–68, 79–80, 86, 92, 95, 109, 127–31, 140–41, 143–52, 162–63, 167–68, 177–81, 224, 231, 247–51, 255, 394, 398, 404–10
discourse, xii–xiv, xvii, 6, 16, 20, 22–27, 38–40, 43, 51–53, 58–59, 61, 68–69, 73, 75, 78–80, 85, 95–96, 98, 101, 103, 109, 111, 113, 115, 117–18, 120–21, 128–30, 136, 141, 143–46, 148, 151, 153–54, 162–64, 167–68, 170–82, 186, 195, 197, 207, 213, 221, 224, 226–27, 231–32, 242, 244–54, 259, 272, 277, 292–93, 300–302, 304, 311–12, 317–33, 336, 339, 349–53, 360, 369, 371, 374, 382, 394, 398, 404–6, 409, 411, 415–17
divine, the/divinity, 15, 54, 105, 153, 239, 334, 338–39, 341, 344, 389, 397
Dondeyne, A., 105, 354, 399
Dostoevsky, Fyodor, 332, 395, 417
Drabinski, John E., 399

economy, 23, 47, 50, 65, 94, 96, 114–15, 119, 125, 132, 135, 138, 140,

143–44, 148, 179, 195, 197, 203, 205, 210, 220–21, 238, 250, 252, 270, 313, 328–29, 352, 361, 389, 397, 407
ego/egoism, 12, 14, 19, 22, 24, 33, 39, 48, 50, 60, 62–68, 79, 83, 86, 88–91, 93–94, 97, 105–6, 110, 115, 119, 121, 125–26, 131–32, 134–35, 137–40, 142, 145–46, 148, 152, 161–62, 171, 196–98, 203–9, 214–23, 229, 248, 256, 273–74, 285–88, 296, 309–10, 320–23, 334–37, 343, 345, 356, 358, 361, 365, 372–73, 377, 379, 382–83, 385–86, 388–91, 393, 396–97, 401, 405, 414, 418
element/al, the, 86, 90–92, 107–8, 119, 126, 131–34, 154, 159, 179, 193, 197, 293, 365, 390–91
empirical/empiricism, 52, 73, 119, 130, 135, 137, 158, 161–62, 173, 176, 188, 203, 221, 235–41, 244, 251, 322, 359–61, 364–68, 371, 373–76, 378, 380–82, 385, 388, 391–92, 399–401, 409
enjoyment/*jouissance*, 11, 48, 50, 61, 79, 86–95, 104, 106–8, 115, 119–21, 125, 127, 130–34, 137–40, 142, 148, 150, 154–55, 157, 159, 179, 193, 196–97, 200, 203–4, 209–10, 213–14, 218–21, 238–39, 250, 252, 336, 362–65, 368, 382–83, 385–93, 399, 401, 416
eternal/eternity, 6, 10, 154, 158–60, 260, 263, 265, 275–76, 278, 290–92, 296–97, 299, 306, 311–12, 353, 373
experience par excellence, 55, 98, 370–72, 377–78, 380–82, 387
expression, 64, 67, 97, 98, 102, 106, 109, 110, 112, 114, 117, 118, 123, 134, 141, 153, 181, 202, 206, 211, 215, 222, 225, 327, 415
exteriority, 8–14, 19, 21, 24–26, 38–39, 47–49, 66, 78–80, 83, 99–100, 104, 114–17, 125, 153–54, 157–58, 203, 205, 248–49, 304, 343, 357, 362–63, 371, 415
father, 221, 239, 256, 269, 277, 390, 395
fecundity, 221, 240, 258, 266, 275–89, 305–6
feminine, 106, 128, 134–40, 150, 160–62, 176, 204–5, 210, 213, 220–21, 223, 238–40, 247, 250, 257–58, 297–98, 312, 345, 389, 392, 401, 417–18
Fichte, Johann Gottlieb, 212
Foucault, Michel, 50, 56
fraternity, 100, 221–22, 235–37, 239, 256, 258, 328, 346–48, 395, 398
freedom, 7–9, 11, 12–20, 22–26, 35, 39, 41, 46–47, 51, 62–64, 66–67, 72–74, 82, 85, 97–98, 100, 104, 108, 116, 125–27, 132, 137–38, 140–44, 146, 148–50, 155, 157–58, 162, 196, 202–5, 208–9, 214, 216–18, 222, 238, 243, 252, 254, 256, 268, 269, 271, 286, 291, 298, 303–4, 326, 331, 339–40, 358, 367, 371–72, 387, 389, 415, 417–18
Freud, Sigmund, 45, 56

Gadamer, Hans-Georg, 52, 255
Gibbs, Robert, 172, 212, 218–20, 231, 252, 256–58, 261–62
gift, 119–20, 126, 142–43, 146, 149–51, 155, 163, 193, 204–5, 213, 215, 240, 247, 276–77, 298, 306, 338, 349, 416
glory, 89, 107–8, 220, 244, 333, 335–38, 340–47, 350–52, 388, 394, 397–98
God, 9, 36, 67, 82, 84, 105, 111, 129, 138, 146, 153, 156, 158, 162, 202, 204, 209, 211, 236–40, 242, 247, 255–57, 273–75, 277, 288, 292, 300, 303, 305–6, 326, 329–30, 336–45, 348–49, 351, 397–98, 403, 408, 410, 417–18
grace/graciousness, 129, 137–38, 146, 158, 162, 204, 210, 220, 236–40, 247, 250–51, 257–59, 262, 297–300, 302, 313, 326, 329, 330, 332–33,

345–47, 349, 352, 389–90, 392–93, 410–11, 417–18

Habermas, Jürgen, 404
Hegel, G. W. F., 12, 15, 16, 19, 31, 45, 52, 77, 103, 183, 212
Heidegger, Martin, 45, 46, 49, 50, 51, 52, 54, 82, 87, 103, 106, 108, 120, 154, 173–74, 180, 185, 192, 212, 237, 260, 267, 356, 361, 362, 363, 375, 387, 400
heterautonomy, 343
history, 6, 13, 16, 19, 28, 35–36, 44–46, 48–49, 51, 53–54, 66, 85, 185, 190, 191, 212, 218, 228, 266–67, 270–76, 282–83, 287, 294, 296–300, 303–6, 311–12, 347, 355, 367, 403, 414
home, 10, 19, 93, 105, 107, 120, 132–35, 137–38, 140, 150, 159–60, 162, 204, 210, 213, 219–22, 238–39, 250, 257, 297, 345, 361, 368, 389, 398, 416
Hobbes, Thomas, 45
Hugo, Victor, 125, 157
Husserl, Edmund, 4, 12, 22, 39, 46, 48, 49, 52, 107, 121, 152, 156, 212, 224–25, 226, 322–23, 331, 355–58, 362, 363, 396, 414

ideology, xvii, 36, 272, 274, 311, 405–6
impossibility/impossible, xiii–xiv, 16, 37–39, 55, 63, 67, 69–72, 90, 96, 98, 117, 133, 152, 167–68, 171–72, 179, 193, 203, 214, 222, 227, 233–35, 243–44, 247–51, 260, 266–67, 269, 284, 301–2, 304, 312, 320, 331, 338, 344, 377, 379, 382, 400, 405, 410
infinity/ the infinite, 33, 35, 38, 44–45, 47, 50, 54, 58, 69, 75–80, 84, 86, 97–99, 103–5, 128, 139, 148, 150, 152, 156, 159–62, 167–74, 176–78, 180, 184, 195, 197–98, 203–5, 210, 212, 218–21, 224, 230, 237–40, 246–49, 252, 256–58, 261, 263–67, 269, 275–79, 289–92, 294–95, 305–6, 310–11, 322, 325, 333, 335–37, 341, 344–46, 348, 352, 354, 359, 361, 364–67, 370, 378, 382–85, 388, 390, 394, 396, 398, 400, 414–15
inspiration, 73, 125, 195, 208–9, 223, 232, 241, 245, 259, 310, 340, 343, 352–53, 401, 412
intentionality, 12, 78, 129, 152–53, 171, 198, 200–201, 214, 222, 227, 233–34, 362–64
interparadigmaticity, xii–xiii, 5, 20, 29, 37–38, 40, 42–43, 57–58, 62, 68, 128, 130, 141, 143–44, 146, 148–51, 163, 167, 247
intersubjectivity, 23, 92, 121
intrigue, xiv, 100, 204, 209, 214, 220–21, 237, 239–40, 257, 262, 297, 312–13, 333, 339, 345–49, 352, 389–90, 392–93
Isaiah, 395

Jaspers, Karl, 54
Jesus, 417
justice, 63, 99, 104, 129–30, 138–39, 149, 157–58, 169, 173, 176, 206, 232–46, 253, 255–56, 258–62, 272, 298–300, 302, 304–5, 317, 321, 324–30, 352, 372–73, 395, 403–4, 408–10, 412

Kant, Immanuel, 88, 101, 103, 186, 373
Kierkegaard, Søren, 299

labor, 50, 107, 132–33, 138, 140, 156, 159, 216, 220, 283, 355, 361, 364, 399, 401–2
language, xiv, 3–4, 21–22, 24, 33, 38, 42, 51–52, 55, 62, 70, 72, 94, 96, 100, 103, 109, 112, 115–17, 120, 123, 125, 130, 134, 136, 143, 146, 152–55, 162, 167–68, 172–73, 176, 179–81, 184, 187–94, 199, 203, 207, 210–11, 213–14, 217–18, 223, 226, 230–32, 245–46, 248, 250–53, 261, 281–82, 292, 302, 311–12, 319, 321–23, 331–32, 340, 347–48, 353–55, 360, 361,

363, 365–67, 375, 378, 380–81, 397, 400, 405, 407, 414–15, 417
Lingis, Alphonso, 107, 212, 214, 222, 254, 257, 305, 309, 312, 395, 396, 398, 414
Llewelyn, John, 101
love, 54, 69, 88–89, 93, 101, 159, 160, 197, 212, 223, 244–45, 256, 258, 297–99, 313, 317–19, 327, 345, 350, 362, 398, 418
Lyotard, Jean-François, 403, 413

MacIntyre, Alasdair, 403, 413
manifestation, 5, 7, 14, 21, 24, 64–65, 73, 100, 109, 111–12, 114, 122, 124–25, 153, 156, 182–83, 185, 213, 259, 279–84, 401
Manning, Robert John Scheffler, 156, 159, 172, 259
Marcel, Gabriel, xv
Marx, Karl, 45, 56
maternity, 138, 161–62, 204, 221, 240, 258
Merleau-Ponty, Maurice, 356, 400
messianic, the, xvi, 54, 263, 265, 278, 290–91, 300, 303, 396
metaphysics, 8–9, 47–48, 70, 100–101, 211, 354, 373, 414
moment, this very/the, xiv, 14, 28, 32, 34, 93, 161, 168, 172, 176, 182, 213, 218, 240, 250–51, 253, 260–61, 264–65, 270, 291–303, 312, 317, 339, 373, 397, 419
mother, 138, 161, 213, 221, 239

Nietzsche, Friedrich, 16, 50–51, 56, 157, 417

objectivity, 78, 85, 120–22, 124–25, 128–30, 134, 140, 142, 144, 153, 176, 407, 408
Odysseus, 11, 19
Olthuis, James H., 260

Parmenides, 47
Pascal, Blaise, 258
peace, xi–xvii, 17, 21, 27–28, 30, 35–37, 42, 53–54, 56, 59, 67, 104, 148–52, 163, 169, 247, 251, 259, 310, 328, 332–33, 346, 349–52, 369, 394, 396, 403–4, 408–12, 417–19
Peperzak, Adriaan, 45, 46, 47, 172, 174–76
phenomenology, 13, 46, 48–49, 55, 62, 97, 163, 212, 281, 307, 355–57, 371, 378, 405, 414
Plato, xv, 8, 14, 16, 22, 26, 32, 33, 45, 46, 49, 88, 89, 100, 113, 151, 153, 173, 176, 214, 226, 255, 404
Plotinus, 45
plurality, xiii, 57, 60–61, 80–81, 83, 85–86, 94–95, 99, 104–5, 129, 145, 413
politics, 18, 46, 50, 54, 80, 104, 149, 242–43, 245, 258–59, 262, 398, 403, 408–9
power, 13, 17–19, 35, 42, 60–61, 63, 65–66, 97–98, 105–6, 116, 119, 140, 158, 292, 303–6, 351, 408–10, 415–16
prophecy/prophetic, xiv, xvii, 153, 163–64, 302, 320, 324–26, 329–33, 344–47, 349, 351–52, 355, 392, 395–96, 398, 418–19
proximity, 43, 53, 56, 150, 155, 158–59, 171, 175–76, 197–202, 205, 207–9, 211, 214–16, 222–23, 227, 229, 233–36, 239–44, 248–49, 255, 258, 260–62, 286, 291, 303, 310, 323, 326, 338, 342, 348, 395, 406, 415

Quintilian, 88

rationality, xii, xv–xvii, 13, 16–17, 25–26, 48–49, 53, 101, 121, 142–43, 196, 238, 257, 327, 355, 403, 405, 407
reason, 3, 7, 15, 24, 28–31, 36, 38–40, 42–43, 49–50, 52–55, 69, 97, 99, 101, 105, 126–27, 150–51, 157, 196–

97, 199, 224, 234, 255, 266, 301, 305, 371, 387, 404, 407–8, 413, 415, 417
recurrence, 208, 217, 221, 223, 248, 285, 287–91, 294, 296–97, 299, 309–12, 373
reduction, 6–7, 20, 27, 46–47, 59, 62, 67, 79, 83, 93, 97, 110, 113, 115, 141, 144, 151, 215, 224, 226–27, 230–32, 245–46, 254, 284, 287, 308–9, 340, 357, 396
religion, 60, 157, 262, 346, 348
responsibility, 6, 58–60, 67, 80, 82, 101, 109–11, 113, 115, 118–19, 124, 128–29, 138–39, 141, 144–46, 149–54, 158, 160–61, 163, 171–72, 175, 180, 193, 195–96, 199–203, 206, 208–9, 211, 215–19, 221–23, 225, 229–31, 233–40, 242–46, 250, 253, 255–57, 259–61, 273, 275, 285–89, 291, 295–300, 303, 306, 308–9, 313, 319, 321, 323–51, 371–72, 374, 379–80, 382, 387, 389–91, 393–96, 398, 406–12, 415, 417
Ricœur, Paul, 56, 356
risk, xiii, 18, 59, 146–50, 152, 207, 214, 291, 302, 410, 412, 417–18
Rolland, Jacques, 44
Rosenzweig, Franz, xv, 219, 258, 396

said, the, xiv, 44, 106, 108, 167–68, 172, 174, 177–81, 187–92, 194–95, 201, 203, 207, 211, 213–15, 221, 223, 226–28, 230–32, 234–35, 237, 240–43, 245–50, 252–57, 260–61, 282–85, 287, 293–94, 300–302, 307–8, 326, 340–41, 344, 348, 395–97
Sartre, Jean-Paul, 127
Saussure, Ferdinand de, 116
saying, the, xiv, 44, 101, 106, 167–68, 171–72, 174, 176–82, 186–88, 190, 192–95, 201–2, 206–9, 211, 214–15, 222–27, 230–35, 240–54, 260–61, 282–83, 285, 300–302, 308, 310, 317, 321, 338, 340–41, 343, 351–52, 394–97
sensibility, 9, 86, 91, 103–4, 133, 148, 171, 176, 199–200, 215–16, 219, 223, 227–29, 249, 280, 335, 415
separation, 58, 60–61, 67, 69, 74–75, 79, 81–86, 92–96, 99, 104–6, 109–11, 120, 125, 130–32, 139, 141, 183–86, 198, 203–4, 218, 220, 266, 270, 279, 361, 363, 366, 382–85, 388–92, 397, 400, 416, 418
Shakespeare, William, 214, 395
skepticism, 172, 192, 300–302, 312
Smith, Steven G., 46, 53
Socrates, 6, 8, 12, 19, 50–51, 143, 414, 417
son, 162, 221, 276–78, 290, 295, 297–98, 390
Spinoza, Benedict de, 15, 33, 54
subjectivity, 32, 49, 53, 96, 121, 132, 147, 152, 163, 171, 174, 183, 200–204, 206–7, 209, 214, 216–19, 222, 225, 227, 230, 240–41, 243, 245, 247–50, 256, 260, 269, 272, 286–91, 297, 299, 303, 305–6, 321–22, 324–25, 331, 334–35, 338–39, 341–44, 347, 394, 397, 415
substitution, 25, 75, 148, 167, 171, 175–76, 200–201, 207–8, 217, 223, 227, 231, 241, 249–50, 254, 287, 291, 299–300, 303, 308, 326, 338, 342, 348, 415
system, 13–17, 19–20, 24, 26, 41, 50–51, 54, 58, 60–61, 68, 81–87, 89–95, 104, 112, 116, 121, 124–26, 129, 142–43, 149, 157, 162, 168, 179–81, 189–92, 195–96, 212–13, 234, 246, 254–55, 272, 280–83, 286, 339, 348, 397, 407, 416

testimony/witness, xii, xiv, xvii, 28, 153, 158, 163, 239, 259, 272, 277–78, 300, 302, 317, 320, 324, 331–33, 337–46, 348–53, 393–94, 396–97, 410–12, 418–19
theology, 211, 338, 340–42, 348, 397
theory/theoretical, 5–6, 8, 20, 29, 38, 44, 46–48, 52, 55, 84, 97–98, 104,

126, 157, 170, 181, 207, 220, 327, 398
Theunissen, Michael, 354, 387, 398
time/temporality, xiv, 8, 10, 30–31, 35–36, 39, 46–50, 69, 84–85, 89, 97, 106, 114, 116, 120, 126, 131–33, 137, 155–57, 159, 161–62, 168, 175, 179–82, 185–87, 191, 210–13, 217, 219, 221, 227–29, 237, 251, 260, 263, 265–311, 313, 317, 325, 335, 338, 340, 347, 349–50, 357, 365, 370, 372–73, 385, 389, 400–401, 416
Tolstoy, Leo, 304
totality, 14–15, 18, 28, 30–31, 50, 58, 60, 67, 74, 76, 79–80, 83–84, 88, 91–96, 103, 105, 110, 116–17, 120–21, 170, 173, 183, 185, 205, 212, 243, 249, 259–61, 272, 275–76, 279, 283, 297, 320, 322, 324, 339, 350, 354, 357, 362, 366, 384, 415, 418
transcendence, 4, 11, 48, 58, 60–61, 63, 66–67, 73, 76–79, 81, 94–96, 98–99, 103, 109, 115, 129–31, 141, 147, 153–54, 175, 180, 198, 211, 236, 248, 253, 274, 277, 289, 290, 304, 306, 309–10, 326, 341, 345, 347, 357, 361, 364–65, 382, 384, 397, 401, 417–18
transcendental/ism, xiv, 11–12, 48, 55, 62, 65, 69, 70, 72–73, 75, 83, 93, 96–97, 99, 103, 112, 130, 135, 137–39, 167, 177, 188, 192, 206, 209, 213, 232, 234, 237, 250, 252, 254, 261–62, 310, 320, 322, 327, 337, 347, 353–82, 386–94, 396, 399–401, 405, 411
truth, xv, 6, 15–16, 18–22, 24–27, 30–36, 41–43, 46, 49, 51, 54–55, 59–60, 67–68, 74, 83, 115–18, 121–30, 143–49, 153–58, 163, 180–86, 193–94, 208, 211–12, 225, 245, 255, 261, 263, 265–66, 272–74, 276–80, 289–91, 301, 305–8, 310–12, 317–19, 321–22, 339, 343–44, 350–51, 403–11, 413–15, 417

Valéry, Paul, 174
violence, xi, xv–xvii, 27–28, 31, 33, 35–36, 40–41, 51, 53–54, 59, 66–67, 79, 97, 99–100, 140, 145, 147–48, 151–52, 157, 163, 217, 259, 267–68, 270–71, 274, 320, 322–24, 331–32, 343, 396, 403–6, 408–9, 411–12, 419

Waelhens, Alphonse de, 55
war, xi, xv–xvii, 18, 27, 35–36, 40, 42, 50, 54, 67, 80, 98, 104, 127, 149, 150, 242, 411, 418
woman, 135–36, 160–61, 401